Exploring Shinto

Exploring Shinto

EDITED BY
MICHAEL PYE

SHEFFIELD UK   BRISTOL CT

Published by Equinox Publishing Ltd.
UK: Office 415, The Workstation, 15 Paternoster Row, Sheffield,
        South Yorkshire S1 2BX
USA: ISD, 70 Enterprise Drive, Bristol, CT 06010

www.equinoxpub.com

First published 2020

© Michael Pye and contributors 2020

All rights reserved. No part of this publication may be reproduced or transmitted in any form or by any means, electronic or mechanical, including photocopying, recording or any information storage or retrieval system, without prior permission in writing from the publishers.

British Library Cataloguing-in-Publication Data
A catalogue record for this book is available from the British Library.

ISBN-13   978 1 78179 959 8   (hardback)
          978 1 78179 960 4   (paperback)
          978 1 78179 961 1   (ePDF)

Library of Congress Cataloging-in-Publication Data
Names: Pye, Michael, editor.
Title: Exploring Shinto / edited by Michael Pye.
Description: Sheffield, South Yorkshire ; Bristol, CT : Equinox Publishing
   Ltd., 2020. | Includes bibliographical references and index. | Summary:
   ""Shinto" is explored in a wide and illuminating perspective by an
   international team of scholars, providing a guide to students and
   general readers through many aspects, both today and in its history"--
   Provided by publisher.
Identifiers: LCCN 2019058981 (print) | LCCN 2019058982 (ebook) | ISBN
   9781781799598 (hardback) | ISBN 9781781799604 (paperback) | ISBN
   9781781799611 (ebook)
Subjects: LCSH: Shinto.
Classification: LCC BL2220 .E97 2020 (print) | LCC BL2220 (ebook) | DDC
   299.5/61--dc23
LC record available at https://lccn.loc.gov/2019058981
LC ebook record available at https://lccn.loc.gov/2019058982

Typeset by S.J.I. Services, New Delhi, India

Contents

Preface and Acknowledgements   vii

Part 1 Concepts and Viewpoints

1   What is Shinto?   3
     Michael Pye

2   Essentialism in early Shinto studies   34
     Gaétan Rappo

3   On writing the history of Shinto   57
     Mark Teeuwen

Part 2 Exploring Borderlands of Shinto

4   Medieval Tendai Buddhist views of kami   79
     Yeonjoo Park

5   Conceptions of kami in the writings of the
     Tendai monk Jien   104
     Vladlena Fedianina

6   Buddhist-Shinto syncretization at the
     medieval Suwa Shrine   121
     Iwasawa Tomoko

7   Underground Buddhism at the Ise Shrines   136
     D. Max Moerman

8   Shinto spaces and shinbutsu interaction in the Noh   151
     Dunja Jelesijevic

9	Buddhist-style pilgrimage with Shinto meanings *Michael Pye*	173
10	Why does Shin Buddhism reject the worship of the kami? *Robert F. Rhodes*	186
11	Multiple divinities in Shin Buddhist temples *Markus Ruesch*	199
12	Responsive reflections on Buddhism and Shinto *Katja Triplett*	218

Part 3 The Puzzle and Fascination of Sect Shintō

13	Sect Shintō and the case of Ooyashirokyō *Michael Pye*	231
14	Meiji government policy, Sect Shintō and Fusōkyō *Shishino Fumio*	250
15	Introducing the faith of Shinshūkyō *Yoshimura Masanori*	260
16	Tenrikyō and Ōmoto in the context of Kyōha Shintō *Avery Morrow*	268
17	A postscript on Shinto diversity *Michael Pye*	305

Index   308

Preface and Acknowledgements

This book has arisen out three international seminars which explored various aspects of Shinto. All the participants were aware that "Shinto" is a contestable concept. They shared the view, or the hope, that to explore it in various ways would lead to greater understanding of what it is all about. The result is a collection of papers which aim to lead both students and a wider readership into what is a fascinating, if sometimes elusive subject.

We are now able to take a much more carefully reflected approach to Shinto than was possible, say, a century or more ago, when it was still being discovered, and in some ways invented, by the world beyond Japan. The first part of our selection therefore explains and discusses the most important conceptual problems which have arisen in the course of modern Shinto studies, whether among Japanese proponents and investigators or among foreign observers and researchers. The authors of the three papers in this section, Gaétan Rappo, Mark Teeuwen and myself, approach these matters in different ways, although many of our perceptions overlap or are complementary.

The many-sided interactions between Shinto and Japanese Buddhism are explored in the second section of this book. These relations dominate much of the history of Japanese religions, and there is very much more that might have been brought in, notably in the areas of Shingon and Nichirenite Buddhism. Nevertheless, the papers assembled here give case studies which may whet the reader's appetite to learn more about this vast subject. Our contributors refer especially to the dominant Tendai school of Buddhism (Yeonjoo Park and Vladlena Fedianina) as well as to the important Shinto shrines at Suwa and Ise (Iwasawa Tomoko and D. Max Moerman respectively), while the delicate case of the relations between Shin Buddhism and the divinities of Shinto is also treated in two very original contributions by Robert Rhodes and Markus Ruesch. The presence of both Shinto and Buddhist elements in Noh dramas, treated by Dunja Jelesijevic, and again in pilgrimage culture, considered in my own contribution, provides further context for the exploration of these themes which are then integrated in an essay of concluding reflections by Katja Triplett.

The third part of the book takes up the fascinating topic of "Sect Shintō" which, if Shinto is regarded as *the* indigenous religion of Japan, might seem to be a contradiction in terms. Two papers on the subject are contributed by "insiders" who are the current leaders of groups that fall into this category. These are Shishino Fumio of Fusōkyō with its links to Mount Fuji, and Yoshimura Masanori of Shinshūkyō which has links to a network of shrines all over the country. Two more papers are by outside observers, namely by myself and Avery Morrow. Though not comprehensive, information about several of the Shinto "sects" will be found in this section, much of which is not available elsewhere.

The papers were all presented at seminars during which mutual questioning and exchange was of great value before they took their final form. Two of them were panels conducted in English at conferences of the European Association for the Study of Religions, firstly at Leuven, Belgium, in 2017, and secondly at Bern, Switzerland, in 2018. Participation in these panels was supported in part by the International Shinto Studies Association (ISSA). The third seminar had already been conducted in Japanese in Tokyo, in 2017, being directly organized by ISSA in its international seminar series. For this support, heartfelt gratitude is extended to the chairman of the trustees, Revd. Miyake Yoshinobu 三宅善信 of the Izuo Konkō Kyōkai in Osaka and to Une Kie 宇根希英 in the administration of ISSA who in various ways made these events possible. Finally, I would like to express my gratitude to all the contributing authors who have made their work available and shown such patience during a complex editorial process.

Michael Pye, 2020
Marburg University, Germany

Part 1
Concepts and Viewpoints

1

What is Shinto?

Michael Pye

Getting started with "Shinto"

Since Shinto is popularly presented in common phrases such as "the indigenous religion of Japan" it may seem at first that what it means is rather obvious. It becomes more problematic however when we hear talk of "the national faith of Japan" or "the fountain of Japanese culture." It is true that Shinto is a very Japanese matter. On the other hand, while a connection with the Japanese ethnos is usually asserted, many Japanese people in fact have little or no concern with it. Moreover it soon becomes very clear that the term "Shinto/Shintō" has meant very different things to different people, and its appropriateness has often been contested by academics writing in various contexts. We must therefore admit that it is not at all easy to use the expression these days, and yet I believe it is not impossible. Let us consider, in an introductory way, where the problems lie and how the term can be deployed. To put it starkly: What is Shinto?

An older, but still very influential account of Shinto from the point of view of a scholarly insider was that of Katō Genchi 加藤玄智 (1873–1965) whose book *A Study of Shinto: The Religion of the Japanese Nation* was published in 1926. This was republished after the second world war (and after his own death) with a new unsigned preface which stated, "The validity of his argument in the meantime has by no means been diminished." It will therefore be well to look at his influential definition of Shinto:

> The present writer [Katō]…advances the view that Shintō – the State Shintō as well as the Sectarian Shintō – is in very

truth a religion, i.e. the original religion of the Japanese people, or, otherwise stated, the religion of the Japanese people from the very beginning down to the present time.[1]

He then goes on to explain, in a modern mode, what he understands to be "a religion," and to outline changing historical features of Shinto. This Shinto, though worked out variously in the history of Japan as a whole, is at the same time presented as "original" and therefore timeless. Since Katō adduces much comparative material as well as various typological considerations his argument should not be oversimplified,[2] and since it was a work of its time, it would be anachronistic to expect account to be taken of more recent arguments about various phases of the *construction* of Shinto. It must be noted however that what we find here is a very influential nationalist statement of apologetics for a Shinto which is conceived in essentialist terms.

Katō Genchi's presentation of "Shinto" would not be problematic if such definitions were no longer advanced. But they are. Unfortunately, brief presentations often take refuge in this misleading simplicity, whether in Japanese or in foreign languages. However, this does not have to be so. Consider the booklet by Sonoda Minoru 園田稔, *The World of Shinto: Reflections of a Shinto Priest* (2002). In this case, while the Foreword does indeed begin with such phrases as "Shinto is the traditional faith of Japan" and "it represents the essence of Japanese culture" what follows is in fact a carefully differentiated and balanced view, written with political sensitivity and cognizance of international scholarship on religion.[3] The combination arises because Sonoda is not only the 30th-generation chief priest (*gūji*) of Chichibu Shrine but also Professor Emeritus of Kyoto University, where he taught sociology of religion.

1   Katō 1926 and 1971, 3.
2   Cf. Hylkema-Vos 1990. This article does not discuss Katō's appraisal of Shinto directly but it brings out the academic background which lent credence to his views. See also Triplett 2004.
3   Tokyo and New York (International Shinto Foundation) 2002.

The interplay of Japanese and foreign viewpoints about Shinto has by now a long history, and one which has been bedeviled by the long tug-of-war over what counts as "religion" during the nineteenth and twentieth centuries. This conceptual debate will not be rehearsed here, and we restrict ourselves to just a few comments about older presentations of Shinto.

Among western observers in the nineteenth and early twentieth centuries there was a widely current idea that Shinto was destined to disappear as being no more than a bundle of local superstitions and customs. The background assumption for this was frequently that "religion" is something which had to be strong and personal (as in a widespread understanding of Christianity current at the time), rather than diffuse and social. Folklore studies were being developed academically not only in the western world but also in Japan, where they went under the name of *minzokugaku* 民俗学.[4] Unfortunately this trend, at a time when an integrated "study of religions" approach had not yet become really visible, led some observers to conclude that "Shinto" was on its way out as a factor in the modern world.[5] It may certainly be admitted that there is a "folk" element to Shinto, but there is also much more.

Notably, the civic and political dimension of Shinto was often ignored, although in fact it was of great importance. It is to the credit of D. C. Holtom (1884–1962) that he highlighted this dimension in his very influential work entitled *The National Faith of Japan*, which was first published in 1938.[6] Interestingly this book, like that of Katō Genchi, was also republished *unchanged* after the war, even though Shinto was then being disestablished from

---

4   A notable leader in this field was Yanagita Kunio 柳田國男 (1875–1962). For a compelling work illustrating the rootedness of much of Shinto in folk practices, though without theorizing it, see his *Nenjūgyōji zusetsu* 年中行事図説 first published in 1928. For his dispute with Katō Genchi over blood sacrifice, see Triplett 2004.

5   For more examples of this "disappearing folk-lore view" of Shinto, see my article "Diversions in the interpretation of Shintō" 1978 and 1981.

6   Cf. also his earlier works: *The Political Philosophy of Modern Shinto* (1922) and *The Japanese Enthronement Ceremonies* (1928), which have both been extensively reprinted.

its privileged position in the state. But the phrase "the national faith" did not originate with Holtom. It was already current for example as a chapter heading in a more popularly conceived but possibly even more widely influential book entitled *Present-day Japan* by Augusta M. Campbell Davidson, first published in 1904.[7] Davidson was writing during the heyday of Japanese nationalism and she saw "the real essence, the soul of Shinto today" as lying in the "heroic spirit" of the people, and by no means in the legends about "Amaterasu and all her divine train," which she regarded as withering away.[8] In this manner Davidson contrived to combine the escape into the "mere folklore" view with a soaking up of the nationalist perspective of insiders.

The postwar period saw the appearance of a massive compilation by the highly qualified French United Nations interpreter Jean Herbert (1897–1980) entitled *Shinto: The Fountainhead of Japan* (1967). Herbert visited many shrines all over the land and offered much circumstantial information, but his political sensitivity regarding Shinto was notably deficient. The title of his work picks up the essentialist idea of "Shinto" as being the starting point *par excellence* for Japanese society and culture in general. Unfortunately, writings of this kind remained the only sources for overseas students for a very long time. Significant updating was to be found in W. H. M. Creemers' careful study entitled *Shrine Shinto after World War II* (1968). W. P. Woodard, who had been centrally involved with the development of the Occupation policy towards Shinto, also published an important study in 1972 entitled *The Allied Occupation of Japan 1945–1952 and Japanese Religions*, which included much source material. However, since the dust had scarcely settled after the war it was not to be expected that his typology of different kinds of Shinto could be adequately rebalanced. The use of phrases such as "Kokutai Cult" and "Kokutai Shintō" was certainly misleading for the postwar situation.[9]

---

   7   It was republished in 1907 with the Preface unchanged, but re-dated. Some of the illustrations were changed or removed. The book has also appeared in a reprint edition.
   8   Davidson 1907, 144.
   9   For a detailed critique see Pye 1981 (originally 1978), 69–72.

One of the most important reasons for multiple strands among the views of what this religion is about is that, while the distant origins are obscure, there have been several new and clear starting points for "Shinto" in the course of Japanese history. At various points in time, claims to some form of seniority or relative authority have been linked to major shrines such as Hiyoshi Taisha, Yoshida Jinja, Ise Jingū or Izumo Taisha. In addition, since early modern times, new religious movements have advanced distinctive teachings which claim to represent "Shinto" in what is claimed to be an especially meaningful sense. It is for this reason that the third part of the present volume is devoted to Shinto "sects" and various demarcation questions which arise. The non-Japanese observer naturally looks for guidance to well organized institutions such as the Association of Shinto Shrines (Jinja Honchō 神社本庁[10]), or the two main institutions of higher education relating to Shinto studies, namely Kokugakuin University in Tokyo and the Kōgakkan at Ise, at each of which many Shinto priests are educated. These institutions have been the most evident centralized institutions since the disestablishment of Shinto after the end of World War II. The situation in the wider field is however not particularly tidy and it would be a mistake to think that there is one authoritative voice which speaks for "Shinto."

Indeed, the diversity of relevant strands of authority is not just a historical matter. Apart from the claims of major shrines and "sects" there have also been in recent times a wide range of unconnected reference points which people associate with "Shintō" even if this diversity is not reflectively articulated. For example, much public attention is paid to the ancient myths and divinities of Japan's oldest text, the *Kojiki*, now explained and depicted in easily assimilable images. This *Kojiki* cult, as it has almost become, is a kind of free-floating cultural event expressed in popular illustrated works, *manga* and exhibitions of various kinds. At the same time the later, immensely popular commerce-friendly god Inari Daimyōjin, who

---

10 This name is often written with the old form of the last character, namely 廳, and this is typical of a certain tendency to calligraphic obscurity in Shinto circles.

is of course not even mentioned in the mythical narratives of the *Kojiki*, attracts mass visits at New Year and other seasons especially by people who seek to ensure their success in commerce. These two areas of interest seem to have rather little to do with each other.

All the while, regardless of such a range, Japanese scholars and communicators who somehow speak for Shinto are usually trying to say what this "Shintō" really is. That is, they do advance an "essentialist" position of some kind as discussed in the paper by Gaétan Rappo in the present volume, or to put it in a phrase made popular by Ninian Smart, they adopt a position within the field.[11] Foreign observers do not usually "adopt a position within the field" though some come close to it when they unreflectively echo talk of "the indigenous religion of Japan" without taking much account of the succession of reinventions which have occurred over the years. More typically, foreign historians of religion and Japanologists with various disciplinary approaches have recently been contesting the very idea of "Shinto," and seek to avoid using it with reference to the earlier periods of Japanese history. This approach is recapitulated in the third paper in the present volume, by Mark Teeuwen, where relevant bibliographical references will be found.[12] The point of this scholarly caution is to avoid sliding into an essentialist position of some kind. The third-party historian cannot be a spokesperson for the Shinto world, thus adopting a *de facto* Shinto theology. On the other hand, those who speak in some sense *for* a Shintoist worldview, from the inside, inevitably maintain a more or less essentialist position about it.[13] That is quite natural. There is an understandable difference between academic non-essentialism and the desire to advocate a normative position.

This still leaves us with the question about how to speak of "Shintō" from the outside. There are several forms of this question,

---

11 Oral tradition from 1968 in the Department of Religious Studies, University of Lancaster.

12 But in particular see Breen and Teeuwen 2010: *A New History of Shinto*.

13 To the writer's knowledge there has not so far been any attempt to mount a position-less Shinto theology or ideology.

but broadly speaking it can be approached either historically or, as a contemporary matter, phenomenologically. In the first case the historian of religions needs to be able to trace continuities and disjunctions in a meaningful sequence. In the second case, the aim is to present a characterization of the religious system in question which would be recognized by other investigators looking into related phenomena. The purpose of it is heuristic. We will now take a look at these two approaches.

Historical complexity and usable categories

Consider first the historical perspective. In order to understand what was going on in earlier periods, and how things changed at later junctures, a certain amount of "category formation" is unavoidable, however cautiously it is advanced.[14] It is too simple to say that the term "Shinto" cannot be used for most of Japanese history because it had not yet been retrospectively "invented." By analogy, it might be thought impossible for geologists to speak of the Jurassic Period, on the grounds that dinosaurs did not have a word for it! In human history, we must recognize that people who lived in the Middle Ages had no idea that they were living in such a period. For them, it was always last year or next year, within the "now" of their own lives. To be realistic therefore, it must be open to historians of religion, at least when writing of the big picture as opposed to studying highly specialized details, to use terms which are broadly appropriate, even if these terms had not yet come into use by representatives of the religions themselves. In fact, there are hardly any names for religions, except those founded in recent modern times, which were first used by their followers at the time of their inception or during the early generations. Used retrospectively they are simply portmanteau terms that, for historians, do not bear any essentialist or normative intention.

There are two problems with essentialist definitions advanced speculatively by apologists for their own view of "Shinto." The

14 Cf. Baird 1971.

first is that they are not earthed in real history, or only misleadingly so. The second is that such definitions usually lay claim to the allegiance of the whole Japanese people without any care for the pluriformity of real religious affiliations. Normative Shinto narratives are not in fact meaningful for, or accepted by, a large number of Japanese people. For example, they may be countenanced in a provisional way in the perspective of Tendai Buddhism, but on the other hand rejected by Shin Buddhists. Or they may be entertained in some new religions, e.g. in Oomoto (in spite of the persecutions), but not by others such as Tenshō Kōtai Jingū Kyō, which has its own conflicting narratives.

To what extent, therefore, does it make sense to use the designation "Shinto" in a historical perspective? The challenge was taken up most effectively, and if one may say so, courageously, by Helen Hardacre in her recent work *Shinto: A History* (2017).[15] She places a strong emphasis on a central office set up as long ago as the 8th century CE to administer shrine affairs, seeing this together with the associated rites and concepts of divinity as a clearly available reference point for speaking of Shinto from then onwards, in whatever varied forms it later took. The office in question was known as the Jingikan 神祇官, literally the "Office of Divinities" but has also been referred to in English rather grandly by the more modern-sounding expression "Department of Shinto Affairs." The expression *jingi* is a compact term linking the gods (*jin*, or *kami*) of heaven, the *amatsukami* 天津神, and the *gi*, or *kunitsukami* 国津神, i.e. the gods of the earth. The full expression *tenjinchigi* in effect means, comprehensively, all the gods of heaven and earth. This provides something of a basis for the choice of side-stepping the term "Shinto," at least for the period in question, while speaking instead of "*kami* worship." Nevertheless, whatever may be said about any antecedents in prehistory, it seems that the history of Shinto, however further differentiated, must at latest begin with the Jingikan. It may be added that these matters are all substantially documented in the *Engishiki*, important and relevant sections of

---

15 Cf. this writer's review in *History of Religions* 58/4 (May 2019).

which have been available for many years in English translations by Felicia Gressitt Bock (Bock 1970).

The views of Shinto in history held by outsiders are immensely complicated by the intimate relations which "Shinto" however conceived has had with the wider flow of Japanese cultural and social development. This includes general artistic matters such as poetry and drama, notably the *nō* drama (also rendered in transcription as noh/Noh). Dunja Jelesijevic, in her article for the second part of this volume, uses the very suggestive title "Shinto spaces and *shinbutsu* interaction in the Noh" and this suggests, quite correctly, that the designation "Shinto" cannot be pinned down by institutions alone. However, quite apart from the general viability of historical categories, it is also necessary in any discussion of religious elements in the arts to be able to refer to them in some appropriate way, e.g. here as pertaining to "Shinto." Admittedly, as the subject matter moves away from any fully structured religious system, the relation to named religious systems with their institutions and behavioural patterns becomes more tenuous. Are miscellaneous references enough? Can gods exist without socially anchored ritual to dynamize them?

We must also consider the complex story of the relations between Shinto and Buddhism, and again the phrasing in the title quoted above is suggestive. It may be recalled that the first element in the term *shinbutsu* 神仏 refers to the *kami* 神 (here pronounced *shin* as in Shinto) while the second, *butsu* 仏, refers to buddhas. While the fuller expression *shinbutsu shūgō* 神仏習合 has long been a standard phrase to refer to syntheses or straight conflations of the respective divinities, the emphasis here is on interactions. To speak of interactions permits the ongoing recognition of alternative identities. In the long run, the perception of alternative identities made it possible for the correlation to be separated out under political direction in a sometimes violent process known as "separation of gods and buddhas" (*shinbutsu bunri* 神仏分離).[16]

---

16 For a recent account and discussion see Rambelli and Reinders 2014.

The relations between Shinto and Buddhism, in its various Japanese forms, have been complex indeed. Quite often it may have seemed as if there were but one single coordinated, if not always totally integrated religious complex. Several case studies about this will be found in the second part of the present volume. Yeonjoo Park and Vladlena Fedianina both consider ways in which the *kami* were considered in the context of Tendai Buddhism. Iwasawa Tomoko and Max Moerman explore Buddhist influences at two major Shinto shrines in medieval times, Suwa Taisha and Ise Jingū respectively, while my own paper reflects on the transfer of Buddhist models of pilgrimage to Shinto. Robert Rhodes and Markus Ruesch carefully test the widely held assumption that Shin Buddhism has been altogether resistant to Shinto influence. An integrated consideration of these papers is found in the final contribution in this section, Katja Triplett's "Responsive reflections on Buddhism and Shinto."

Suffice it to mention at this point just one underlying complex of questions. Was there any kind of *continuity* in Shinto identity during the (religiously speaking) long medieval period? Did such Shinto identity disappear, or could it even not yet clearly emerge because of the endless fluidity of religious networks and patterns, as is suggested in the excellent title of Bernard Faure's recently published *Gods of Medieval Japan Vol. 1: The Fluid Pantheon* (2016)? It is notable that in his largely historically positioned "pantheon" Faure presents above all divinities who may be regarded as marginal between Buddhism and Shinto, such as Benzaiten and Daikokuten. His argument is that "reductionist" concepts such as Buddhism and Shinto do not do justice to the complexities of "medieval" times. Clearly, if such categories are used naively and anachronistically, this is so. At the same time it should not be overlooked that Japan has been post-medieval for a long time now.

There has been a long tug-of-war over Benzaiten, a goddess of music and eloquence derived from India. The notable case is that of the island of Chikubushima in Lake Biwa, where she was extracted from the Shinto shrine in the interests of ideological purification and set up instead in a Shingon Buddhist temple. In recent years however, there has been a tentative attempt to reclaim her in proximity to the Shinto shrine.[17] A neat solution has been achieved at Demachi in Kyoto, where the entrance to the shrine of Myōon Benzaiten[18] is marked by a substantial Shinto-style gate (*torii*) while regular sutra recitations are performed by monks from the nearby Rinzai Zen temple Shōkokuji. Myōon Benzaiten also has an "affinity day" (*ennichi* 縁日), a feature which is usual for buddhas and bodhisattvas but not for Shinto *kami*.[19] This settlement follows a considerable period during which the shrine had languished due to the enforced separation of Buddhism and Shinto. It was restored in postwar years at the strong wish of the local community, which feared for the loss of their this-worldly benefits. Is this a "Shinto" shrine? In a purist, essentialist sense, no. But it is a shrine which blurs the edges of the concept "Shinto."

Another example of such a blurring of the edges is the third most important Inari shrine of Japan, at Toyokawa in central Japan, which is at the same time a temple of the Sōtō Zen Buddhist denomination. The temple itself is formally called Myōgonji 妙厳寺 but the popular name for the whole complex is Toyokawa Inari 豊川稲荷. This is the result of a decision taken during the time of the *shinbutsu bunri* policy, when the shrine authorities had to decide which way to jump. Today the distinction is no longer relevant for the petitioners who swarm the area on occasion, contributing their money for the ever-growing number of votive fox figures, the messenger of Inari Daimyōjin. Nor will they notice that the huge *torii* in front of the main worship hall has small Buddhist-style swastikas[20] at the ends of the cross-pieces. These are just examples of cases where "fluidity" was never completely abandoned or where it has been resurfacing. In spite of the haunting, almost

---

17 Cf. "Buddhism and Shinto on one island" in: Pye 2013, Vol. II, 278–86.

18 Benzaiten of Exquisite Sound. We recall that Benzaiten is the personification of the Indian river Sarasvatī and is for this reason a divinity of eloquence and music.

19 A notable exception is the memorial day on the 25th of each month commemorating Sugawara Michizane or Tenjin-sama, although this is not specifically referred to as an *ennichi* at the relevant shrines.

20 The left-turning swastika is a regular symbol for Buddhist temples, also used on maps to show their location.

minimalist clarity of some of the major shrines such as Atsuta or Ise, the overall contours of what people call "Shinto" cannot ever be completely tidy.

In this context a word of warning is in order against any mere conflation of the expressions "syncretism" and "synthesis," which after all are not quite the same.[21] A synthesis is an integrated result in which the contributory elements are totally taken up, whereas "syncretism" allows for continued perception of the diverse elements and even suggests that they could be drawn apart again. In the case of Buddhist-Shintō interactions there are other considerations which encourage this view, not least the fact that Buddhist thought itself had and maintains an emic theory of correlation, one which implies reflective awareness of the diversity of the elements involved and therefore a recognition of their latent distinctiveness. The concept of skilful means in Buddhism entails the recognition that provisional expressions of a deeper truth will eventually be set aside; and for this they need to be recognizable. In the Shinto perception, as already argued above, the very fact that it was possible for political leaders in the nineteenth century to insist on the "separation of gods and buddhas" (*shinbutsu bunri* 神仏分離) shows that the previous arrangements had been syncretistic and not totally synthesized. To take just one example, it was quite possible for the Buddhist images which had once been set up at various locations on Haku-san, the well-known pilgrimage mountain in western Japan, to be extracted from their reverential sites and gathered together in one single location, where they can still be seen. The point to note here is that the people in charge knew very well which images they were taking away: Buddhist ones, not Shinto ones.

It will be clear even from the few indications given here, that the expression "Shinto" cannot be used simply to refer to one clear-cut stream of religious tradition that has maintained an orthodox coherence since ancient beginnings. While different investigators concentrate on different junctures at which there have been fresh departures, the recognition that there is this complexity seems to

---

21 See Pye 2013, Vol. II Part 6, pp. 243–306.

be widely shared and stands in some tension to insider expressions of religio-ideological purity.

In the contemporary Shinto world itself, the past continues to be present, indeed massively so. Note must therefore be taken of the various "inside" positions of apologists, who all have their own view of the past, whether by choice or in accordance with an inherited religious role. In their explanations, history, tradition and legend are interwoven in support of a distinctive religious agenda. It is not necessary to agree with these perspectives, but they are themselves part of the phenomenon. A distinct lack of historico-critical grasp may be noted, and indeed it is a typical feature that Shinto apologists seek to harness the past without being very interested in checking it over. This is illustrated by the frequency with which the phrase "...*to iwarete imasu*" is used, which means "so it is said," when explaining something about the story of a particular shrine. In this sense, even leaving aside the so-called "origins" in mythical narratives, the undiscerning observer may be confronted with the assertion that "Shinto" somehow began in the iron-age Yayoi Period (c. 300 BCE to c. 300 CE), even though there is simply no evidence for anything discernible as "Shinto" at that time. All we can say is that the wish to perceive such origins is a feature of the modern Shinto mentality, at least in many cases. At the same time, it is fair to say that beyond a certain point the origins of Shinto get lost in the mists of time.

Characterizing Shinto today

Getting the history right is one thing, but the second task of an external observer or researcher into religions is to present a synchronic characterization of "Shinto" in contemporary times in such a way that this can be recognized both by Shintoists themselves and by others who study religions in the field. Such a characterization needs to be a recurring, if varying and renegotiable pattern, based on embedded research, or fieldwork, with varying degrees of participant observation depending on the occasions and personal relationships in the contemporary situation. This task is inevitably complex precisely because there is no one self-evidently coherent field of "Shinto." If we are not to be speaking on behalf of some internal *parti pris*, we need to approach the matter by "adumbrating" the field to which we seek to refer. This process is analogous to the task which specialists in the study of religions face when seeking to set out what it is that they are studying.[22] At the risk of oversimplification, at least six major strands or areas must be taken into consideration.

First there is the concept of "shrine Shinto" espoused particularly by the Association of Shinto Shrines (Jinja Honchō) and broadly presupposed by Kokugakuin Daigaku, the leading Shinto-oriented university mentioned earlier. Most of the major Shinto shrines are affiliated to the Jinja Honchō. Broadly speaking, "shrine Shinto" follows on from what was formerly "state Shinto" (*kokka Shinto*), but this latter term is no longer applicable. On the other hand, that there is a specific connection between the Imperial Household and the Ise Shrine (often referred to simply as "Jingū") must be noted. Shrines affiliated to the Jinja Honchō usually display centrally issued posters, relating for example to Ise Jingū and its periodic rebuilding, and to imperial accession rites when relevant. There is also a standard notice about the correct sequence to observe when praying before a shrine. The numerous shrines in this category by no means exhaust the field of contemporary Shinto.

Second therefore, cognizance must be taken of a significant number of shrines, even large ones, that are not linked to the Jinja Honchō and to some extent develop an independent profile. A clear example of such is Tsubaki Ōkami Yashiro 椿大神社, located at Suzuka in Mie Prefecture. Tsubaki Grand Shrine, as it is also known, not only projects itself as the true guardian of ancient and authentic Shinto tradition but also has an international outreach beyond the Japanese ethnos. There is an American version of Tsubaki Grand Shrine at Granite Falls, Washington with a non-Japanese priest in charge. This outreach involves the delineation of

---

22 On "adumbrating the field" see "Field and Theory in the Study of Religions" in: Pye 2013, Vol. I, 33–49 (esp. 34–6).

a distinctive "teaching," and so visiting guests, whether in Japan or the US, must take care not to assume that this is a common teaching of Shinto in general. Typologically Tsubaki Grand Shrine comes close to being a Shinto "sect" though it does not present itself as such.

Third must be noted the existence of innumerable very small, neighbourhood shrines tucked away in residential back-streets and looked after by local voluntary groups. While such shrines may on occasion be visited for ritual actions by the priest of a larger shrine, they are simply not sufficiently organized for any regular formal affiliation. There is usually an oral tradition about their provenance, i.e. about which *kami* came to be settled in any one location, and from where. The relations with larger shrines are so loose that, viewed by an observer, these can only be regarded as more or less independent shrines.

Fourth, larger shrines themselves quite often include tiny shrines within their grounds which correspond to larger shrines elsewhere. Such sub-shrines, known as *sessha* 摂社 or (of lower status) *massha* 末社, represent a local focus for paying reverence to the divinity of a major shrine located elsewhere, e.g. the *kami* of Suwa Taisha or Tenmangū. Imamiya Jinja in Kyoto, for example, has eleven such sub-shrines, some of which are the result of relocations within the city.[23] Most frequently these sub-shrines cannot be entered physically by humans; they are little more than raised wooden shelters (*hokora* 祠)[24] in which only the *kami* reside. The *kami* do not require a large space. Sometimes there is a small area before the shrine itself that can be entered on foot, as in the Inari shrine in the grounds of Imamiya Jinja. There is therefore a sliding scale in terms of size and access. Yet they are all true shrines in that the *kami* reside in them and can be venerated there. Slightly different are specially marked places for "worshipping from afar" (*yōhai* 遥拝). Here we usually find a *torii*, the symbolic entrance gate, and beside it, or looking through it, a stone marker with the name of the

---

23 See Pye 2004, 35–6 and 44.
24 The term is also used for the small wayside shelters in which Buddhist images, notably Jizō or Dainichi Nyorai are positioned.

distant shrine in question. Although this little spot might look like a shrine, it is not. The shrine is not here, nor is or are the *kami*. It is quite common to find such positions for worshipping towards Ise Jingū "from afar." But they may also be found on the lower reaches of a mountain when the real shrine is at a summit which can only be reached with difficulty.

Fifth, there are independently active Shinto-related religious groups to be taken into account, some of which are classified under the concept of Sect Shintō (Kyōha Shintō). A number of these groups or movements, notably Kurozumikyō, Ooyashirokyō (earlier known as Taishakyō) and Shinshūkyō arose in the context of shrines with a clearly marked Shinto character, while others which have no such origin also have a number of features which bring them more loosely into the Shinto fold. A very clear example of the latter type is Konkōkyō. This field of so-called Sect Shintō is introduced and discussed in more detail in the third section of the present volume.

Sixth in this broad spectrum is the wide field of Shinto-oriented presence in the media. This includes a plethora of free-wheeling publications about how and when to visit individual shrines and for what purpose, about various *kami* and their attributes, or about the myths of the ancient *Kojiki* which are currently enjoying much popular attention in illustrated works, in *manga* and in *anime*. A couple of popular titles, here translated, will give the flavour: "What we, as Japanese, should know about Shinto" or "Book for Understanding the Kojiki and the Gods of Japan."[25] In such books the various *kami* of the mythical narratives and the presumed imperial ancestors are illustrated in near-*manga* style, even though in ancient times, as is often pointed out, they escaped depiction. The *Kojiki* itself also receives considerable attention as a free-standing reference point in Japanese culture. The Nara Prefectural Museum of Art, for example, mounted "The Grand Kojiki Exhibition" in 2014, subtitling its catalogue in English with "Feelings and words handed down from past generations to the future" and "Stories of love and creation for all five senses." On a different tack the

---

25 See Takemitsu 2003 and Yoshida 2015 respectively.

1300th anniversary of the *Kojiki*'s appearance was celebrated by the publication of a book of maps showing 165 places somehow connected with it (*kojiki yukari chi* 古事記ゆかり地) ranging from Kyūshū in the south through Honshū all the way to present-day Ibaraki Prefecture in the East.[26] The fact that these are numbered and shown with clear transport instructions makes it effectively an invitation to pilgrimage. The large-format book is also proved with a few manga-style depictions of important *kami* such as Ōkuninushi no kami, Ninigi no Mikoto, and heroes including the first emperor Jinmu Tennō and Yamato Takeru no Mikoto. As a field, these elements of medial culture escape any institutionalized standing or formalized definition but may nevertheless be viewed as being in some way a part of the Shinto world today.[27]

The idea of setting out various elements which make up "Shinto" has arisen in various contexts. Earlier typologies are somewhat helpful but are usually in need of some qualification. In his substantial book *Shintō no kisochishiki to kisomondai* (1973, "Fundamental knowledge and fundamental problems of Shintō"), the influential Shinto scholar Ono Sokyō listed the following elements: (1) Imperial Household Shintō, (2) Jinja Shintō (Jingū), (3) Jinja Shintō (Jinja), (4) Kyōha Shintō (13 sects), (5) Shinkyō Shintō (i.e. new sectarian Shintō) and (6) Folk Shintō. While "state Shinto" has disappeared here, following its disestablishment, it is notable that a spectrum is suggested which runs from the politically significant to the politically insignificant. It begins by highlighting Imperial Household Shinto, then gives precedence within shrine Shinto to *jingū* and then moves through various voluntary elements to land with, in full, "common folk Shintō" (*minkantsūzokuteki shintō* 民間通俗的神道). This sequencing by Ono clearly reflects an ideological preference within the field. The formal term Jingū can refer specifically to Ise Shrine, and Atsuta Jingū and Meiji Jingū both have deep connections with the Imperial Household. It should not be overlooked however that *jingū* or even *daijingū* can

---

26 Oikawa 2013.
27 The International Shinto Studies Association (ISSA) recently held a public symposium on Shinto and *anime* (Kyoto, 2018).

occur in other shrine names, and others such as Hachimangū or Tenmangū incorporate the designation *-gū*.

A discursive description

Again and again we find that voices from within the shrine world are not slow to tell us what "Shinto" is supposed to be. Though diverse, they have in common that they express a normative, even essentialist position. These are voices *from inside*. An approach from outside needs to be more circumspect and to include as many relevant elements and aspects as possible. How can this be done? One way is to offer an open-ended, briefly discursive account of what amounts to "Shinto" while taking the wide variety of relevant features into account. Consider first then, as a way into this approach, a relatively short discursive description of this kind. The example may be thought of as *hybrid* in that it was initially drafted by an observer on request and then adapted at the suggestion of insiders before being adopted by what is now the International Shinto Studies Association.[28] It runs:

> Shintō is a set of notions, ritual practices and values of which the early origins are lost in the mists of ancient Japanese history. There are some 90,000 Shintō shrines across the country today, most of which are linked in the Association of Shintō Shrines (Jinja Honchō). At the same time each shrine has its own strong local roots and history. The shrines are dedicated to one or several divinities called *kami*, regarded as representing various natural and cultural forces. Their power is tamed, pacified, enhanced or appropriated through rituals which are performed in particular by priests. Shintō can be said to foster a strong sense of communal identity, and many ordinary persons participate with offerings, special visits or pilgrimages to the shrines and membership in cultic associations. The ritual

---

[28] International Shinto Studies Association (ISSA) is the English designation for the non-profit organization Shintō Kokusai Gakkai 神道国際学会, based in Tokyo, which should not be confused with the International Shinto Foundation, based in New York. The "observer" was the present writer.

> calendar typically includes both rites which are carried out across the whole country and rites which are characteristic of the shrine in question. Having been influenced over the centuries by various Asian religious, as well as being redefined and adjusted at various times, Shintō today is a rich storehouse of resources from which people seek various kinds of guidance and succor. When they visit shrines, foreign visitors are requested to maintain a respectful attitude at all times. In particular, it is a matter of courtesy to rinse the mouth and hands before approaching the main shrine. Visitors are welcome to ask questions and to participate as appropriate.

Because this is a hybrid statement, it hovers between open-ended description and a tendency towards summarization. Summarization may lead into essentialism, for some. For others it is a necessary result of compactness without further commitment. Hence the matter is moot and judgement about it should remain suspended. Normative assertions about origins such as are made in the definition by Katō Genchi quoted earlier are avoided. Without going into details, the justified caution of professional historians about so-called origins has been taken into account.

Even with due care, it is not possible to resolve all the tensions between "Shinto from outside" and "Shinto from inside." Those who study religions in the field with attention to what is actually going on will frequently find that the standpoints and statements of believers and dispassionate observers are not consistent with each other. W. Brede Kristensen famously stated "For the historian only one evaluation is possible: 'The believers were completely right.'"[29] The purpose of this striking statement was to shift the focus from what some might regard as "mere" history to the consciousness of believers in their own self-proclaimed authenticity. But the assertion cannot really be maintained. For one thing, many fraudulent claims are advanced in religious contexts. To illustrate, it has been suggested that if all the fragments claimed to be bits

---

29 Kristensen 1960, 14. Similarly, Wilfred Cantwell Smith had enunciated the principle "no statement about a religion is valid unless it can be acknowledged by that religion's believers." (Smith 1959, 42.)

of the true cross on which Christ was crucified were gathered together they would fill up several huge transport trucks. And there are many other religious statements which do not stand up to critical examination, especially hagiographical accounts of events purported to have happened in the past. Charming though it is to hear such things, our realistic historical awareness must also claim its due. When we study religions, including Shinto, we may therefore experience what I refer to as "tension with the believers."[30] However, this is normal. We are most likely to experience tension with the believers or participants (for the word "believers" is not always particularly relevant) if we get into the field and become involved with them. Desk-top study is not enough.

Three further points may be noted on the statement cited above. First, the three concluding sentences are not descriptive, but simply give a request and guidance to visitors, presumed to be non-Japanese, to shrines. This reflects an understandable concern from within Shinto circles, and at the same time underlines the importance of the shrine itself (any shrine) as locating the presence of *kami*. Second, there is no attempt to set out a typology of the elements of Shinto along the lines discussed earlier. This was avoided because no one account would have gained final assent. Third, there is no reference to any named shrines. This is because in a concise statement it would not be possible to know where to start and to stop with the naming of shrines. The approach taken avoided a potentially controversial typology of shrines and shrine groups as well as decisions about which ones are more important than others.

For these reasons the statement is only of limited value as a discursive answer to the question "What is Shinto?" It needed to be closed off briefly in the interests of compactness and ease of general consent. For a more satisfactory discursive delineation or adumbration of this field, more is required. The matter of the

---

30 Discussed in detail in my article "Getting into trouble with the believers" in Pye 2013, Vol. I, 86–106. In the case of Shinto a significant tension occurs when the observer does not full-heartedly concur with statements about the distant past of "Shinto" which evidently cannot be upheld in a sober fashion.

typology of the elements of Shinto was addressed earlier, and some earlier typologies were criticized. Taking that into account, six different areas were adduced that all form a part of the overall field of Shinto. In particular, some specific, real shrines do need to be named. It might seem that from among such a huge number of shrines it is impossible to decide which ones to choose as examples. In prewar times it might have been appropriate to rehearse the official lists known as the *kanpei taisha* in order to make a start. These lists are of interest historically, but would now be an inappropriate starting point because they were politically normed. As an alternative, it is convenient to start by naming those shrines which attract a particularly large number of visitors at New Year, such as: Meiji Jingū, Kasama Inari Taisha, Fushimi Inari Taisha, Atsuta Jingū, Kitano Tenmangū or Kotohiragū. Such shrines compete with various extremely popular Buddhist temples for visitors on January 1st to 3rd. The Jinja Honchō, evidently recognizing the importance of these numbers, recently ran a campaign to encourage people to visit their local shrine *first* on New Year's Day. This campaign implies granting a priority to the local "clan divinity" (*ujigami* 氏神) as the initial locus of Shinto identity. In fact, it is well known that the idea that people are the "clan children" (*ujiko* 氏子) is now little more than a pious fiction, on account of vast demographic changes. Nevertheless it is used as a courtesy designation for all those who support major festivals with processions and much drinking of saké.

As a complementary starting point, mention may be made of shrines which have special civil or political associations. Ise Jingū and Atsuta Jingū are prominent because they house two of the three original imperial regalia, the mirror and the sword respectively. The other one of the three, the curved jewel, is enshrined in the Imperial Palace. There is also a duplicate sword used when these regalia are ceremonially handed to the new emperor. Ise Jingū provides the most important link to the Imperial Household, being the normal residence of the sun-goddess Amaterasu, the presumed ancestor of the imperial family. Of broader civil significance are Meiji Jingū, with its huge grounds in Tokyo, because it honours the great modernizing emperor of the nineteenth century who is still so respected today, and Yasukuni Jinja which was founded in the Meiji Period to honour all who died in the service of the emperor, or by extension of the Japanese state in its various wars. Yasukuni Shine is politically controversial, but that is not our present subject.[31] Uncontroversial, but of major significance because of its ancient and intimate connections with the mythical narratives of the *Kojiki*, is Izumo Taisha, located in Shimane Prefecture and far from both the ancient and the modern capitals of the country. The very existence of Izumo Taisha counteracts tendencies to focus Shinto exclusively on the Ise Shrine and the Imperial Household. In this connection the existence of the "Shinto sect" Taishakyō (later Ooyashirokyō) is significant, as discussed in the third part of this volume.

Such major shrines, all important for various reasons, need to be named, and yet there are supposedly 90,000 shrines all over the country which can all tell us something about what Shinto is. In fact there are more than this number, because many of the tiny local shrines mentioned earlier are simply disregarded or taken for granted.

What is a shrine?

This leads into a second approach towards defining Shinto by posing the apparently elementary question: What is a shrine? Admittedly, as seen, even this question is not quite as simple as it may first sound, for the shrines are so varied. However, if we have a generic idea of what a Shinto shrine is, then we will be able to recognize the family resemblances and thus acquire a balanced idea of what Shinto is about. Indulgence is requested on the part of readers already familiar with all these features, but their mention is an essential part of the wider argument.

There are several Japanese terms for shrine of which the most generic is *yashiro*, written with the expressive character 社. This character consists of two elements, the part on the left means

---

31 See Antoni 1991, especially 155–89; Pye 1996b, 2003; Breen 2013.

"pointing to," and the part on the right means "earth." A *yashiro* is a place where a *kami* is enshrined for care and reverence. It may or may not have a building on it.[32] However that may be the place is marked off in some way, typically by a rope (*shimenawa*) often with white papers (*shide*) attached to it, or by an open, framed entrance known as a *torii*. There is commonly a structure in which the *kami* is presumed to reside, having been ceremoniously escorted there. This is at the highest position in the area, or it is raised; however it is usually not the largest structure, because the *kami* are a spiritual force which can be concentrated in a small space, whereas the people who revere it, or them, may need to be fitted in to a larger structure to the fore. The two structures are known as the *honden* (main hall) and the *haiden* (reverencing hall) respectively.

Secondary but not essential features typically include: a fence all around the wider enclosed area; a *temizuya* just inside the entrance, that is, a covered stand with clean flowing water and bamboo (or plastic) ladles for preliminary ablutions; a shrine office (*shamusho*); a counter served by assistants for the sale of amulets and votive tablets, and other accessories; a stand for hanging up votive tablets (*ema*) after they have been inscribed with wishes or prayers; a depository for the return of out-of-date amulets and so on, which await ritual disposal; a hanging gong at the front of the reverencing hall, to attract the attention of the *kami* before praying; various sub-shrines. These elements will be found in all Shinto shrines above a certain size. Incidentally, the *temizuya*, hanging gong and stand for votive tablets are also found at many Buddhist temples, depending on the denomination.

The key element which makes any one spot, or situational complex, into a shrine in the more general sense, is the *yashiro*, whether this is architecturally structured or not. This residence of the *kami* is marked by physical separation, however minimal. Since the character for *yashiro* 社 can also be read in compound words as *-sha* or *-ja* (cf. the modern Chinese pronunciation *shè*), it appears, in some form, in the names of the great majority of shrines, as in

---

32 Cf. Sonoda 2002, 9.

26 *Exploring Shinto*

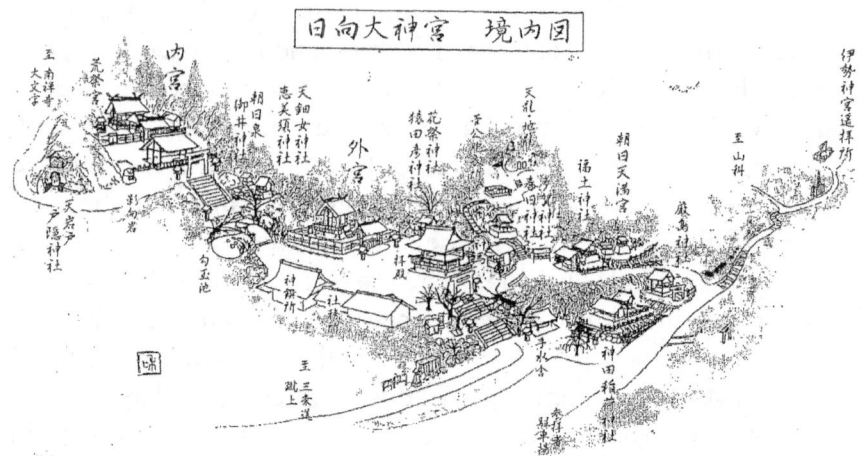

Figure 1 Sketch of Himukai Daijingū shrine grounds.

-jinja (literally "*kami* shrine") or *-taisha* ("great shrine").[33] These variations conveniently light up the generic quality of the term *yashiro* when we are thinking of Shinto shrines.

In spite of the consistency of all of these typical features, it should not be overlooked that there is always *a reason* why particular *kami* are enshrined at a particular spot. In the case of larger shrines, such a reason (the *yurai* 由来) is usually explained in a pamphlet. This means that there are always specifics, often mythical or historical stories (which do not need to be historically accurate). It pertains to the *generic* nature of "shrines" that there are such specifics and that these vary from case to case.

This approach will now be illustrated with reference to one selected shrine, Himukai Daijingū 日向大神宮, which is located on a relatively isolated hillside near the city of Kyoto (administratively within it). The slightly unusual formal name of this shrine will become clear below. The entrance to this shrine is shown on the cover of this book. Here we show a sketch of the shrine grounds (**Figure 1**). In the lower foreground can be seen two flights of steps

---

33 The Chinese-derived pronunciation for *kami* is *-shin* or *-jin*, hence the common term *jinja*. The relatively unusual term *jingū* arises because the *-gū* means "palace" and is reserved for very special places indeed.

leading up to the *torii* at the entrance. To the left, just inside the *torii*, is the shrine office and a counter for the sale of amulets. To the immediate right of the *torii* is the reverencing hall (*haiden*). In the upper part to the left, above another flight of steps, is the main shrine, fenced off and with nothing but trees behind it. Now come the specific features. The high shrine in this case is not called a *honden* as usual, but is referred to as the *naikū*, which means "inner palace." Moreover, below it, at the foot of the steps, but after the *haiden*, there is another structure referred to as the *gekū*, which means "outer palace." This is positioned delicately to the right of the onward steps, so that it also has its own situational finality. Himukai Jingū is therefore a double shrine, and the reason for this distinctive, non-generic feature is that the complex corresponds to the two main shrines of Ise, known there as the *gekū* and the *naikū* respectively. At Ise itself, in distant Mie Prefecture, these two are in effect separate shrines (phenomenologically speaking) with their own separate sites and entrances; at the same time they are referred to collectively as Jingū, the "*kami* palace." Thus at Himukai Daijingū both the *gekū* and the *naikū* are referred to as "main palace" (*hongū*), being the "lower" *hongū* and the "upper" *hongū* respectively. It is in the upper main palace that the sun-goddess Amaterasu is enshrined. Here at the Himukai Daijingū, therefore, we have a small-scale substitute for Ise Jingū itself that can be reached relatively easily by citizens of Kyoto. In other words, it is rather like a grand version of "worshipping from afar" (*yōhai*) but, because the *kami* are enshrined there it is at the same time a stand-alone shrine in its own right.

The wider picture

It is very tempting to assert that if we know what a shrine is, we know what Shinto is. I am in fact convinced that this is the best place to start, and that the question should be asked for preference in the context of the field itself, where we always come up against the fascinating interplay of the generic and the specific. But we also have to consider what people do when they visit the *kami*, what they think and feel, how they are organized insofar as they are not casual individual visitors, how one shrine fits in with other similar ones, how the shrines relate to wider cultural, social and political matters, what points of interest are hidden in their endlessly complicated narratives, and much more besides. There can therefore be no very short, single statement that does justice to the whole field of Shinto. Yet part of the task of those who study religions is to offer compact characterizations which may have a heuristic value in an ongoing process of observation and analysis. In this spirit I conclude with one final attempt at a discursive statement which may be regarded as a tentative personal answer to the question "What is Shinto?" from an observer's point of view. The observer has indeed looked at it from the outside, but after listening and watching from the inside, and this interaction is also reflected below.

> Shinto is usually presented by its priestly and academic representatives as the indigenous religion of the Japanese people which has roots in prehistoric times. At the same time, Shinto as we know it today is the result of a series of inventions and reconstructions. The earliest major construction is to be found in the mythical narratives of the eighth century *Kojiki* and *Nihonshoki* (or *Nihongi*). This was followed by Watarai Shintō, Yoshida (or Yuiitsu) Shintō, the Kokugaku movement, and so on. Then came the ideologically heightened form of Shinto related to the Tennō cult in the nineteenth and early twentieth centuries, and the redefined form of Shinto which was created after the separation of religion and the state at the end of the second world war. This current form is defined largely by the guidelines of the Association of Shinto Shrines (Jinja Honchō), which is a religious corporation registered in law but independent of the state. At the same time there is a spectrum of less clearly defined phenomena which also belong to the world of Shinto.
>
> Literally, Shinto means "the way of the *kami*", that is, the way of the gods or spirits. The *kami* are mythical figures whose stories are told in the *Kojiki* and the *Nihongi*; various forces

of nature found in the mountains, the forests, the springs and rivers, and so on; human figures who have a special place in the common memory: and, more vaguely, all the ancestors of the Japanese people. All these different kinds of *kami* may be revered in the various shrines of Shinto, which provide a focus for their sacred power. In Shinto, therefore, the sacred is localised in a defined space. Though invisible, it is felt to be present in particular places which are important to the people who live in the area and even beyond. Many *kami* are of local or regional importance. Every village has at least one *kami* in its own shrine, which may be related notionally and ritually to other shrines elsewhere. The festivals centred on these shrines serve to reinforce the common identity of the people in the area. Some of the more prominent *kami* are of national importance, especially those named in the mythical narratives, previous emperors, and other widely respected heroes. Notable ancient shrines of this kind are Izumo Taisha, the residence of Ōkuninushi who established the land, and Ise Jingū, the residence of Amaterasu Ōmikami, the presumed ancestress of the imperial line. A more recent, very substantial foundation is Meiji Jingū in Tokyo, where the nineteenth century Emperor Meiji and his consort Empress are revered. This and others contribute to a political narrative relating to the imperial line, reverence for which continues to be promoted by the Association of Shinto Shrines. Other shrines, such as the well-known Inari shrines at Fushimi in western Japan and Kasama in eastern Japan, cater for popular interests and are mainly visited in order to pray for commercial and personal benefits.

Socially, Shinto is in the first instance understood to be the religion of the immediate social group surrounding a given shrine, then of the wider group, extending further afield until it covers the whole nation of Japanese people. The extension of Japanese power over Korea and Taiwan in earlier times led to an attempted extension of Shinto along the lines drawn by political control. Nowadays the overseas extension of Shinto is limited to the provision of a small number of shrines which serve the *émigré* and business communities.

The main rituals associated with Shinto are purifications of the people on the one hand and offerings to the *kami* on the other hand. The ritual of purification, performed by a Shinto priest, is understood to bring about a cancellation of impurity (*kegare*) which arises from the staining effect of daily life, and in a positive direction a clarification of the human spirit, that is, a cleansing of attitudes and motivations. This leads to a sharpened sense of resolve and increased loyalty to one's family, one's associates and the Japanese nation. The offerings to the *kami* usually consist of rice-cakes, rice-wine and citrus fruits, but traditionally they also include "the harvest of the sea" and "the harvest of the mountains" (*umi no sachi* and *yama no sachi*) and in some cases materials for clothing (e.g. for the goddess Amaterasu at Ise Jingū). These offerings express care for the needs of the *kami*. They are intended to ensure that the *kami* will be content and thereby benevolent towards human beings. When members of the public take part in Shinto rites a small branch of the *sakaki* tree is usually offered in the presence of the Shinto priest. The correct way of performing such an offering is occasionally described with illustrations. Since the ritual functions of Shinto are mainly social, the rites relating to the individual are the so-called "life rites", following the passage of the individual through the various stages from infancy through marriage up until death. The provision of death rites, on the other hand, has largely been taken over by the various denominations of Buddhism. Other occasional rituals serve this-worldly needs, such as safety at work and on journeys, success in examinations and commerce, and the assistance of the *kami* in finding a marriage partner. These rites are essentially *transactional* and, together with the life-rites, meet the this-worldly needs which play a normal role in the *primal* religion of undifferentiated societies. We should remember however, that Shinto has a long history and, as noted above, has been reconstructed several times in accordance with the political and economic development of Japan; for this reason contemporary Shinto may be described as an "adapted primal religion."[34]

---

34 Cf. Pye 2003 for an earlier version of this statement, headed "Some general features of Shinto." I proposed the use of the phrase "adapted primal

Although this statement touches on various aspects of cultural and social life, the highlighted central feature is certainly religious.[35] The central focus of Shinto is always on the shrine, that is, on the spot which is indicated as being the residence of the *kami*. Without doubt, a characterization like this could be set out in other ways and with different emphases. Yet, however the details might vary, such a formulation can provide a general indication of what it is that we are studying. In this sense it is an attempt to answer the question "What is Shinto?"

References

Antoni, Klaus 1991. *Der himmlische Herrscher und sein Staat: Essays zur Stellung des Tennō im modernen Japan.* München (Judicium).
Baird, Robert D. 1971. *Category Formation and the History of Religions.* The Hague (Mouton). https://doi.org/10.1515/9783111375137
Bock, Felicia Gressitt 1970. *Engi-Shiki. Procedures of the Engi Era* (2 vols.). Tokyo (Sophia University / Monumenta Nipponica Monographs).
Breen, John (ed.) 2013. *Yasukuni, the War Dead and the Struggle for Japan's Past.* Oxford (Oxford University Press). Reprint from 2008 (Hurst/Columbia University Press). https://doi.org/10.1002/9781444317190
Breen, John and Teeuwen, Mark 2010. *A New History of Shinto.* Oxford (Wiley-Blackwell).
Creemers, W. H. M. 1968. *Shrine Shinto after World War II.* Leiden (Brill).
Davidson, Augusta M. Campbell 1904 and 1907. *Present-day Japan.* London (Fisher Unwin).
Faure, Bernard 2016. *Gods of Medieval Japan Vol. 1: The Fluid Pantheon.* Honolulu (University of Hawaii Press).
https://doi.org/10.21313/hawaii/9780824839338.003.0001

---

religion" earlier (Pye 1996a). It is arguable that it could also be applied to Brahmanism/Hinduism, especially when we take account of the parallels considered by Mark Teeuwen in this volume.

35 This can be important for extraneous reasons, socio-political but not in themselves religious. For example, the instructions on how to offer a *sakaki* branch to the *kami* are illustrated in a booklet published by Yasukuni Shrine. Making such an offering is a religious act, but indirectly it provides politically significant evidence that this controversial shrine, sometimes said to be "non-religious," participates in the normal ritual patterns of Shinto.

Hardacre, Helen 2017. *Shinto: A History*. Oxford (OUP).
https://doi.org/10.1093/acprof:oso/9780190621711.001.0001
Herbert, Jean 1967. *Shinto. The Fountainhead of Japan*. London (George Allen and Unwin).
Holtom, Daniel Clarence 1922. *The Political Philosophy of Modern Shinto. A Study of the State Religion of Japan*. Tokyo (The Asiatic Society of Japan).
Holtom, Daniel Clarence 1928. *The Japanese Enthronement Ceremonies*. Tokyo (Kyo Bun Kwan).
Holtom, Daniel Clarence 1938. *The National Faith of Japan: A Study in Modern Shinto*. London (Kegan Paul, Trench and Trubner).
Hylkema-Vos, Naomi 1990. "Katō Genchi: A Neglected Pioneer in Comparative Religion." *Japanese Journal of Religious Studies* 17/4 (December), 375–95.
https://doi.org/10.18874/jjrs.17.4.1990.375-395
Katō, Genchi 1926. *A Study of Shinto. The Religion of the Japanese Nation*. Tokyo (Meiji Japan Society). Second edition: London and Dublin (Curzon) 1971.
Kristensen, W. Brede 1960. *The Meaning of Religion: Lectures in the Phenomenology of Religion*. The Hague (Mouton).
https://doi.org/10.1007/978-94-017-6580-0
Nara Prefecture (ed.) 2014. *Daikojikiten / The Grand Kojiki Exhibition*. Nara (Nara Prefecture).
Oikawa Chihaya 及川千早 2013. *Kojiki yukarichi mappu* 古事記ゆかり地マップ. Tokyo (Buyōdō).
Ono, Sokyō 小野祖教 1973. *Shintō no kisochishiki to kisomondai* 神道の基礎知識と基礎問題. Tokyo (Jinja Shinpōsha).
Pye, Michael 1978. "Diversions in the interpretation of Shinto" in: D. W. Anthony (ed.), *Proceedings of the British Association for Japanese Studies (Volume Two: 1977, Part Two: Social Sciences)*. Published in 1978 by The Centre of Japanese Studies, The University, Sheffield, 77–92. Republished in: *Religion* 11 (1981), 61–74. https://doi.org/10.1016/S0048-721X(81)80060-7
Pye, M. 1996a. "Shinto, primal religion and international identity." *Marburg Journal of Religion* 1/1, 5.
Pye, M. 1996b. "Yasukuni Jinja als umstrittene Kriegsgedenkstätte" in: Konvent der Philipps-Universität (ed.), *Die Philipps-Universität Marburg im Nationalsozialismus*. Marburg (Konvent der Philipps-Universität Marburg), 267–72.
Pye, Michael 2003. "Religion and conflict in Japan with special reference to Shinto and Yasukuni Shrine." *Diogenes* 50/3, 45–59.
https://doi.org/10.1177/03921921030503004
Pye, Michael 2004. *The Structure of Religious Systems in Contemporary Japan: Shintō Variations on Buddhist Pilgrimage*. Marburg (Centre for Japanese Studies, Occasional Papers 30).
Pye, Michael 2013. *Strategies in the Study of Religions Volumes I and II*. Berlin (de Gruyter).

Rambelli, Fabio and Reinders, Eric 2014. *Buddhism and Iconoclasm in East Asia: A History.* London etc. (Bloomsbury).

Smith, Wilfred Cantwell 1959. "Comparative Religion: Whither and Why?" in: M. Eliade and J. M. Kitagawa (eds.), *The History of Religions.* Chicago (University of Chicago Press).

Sonoda, Minoru 2002. *The World of Shinto: Reflections of a Shinto Priest.* Tokyo and New York (International Shinto Foundation).

Takemitsu, Makoto 武光誠 2003. *Nihonjin nara shitte okitai shintō* 日本人なら知っておきたいと神道. Tokyo (Kawade Shobō).

Triplett, Katja 2004. "Katō Genchi and the History of the Study of Religions in Japan" in: Katja Triplett, Christoph Kleine and Monika Schrimpf (eds.), *Unterwegs. Neue Pfade in der Religionswissenschaft / New Paths in the Study of Religions (Festschrift für Michael Pye zum 65. Geburtstag).* München (Biblion), 319–72.

Woodard, W. P. 1972. *The Allied Occupation of Japan 1945–1952 and Japanese Religions.* Leiden (Brill).

Yanagita Kunio 柳田國男 1928, reprint 1975. *Nenjūgyōji zusetsu* 年中行事図説. Tokyo (Minzokugaku Kenkyūsho).

Yomiuri Shinbunsha (ed.) 1990. *Nihon no kamigami to yashiro. Gendai ni tsutaeru nihonbunka no genten* 日本の神々と社。現代に伝える日本文化の原点. Tokyo (Yomiuri Shinbunsha).

Yoshida, Kunihiro 吉田邦博 2015. *Kojiki to nihon no kamigami ga wakaru hon* 古事記と日本の神々がわくる本. Tokyo (Kenkyū Publishing).

About the author

Michael Pye (born 1939) first resided in Japan from 1961 onwards. From 1968 he taught Religious Studies in England and in 1982 became professor for the Study of Religions at Marburg University, Germany. He was president of the International Association for the History of Religions from 1995 to 2000. On retirement he returned to Japan for several years, being associated with Otani University, Kyoto. Publications include *Strategies in the Study of Religions* (2013) and *Japanese Buddhist Pilgrimage* (2015).

2

Essentialism in early Shinto studies

Gaétan Rappo

In a recent book on the links between Shinto and Nationalist discourses in prewar Japan and Europe, Bernhard Scheid remarked that early studies on the subject were, in the West, influenced by nativist ideas (*kokugaku* 国学). They thus tended to showcase a very "essentialist" view of Shinto, neglecting its undoubtedly composite nature in favour of narratives presenting it as the "soul of Japan."[1] Despite the recent focus of the composite, medieval Shinto, especially after the work of Kuroda Toshio, such views still have a large impact, even today.[2]

This article will show how – despite the Kokugaku narrative – essentialism, and by extension the later form of state Shinto, seems to have been the product of both the lineage of nativism in Japan itself, and the influence of Western ideas on prewar Japanese thinkers. This was especially the case with Hiraizumi Kiyoshi, a scholar who would become a major figure in the production of the extreme imperialist ideology of the early Shōwa Period. He was also one of the main sources of the discourses comparing the Japanese spirit to the Nazi ideals, which were created mostly by contemporary German scholars. The origins of this process can actually be seen in Hiraizumi's stay in Europe, especially in France, Germany and England, from 1930 to 1931.

Shinto in the west, and the quest for a "Japanese spirit"

While, as we will see, Hiraizumi was not directly concerned with Shinto studies in the West during his trip, as an introduction to

---

1 Scheid 2013b, 15.
2 In English, see Kuroda 1996.

this paper, I will briefly showcase how early Shinto inherited ideas of the *kokugaku* movement. Since before the war, Shinto studies have been largely defined by an essentialist view of "Shinto" as the "native religion" of the Japanese. What is today called medieval Shinto was either seen as a corruption of a pure ancient form, or as a negligible evolution.

Any study on the history of early Shinto scholarship must mention the work of William George Aston. A British diplomat posted in Asia in the late 19th century, he is the author of many works on Japanese grammar, literature and religion, including a famous translation of the *Nihongi*, published in 1896.[3]

Aston's first book on Shinto was published in 1905, and is called *Shinto, The Way of the Gods*.[4] It is solely focused on what he calls "ancient Shinto," centred on the *Kojiki* and the *Nihongi*. However, an entire chapter is also devoted to what he calls the "decay of Shinto."[5] This basically describes the assimilation of Shinto by Buddhism. He then mentions a "revival of pure Shinto" with Motoori Norinaga.[6]

His ideas of a pure, ancient Shinto – opposed to its later development, which he views as a "decay" through the influence of Buddhism – are perfectly in line with the official discourse on Shinto in Japan during his times. He also clearly established the main framework on interpretation of Shinto in the West, which we can define as a form of "extreme essentialism," that would be the main current until after the war. While the general tone sounds very negative, in his 1907 book, Aston also has a short chapter on "Ryōbu Shintō," (両部神道; a form of medieval Shinto combined with Buddhism). Here, he does also credit Buddhism with bringing a moral aspect to Shinto, which he views as absent from its original form.[7]

Around the same time as Aston, the French jurist-turned-Japanologist Michel Revon published in 1905 a book called *Le*

3   Aston 1896.
4   Aston 1905.
5   Ibid., 359.
6   Ibid., 372.
7   Aston 1907, 78–9.

36 *Exploring Shinto*

Shinntoïsme.⁸ This scholar, criticized by his peers in France such as Noël Péri,⁹ was influenced by Ernest Satow and critical of Basil H. Chamberlain. His goal was to restore a primitive Shinto, a term he did not view negatively, with the methods of comparative science. He thus establishes, in similar ways to Aston, a distinction between primitive Shinto (*Shinto primitif*) and "shinto mélangé" (mixed), a concrete example of which is what he calls "Riyôbou shintou."[10] He views Buddhism and Confucianism as elements that corrupted the pure Shinto, and that should have been rejected.

This approach is continued in France through the work of vulgarizers such as Father Jean-Marie Martin, a member of the Missions Étrangères de Paris, who published two volumes on Shinto in 1924 and 1927. Following the trend in Japan, Martin, a more acute observer of Japanese religions than Revon, also was mainly interested in early Shinto. He, however, gives a very negative vision of it, as a primitive state of religion that just got out of animism in a line of evolutionist view of religions, which sees Christendom as the ultimate stage of development. He speaks of "infiltration of Buddhist thought" in Shinto during the Middle Ages.[11]

While such approaches were still following a certain trend of positivism, this was not the case of the next generation of scholars, where Shintō essentialism would become not only a way to look at historical phenomena, but also a political discourse. It would indeed play, as we will play, a crucial role in the 1930s works trying to blend Nazi concepts of the "spirit of the people" with Japanese ideas such as "essence of the state" (*kokutai* 国体). They were particularly prominent in the work of Hermann Bohner and in the early Monumenta Nipponica school of German scholars in Japan.[12]

---

8 Revon 1905. There is also a 1907 edition, Revon 1907. On early French Shinto studies, see Berthon 2013.
9 Especially his work on Japanese literature. See Péri 1911.
10 Revon 1907, 5–7.
11 Martin 1924, 54.
12 See Wachutka 2012.

Essentialism imported from the west? The case of Hiraizumi Kiyoshi

Essentialism was not a one-way street. Such discourses, deeply rooted in Nazi terminology, perfectly mirror the thought of temporary Japanese thinkers such as Hiraizumi Kiyoshi. Originally from a family of priests of the Hakusan shrine in Toyama, Hiraizumi became one of the most influential scholars in prewar Japan with his conception of extreme imperial loyalism.[13] He was largely disregarded after the war, but the University of Tokyo, where he used to teach, kept a very interesting souvenir of him. In an interview online, Professor Matsukata Fuyuko 松方冬子 of the Historiographical Institute (Tōkyō daigaku shiryō hensanjo 東京大学史料編纂所) affirmed that Hiraizumi was used as an example to discourage young researchers from studying abroad. A popular legend in the university effectively said that Hiraizumi was a normal guy before going to Europe, but when he came back, he was effectively "crazy."[14]

This is certainly an exaggeration. In fact, a lot of the ideas that he would express during and after his trip were already present in some way in his writings from the mid-1920s. Even earlier, in 1911, Hiraizumi reacted strongly to the end of the trial for the perpetrators of the 1910 *Taigyaku jiken* 大逆事件 (Great Treason Incident), when the anarchist Kōtoku Shusui and some of his companions were executed for an alleged plan to assassinate the emperor.[15] The scandal had in fact evolved to a vast debate of history at school.[16] In a letter sent to a friend, Hiraizumi, in a reaction to the general climate, actually declared his intention to purify Japanese schools and the way history was taught, basically in order to instil loyalty to the emperor.[17]

13 For a general presentation of Hiraizumi's life and work, see Wakai 2006.
14 See the interview given at: http://gjs.ioc.u-tokyo.ac.jp/ja/interviews/post/20170303_matsukata/ (accessed on March 8, 2020).
15 On this event, see Lévy 2010; Brownlee 1997, 120.
16 This would also lead to a vast debate on the legitimacy of the two imperial courts of the fourteenth century. On this see Brownlee 1997, 121–31; Rappo 2017, 41–5.
17 Tani 1985, 26.

Such personal inclinations and his background would naturally lead him to become a defender of the Imperialistic view of history (*kōkoku shikan* 皇国史観), as well as a prominent critique of the positivist school (*kōshōgaku* 考証学),[18] and he saw Shinto as a key concept at the core of Japanese values. He also directly inherited the ideas of the founders of modern Shinto studies, such as Tanaka Yoshitō, who saw it as a weapon against Marxism and materialism.[19]

In fact, during the 1920s, Hiraizumi described what can be seen as a very essentialist view of Shinto. In 1927, he wrote an article on the famous separation of Buddhism and Shinto undertaken by the Meiji government. Here, while he does value Buddhism as a religion that tried to adapt to Japan and brought valuable teachings, he clearly states that Shinto represented the traditions of the Japanese state.[20] It was the true religion of Japan, and, as he says with more detail in his 1926 *Chūsei ni okeru seishin seikatsu*, it was only because of the state's weakness, especially in the medieval period, that Buddhism was able to dominate Japanese society and affect all its aspects.[21] His logical conclusion is that when the state recovered its authority in the Meiji Period, it was only natural that Buddhism would be rejected. For Hiraizumi, even before his stay in Europe, Buddhism was just a superfluous, but sometimes appreciable, decoration on the Japanese religious landscape, which was defined by Shinto.[22]

Hiraizumi was thus already an imperial loyalist, and a proponent of essentialism in the 1920s. However, the record of his stay in Europe strongly suggests that he was also deeply affected and inspired by what he saw and heard during his times in the west, and his foreign experience was clearly a catalyst to the more extreme views of the emperor, the state and Shinto that he would develop in the 1930s and even further expand after the war.

18 On this debate, see Souyri 2010.
19 Isomae 2000.
20 Hiraizumi 1927c.
21 Hiraizumi 1926.
22 Matsuo 1985, 16–18.

Hiraizumi's trip to the west

Hiraizumi, at the time an assistant professor in the University of Tokyo, travelled to Europe and America from March 1930 to July 1931. He visited several countries, including France, Germany, Italy, Greece, Czechoslovakia, Hungary, England and the United States. While he wrote some articles relating his experiences after his return to Japan,[23] he also kept a diary, which has been partially published recently.[24]

Hiraizumi's journal appears at first as a very ordinary travel log combined with notes on the various languages the author studied. However, the very first page, with a long description of the importance of race (*minzoku* 民族), shows that most of his observations were already oriented in a certain narrative that also largely determined the people he went to see and his range of interests.[25]

This was already the case of his discussions with the German historian Friedrich Meinecke (1862–1954) in Berlin. His diary tells us that Hiraizumi's motivation in seeking out such scholars was his dissatisfaction with what he saw as the ordinary way of writing history in Japan. He dismissed it as a mere record of how events happened chronologically.[26] The reason he wanted to go to Germany was to study how historians were contributing directly to society. Meinecke actually shared such concerns, and Hiraizumi mentions a passionate discussion with the German scholar.[27] The

---

23 Several of such are included in his Hiraizumi 1933a. A record of his stay in Europe can be found in Hiraizumi 1980.

24 The publication takes the form of facsimiles (*ei'in* 影印) of the original manuscript, in eight parts: Uemura 2014a; Uemura 2014b; Uemura 2015a; Uemura 2016b; Uemura 2016a; Uemura 2017a; Uemura 2017b; Uemura 2018.

25 For the first page of the diary, see Uemura 2014a, 7. Hiraizumi kept a very racist view of the particularity of Japanese people until his death. See Brownlee 1997, 172.

26 Uemura 2015b, 36.

27 See Tani 1985, 32–3. Hiraizumi's record of his talk with Meinecke can be found in an unpublished book called *Kanrin nenpu* 寒林年譜. On this text, see Uemura 2015b, 53, note 2.

fact that Meinecke had anti-semitic views and would later support Nazism foreshadows a link that we will mention below.[28]

After five months in Germany, from May to October 1930, Hiraizumi travelled to Czechoslovakia and Italy, and met the Italian thinker Benedetto Croce in Naples.[29] Hiraizumi knew his work, and meeting him was a key motivation for his trip to Europe, and especially to Italy.[30] On a philosophical level, it appears that Croce had a great appeal for the young Hiraizumi. As he relates in his diary, he considers that they shared a similar view of history, philosophy and also their rejection of Marxist materialism.[31] Croce's idea of blending philosophy and history was also something that Hiraizumi appreciated and that he would expand upon.[32]

Hiraizumi then arrived in Paris in late November the same year. In France, Hiraizumi was particularly interested in the great revolution of 1789 and especially in the work of figures such as François Ferret, who tended to relativize it and even criticize its impact from a royalist point of view.[33] His own interests also led him to study the idea of traditionalism, which he saw as prominent in France, and would provide the nucleus for his 1940 book called *Tradition* (*Dentō* 伝統).[34] Hiraizumi left Paris in early April 1931,

28 However, Hiraizumi did not really think much of the Nazi party itself. See Brownlee 1997, 172.

29 Brownlee 1997, 171–2.

30 In fact Hiraizumi met with Meinecke because the latter quoted Croce in his *Weltbürgertum und Nationalstaat, Studien zur Genesis des deutschen Nationalstaates*, Freiburg, 1911. See Nihongaku kyōkai 2014a, 480.

31 Uemura Kazuhide 2015b, 35. Hiraizumi is extremely elogious on Croce, whom he visited in October 1930 without any invitation, in Hiraizumi 1951. Also found in Nihongaku kyōkai 2014a, 172–82.

32 Tani 1985, 33. However, Hiraizumi's understanding of Croce was quite selective. He did not, of course, take into account Croce's antifascist stance, which became a major feature of his thought after 1925. Even in the process of writing history, Croce was more an inspiration. While Hiraizumi was quite influenced by his distinction between the "certum" and the "verum" in history (which Hiraizumi translates as *jitsu* 実 and *shin* 真), his final goal was to create a "narrative history" for political and moral purposes. See Karube 1996, 272. For a more thorough discussion of Croce's reception in the West, see Ginzburg 2012.

33 Uemura 2015b, 37.

34 Hiraizumi, 1940.

and then stayed briefly in England, where he studied the thought of anti-Revolution thinkers such as Edmund Burke (1729–97). However, he decided to cut his trip short, and he went back to Japan, through the United States, in May 1931.[35]

Hiraizumi's view of Shinto after his stay in Europe

Hiraizumi was thus an idealist who had a very militant view of history. However, did his European experience change his view of what remained one of his main subjects, Shinto? We have seen that Hiraizumi was already, before his departure, a proponent of the idea that Shinto was the original Japanese religion, and that Buddhism was nothing more than a decoration – albeit sometimes appreciable or even admirable. In fact, previous studies have already suggested that European thought shaped Hiraizumi's view of history and his extreme imperial loyalism.[36] However, his journal gives further substance to this claim, and his whole trip can be seen as a continuation of the initial quest he undertook after the *Taigyaku jiken*: a search of not only the meaning of history, but also for the essence of Japan and the implications of being Japanese.

To understand this, let us begin with another anecdote from his journal. Mentioning other Japanese scholars in the West such as the economist Kawai Eijirō 河合栄治郎 (1891–1944), Hiraizumi describes them as being too westernized, and not being aware of their own nature as Japanese. According to him, intellectuals should strive not to be "fake Japanese." Rather, he saw embracing "Japanese purity" as the only way to "save the country."[37]

In his comments regarding another major event of the time, Hiraizumi even clearly mentions Shinto as the only solution to what he perceived as Japan's problems. In 1930, when Hiraizumi was in Europe, Mahatma Gandhi started the famous Dandi Salt March. Learning about it through the work of Yoneda Minoru

---

35 Tani 1985, 34.
36 Especially Brownlee 1997.
37 Uemura 2014a, 19.

米田實 (1863–1926),[38] Hiraizumi makes the following comments on the situation: "Without using the heritage from Europe, starting with England, Gandhi urged to use the Indian heritage. He also told his compatriots not to defile the pure Indian soul." He adds, "For Gandhi, there was meaning in restoring Indian culture. He wanted to erase English education, and also for Hinduism to flourish." His comments show that he shared Yoneda's view of Gandhi as a manifestation of the high spirit of a nation who just had to resist colonialism.[39]

He also adds the following comment, which tells us clearly that he saw Shinto as an alternative to the Hinduism that he attributed to Gandhi: "Moreover, if I am sympathetic with him, it is not only out of intellectual interest. I truly believe that his goal itself will be what will save contemporary Japan. For the Japanese to lead a sensible life, it is absolutely necessary that they free themselves from the shackles of liberty or individualism, in a way of the Western civilization, and reject the domination or Marx and Lenin. The Japanese have to abandon their admiration of things brought from outside. It is indispensable if they want to keep the pure spirit of the Japanese who admire their own culture. We put too much emphasis on foreign education. Now, we have to put Shintō forward even more. Japanese, do not defile your pure souls. This is my only goal."[40]

Shinto and history

As we can see, Shinto was the answer that Hiraizumi found for the problems of his times. In fact, such ideas directly follow the concerns expressed in a series of articles from before his trip. His experience in the west allowed him to provide more refined, or more extreme, answers to them. To show this, let us try to define what Hiraizumi thought of Shinto and its place in Japanese history before his departure.

38 Yoneda 1931.
39 Uemura 2018, 31.
40 Ibid., 31.

In his critique of contemporary historians found in his journal, Hiraizumi showed that he was in search of a way to go beyond merely recording old events. An older article, published in 1925, gives a better idea of his position. There, he first seems to admit that facts must be analysed and synthesized. This then leads him to the surprisingly modern conclusion that history is closer to an art than to science. However, his conclusion has nothing in common with what postmodern researchers would say. He suddenly concludes that "faith" (*shinkō* 信仰) is the missing link needed to perform such tasks – a pure nativist concept.[41]

This concept of faith is a part of a set of ideas that largely defined his stay in Europe, and is at the core of his very mystical and nationalist view of Shinto. In 1927, Hiraizumi published the first of a series of studies on the text that, according to him, brought an answer to this question, the famous *Jinnō shōtōki*, written by Kitabatake Chikafusa around 1339. According to Hiraizumi, this text was different from the usual Japanese historical works. As shown by its first sentence – "Japan is the country of the gods" – the *Shōtōki* was a product of "pure Japanese thought, Shintō spirit, and non-materialism." The fact that the text did not, as other similar works do, mention China, India, or Buddhist narratives (*setsuwa* 説話) – in other words its perceived ideological purity – was another reason why it was worthy of extreme praise.[42]

In Hiraizumi's thought, Kitabatake Chikafusa touched upon another key concept appearing in his 1920s work: the idea of a fundamental spirit of the nation of Japan, which was revived through the *Jinnō shōtōki* and became the basis of the Meiji restoration.[43] Hiraizumi even went further, describing this kind of phenomenon as a mystical force guiding Japan throughout history. This is precisely what he stated during a lecture to Japanese marines, which

---

41 See Hiraizumi 1925. Found in Nihongaku kyōkai 2014a, 42. This article actually discusses Croce's concept of "certum" and "verum" in historical writing.

42 Hiraizumi 1927a. See Nihongaku kyōkai 2014a, 78–9.

43 Hiraizumi 1927b. See Nihongaku kyōkai 2014a, 88.

was published in 1928: "The Mystical Force Permeating Through History."⁴⁴

Shinto as a cultural weapon against western paradigms

Such ideas guided Hiraizumi's trip to Europe, and they can clearly be seen in either his discussions with scholars or his later recollection of the various steps of stay. And in fact, after his return to Japan, Hiraizumi became even more focused on the *Shōtōki*. We can count twelve articles on the subject from his return to the war.⁴⁵ However, his views were not only a continuation of his studies from the 1920s. They were also an answer to the challenges he encountered in Europe. In fact, as his observations on Gandhi's movement show, Hiraizumi's stay in Europe allowed him to further blend several narratives into a single one, focused heavily on Shinto as the expression of the original Japanese mind, and on imperial loyalism. In his work, Shinto, in a broad sense, clearly appears as an alternative to western models.

The general idea connecting it all was another product of Hiraizumi's stay in Europe, and especially in Germany, nationalist thought. His 1933 book *Bushidō no fukkatsu* reflects the influence of German thought on Hiraizumi and explains his motivations for trying to promote national spirit in the 1930s. One of the solutions given is a conception of Bushido – the alleged ethical code of Japanese samurai – with imperial loyalism. The whole ensemble is combined into a rather extreme Japanese nationalism, which

---

44 Hiraizumi 1928. Both this article and the precedent would later be included in Hiraizumi 1932d. Can also be found in Nihongaku kyōkai 2014a, 94–101.

45 Here is a list: Hiraizumi 1932c, Hiraizumi 1933c, Hiraizumi 1933b, Hiraizumi 1932b. A book on the copy of the text held at the Hakusan shrine was also published in Hiraizumi 1934a. Also, Hiraizumi 1932a, Hiraizumi 1934c, Hiraizumi 1942a. Articles on the *Jinnō shōtōki* can also be found in Hiraizumi 1940. After the war, Hiraizumi continued publishing on this topic. See, for example, Hiraizumi 1953, reprint in Hiraizumi 1964, 147–65. For a modern edition of a part of Hiraizumi's work on Shinto, see Nihongaku kyōkai 2014a, and especially 2014b and 2014c.

opposed an alleged western materialism with supposed Japanese spiritualism.⁴⁶

While the book focuses on Bushido, it also draws on a series of previous articles centred on the role of Shinto as the identity of Japan. In 1932, after his return, he wrote *Minzoku no tokuisei to rekishi no kōkyūsei*, an essay heavily inspired by his stay in Europe. Here, in a global advocacy for tradition and nationalism against communism, he gives the example of traditionalism in France, but he also explains how he was impressed by Jews in Praha who were able to keep their own customs and calendar in a fully Christian environment.⁴⁷ He was so moved that he even insisted on witnessing their rituals. He concludes that this kind of spirit was exactly what Japan needed in order to keep its own "independence as a race" (*minzoku no tokuisei*),⁴⁸ and adds that it had to be done through the cultivation of Shinto.⁴⁹

This combination of Shinto and the imperial system regularly appears in several of his works from the same period, and forms the nucleus of his project to re-educate the country – a necessity he had felt since the 1910s, but which became even more crucial for him after his return. This can be seen in *Kokushika to shite ōbei wo miru*, an account of his stay in Europe given in 1931.⁵⁰ This gives Hiraizumi's main impressions of Europe, and how history was used there. He concludes by saying that everything was different from what he had read in books, and affirms that one of his main findings was the discovery of historians and thinkers who were against the ubiquity of Marxism.⁵¹

Kōshitsu to kokumin dōtoku, published in 1932,⁵² develops an argument on the deep link between public morals and the imperial system. Concretely, he uses the concept of revolution (*kakumei*

---

46 Benesch 2014, 183–5.
47 Nihongaku kyōkai 2014a, 207–8.
48 Ibid., 214.
49 Ibid., 214.
50 The conference was published in the journal of the Kaigun Yūshūkai 海軍有終会. It can be found in Nihongaku kyōkai 2014a, 169–202.
51 Ibid., 202.
52 Hiraizumi, 1932e. Can also be found in Nihongaku kyōkai 2014a.

革命) in various cultures to propose a definition of the relation between the sovereign and his subjects. His argument is that the absence of revolution is a unique beauty of Japan.[53] In fact, he even uses the example of France, and of Rousseau, whose vision of a practical contract between the people and the king he mentions as the complete opposite of the Japanese model.[54] The second part deals the idea of revolution in Mencius 孟子, and Hiraizumi claims that it was not fully adopted and often criticized in Japan. His conclusion links Rousseau and Mencius, saying that Rousseau's ideas were already present in Japan through Mencius for a long time. The process of rejecting such "heretical and nefarious theories" (*itan jasetsu* 異端邪説) is seen as a step in the manifestation of the "essence" (*kokutai* 国体) of Japan, and imperial loyalism becomes a tool to dispel the chaos of contemporary thought.[55]

As a whole, the negation of the idea of revolution – which can also be seen as anti-communism – also leads to a reaffirmation of Hiraizumi's belief in a continuous line of emperors since times immemorial, a belief that was strengthened by what he saw in Europe. This text is thus clearly an important step in his march towards extreme loyalism, which he sees as a devotion to the main figure of his vision of Shinto: the emperor.

Kenmu, Shinto and imperial loyalism

In the 1930s, Hiraizumi's influence grew and saw him become a major figure in the universities of Japan. His thought culminated in a certain synthesis in the 1930s, through a famous historical theme, which was already invoked as a precedent to the Meiji restoration: the Kenmu government. This term describes the famous overthrow of the Kamakura shogunate by Emperor Go Daigo and his allies in 1333. This brief regime, which was already seen as a precedent to the Meiji era, became an important model in prewar

---

53 Ibid., 215–249.
54 Ibid., 218.
55 Ibid., 248.

Japan. During the 1910s, the government had already laid the groundwork for this official celebration of Kenmu and especially of Go Daigo's branch of the imperial lineage. When Go Daigo lost power, he fled and opened another imperial court in Yoshino, in 1336. This became the Southern Court, and it was opposed to a rival lineage, the Northern one, which stayed in Kyoto. In the 1910s, following the debate known as *Nanbokuchō seijunron* 南北朝正閏論, it was officially decided that the Southern Court was legitimate, and the period – formerly known as the "period of the Northern and Southern Court" – was renamed the "period of the Yoshino court."[56]

During the early Shōwa years, the heroes of the Southern Court, such as Kusunoki Masashige – the very embodiment of Hiraizumi's Imperialist Bushido[57] – with his statue near the imperial palace, were seen as model loyalists, and they became the subject of state-sponsored cults. Go Daigo himself became a Shinto deity revered at Yoshino jingū, built on the ruins of a part of Kinpusenji.[58]

Hiraizumi himself was a strong promoter of this movement, and he published more than ten books or articles on Kenmu,[59] including his famous "The True Meaning of the Kenmu Restoration"[60] in 1934. Here he combines his vision of history as a state tool with his idea of Shinto as the essence of the nation and the imperial system. The conclusion of the book is very clear on this matter. The Kenmu restoration should not be seen as a thing of the past, but rather as something that should be reflected upon in order to deal with the problems of his times. In fact, the reasons he uses to explain the fall of the Kenmu government are especially in line with his general narrative on Shinto. Kenmu failed because people forgot what is, according to Hiraizumi, the key value of Japan: their obligation of loyalty towards the emperor.[61] This can be seen

56 Brownlee 1997, 118–30.
57 On Masashige's posthumous image, see Maeda 2012.
58 Rappo 2017, 37–8.
59 Most of them were written between 1934 and 1941. For a complete list, see Ban 2014, 589–91.
60 Hiraizumi 1934b. On this book, also see Nagoya 1985, 96.
61 Hiraizumi 1934b.

as another formulation for his earlier mystical force guiding the country in its history.

This conception of imperial loyalism as the core value, or essence, of Japan is expanded two years later, after his nomination as a full professor of the Imperial University of Tokyo in 1935, in a publication that can be seen as another product of his stay in Europe: *Banbutsu ruten* 万物流転 ("On the Impermanence of Things"). The subject of what remains in the never-ending flow of history was actually one of the topics Hiraizumi discussed with Meinecke.[62] In this book, he recognizes the impermanence of history, but also defines the Imperial State as the only permanent object in this endless stream. He then proceeds to give his view of Shinto. According to him, the prayers of Shinto must do their utmost to protect the Imperial State, and one of the main purposes of this militant, or even warlike Shinto is to become a weapon against revolutionary thought.[63] This is even clear in his *Kōkoku goji no michi*, published by the military school of the Japanese marines in 1942, during the Pacific War.

This definition can actually be seen as a way to link all of Hiraizumi's concerns during his stay in Europe: his search of meaning in history, his anti-communist ideas, and even his critique of the French Revolution.

Hiraizumi and the Monumenta Nipponica school

Hiraizumi's impact should not be overstated, especially as he was prone to exaggeration in his recollections after the war. However, he played an active part in creating an extreme view of Shinto as the essence of Japan, which would be at the centre of the discourses edited by German scholars in the late 1930s and '40s.

In fact, Hiraizumi's work was prominently used by figures such as Hermann Bohner and even translated into English in the early issues of *Monumenta Nipponica*. The fact that Nazi terminology

---

62 See section above, *Hiraizumi's trip to the west*.
63 Tani 1985, 35–6.

was used in such translations shows the many parallels that were seen between his work and the ideas that the scholars of Sophia University tried to spread, partly in order to justify the Axis alliance.[64] Interestingly, Hiraizumi's brief friendship, a decade earlier, with Meinecke – another supporter of the Nazi ideas – shows that such figures shared not only political views of positions, but also a certain concept of history and religion.

Similar reliance on Hiraizumi can be found in the work of another German missionary, Heinrich Dumoulin. Dumoulin, who later distanced himself from such ideas and became a major specialist of Zen, was first interested in Kokugaku in his early days in Japan. He published in 1943 a study called *Kamo Mabuchi: (1697–1769): ein Beitrag zur japanischen Religions und Geistesgeschichte.* This book, which contains a full translation of a work by Yoshida Kanetomo, presents the Japanese Middle Ages as a high point of syncretism: a syncretism that the Kokugaku movement fought against.

While quite precise and interesting, this work gives the sense that medieval Shinto was a corruption of the original pure Shinto seen as the source of the Japanese spirit. This general orientation of his work can be seen in the last chapter, where the author compares the fight against foreign influences on the national spirit in Japan and Germany.

As a whole, works of German scholars on Shinto in prewar Japan make abundant use of Nazi rhetoric. Johannes Kraus, the first editor of *Monumenta Nipponica*, in his review of Bohner's translation of the *Jinnō shōtōki*, says the book was a "a picture-book of Japan's popular national worldview" ("Bilderbuch der völkisch nationalen Weltanschauung Japans").

Although not always that extreme, studies in medieval Shinto, following larger trends in Shinto discourses in Japan, thus tended to emphasize the "original" "pure Shinto," and view later developments as corruptions that needed to be purged or, in the best case, as negligible accidents. Even Heinrich Dumoulin, while recognizing some value to the medieval "syncretism," embraces this

64 See Hiraizumi 1938, quoted in Scheid 2013a, 247.

essentialist framework, and, like his peers, he uses Shinto to showcase what he sees as fragments of the Japanese national spirit.[65]

Conclusion: Hiraizumi's scholarship and contemporary studies on Shinto

Despite his extreme positions, Hiraizumi was not condemned after the war, but just sent back to his hometown. This allowed him to continue developing his thought, especially on Shinto, as well as to organize a group of students around the Hakusan shrine. In 1958, he wrote an article titled "*Shintō no ganmoku*," where he reiterates his idea of Shinto as a means to protect the Imperial State.[66] He also goes on to say that while it may be blended with other things in parts, Kitabatake Chikafusa's *Jinnō shōtōki* is the essence of Shinto at its core, because it was written for an emperor and for the Imperial State.[67]

In 1971, he published an introduction to his disciple Tani Seigo's book *Shintō genron*.[68] Here, after criticizing the postwar studies for their lack of interest for the mystical aspect of Shinto, Hiraizumi gives his definitive vision of Shinto. He calls it the indigenous religion of Japan, which managed to survive throughout the times and despite foreign influences, something that original European religions were not able to do, as they were destroyed by Christianity.

---

65 Scheid 2013a, 244–6.
66 Hiraizumi 1958. Also found in Nihongaku kyōkai 2014b. This text, as well as the impact of Shinto on Hiraizumi's view of history is analysed in Uemura 2004, 73–4.
67 "To move away from the lord Chikafusa means to move away from the true essence of Shinto. When it forgets its unique great purpose of the Imperial State, then Shinto degrades itself either to a primitive religion, or to vulgar popular customs. Such things have nothing in common with the original Shinto. Moreover, Shinto was improved and bolstered with the establishment of the Japanese state. The State of Japan cannot be adorned in its full glory as a paradise by any other thing than Shintō." Nihongaku kyōkai 2016, chapter 2; Tani 1985, 31.
68 Tani 1971. Also found in Nihongaku kyōkai 2014b.

This leads him to stress the importance of keeping the original spirit of Shinto in Japan, even after the War.[69]

This article has shown that Hiraizumi's stay in Europe largely contributed to accentuating his conception of Shinto as a manifestation of the unique Japanese spirit. It also provided him with the theoretical background and the incentive to further develop his ideas of imperial loyalism, and of Shinto as an almost warlike, military concept used to defend the "Japanese race." His mostly indirect similitudes with the thought of leading Nazi scholars also explains clearly why he was actively used by the German scholars of Shinto, who were identifying his idea of Japanese spirit with the core concepts of Nazism.

Although such ideas are mostly rejected in academic circles, Hiraizumi's insistence on Shinto as the core of the "Japaneseness" (*Nihonjinron* 日本人論) is largely shared by some scholars, priests and more generally in the public. While his conclusions and his ideological uses of history are, of course, extremely problematic, Hiraizumi can still be seen as an interesting figure. In fact, parts of his work are extremely erudite and interesting, and his effort to establish an alternative to western thought in Japan can be seen as parallel to that of the far more successful, and accepted, Watsuji Tetsurō. However, while he may give some interesting factual information, his work on Shinto should be understood as something that needs to be criticized and studied as the produce of a specific period and also of an extremely influential current in the history of this religion, rather than as a valid academic source.

Essentialism was in fact a deep component of modern Shinto. It also draws on the persistent ideas, at various times in Japanese history, of a certain continuity in Shinto, which has been developed in the recent book by Helen Hardacre. Of course, studies on the medieval period have shown that such continuity is in fact misleading: Shinto changed so much, especially through its contact with Buddhism and other Asian religious traditions, that, on a purely historical level, a deconstruction of the very pervasive and powerful illusion of continuity in Shinto had to be undertaken. However,

---

69   For a comment on this, see Tani 1985, 41–5.

this notion of continuity has its history, from the most vague perception of the existence of indigenous, or originally indigenous gods, held by most people in Japanese history, to the more extreme political uses of it by figures such as Hiraizumi. The idea of continuity in Shinto should thus at least be recognized and studied on its own, but with a clear idea of the various changes Shinto itself encountered, and avoiding the pitfall of essentialism and its political or ideological implications that can still be seen today.

References

Aston, William G. 1896. *Nihongi, chronicles of Japan from the earliest times to A.D. 697.* London (K. Paul, Trench & Trübner).

Aston, William G. 1905. *Shinto, The Way of the Gods.* London (Longmans).

Aston, William G. 1907. *Shinto, The Ancient Religion of Japan.* London (A. Constable & Co. Ltd).

Ban Isoshirō 伴五十嗣郎 2014. "Kaidai" 解題 in: Nihongaku kyōkai 日本学協会 (ed.), *Hiraizumi hakase shironshō* 平泉博士史論抄. Tōkyō (Kinseisha), 573–96.

Benesch, Oleg 2014. *Inventing the Way of the Samurai: Nationalism, Internationalism, and Bushido in Modern Japan.* Oxford, England; New York, NY (Oxford University Press).
https://doi.org/10.1093/acprof:oso/9780198706625.001.0001

Berthon, Jean-Pierre 2013. "The Ethnographer, the Scholar, and the Missionary: French Studies on Shinto at the Beginning of the Twentieth Century" in: Bernhard Scheid and Kate Wildman Nakai (eds.), *Kami Ways in Nationalist Territory: Shinto Studies in Prewar Japan and the West.* Wien (Verlag der Österreichischen Akademie der Wissenschaften), 179–202.
https://doi.org/10.2307/j.ctt1vw0r67.12

Brownlee, John S. 1997. *Japanese Historians and the National Myths, 1600–1945: The Age of the Gods and Emperor Jinmu.* Vancouver, BC (University of British Columbia, University of Tokyo Press).

Ginzburg, Carlo 2012. *Threads and Traces: True, False, Fiction.* Berkeley; Los Angeles; London (California University Press).

Hiraizumi Kiyoshi 平泉澄 1925. "Rekishi ni okeru shin to bi" 歴史における真と美. *Shigaku zasshi* 史学雑誌 36/5.

Hiraizumi Kiyoshi 1926. *Chūsei ni okeru seishin seikatsu* 中世に於ける精神生活. Tōkyō (Shibundō).

Hiraizumi Kiyoshi 1927a. "Jinnō shōtōki kenkyū" 神皇正統記研究 in: *Nihon bungaku kōza 8* 日本文学講座 第八巻. Tōkyō (Shinchōsha), 66–74.

Hiraizumi Kiyoshi 1927b. "Kokushigaku no kotsuzui" 国史学の骨髄. *Shigaku zasshi* 史学雑誌 38/8.

Hiraizumi Kiyoshi 1927c. "Shinbutsu bunri no igi" 神仏分離の異議. *Nihon* 日本 11.

Hiraizumi Kiyoshi 1928. "Rekishi wo tsuranuku meimei no chikara" 歴史を貫く冥々の力. *Gakushū kenkyū* 学習研究 7/6.

Hiraizumi Kiyoshi 1932a. "Jinnō shōtōki kaisetsu" 神皇正統記解説 in: Monbushō shakai kyōikukyoku 文部省社会教育局 (ed.), *Nihon shisō sōsho 10 Jinnō shōtōki* 日本思想叢書 (第 10 編) 神皇正統記. Tōkyō (Monbushō shakai kyōikukyoku), 8–15.

Hiraizumi Kiyoshi 1932b. "Jinnō shōtōki shohon no kenkyū" 神皇正統記諸本の研究. *Shigaku zasshi* 史学雑誌 43/9.

Hiraizumi Kiyoshi 1932c. "Kitabatake Chikafusa no Kokinshū-chū" 北畠親房の古今集註. In: Sadaki hakase kanreki kinenkai 佐佐木博士還暦記念会 (ed.), *Nihon bungaku ronsan* 日本文学論纂. Tōkyō (Meiji sho'in), 185–98.

Hiraizumi Kiyoshi 1932d. *Kokushigaku no kotsuzui* 国史学の骨髄. Tōkyō (Shibundō).

Hiraizumi Kiyoshi 1932e. "Kōshitsu to kokumin dōtoku; sono ichi" 皇室と國民道德 其の一 in: Higashi Fushimi no miya-ke 東伏見宮家 (ed.), *Kōshitsushi no kenkyū* 皇室史の研究. Tōkyō (Higashi Fushimi no miya-ke), 30–71.

Hiraizumi Kiyoshi 1933a. *Bushidō no fukkatsu* 武士道の復活. Tōkyō (Shibundō).

Hiraizumi Kiyoshi 1933b. "Jinnō shōtōki no naiyō" 神皇正統記の内容 in: *Bushidō no fukkatsu* 武士道の復活. Tōkyō (Shibundō), 127–43.

Hiraizumi Kiyoshi 1933c. "Jinnō shōtōki no seiritsu" 神皇正統記の成立 in: *Bushidō no fukkatsu* 武士道の復活. Tōkyō (Shibundō), 114–261.

Hiraizumi Kiyoshi (ed.) 1934a. *Jinnō shōtōki* 神皇正統記. Hakusan, Ishikawa (Shirayama hime jinja).

Hiraizumi Kiyoshi 1934b. *Kenmu chūkō no hongi* 建武中興の本義. Tōkyō (Shibundō).

Hiraizumi Kiyoshi 1934c. "Kitabatake Chikafusa no shikan" 北畠親房の史観. *Meiji shōtoku kinenkan kiyō* 明治聖徳記念学会紀要 41, 61–76.

Hiraizumi Kiyoshi 1938. "Der Einfluss der Mappo-Lehre in der japanischen Geschichte." *Monumenta Nipponica* 1/1, 58–69.
https://doi.org/10.2307/2382445

Hiraizumi Kiyoshi 1940. *Dentō* 伝統. Tōkyō (Shibundō).

Hiraizumi Kiyoshi 1942a. "Kaidai" 解題 in: Dainihon bunko kankōkai 大日本文庫刊行会 (ed.), *Dainihon bunko 31 Kokushihen 4* 大日本文庫 31 国史篇〔第 4. Tōkyō (Dainihon bunko kankōkai), 5–11.

Hiraizumi Kiyoshi 1942b. *Kōkoku goji no michi* 皇國護持の道. Tōkyō (Kaigun heigakkō).

Hiraizumi Kiyoshi 1951. "Napoli no Tetsujin" ナポリの哲人. *Geirin* 藝林 4/3.

Hiraizumi Kiyoshi 1953. "Tōka hiden no shikiken" 東家秘伝の識見. *Shintōshi kenkyū* 神道史研究 1/2.

Hiraizumi Kiyoshi 1958. "Shintō no ganmoku" 神道の眼目 in: *Senge Takanobu sensei kanreki kinen ronbunshū* 千家尊宣先生還暦記念神道論文集, 千家尊宣先生還暦記念神道論文集編纂委員会. Tōkyō (Shintō gakkai), 14–17.

Hiraizumi Kiyoshi 1964. *Kanrin shihitsu* 寒林史筆. Tōkyō (Tachibana shobō).

Hiraizumi Kiyoshi 1980. *Higeki jūsō* 悲劇縦走. Ise (Kōgakkan daigaku shuppanbu).

Isomae, Jun'ichi 2000. "Tanaka Yoshitō and the Beginnings of *Shintōgaku*" in: Mark Teeuwen and John Breen (eds.), *Shinto in History: Ways of the Kami*. Richmond (Curzon), 318–39.

Karube Tadashi 苅部直 1996. "Rekishika No Yume – Hiraizumi Kiyoshi wo megutte" 歴史家の夢 – 平泉清をめぐって in: *Nenpō Kindai Nihon kenkyū, 18, Hikaku no naka no Kindai Nihon shisō* 年報近代日本思想 18 比較の中の近代日本思想, 259–88. Tōkyō (Yamakawa shuppansha).

Kuroda, Toshio 1996. "The Discourse on the "Land of Kami" (Shinkoku) in Medieval Japan: National Consciousness and International Awareness." *Japanese Journal of Religious Studies* 23/3–4, 353–85. https://doi.org/10.18874/jjrs.23.3-4.1996.353-385

Lévy, Christine 2010. "Autour de l'Affaire du crime de lèse-majesté : modernité politique et répression." *Ebisu : Études Japonaises* 44, 87–109. https://doi.org/10.3406/ebisu.2010.1780

Maeda, Tamaki 2012. "From Feudal Hero to National Icon: The Kusunoki Masashige Image, 1660–1945." *Artibus Asiae* 72/2, 201–58.

Martin, Jean-Marie 1924. *Le Shintoïsme, religion nationale I. Les origines. Essai d'histoire ancienne du Japon.* Hong Kong (Imprimerie de Nazareth).

Matsuo Jirō 村尾次郎 1985. "Sensei Hiraizumi Kiyoshi hakase ni okeru shintō" 先師平泉澄博士における神. *Shintōshi kenkyū* 神道史研究 33/1, 2–25.

Nagoya Tokimasa 名越時正 1985. "Hiraizumi sensei no nihongaku to iwayuru Mito-gaku" 平泉先生の日本学といはゆる水戸学. *Shintōshi kenkyū* 神道史研究 33/1, 83–101.

Nihongaku kyōkai 日本学協会 (ed.) 2014a. *Hiraizumi hakase shironshō* 平泉博士史論抄. Tōkyō (Kinseisha).

Nihongaku kyōkai 日本学協会 (ed.) 2014b. *Hiraizumi Kiyoshi hakase shintōronshō* 平泉澄博士神道論抄. Tōkyō (Kinseisha).

Nihongaku kyōkai 日本学協会 (ed.) 2014c. *Hiraizumi Kiyoshi hakase shintōronshō zoku* 平泉澄博士神道論抄続. Tōkyō (Kinseisha).

Péri, Noël 1911. "Michel Revon: Anthologie de la littérature japonaise des origines au XXe siècle [compte-rendu]." *Bulletin de l'École française d'Extrême-Orient* 11, 226–31.

Rappo, Gaétan 2017. *Rhétoriques de l'hérésie dans le Japon médiéval et moderne: Le moine Monkan (1278–1357) et sa réputation posthume – Préface de Philippe Borgeaud.* Paris (L'Harmattan).

Revon, Michel 1905; second revised edition 1907. *Le Shinntoïsme.* Paris (E. Leroux).

Scheid, Bernhard 2013a. "In Search of Lost Essence: Nationalist Projections in German Shinto Studies" in: Bernhard Scheid and Kate Wildman Nakai (eds.), *Kami Ways in Nationalist Territory: Shinto Studies in Prewar Japan and the West*. Wien (Verlag der Österreichischen Akademie der Wissenschaften), 237–64. https://doi.org/10.2307/j.ctt1vw0r67.14

Scheid, Bernhard 2013b. "Introduction" in: Bernhard Scheid and Kate Wildman Nakai (eds.), *Kami Ways in Nationalist Territory: Shinto Studies in Prewar Japan and the West*. Wien (Verlag der Österreichischen Akademie der Wissenschaften), 2–22.

Souyri, Pierre-François 2010. "L'histoire à l'époque Meiji : enjeux de domination, contrôle du passé, résistances." *Ebisu: Études Japonaises* 44, 33–47. https://doi.org/10.3406/ebisu.2010.1777

Tani Seigo 谷省吾 1971. *Shintō genron* 神道原論. Tōkyō (Kōgakkan daigaku Shuppanbu).

Tani Seigo 1985. "Hiraizumi Kiyoshi sensei to shintō" 平泉澄先生と神道. *Shintōshi kenkyū* 神道史研究 33/1, 26–46.

Uemura Kazuhide 植村和秀 2004. "Rekishigakusha Hiraizumi Kiyoshi (2, kan)" 歴史神学者平泉澄 (二・完), *Sandai hōgaku* 産大法学, 38/1, 42–87.

Uemura Kazuhide 2014a. "Hiraizumi Kiyoshi hakase no taiō kenkyū nikki (sono ichi)" 平泉澄博士の滞欧研究日記(その1). *Geirin* 藝林 63/1, 2–62.

Uemura Kazuhide 2014b. "Hiraizumi Kiyoshi hakase no taiō kenkyū nikki (sono ni)" 平泉澄博士の滞欧研究日記(その2). *Geirin* 63/2, 2–57.

Uemura Kazuhide 2015a. "Hiraizumi Kiyoshi hakase no taiō kenkyū nikki (sono san)" 平泉澄博士の滞欧研究日記(その3). *Geirin* 64/2, 2–52.

Uemura Kazuhide 2015b. "Taiō kenkyū nikki ni mieru Hiraizumi Kiyoshi hakase" 滞欧研究日記にみる平泉澄博士. *Geirin* 64/1, 33–56.

Uemura Kazuhide 2016a. "Hiraizumi Kiyoshi hakase no taiō kenkyū nikki (sono yon)" 平泉澄博士の滞欧研究日記(その4). *Geirin* 65/1, 2–32.

Uemura Kazuhide 2016b. "Hiraizumi Kiyoshi hakase no taiō kenkyū nikki (sono go)" 平泉澄博士の滞欧研究日記(その5). *Geirin* 65/2, 2–32.

Uemura Kazuhide 2017a. "Hiraizumi Kiyoshi hakase no taiō kenkyū nikki (sono roku)" 平泉澄博士の滞欧研究日記(その6). *Geirin* 66/1, 2–30.

Uemura Kazuhide 2017b. "Hiraizumi Kiyoshi hakase no taiō kenkyū nikki (sono nana)" 平泉澄博士の滞欧研究日記(その7). *Geirin* 66/2, 2–60.

Uemura Kazuhide 2018. "Hiraizumi Kiyoshi hakase no taiō kenkyū nikki (sono hachi; kan)" 平泉澄博士の滞欧研究日記(その8・完). *Geirin* 67/1, 2–48.

Wachutka, Michael 2012. "A Living Past as the Nation's Personality: 'Jinnō shōtōki,' Early Shōwa Nationalism, and 'Das Dritte Reich'." *Japan Review* 24, 127–50.

Wakai Toshiaki 若井敏明 2006. "Hiraizumi Kiyoshi: Mikuni no tame ni ware tsukusanamu" 平泉澄　み国のために我つくさなむ. Tōkyō (Minerva shobō).

Yoneda Minoru 米田實 1931. "Indo no kōei undō" 印度の抗英運動. *Kaizō* 改造 13/3, 75.

About the author

Gaétan Rappo received his doctorate from the University of Geneva in 2014. In his dissertation, published as a book under the title *Rhétoriques de l'hérésie dans le Japon médiéval et moderne*, he analysed the life and work of the Shingon monk Monkan (1278–1357) juxtaposing primary sources with posthumous depictions of Monkan as a "heretic." He has also published several articles on medieval Japanese religions with a focus on Shingon Buddhism and Shinto; these articles include editions of medieval manuscripts. He is currently a Hakubi associate professor at the Institute for Research in Humanities, Kyoto University.

3

On writing the history of Shinto

Mark Teeuwen

This essay first surveys recent approaches to writing "Shinto history," and reflects on the problems that are inherent in this genre. Does the very notion of a Shinto history force writers to adopt a particular perspective on the past, due to the semantic and discursive structure of the concept of Shinto itself? Is it possible to write a Shinto history without constructing, once again and in new words, that same ideological concept – even while one is determined not to fall into this trap? Can the genre of Shinto history be reinvented and saved from this conundrum?

In the second part of the essay, I try to gain a new perspective on Shinto historiography by comparative means. Shinto is part of a family of national-religious categories that gained prominence in the nineteenth century, and Shinto history is a modern genre that arose to supply that category with a venerable past. It may be enlightening to analyse the dynamics of Shinto's modern conceptualization through the lens of another such category from another cultural and political context. Here I will attempt to view Shinto through the lens of its distant cousin Hinduism.

The history of Shinto historiography

Shinto history is a genre that first emerged in the 1910s and came into its own in the 1930s. The earliest publication to carry the phrase *shintōshi* ("Shinto history") in its title is a seventy-page work by Tanaka Yoshitō (1872–1946), titled *Shintōshi kōyō*, "Essentials of Shinto History." This work, published in 1915, drew on an earlier "Outline of Shinto History" (*Shintōshi gaikan*) that Tanaka had published in 1909 in *Kokugakuin zasshi*, the journal of the country's imperial educational facility for Shinto priests (Tanaka 1909). Tanaka, however, was not a Shinto priest or even an expert on Japanese history by training. His first book, published in 1908, had offered a "systematic history of Western pedagogy" (*Keitōteki seiyō kyōikushi*). When Tanaka turned his attention to Shinto, his agenda was to enlist this imperial "philosophy," as he called it, as the basis for a new pedagogy that was both scientific and patriotic, and that could foster what Tanaka's teacher Inoue Tetsujirō had termed Japan's National Morality (Isomae 2000). This is made abundantly clear in *Shintō hongi* ("The Essence of Shinto"), a book Tanaka published in 1910: the first page of this work carries the full text of the 1890 Rescript on Education, presenting it as the gist of that essence. In his 1915 history, Tanaka identified Shinto as the source of the virtues of loyalty and filial piety that constituted National Morality, and as the timeless foundation of the imperial national essence or *kokutai*. With these and other publications on similar topics, Tanaka became a central figure of Shinto studies: he taught at Tokyo University's first Shinto programme from 1921 onwards, and in the late 1920s became a central advocate of *Shintōgaku*, a new academic discipline that sought to provide Shinto ideology with an historical basis.

Shinto history, then, began in the first decades of the twentieth century as a highly politicized discipline. As short and relatively bland as it was, *Shintōshi kōyō* set the tone of the genre. Tanaka argues that "Shinto had an extraordinary strength already in ancient times, and responded to the intellect, the emotions, and the will of the people (*kokumin*) of that period" (Tanaka 1915, 5). He describes how the people were seduced by Buddhist promises of wealth and good fortune, leading to the emergence of Buddhist Shinto schools such as Sannō and Ryōbu Shintō; but these ultimately failed to satisfy the "national spirit" of the people (ibid., 16), not least because the court countered the Buddhist threat by making Shinto philosophy explicit in *Kojiki* and *Nihon shoki*. Tanaka introduces a series of Shinto thinkers, including Kitabatake Chikafusa, Yoshida Kanetomo and Yamazaki Ansai, and warns the reader that "while these all strove to express the authentic Shinto of our country, they remained under the influence of Buddhism and Confucianism" (ibid., 25). Only with the work of Motoori Norinaga and the Kokugaku school did the true "Great Way of Japan" re-emerge, enabling ritual and government to be unified once again after the Meiji Restoration (ibid., 5).

What was innovative about this first Shinto history was not necessarily the lineage of thinkers that Tanaka includes, but rather the fact that he subsumed the narrative of ancient imperial *kami* worship, its medieval demise, and its modern revival under the concept of "Shinto." This stands in contrast to, for example, the "History of Japanese Religion" (*Nihon shūkyōshi*) published in 1907 by Tsuchiya Senkyō (1872–1956). Tsuchiya, a Buddhist scholar who spent much of his career at Waseda University, argued that Shinto began with Kitabatake Chikafusa in the fourteenth century. Tsuchiya dedicates a few pages to the classical "rituals to the gods of heaven and earth" (*jingi saishi*) of ancient times, but he does not identify these as expressions of Shinto, nor does he link these rituals to the writings of Kitabatake and later Shinto thinkers. This was a direct reflection of the current legal standing of *saishi* ritual as non-religious, public ceremonial, and therefore as fundamentally different from the private traditions of religious Shinto. As a religion, Tsuchiya argued, Shinto began with the theology of Kitabatake and survived into modern times as the "New Shinto" of such religious movements as Shinshūkyō, Misogikyō and Kurozumikyō (Tsuchiya 1907, 267–70). Tsuchiya's taxonomy was in line with contemporary administrative arrangements; it was by knowingly "confounding" *saishi* ceremonial with the teachings of (sect) Shinto that Tanaka opened up for a new and more expansive historical narrative.

While Tanaka's Shinto history bears all the marks of prewar imperial ideology, its larger structure is also replicated with few modifications in postwar Shinto histories. Recent histories written for the popular market repeat the formula faithfully, although the theme of imperial loyalty is now replaced with other purported ethnic Japanese values, such as tolerance and an innate respect for nature (contrasted with monotheistic fundamentalism and utilitarian views on nature). Academic Shinto histories, written by specialists, address a much broader spectrum of issues than

Tanaka's simple template, but even so most end up tracing the same plotline, only with a different emphasis and added caveats. Let me illustrate this on the basis of two examples: Inoue Nobutaka's *Shintō: Nihon-umare no shūkyō shisutemu* (1998, translated as Teeuwen and Breen, *Shinto – A Short History*, 2003), and Okada Shōji, *Nihon shintōshi* ("History of Shinto," 2010). Both of these books, which are written by teams of historians, are edited by professors of Kokugakuin, one of the two universities that educate Shinto priests, and aim to present the latest findings on the history of Shinto to an informed audience.

Inoue starts out by questioning traditional definitions of Shinto, notably the view that all "traditional religious folklore" constitutes Shinto (Inoue 1998, 12). He rejects the notion of an authentic, pure Shinto that functioned as the archaic prototype of later stages of Shinto, and he spurns all attempts to define Shinto on the basis of a reconstructed "original essence" (ibid., 14). Rather than such vagaries, he seeks to trace the history of Shinto as a "religious system," consisting of constituents (the people who carry and maintain it), networks (physical and organizational structures) and substance (teachings, practices and rituals). This leads him to identify a well-developed and complete Shinto religious system in classical times, when the imperial court took nominal control over *kami* cults at major shrines and incorporated these in the ceremonial of the Ritsuryō state (c. 700). In medieval times, however, the Ritsuryō state withered away and Shinto ceased to function as a "distinct religious system" (ibid., 18); yet, parts of that now broken system were encapsulated in other religious systems and survived in that way, allowing a new complete Shinto system to re-emerge in modern times. In this manner, Inoue explicitly rejects some of the most crucial premises of Tanaka's historical narrative, notably the idea of an ancient, pre-Buddhist, purely native Shinto philosophy; but even so, he ends up with a very similar storyline that leads the reader from a fully developed classical Shinto, by way of a period of incubation as a component of medieval Buddhism, to a renaissance in the form of sect and shrine Shinto as fully developed religious systems in modern times.

For Okada, the red thread that held Shinto together throughout history is found not in a system with multiple components but in *saishi* ritual. Okada starts his Shinto history by quoting a poem from the classical poetry collection *Man'yōshū* (13/3253): "This land of reed plains, filled with plentiful rice ears, is a land that heeds the gods and does not raise words (*kotoage senu kuni*)." This poem, and this phrase, were highlighted by Kokugaku thinkers as the essence of the Japanese spirit, and therefore of Shinto, by contrasting the wordiness of the thinkers of China with the intuitive responsiveness to the gods of the worshippers of Japan. Okada then leads the reader to an even earlier, prehistoric age when ancient sites where local communities worshipped the *kami* constituted "concrete expressions of Shinto faith" (Okada 2010, 3). In contrast to Inoue, Okada holds on to the notion of an Ur-Shinto that constitutes the fountainhead of a continuous Shinto tradition.

After introducing this notion of an ancient Shinto faith, Okada offers an overview of different theories about "the origins of Shinto." He lists four such theories (ibid., 14–17). The first two refer to the systematization of *kami* worship as Ritsuryō ceremonial, and differ only in dating that systematization to either c. 700 or c. 800; the latter two look to the development of Shinto thought, which they date either to the c. 1100 or to the fifteenth century. Okada dismisses the "raising of words" highlighted by the latter theories as secondary, and insists that *kami* ritual, in all its forms, can be described as a coherent "system" (*taikei*) across the ages. He further places the origins of this body of ritual in prehistorical times, referring to excavated ritual sites from the Tomb (*kofun*) Period which lasted from the third to the seventh century. His history traces the development of this ritual system via the development of the classical court cult, by way of a phase of medieval "diversification" and "theorizing," via early modern "restructuring," to the establishment of a new "Shinto system" in the Meiji Period.

These two histories posit a form of continuity from ancient times until today that may be termed Shinto. They do so, however, in different ways. Before the war, Tanaka stressed the continuity of an intangible Shinto "national spirit," expressed first and foremost in the form of a moral philosophy and practice. In the radically altered setting of postwar Japan, neither Inoue nor Okada supports the notion of an unbroken tradition of Shinto thought or philosophy, let alone morality; rather, they stress the continued existence, from ancient times until today, of "systems," institutions (shrines) and rituals (*saishi*). They leave it to less academic writers to answer the obvious questions about what the survival of shrines and rituals signifies, and what factors made it possible. Priests, journalists, politicians, travel writers and the authors of tourist guides on occasion fill in this blank by claiming enduring ethnic traditions of nature worship, or by pointing to the place of the emperor in Japanese society as the linchpin that has held the country together by means of unbroken traditions of *kami* worship.

This silence is perhaps the only way to deal with an acute historiographical problem. There is no doubt that shrines, and also at least a small selection of rituals that are today classified as Shinto, have long histories that go back to classical or even prehistoric times. At the same time, the sources abound with evidence of radical breaks, not only in the layout and architecture of these sites or the structure of these rituals, but also in their social and political contexts, the networks of actors involved in them, and their conceptualization and signification. This raises the question whether the histories of these sites and rituals are best analysed within the framework of "Shinto history" – in spite of the fact that the main actors involved in them were Buddhist priests, Yin Yang diviners, or folk shamans who not only failed to conceptualize their practices as Shinto, but often even were unaware of that concept altogether.

This point has been made forcefully since the 1970s, most famously by Kuroda Toshio (cf. Kuroda 1981), and there is no need to rehearse it further here. In my own work, I lean to a position closer to Kuroda than to Inoue or Okada. I make two basic arguments. First, the establishment of Shinto as a concept and a category (rather than merely as a word) was an important landmark in the history of the sites, rituals and actors whenever that concept became normative and forced concrete changes upon them. The conceptualization of Shinto was a complicated process that went through a number of phases; in fact, it is more accurate to talk of multiple conceptualizations. Not only did the meanings of these different Shinto concepts diverge radically; so did the impact that they had beyond the circles where they were first developed. Some sites, rituals, or actors went through multiple bouts of "Shintoization" (conceptual redefinition and physical reforms inspired by a new notion of Shinto), while others remained beyond its influence and developed along different paths. In my view, it is the task of "Shinto history" to map these dynamics. However, those dynamics become untraceable, or even unimaginable, if one departs from the premise that the sites, rituals and actors one studies are and always have been inherently Shinto.

My second argument addresses the fact that the concept of Shinto always post-dated the phenomena that it has sought to conceptualize. This implies that later concepts of Shinto can never be applied to periods that pre-date their formation. This is a simple matter of logic, but still worth pointing out because blatant anachronisms that ignore this fact are so common. Tanaka's projection of a Japanese "national spirit" onto ancient and medieval "Shinto" is one example; the current "ecological paradigm" (Rots 2017) that defines Shinto as a nature religion with archaic roots is just as obvious.

As soon as one Shinto conceptualization (or paradigm) gives way to another, the historical narratives that were constructed around it collapse. In fourteenth-century Ise, for example, priests adopted the term "Shinto" to refer to the knowledge of Ise priests concerning the shrines' true identity as the palace of the World Buddha in the Sahā world – a site of mandalic suchness in the karmic realm. This was the first conceptualization of this older term, which ultimately derived from a Buddhist context (Teeuwen 2002). This particular Shinto concept generated new narratives, secret transmissions and ritual practices based on radical reinterpretations of selected physical properties of the Ise shrines, such as their gables and their mirrors. Of course, those gables and mirrors pre-dated the concept of Shinto as pioneered by Ise priests of that period. It goes without saying that Ise's medieval Shinto cannot be used to explain the meanings of those gables and mirrors in the eighth or the tenth century. Yet, it appears less obvious to many that modern conceptualizations of Shinto cannot be used to explain the meaning of shrine practices in periods before those Shinto concepts emerged.

Taking these two arguments together, it becomes possible to study the context in which the particular conceptualization of Shinto in fourteenth-century Ise occurred, as well as its impact. To give an example: it is possible that the gables of the Ise shrines were redesigned on the basis of the esoteric knowledge that constituted "Shinto" for their priests at this juncture. This cannot be proven due to a lack of sources, but even if the physical gables were not recarved, they now took on a new meaning that was defined by that Shinto concept, and there are sources that allow us to trace rituals inspired by this new meaning. One might describe this as the first instance of Shintoization. In this case, the term Shinto referred only to knowledge about Ise, and there was as yet no sign of a Shinto concept that extended to all shrines and their rituals in general; but soon, the Miwa and Hie shrines were Shintoized in ways that betray obvious influence from Ise. When new and broader conceptualizations of Shinto emerged in later centuries, their influence reached much further, transforming shrines in many different ways; Yoshida Shintō in the fifteenth century and the Shinto concepts developed by Kokugaku and Mitogaku scholars in the eighteenth and early nineteenth centuries were particularly influential. A history of Shintoization would bring out the mutual influence of such conceptualizations of Shinto on the one hand, and shrines, rituals and myths on the other. Also, it would help us to avoid anachronisms of the kind mentioned above, and to think about the meanings and functions of shrines and *saishi* rituals in settings where Shinto was not a significant concept, or where other conceptualizations of Shinto were current.

This is a different course from that taken recently by Helen Hardacre in her magisterial *Shinto: A History* (2017). Hardacre treats the term Shinto as a descriptive, analytical category that can be applied to disparate phenomena throughout Japanese history, rather than a historical construct that has its own history and that has created its own reality (or realities) by way of processes of Shintoization. This leads her to posit the existence of a distinct category of Shinto that goes back to the prehistoric Yayoi Period. This category, Hardacre argues, denotes a distinct set of traditions that share a number of characteristics. She defines the distinctness of Shinto in terms of its indigeneity and its public nature – two characteristics that are typically used to describe the classical Ritsuryō cult of the "gods of heaven and earth" (*jingi saishi*) and post-Meiji forms of Shinto, notably state and shrine Shinto.

It is questionable, however, whether the Ritsuryō cult was understood, let alone broadcast, as indigenous and public even in classical times. As many have pointed out, there is at least a heavy overlay of Chinese (Tang) elements, as one would expect in a ritual system that sought to convert Japan's kings into Chinese-style emperors.[1] Defining Japan ("the indigenous") as different from China and India ("the foreign") was not an aim of Ritsuryō ritual, nor was it a theme of the mythologies of *Kojiki* or *Nihon shoki*; rather, these rituals and narratives served to enhance imperial authority by drawing on both continental and local practice and imagery.[2] Moreover, Ritsuryō ceremonial combined "public" rituals, performed in the presence of court officials and priests from the provinces, with "private" ones that focused on the person of the emperor, his lineage and his palace. Ritsuryō ceremonial as a whole can be defined as public only if we accept the East-Asian premise that everything imperial is by definition public. Also, even those rituals that were public, in the sense that they were performed in front of the entire bureaucracy and many priests, were in fact intramural affairs when regarded through Meiji glasses: they did not seek to speak to or involve "the people" in any manner, other than as producers of tribute.

Hardacre's selection of indigeneity and publicness as Shinto's two characteristics replicates the central dogma of modern Shinto theology: that classical, indigenous and public Shinto (that is, the Ritsuryō system of *jingi saishi* – but also, in its shadow, "Shinto" in a much broader sense, as Japanese *kami* worship in general) was

1 E.g., Naumann 1997; Ooms 2009.
2 It is worth pointing out that also *kami* cults beyond the court (of which we know little) were likely less "native" than usually assumed (Como 2009).

restored in Meiji after an intervening period of decline. Hardacre warns against such an ideological and a-historic view on almost every page of her book; but when she stresses multiple times that "Shinto originates with the Jingikan" (the Council of the Gods of Heaven and Earth, which coordinated *jingi saishi*),[3] she cannot avoid validating the post-Meiji narrative of Shinto as Japan's enduring indigenous religion, guarded as an unbroken tradition by the imperial court. This is certainly not her intention, as is also demonstrated beyond any doubt in her earlier work on Shinto and the state in the Meiji Period (e.g., Hardacre 1989). In her Shinto history, Hardacre's failure to address the conceptualization of the category of Shinto itself and the effects of that conceptualization lures her into a trap, set by the discursive structure of the concept of Shinto itself. That this can happen to an immensely knowledgeable historian of Hardacre's calibre is perhaps the best demonstration of the dilemmas that are inherent in the very act of writing "Shinto history" in any shape or form.

Attempting a comparative perspective: Hinduism

The history of shrines, Shinto and Shintoization is, of course, unique in its particulars. Yet at the same time it follows a pattern that, on some level of abstraction, may be recognized also in other settings. I have earlier attempted a comparative study of Buddhist cults of local deities in and beyond Japan, focusing on medieval Shinto and the *nat* cult in Myanmar (Teeuwen 2007). This revealed some striking parallels and, not least, differences that helped me pose new questions to the Japanese material. In this essay, as then, my principal aim is not to construe a grand taxonomy of structural commonalities across Asia, but merely to gain a fresh perspective on Japanese developments by observing them through the prism of another tradition that, in an impressionistic way, appears analogous enough to raise new questions. There are multiple candidates for such a comparison, but I will here try my hand at Hinduism.

---

3   E.g., Hardacre 2017, 45.

What stands out about Shinto historiography when it is juxtaposed to the historiography of Hinduism?

The concept of Hinduism is profoundly different from Shinto in crucial ways. Perhaps most critical is the simple fact that while a billion people identify as Hindus, Shinto has hardly functioned as an identity marker at all, neither in the past nor in modern times. The term Hindu, which started out as a geographical designation, gained religious and cultural connotations as an identity tag for non-Muslims in India's late medieval period (Lorenzen 1999; Sharma 2002). Shinto, in contrast, did not function as a sectarian identity in the Edo Period (when even Shinto priests were legally bound to affiliate with a Buddhist temple), and abortive attempts to transform it into a religious identity failed in the early years of Meiji.

These two traditions do, however, share some of the same historiographical quandaries. Like Meiji Period Shinto, Hinduism was a post-facto concept construed on the basis of creative reinterpretations of a national or ethnic past. In both cases, these reinterpretations occurred in a context of dominance by the Christian west – in India in the form of British rule, and in Japan, more indirectly, through the forced opening of the country to American and European powers, which inspired a justified fear of western intentions. Historians both of Hinduism and of Shinto have struggled with the question whether these religions were nineteenth-century "inventions" or pre-existing categories that were merely recalibrated as they encountered modernity – or, to be more accurate, the question in what measure they were both of those things. In both cases, the same historiographical problem arises: it is clear that neither Hinduism nor Shinto was invented out of thin air, while at the same time, modernity fundamentally altered the way Hinduism and Shinto were conceived, the position they occupied in society, and the way they were practiced.

In the historiography of Hinduism, there is much controversy around questions of who did the invention/recalibration, and with what aims. Was Hinduism designed by an "unholy alliance" (Halbfass 2005, 23) between India's British masters and their Brahman allies to serve the interests of both, or did Hinduism "crystallize in the Indian cultural imaginaire" (Fisher 2017, 3) already before the colonial period? This question is not just an academic one, asked in order to set history right; it puts the very authenticity of Hinduism as a category at stake. If Hinduism is a nineteenth-century "conceit," it is devoid of legitimacy. Are critical historians giving too much credit to the European colonialists, and turning a blind eye to patchy but real evidence of both precolonial and colonial expressions of Hindu identity, as articulated in native sources? The very fact that the concept of Hinduism made sense to Hindus and survived Britain's exit demonstrates that it was not a mere figment of outsiders' imagination. On the other hand, the changes from the fragmented landscape of precolonial Hindu religion(s) to modern ideas of a monolithic "neo-Hinduism" are profound. Where does continuity end and discontinuity begin? And what is more: is it even ethical for an outsider to deconstruct an identity that is central to the self-understanding of millions? Or would it be unethical *not* to deconstruct an identity discourse that inspires harmful identity politics?

It appears that both in the case of Hinduism and that of Shinto, new research into medieval and early modern conceptualizations has inspired more moderate and balanced assessments of the modern novelty of these categories. This tendency is strengthened further by a more general turn away from the once popular idea that "everything was invented in the nineteenth century," and criticism of studies that employ Hobsbawm's concept of "invented traditions" in a manner that is too cynical and top-down. In the case of Hinduism, the question is not whether there was a notion of Hindus as a category of people in premodern (or at least early modern) times, but rather whether they shared a "religion," or even a "metareligion," beyond the local communities to which they belonged. Lipner points at the Vedas as a common frame of reference for the "vast array of different sects, cults, and denominations" (Lipner 2006, 100) that constituted the "jungle" of Hindu religious life. Discussions within the different schools of medieval Vedānta, while failing to agree on most matters, at least created a joint arena that may have suggested an abstract notion of "orthodox" (*āstika*) Hinduism, in the limited sense of a family of cults that agree to disagree about the same things – in contrast to, for example, the Muslims, who were not part of that family discussion (Fisher 2017, 5). Elsewhere, Lipner has argued that it is the historian's task to explore the "distinctive characteristic of 'Hinduness'" that typifies Hinduism as "a family of religious traditions," and he suggests that paradoxality, relativism and polycentrism are central traits of this family (Lipner 1996). To this, Richard King objects that such an approach remains profoundly anti-historical, because it postulates a timeless, *a priori* "essence" that is then considered central to all forms of later "Hinduism" (King 1999). King points out that the commonalities adduced by Lipner are rooted in Sanskritized philosophical traditions (notably Vedānta), and therefore hardly representative; and that even within this limitation, those traditions are very indistinct and incoherent. Lipner proposes to imagine Hinduism metaphorically as a banyan tree, a plant that might be described as something between a tree and a forest. Such an image would imply that Hinduism grew from a single seed. King, on the other hand, denies even this limited notion of organic unity as a modern construct.

The problem is compounded by the fact that the term Hinduism was coined around 1800 and gained wider currency only in the latter half of the same century. The Sanskrit equivalent *Hindu-dharma,* while not completely absent from premodern sources, spread as a translation of that English term in the same period. As with Shinto, this was not simply a matter of naming what was already there; behind the appearance of these new terms was a process of conceptualization that had profound consequences for those who were being reconceptualized. Pennington warns against regarding this "development of Hinduism in the nineteenth century as principally a response to the West, whether to Christianity, Western education, or colonial rule" (Pennington 2005, 161); rather, he stresses the agency of Hindu reformers, like Rammohan Roy and Vivekananda, and their Hindu critics, like Bhabanicaran Bandhyopadhyay, editor of a Bengali-language newspaper in Calcutta. Both the reformers and their more conservative critics appealed to ancient Hindu traditions to create a modern Hinduism for a new age. That new age was an age where western ideas were dominant and normative.

When Hinduism was defined as India's indigenous religion, it entered a category in which it could not escape being measured against Christianity, as the defining archetype of "religion" in its most evolved form. Hindu reformers took the hint by reimagining Hinduism as "at core" a monotheistic, rational, egalitarian religion, sadly ridden by such corruptions as polytheism, ritualism and the discriminatory caste system. Modernization, then, implied a return to a pure Hindu tradition rooted in (new interpretations of) the Vedas, and also a refutation of existing Hindu traditions as they were actually practised across the Indian subcontinent – a fact that unleashed a storm of criticism among Hindu leaders against the movements instigated by Roy and Vivekananda.

At first, this new Hinduism was not necessarily nationalist or anti-colonialist in nature. Pennington urges us not to downplay the motivational power of religion, and argues that rather than resisting colonialism, the creators of the new Hinduism sought to "demonstrate that ancient traditional understandings could find wholly appropriate expression through the new formulations that modernity suggested" (ibid., 164). It should be noted that the "ancient" understandings that the reformers sought to modernize were to no small measure modern imaginings. Most importantly, their neo-Hinduism was premised on the notion of an ancient ancestral religion that tied all Hindus together.

Modern Hinduism carried forward the ambiguity of the older term Hindu, in combining geographical with religious/cultural meanings. This ambiguity came to the fore in early twentieth-century developments of the term, when the Indian independence movement was well underway. The concept of Hinduism was expanded into a vision of a cultural, ethnic and racial identity that was to define the new polity that independence would bring about. Famously, the nationalist ideologue V. D. Savarkar distinguished between *Hindu-dharma* (Hinduism) as a religion and *Hindutva* ("Hindudom") as a much broader unifying cultural identity shared by all Hindus (Lipner 2006, 103; Sharma 2002, 22). Savarkar, who did much of his writing in British prisons, expanded the term Hindu to include all religious groups of Indian origin (Buddhists, Jains and Sikhs), while excluding religions of foreign origin, even if they had a long history in India (most notably Muslims, Christians and Jews). His notion of *Hindutva* was a further extension of Hinduism: it qualified for Hindu nationality a population that belonged to a diverse group of distinct religions, by constructing an overarching umbrella that was even more of an ideological invention than Hinduism itself, while excluding all others.

Can we gauge new perspectives on the modern conceptualization of Shinto when we consider it through the lens of Hinduism? In spite of the radically different political and social context, there are many obvious parallels between nineteenth- and twentieth-century Hinduism and Shinto when it comes to the process of conceptualization. As already noted, both were created as answers to new questions, notably about national identity in a nation-state and about the role of religion in that identity. As pointed out by Maxey (2014), answering these questions constituted no less than "the greatest problem" in the late nineteenth-century efforts to build a modern Japanese nation-state. Here too, reformers clashed with critics, and a complicated process of negotiation, power-play and compromise resulted in a constellation where Shinto, at least officially, was at the same time elevated to a public body of ceremonial that was fundamental to the Japanese Imperial State, and excluded from the category of religion, which came to be understood to denote a realm of private, optional faith. As we have seen, the first author of a "Shinto history," Tanaka Yoshitō, broke with this official definition of Shinto and proposed that Shinto should be studied as Japan's ethnic moral philosophy. Soon, others were to argue that the Shinto history that Tanaka had constructed was the history not of a philosophy but of a "super-religion" (*chō-shūkyō*) that was at the core of all Japanese cultural, moral and religious practice, even if on the surface, it took the form of Buddhism or Confucianism. This ambiguity about the status of Shinto finds a parallel in the tension between a sectarian *Hindu-dharma* and the much broader notion of *Hindutva*, which is both religious (as a kind of super-religion binding together all Hindus, even if they do not follow a religion that is part of Hinduism in the narrow sense of the term) and ethno-cultural.

Both neo-Hinduism and modern Shinto may be described as attempts to create national ethno-cultural and (semi-)religious identities out of local traditions with great local variety and little coherence. In both cases, this was done by means of a narrative that assumed ancient unity and purity. Ancient purity was then followed by latter-day perversion, causing superstition, syncretism and sectarianism to obscure the original essence of the tradition. Reform, however, could recover that original essence by removing the accumulated layers of corruption. In the case of Shinto, it was the inclusion of the classical Ritsuryō cult in the historical narrative of Shinto that made it possible to create a plotline that passed from classical purity, by way of medieval confusion (typically blamed on "foreign" Buddhism and/or Confucianism), to a modern clarity that was achieved by anti-syncretic cleansing of truly revolutionary proportions. According to Richard King, the standard narrative of the history of Hinduism is likewise structured as a three-act play: (i) Hinduism as a single, unified religion rooted in the Vedas, (ii) stagnation from the medieval period onwards (most typically, the tenth century) and (iii) modern renewal, as reformers restored their now decadent religion into something approaching its former glory (King 1999). Strikingly, even the timing of the major turns in this play line up perfectly with the Japanese narrative on Shinto: in Japan, the tenth century saw the collapse of the Ritsuryō cult, which was replaced by the Buddhist-dominated system of twenty-two court-sponsored shrines,[4] and "modern renewal" likewise occurred in the nineteenth century.

It is difficult to imagine a Shinto narrative that does not replicate this three-act structure. At the same time, it is impossible to imagine such a narrative doing justice to the complicated history of *kami* shrines, practices and agents. If the three-act structure is inherent in the very concept of Shinto, then this concept cannot be used to structure historical work. Likewise, if anti-syncretism is inherent in the very word Shinto, then that word is best avoided

---

4 In his alternative history of Shinto, Inoue Hiroshi (2011) refers to this transition as the starting point of the development of Shinto as a concept.

when one tries to understand the place of shrines or shrine rituals in premodern times.

I believe that focusing on questions of Shintoization is helpful as a way to avoid projecting modern understandings of Shinto onto the past, but even this method approaches shrine cults and *kami* worship through the lens of consecutive conceptualizations of Shinto. That begs the question how important Shintoization was in different periods of shrines' lives. In our own Shinto history (Breen and Teeuwen 2010), we came to the conclusion that Shintoization had a great impact at least on larger shrines after the Meiji Restoration, and some impact already in the seventeenth century. We found that before that time, other historical processes were much more important. This became all the more clear to me while John Breen and I wrote a history of the Ise shrines (Teeuwen and Breen 2017). In this book, we identify and analyse eight moments of profound change in the 1,300-year history of this central shrine complex. Only a few of those moments had anything to do with reconceptualizations of Shinto and the implementation of such new concepts in Ise. Again, such Shinto-inspired changes occurred in the seventeenth and, much more dramatically, in the nineteenth century. In 1675, Buddhist actors were formally excluded from Ise's pilgrimage business after Ise had been defined as a Shinto site; and between 1871 and 1873, Ise was radically redesigned to serve as an imperial site of state ritual. These reforms had a great impact on the site, not only theologically but also physically, socially, economically and politically. At the same time, however, Ise experienced many other transformations that were equally revolutionary, but that can hardly be described as moments of Shintoization. Often, these transformations signalled shifts in the economic model that allowed the shrines to thrive or survive. They occurred when court taxes dwindled and shrine priests developed a system of soliciting land donations from Kanto warriors; and again when these priests lost control over their lands, and their position was challenged by pilgrimage entrepreneurs who welcomed pilgrims to their private compounds. In the postwar period, Ise changed radically again after it was privatized as a religious charity.

Such changes and their causes can easily fall out of the historical narrative if, defined as a "Shinto history," it sets itself the task to fill that abstract concept with meaning in different periods. For this reason, I doubt that I will attempt to write another Shinto history in the future.

References

Breen, John and Teeuwen, Mark 2010. *A New History of Shinto*. Oxford (Wiley-Blackwell).

Como, Michael 2009. *Weaving and Binding: Immigrant Gods and Female Immortals in Ancient Japan*. Honolulu (University of Hawai'i Press).

Fisher, Elaine M. 2017. *Hindu Pluralism: Religion and the Public Sphere in Early Modern South India*. Oakland (University of California Press).

Halbfass, Wilhelm 2005. "The Idea of the Veda and the Identity of Hinduism" in: J. E. Llewellyn (ed.), *Defining Hinduism: A Reader*. New York (Routledge), 16–29. https://doi.org/10.4324/9781315475653-3

Hardacre, Helen 1989. *Shinto and the State, 1868–1989*. Princeton (Princeton University Press).

Hardacre, Helen 2017. *Shinto: A History*. Oxford (Oxford University Press).

Inoue Hiroshi 2011. *Shintō no kyozō to jitsuzō*. Tokyo (Kōdansha).

Inoue Nobutaka (ed.) 1998. *Shintō: Nihon-umare no shūkyō shisutemu*. Tokyo (Shin'yōsha).

Isomae Jun'ichi 2000. "Tanaka Yoshitō and the Beginnings of *Shintōgaku*" in: John Breen and Mark Teeuwen (eds.), *Shinto in History*. Richmond (Curzon), 318–39.

King, Richard 1999. "Orientalism and the Modern Myth of 'Hinduism.'" *Numen* 46/2, 146–85. https://doi.org/10.1163/1568527991517950

Kuroda Toshio 1981. "Shinto in the History of Japanese Religion" (tr. James C. Dobbins and Suzanne Gay). *The Journal of Japanese Studies* 7/1, 1–21. https://doi.org/10.2307/132163

Lipner, Julius J. 1996. "Ancient Banyan: An Inquiry into the Meaning of 'Hinduness.'" *Religious Studies* 31/1, 109–26. https://doi.org/10.1017/S0034412500024100

Lipner, Julius J. 2006. "The Rise of 'Hinduism'; Or, How to Invent a World Religion with Only Moderate Success." *International Journal of Hindu Studies* 10/1, 91–104. https://doi.org/10.1007/s11407-006-9004-6

Lorenzen, David N. 1999. "Who Invented Hinduism?" *Comparative Studies in Society and History* 41/4, 630–59. https://doi.org/10.1017/S0010417599003084

Maxey, Trent E. 2014. *The "Greatest Problem": Religion and State Formation in Meiji Japan*. Cambridge, MA (Harvard University Press).

Naumann, Nelly 1997. *Die einheimische Religion Japans. Bis zum Ende der Heian-Zeit.* Leiden (Brill).
Okada Shōji 2010. *Nihon shintōshi.* Tokyo (Yoshikawa Kōbunkan).
Ooms, Herman 2009. *Imperial Politics and Symbols in Ancient Japan: The Tenmu Dynasty.* Honolulu (University of Hawaii Press).
Pennington, Brian K. 2005. *Was Hinduism Invented? Britons, Indians, and the Colonial Construction of Religion.* Oxford (Oxford University Press).
Rots, Aike Peter 2017. *Shinto, Nature and Ideology in Contemporary Japan.* London (Bloomsbury).
Sharma, Arvind 2002. "On Hindu, Hindustān, Hinduism and Hindutva." *Numen* 49/1, 1–36. https://doi.org/10.1163/15685270252772759
Tanaka Yoshitō 1909. "Shintōshi gaikan." *Kokugakuin zasshi* 15.
Tanaka Yoshitō 1910. *Shintō hongi.* Tokyo (Nihon Gakujutsu Kenkyūkai).
Tanaka Yoshitō 1915. *Shintōshi kōyō.* Tokyo (Nihon Gakujutsu Kenkyūkai).
Teeuwen, Mark 2002. "From *Jindō* to Shinto: A Concept Takes Shape." *Japanese Journal of Religious Studies* 29/3–4, 233–63.
Teeuwen, Mark 2007. "Comparative Perspectives on the Emergence of Jindō and Shinto." *Bulletin of the School of Oriental and African Studies* 70/2, 373–402. https://doi.org/10.1017/S0041977X07000456
Teeuwen, Mark and Breen, John 2017. *A Social History of the Ise Shrines: Divine Capital.* London (Bloomsbury).
Tsuchiya Senkyō 1907. *Nihon shūkyōshi.* Tokyo (Waseda Daigaku Shuppanbu).

About the author

Mark Teeuwen is professor of Japanese studies at the University of Oslo, Norway. He has published widely on the history of Japanese religion, with a focus on Shinto. Recent publications include *A New History of Shinto* and *A Social History of the Ise Shrines: Divine Capital* (2010 and 2017, both co-authored with John Breen).

Part 2

Exploring Borderlands of Shinto

4

Medieval Tendai Buddhist views of kami[1]

Yeonjoo Park

Introduction

There are a multitude of positions and angles from which one can understand Shinto – Japan's indigenous religious practice that is based on the worship of a myriad of *kami*. Among them are a succession of comparative studies that have explored common elements between Shinto and other native religious beliefs or practices, specifically shamanic religions in northeast Asia, in an effort to trace their origins and archetypes. Aside from the ultimate objectives of comparative studies, there are indeed many shared features among these religious practices, such as a belief in the spirit of all beings and things. It is the so-called animistic element that constitutes the main characteristics of many folk religions in the world. This element also constitutes a central religious concept that is revealed through numerous folk legends, mythic tales, religious symbols and rituals in East Asia. These tales and rites exhibit people's faith in spirits that are possessed by trees, rocks, rivers and so on, and their worship of spirits as sacred divinities that influence human affairs to varying degrees. Typically in these beliefs there exists a medium or a shaman who takes charge of communication between spirits and humans. However, a shaman is simply the recognized expert of this communication. At a fundamental level, the common notion of the spirit in East Asian shamanism is based on a belief that humans, all beings and nature itself can mutually communicate and interact with one another. Although often regarded as primitive by modern standards, these types of animistic beliefs and

1 This paper is for the most part based on my previous article in Korean which was published in a collection of monographs on various shamanic religions in East Asia (Park 2017).

folk or shamanic practices suggest an ontological principle that demonstrates the oneness of all beings, the central importance of such knowledge, and efforts for the confirmation and transmission of the ideal principle. In other words, philosophical or theoretical grounds for a religion can sufficiently be gleaned from such shamanic practices. On the other hand, the lack of intellectual tools with which to elucidate those grounds is the major obstruction to fathoming the original nature of shamanism. Most of these religious practices, as well as ancient Shinto, are not equipped with systematic doctrinal scriptures or teachings, which clarify what their beliefs and venerating practices – including rituals of spirit worship – are about. Nor have these practices and beliefs been explained or studied in and of themselves by scholars who study the way in which one can recognize the object of veneration or explain the meaning of various rituals and symbols.

In this light, Shinto of Japan is a remarkable case, in that it was first examined and explained by another religion. Since the arrival of Buddhism in Japan in the sixth century, a wide array of non-Buddhist beliefs and practices that were largely based on *kami* worship had established an exceptionally close relationship with Buddhism, until separated by the Meiji government in the nineteenth century. In particular, in textual terms, medieval Japanese Buddhist writings, such as tales, commentaries and preaching texts, featured syncretic discourse in which *kami* (alt. *shin* or *jin*), an umbrella term for non-Buddhist folk deities, were merged into the Buddhist pantheon. This medieval Japanese syncretic discourse was typically viewed by scholars of the past several decades as an expression of a larger development called "Kami-Buddha amalgamation" (*shinbutsu shūgō* 神仏習合) or "combination." In this context, the term amalgamation or combination does not indicate something like a "mixture" of *kami* and buddhas, but, rather, signifies that these two are one and the same. In other words, *shinbutsu shūgō* is ultimately a noetic or cognitive idea that emphasizes the oneness of *kami* and buddhas.[2]

2 *Shinbutsu shūgō* is of course a general term that refers to a wide scope of religious syncretism in medieval Japan, including the physical cohabitation

What is more remarkable in the course of the development of the Kami-Buddha combinatory system is the very logic that combines *kami* and buddhas. Kami-Buddha combinatory discourses are featured throughout a variety of medieval Buddhist – Tendai in particular – writings in which *kami* were merged into the Buddhist pantheonic structure, typically as the "traces," that is, local manifestations of various buddhas, which are construed to be the "original ground." The structure of the original ground-trace (*honji suijaku* 本地垂迹), or the origin-trace (*hon-jaku*), operates as the basic paradigm for Kami-Buddha combinatory discourse, based on many Buddhist writings. These writings include Buddhist tales, commentaries and preaching texts that emphasize the seemingly hierarchical yet inconceivably nondual associations between *kami* and buddhas. For the first time in the history of Japan the native, animistic and shamanic practice of *kami* worship in that country was "studied" and "explained," and treated as the object of academic discourse by Tendai scholar-monks. Indeed, as viewed from the Tendai Buddhist perspective, the explanation of *kami* worship practice was performed within a rather asymmetrical power dynamic. However, one can also argue that it was through the *honji suijaku* paradigm that Buddhist scholars' understanding of *kami* was enhanced and deepened, and consequently, generated a more theorized and ritualized worshipping of *kami*. In particular, Tendai's interpretation of *kami*'s salvific role for people because of their marvellous capacity for non-obstructive communication is noteworthy. Even though we are able to see/access the nature of *kami* worship through the lenses of Tendai esoteric ideals such as nonduality, non-obstruction and original enlightenment, examining the medieval Tendai discourse of *kami* can offer an important key for understanding the previously unspoken meaning of the spirit that dwells in all things.[3]

---

of Buddhist temples and *kami* shrines. However, this type of phenomenon was inseparable from the perception of the oneness of *kami* and buddhas.

3 As is well known in the field of Japanese religion, the medieval Tendai discourse of *kami* and Kami-Buddha combination had a crucial influence on the emergence of later independent Shintoist thought.

This paper will first sketch the development of the Kami-Buddha amalgamation and the *honji suijaku* structure.[4] Then it will introduce the fourteenth-century Tendai text *Keiran shūyōshū* 渓嵐拾葉集 (c. 1318–48), compiled by one of Tendai's unique groups of scholar-monks, called "chroniclers" (*kike* 記家), who made primary contributions to the systemic development and dissemination of the Kami-Buddha combinatory discourse. As *Keiran shūyōshū* represents the pinnacle of fully-grown medieval Tendai scholasticism, ample discussions about *kami* and the *honji suijaku* relationship therein will successfully lead us to grasp the way in which medieval Tendai scholars understood *kami*.

A short outline of Kami-Buddha combination and Keiran shūyōshū

After a long and complicated process of introduction, Buddhism came to be incorporated into court rituals (*jingisaishi* 神祇祭祀) in Japan by the seventh century. At first, the Buddha or Buddhist divinities were worshipped as the new, foreign *kami*, which had different origins and names from existing Japanese *kami* but were equivalent in their numinous and awe-inspiring power and sacredness. This was not at all a rarity: there had already been veneration of various deities (*jin*, *shin* or *kami* 神) from areas beyond the Japanese isles, including regions of continental East Asia.

It was in the eighth century that environs around *kami* and buddhas began to change, and as generally agreed among scholars of Japanese religion, there were combinatory relations between *kami* and Buddhist divinities (*shinbutsu shūgō*) from this period onward. The amalgamation process can be divided into three stages: the first took place when the "downgrade" of *kami* occurred, during

---

4 Since a sufficient number of studies in the English language have discussed the history of Kami-Buddha amalgamation and the *honji suijaku*, this paper will limit that aspect to an essential minimum that offers enough background for understanding the main discussion here. In particular see Rambelli and Teeuwen (2003) and Inoue (2003).

which *kami* were portrayed in Buddhist writings as ordinary sentient beings, similar to humans who carried evil karma and thus must be saved and tamed by means of the Buddha and Buddhist teachings. This first phase was undoubtedly intimately related to the subsequent development of the status of *kami*. As deluded beings, *kami* were guided by Buddhist teachings and thus reformed and converted into becoming "protectors" of the Buddha's teachings and Buddhist deities (Skt. *dharmapāla*; J. *gohō zenshin* 護法善神). This was the second stage in the history of Kami-Buddha amalgamation.

The third stage occurred when the concept of the *honji suijaku* 本地垂迹 was formulated and developed by Buddhist scholar-monks.[5] By the late Heian Period, the concept of *honji suijaku* and buddhas as the original ground of *kami* became a religious idiom and was increasingly prominent in many medieval Buddhist doctrinal writings, as well as in non-Buddhist, general literature.[6] This concept was gradually disseminated into the general populace through the process of proselytization of Buddhist teachings. The success of this process was contributed to in particular by various types of mobile or "networking" monks and ascetic practitioners[7] who were closely associated with the major Buddhist institutions, such as Tendai's main temple, Enryakuji 延暦寺 on Mt Hiei. This can be attributed to their dedication to learning high Buddhist teachings and practices, and the transmission of that knowledge to

---

5 According to Yoshida Kazuhiko, the notion of *honji suijaku* was not at once simultaneously formulated: rather, the idea of *suijaku* 垂迹, that is, the Buddhist interpretation of *kami* as the manifestation of Buddha, was discussed and disseminated for the first time around the ninth century. Then, over the course of time, the notion of *honji* 本地 in the midst of continental Buddhist commentarial discourses was illuminated, combined with the then-existing view of *kami* as *suijaku*, and together began to be formulated as the dominant framework that defines the combinatory relationship between *kami* and buddhas. Yoshida 2006, 199.

6 Ibid., 203–20; Itō 2012, 55–8.

7 These ascetics include itinerant ascetics *hijiri* (holy ones), practitioners of mountain asceticism (*shugenja* 修験者), and upholders of the Lotus Sūtra (*jikyōsha* 持経者).

diverse Buddhist circles, as well as to the general populace in the Japanese isles.[8]

The *honji suijaku* structure provided the rationale for the combination of buddhas and *kami* in the *shinbutsu shūgō* discourse, which means that buddhas and bodhisattvas, or the origin(s), manifest as various *kami*, or the trace(s). Although a sense of hierarchy and asymmetry between buddhas and *kami* in this structure is detected, over time the asymmetry between them became less distinct, as illustrated by the scholarship in the history of the Kami-Buddha combination. As the *honji suijaku* grew to be a dominant rhetorical and discursive structure in Japanese religious culture, the relationship between the origin, *hon*, and the trace, *jaku*, gradually came to be interpreted as "identical." This was specifically grounded upon Tendai's crucial doctrinal concept of nonduality (*funi* 不二) or mutual identity (*sōsoku* 相即), which emphasizes the inconceivable oneness between concepts that are conventionally considered polar opposites. Tendai's theoretical development of the nondual identity of *kami* and buddhas eventually led to the formulation and dissemination of the so-called inverted *honji suijaku* theory (*han honji suijaku setsu* 反本地垂迹説) within Tendai scholastic and monastic circles, which gave prime importance to *kami*. This further influenced the independent establishment and development of "Shinto" from the late fifteenth century on.

Even a brief outline of the Kami-Buddha relations as described above would be sufficient to highlight the gravity of the *honji suijaku* in Japanese religion and call for attention to the fact that the core of the *honji suijaku* scheme lies in understanding the relationship between the origin and the trace. A vital key to fathoming this relationship hinges upon how to interpret the meaning of the trace, or, *suijaku*. As noted in previous studies on the historical development of the *honji suijaku* paradigm, the term *suijaku* was formed within the Buddhist hermeneutical tradition in East Asia, particularly through exegetical efforts to comprehend what the

---

8   For more on the important roles of networking monks in the development of Buddhism in medieval Japan, see Ruppert 2014, 369–93. See also Deal and Ruppert 2015, 153–60.

Buddha truly was. Scholars have paid attention to Sengzhao 僧肇 (384 [alt. 374]–414)'s use of the terms "origin" and "trace" in his commentary on the *Vimalakīrti Nirdeśa Sūtra* (J. *Yuimakyō* 維摩経). Discussing the relationship between true wisdom and expedient means, he commented, "[the origin] casts (*chui* 垂) [its] traces (*ji* 跡)."[9]

Although Sengzhao's comment is generally considered to be the first usage of *hon-jaku* terminology, one can find the *Lotus Sūtra* as the hermeneutic ground for the formation and the development of the notion that the Buddha, the everlasting truth (origin), can manifest in various forms (trace) as expedient means. Zhiyi 智顗 (538–598), the founder of the Tiantai school, employed Sengzhao's terminology as an exegetic tool to appreciate the teachings of the *Lotus Sūtra* and paved the way for the foundation of Tendai-*Lotus* hermeneutics.[10] Additionally, this notion of the origin and trace came to be broadly applied by Japanese Tendai scholar-monks, to the extent that the notion of the origin and trace(s) became a broader pantheonic structure that defined the relationships among Buddhist and non-Buddhist deities alike. Japanese Tendai further developed the *hon-jaku* tool to explain the inconceivable identity of Buddha and *kami*, highlighting the nonduality between origin and trace (*honjaku funi* 本迹不二). This emphasis on *hon-jaku* nonduality was a natural outcome of medieval Tendai's efforts toward esotericization of the *Lotus Sūtra* and Śākyamuni, which were respectively the central scripture and the main buddha in the Tendai school. Tendai's integration of esoteric Buddhism (Mikkyō 密教) and the *Lotus*-based Tendai teachings led to the exaltation of Śākyamuni as identical with Vairocana, the cosmic Buddha of esoteric teaching. This process called for Tendai's redefinition of the

9 T.38, 1775: 327b3–5 (*Commentary on the Vimalakīrti Nirdeśa Sūtra* 注維摩詰經). See Yoshida 2006, 201–2 and Stone 1999, 170.

10 Zhiyi employed the two terms "origin" and "trace" in his twofold interpretation of the *Lotus Sūtra*: origin teaching (*honmon* 本門) and trace teaching (*shakumon* 迹門). The distinction between the two teachings is grounded upon the previous ideas of expedient device (*hōben* 方便) and the manifestation of absolute truth. See Stone, *Original Enlightenment*, 170–1, for a detailed discussion.

relationship between the original Dharma body and the manifested body, and, consequently, the inconceivable identity of the two was strengthened.[11] The nondual identity of the essential Dharma body and the manifested body established the basis for Tendai/Taimitsu's hermeneutics of nonduality and provided a fundamental perspective for understanding either Buddhist or non-Buddhist matters.

The rationale for the nondual identity between Buddha and Kami was developed on the ground of *hon-jaku* nonduality, and constituted the fundamental premise in the discourse on *kami* by medieval Tendai scholar-monks on Mt Hiei. In particular, a specific group of scholar-monks, called "chroniclers" (*kike*), contributed to the systemic development and dissemination of the Kami-Buddha combinatory discourse, which was based on *hon-jaku* nonduality, centring on religious beliefs and practices on Sannō, the supreme *kami* of Mt Hiei.

Tendai chroniclers were erudite scholar-monks who collected various types of records, such as oral transmission (*kuden* 口伝) and secret texts, studied them thoroughly, added interpretations and transmitted those records.[12] The tradition of chroniclers was deeply related to medieval Tendai's peculiar culture of oral transmission, which typically was written on thin and small cut papers called *kirikami* (alt. *kirigami* 切紙). Hence, the content written on them was naturally compact and not reader-friendly. In that sense, chroniclers' organizational and editing skills must have been very useful. *Kike* transmissions are considered to have been systematized by Gigen 義源 (c. 1289–1351), who compiled *Sanke yōryakuki* 山家要略記 – an instrumental collection of transmissions regarding Sannō worship – and the compiler of *Keiran shūyōshū*, Kōshū

---

11 Medieval Tendai's commentarial texts, such as *Keiran shūyōshū*, the main text in this study, constantly emphasize the nondual identity between Śākyamuni and the cosmic, essential Buddha, particularly through discussions and comments on Śākyamuni's action of sitting with the Abundant Treasure Buddha (*Tahō Nyorai* 多宝如来) as recounted in Chapter 11 of the *Lotus* (T.9, 262: 32b16–34b22). Often referred to as the "co-sitting of the two buddhas (*nibutsu byōza* 二仏並座)," this episode was interpreted in the text to epitomize *hon-jaku* nonduality, as well as authenticating Śākyamuni as the eternal Buddha.

12 Tanaka 2003, 7.

光宗 (1276–1350). Ever since his entry to Mt Hiei to become a monk, Kōshū became dedicated to learning and training, as taken from various lineages and schools on Mt Hiei.[13]

Kōshū's *Keiran shūyōshū* is presumably the largest collection (extant fascicles of one hundred and thirteen in all) of Tendai *kuden* transmissions edited by chroniclers. Often labelled "encyclopedic" due to the all-inclusive quality of its content, *Keiran* records transmissions pertain to a wide variety of matters – not only Tendai/Taimitsu teachings and practices but also religious, historical and cultural traditions of Mt Hiei. But most of all, scholarly attention has been drawn to numerous discussions of *kami* in *Keiran*, as this work presents a fully-grown and well-elaborated medieval Tendai discourse on the Kami-Buddha combination.[14]

Kami in Keiran shūyōshū

Keiran is a massive volume: according to other records, it was originally composed of more than three hundred fascicles. Even what remains today comprises one hundred and thirteen fascicles. *Keiran*'s structure typically includes four divisions: sections on exoteric teachings (*kenbu* 顯部), esoteric teachings (*mitsubu* 密部), precepts (*kaibu* 戒部) and records (*kirokubu* 記録部). This was a typical curricular category of the medieval Hiei educational system. The first *kenbu* part is divided into four subsections. One of them is titled *shinmeibu* 神明部 (*kami* section), wherein most of *Keiran*'s discussions on *kami* is concentrated. Discussions on *kami* in the *shinmeibu* – mostly focused on Sannō, the tutelary deity of Mt Hiei, as well as Amaterasu for her importance as the

---

13 Tendai chroniclers were typically affiliated with several different lineages, because their work required knowledge of transmissions emanating from various lineages. Thus Kōshū was affiliated with a variety of lineages, although there were two main lineages for which he had a particularly strong sense of bondage. For a fuller discussion about Kōshū's lineages, see Tanaka 2003 and Park 2016, Chapter 1.

14 Previous studies that treated *Keiran* as a main text or topic include Grapard 1998; Tanaka 2003; Faure 2015.

ancestor *kami* of Japan – pivot on their *hon-jaku* associations and the Tendai doctrinal interpretation of those associations. For example, Amaterasu is the manifestation (*suijaku*) of Dainichi Nyorai and becomes "one" with Sannō, the manifestation of Śākyamuni. This association is grounded upon the rationale that Dainichi and Śākyamuni are nondually one; however, I will spare further elaboration on this logic, as this particular subject is beyond the scope of this study.[15] An important point here is that the *hon-jaku* relations in *Keiran* are all explained as forming the inconceivable oneness of nonduality. Various sets of terms and phrases associated with the idea of nonduality, such as "mutual identity" (*sōsoku* 相即), "neither one nor two" (*funi* 不二), "mysterious unity" (*myōgō* 冥合), "non-obstruction" (*muge* 無礙), and "mutual correspondence" (*sō-ō* 相応) are the key words found throughout *Keiran,* which represents the Tendai/Taimitsu ideal of perfect integration (*enyū* 円融). The notion of nonduality is at the core of Tendai's doctrinal understanding of the *honji suijaku* paradigm. Specifically speaking, nonduality provides the logical ground for the *hon-jaku* scheme. On the other hand, the *hon-jaku* structure offers an explanation for the rationale of nonduality, that is, how a nondual relationship actually works between two, seemingly polar-opposite elements.

Overall, there is a noteworthy tendency in *Keiran*'s discussions of *kami*: *Keiran* repeatedly emphasizes the "role" of *kami*, namely, what *kami* do, accompanied with the explanation of its rationale. To put it concisely, what *kami* do – and do very well – is to "manifest," which is expressed in a variety of ways such as *ōjaku* 應迹 *ōgen* 應現, *kegen* 化現, and so on, in addition to *suijaku* or *shaku* 迹. Nevertheless, the most poetic expression in *Keiran* that refers to *kami*'s ability to manifest would be the one that describes *kami* "dimming the light and becoming like the dust" (*wakō dōjin* 和光同塵).[16] Originating in the discussion of the "Way" in the

15 For an elaborate discussion on this subject, see Yeon Joo (Yeonjoo) Park's doctoral dissertation (2016), and an article on Sannō in *Keiran*, in the *Japanese Journal of Religious Studies* 47/1 (Spring 2020).

16 In the context of traditional East Asian thought, the *wakō dōjin* phrase from the *Dao de jing* was often appropriated by Buddhists in a metaphorical

Chinese classic, *Dao de jing* 道德経, in Japan this term had specifically been appropriated to allegorize *suijaku* or manifestation. Throughout *Keiran* this term often appears in a more concise form as "dimming light and manifesting" (*wakō suijaku* 和光垂迹), and indicates the manifestation of either *kami* in general or a specific *kami*, such as Sannō. One important point to note is that there is a special mission with regard to *kami*'s manifestation: it takes place for the salvation of all beings. Medieval Tendai thought, as voiced through *Keiran*, declares that *kami* guide all sentient beings to enlightenment through their ability to dim light and manifest. Seen in this light, the relevance of the expression, "dimming the light and becoming like the dust," with respect to the meaning of *kami*'s manifestation, becomes clearer, given that the expression connotes *kami*'s ability to "access" ordinary beings such as human beings by their appearances.

Through the development of medieval Tendai's Kami-Buddha discourse, *wakō dōjin* or *wakō suijaku* was adopted as a specific term that signifies appearance, disclosure or manifestation of that which is normally hidden, divine, enigmatic or salvific. In that sense, the Daoist concept of the Way, deities – either Buddhist or non-Buddhist – or absolute truth can all be viewed as the subject of the act of dimming light and becoming like dust. At this juncture Kōshū's interpretation of "recording" is remarkable. In the taxonomical discussion that centres on the main sections of *Keiran*, Kōshū emphasizes significance and responsibility attached to recording, and in particular, reveals his view of recording as an

---

way to stress the spirit of "transforming ordinary beings below" (下化衆生). Therefore, in this context, the meaning of "dust" implies something impure and represents ordinary people. This type of interpretation does not specifically conflict with our above discussion of *kami*'s role; in my view, however, the *wakō dōjin* of *kami* would be better understood as meaning their mysterious action as such small entities as dust. Consequently, "dust" implies something almost invisible and highlights *kami*'s subtle and inconceivable working on our minds. That said, it is also true that either interpretation links dust to ordinary beings. Therefore, in this case it would be not such a critical matter to choose the "correct" translation.

act of *wakō dōjin* that benefits people. As pointed out by previous scholarship, for medieval Tendai chroniclers faithful engagement in "recording" must have been in and of itself a bodhisattva practice that benefits all people by manifesting and transmitting Dharma.[17] Throughout the text we can also peek at Kōshū's pride as a chronicler and perceive his solemnity toward transmissions, which is comparable to manifestations of buddhas and bodhisattvas.

Throughout the above discussions about the meaning of manifestation, an important point rises slowly to the surface: Tendai's view of *kami*'s manifestation seems to be deeply related to humans' cognitive ability and the faculty of thinking. All in all, *Keiran* states that people[18] can approach the truth through *kami*'s manifestation. Of course, it is not only *kami* who can manifest and lead us to awakening. Buddhas and bodhisattvas also are well known to manifest in a variety of forms, i.e., the *nirmaṇakāya* or manifested body (*keshin* 化身), or the response body (*ōjin* 応身). However, there seems to be a special significance placed upon *kami*'s manifestation.

According to *Keiran*, *kami* can manifest freely due to their supernatural ability to penetrate anything (*jinzūriki* 神通力). What draws our attention in particular is the way *Keiran* explains this special ability of *kami* in an esoteric, allegorical language. One of the paragraphs that discuss Sannō, the supreme divinity of Mt Hiei, reads:

> The reason why the monkey should be the messenger of Sannō [is] because monkeys (申) have nothing to hinder or stop them.
> That is why they are called kami (神).

---

17 See Sueki 2003; Tanaka 2003, 7; Stone 1999, 124.

18 *Keiran* uses the word "(*issai*) *shujō*" (一切) 衆生; Skt. *sattva*) for the beneficiary of *wakō dōjin*. Of course, this term indicates all sentient beings, and strictly speaking, enlightenment is not a concept limited to human beings. However, only humans can read recorded texts, and Tendai's original enlightenment thought placed a great emphasis on mind practice. Thus, I limit the beneficiary influenced by *wakō dōjin* to human beings, who can benefit others through the act of transmission, or by "manifesting" the Dharma.

Monkeys are animals but have human forms; they can freely exist (*jizai* 自在) both in the sky and on earth.[19] There is nowhere that obstructs or stops them.[20]

The homology between the monkey and *kami* that is seen in the above passage cannot be perceived based on a mere word play (see the characters above). The character for *kami* is made up of a right-hand part which is the same as the character for monkey, and a left-hand part which means to point out or to show. *Keiran* repeatedly links the monkey and *kami* through the symbolism of the act of "showing", and thereby connects the two discussions, i.e., the symbolism of the monkey as the messenger of Sannō and *kami*'s ability to manifest unobstructively. Throughout *Keiran* it is remarkable that what is represented by the unobstructive, all-penetrating power of *kami* is the truth of nondual realities. This truth declares that those elements that are seemingly in a mutually contrasting, incompatible relationship, e.g., the human world and the divine, do in fact penetrate, communicate and identify with each other. Thus *kami* represent the nonduality or mysterious unity of all things as they communicate with ordinary people by their ability to *wakō dōjin*.[21]

This magical power of penetration is often explained with the notion of non-obstruction (*muge*); the nondual, perfect integration; and mysterious unity (*myōgō*). Integrating various representations of *kami* in *Keiran*, including the *wakō dōjin* and manifestation, one concept becomes clear concerning Tendai's interpretation of *kami*: it is associated with the act of transmission (let us recall the discussion of recording and Sannō's messenger), which makes an impact on humans' level of cognition. Given the earlier discussion on *wakō dōjin,* one can infer that *kami* play a crucial role in transmitting some important message to us, which must be related

---

19 This means that monkeys reside on earth and yet jump to the air (T.76, 2410: 672b16).
20 T.76, 2410: 518b14–16; 672b14–16.
21 On numerous occasions, *Keiran* emphasizes *kami*'s representation of nonduality, and Sannō, as the best among the myriad of *kami*, is the embodiment of the principle of nonduality. See Park 2016, Chapter 2.

92 *Exploring Shinto*

to our enlightenment. Still, questions remain: precisely what type of message would that be, and more importantly, exactly through what kind of method do *kami* deliver the message to us? *Keiran* presents clues to these questions through its compact allegorical language, as illustrated below.

The tiny snake inside us

Tendai chroniclers' records such as *Keiran* include a large portion of the collected oral transmissions passed on from masters to disciples. Naturally, discussions structured in a dialogue style – between the hypothetical master and disciple – are not rare in *Keiran.* Among its discussions about *kami*, the following hypothetical dialogue requires special attention:

> Question: Why must kami's manifestation always appear in the form of the snake?
> Answer: Kami are the essence of [softening light and/or] sitting/positioning with the dust (or the sentient beings). Thus they become like ordinary beings. Ordinary beings are the form composed of the Three Poisons in their most powerful and perfected condition. The original, uncreated form of the Three Poisons – when they are most powerful – is the form of the snake. Thus, the discussion of the Ono school in *Shijū jōketsu* 四十帖決[22] says: it is known that all kinds of kami's transformation and manifestation (must) come back to the worm species. Transformation here indicates kami's responsive manifestation. The worm species refers to beings that have the body of the snake, and so on…
> That kami always manifest themselves in the body of the snake; the uncreated original form of all sentient beings has the shape of the snake, which indicates the original body of the Dharma that opens enlightenment (*kaku* 覚). There is a tiny snake that is even smaller than 3 *sun* 寸, deep inside the entrails of all sentient beings…[23]

---

22 By Chōen 長宴 (1016–81). His lineage was known to have stemmed from orthodox Tendai esoteric teachings (Taimitsu).

23 T.76, 2410: 517c.

Previously, the first passage was briefly examined by Mark Teeuwen.²⁴ As Teeuwen notes, this passage deserves careful attention, as it reveals a radical nondualistic thought about worldly matters and enlightenment, a thought that was developed under the original enlightenment (*hongaku* 本覚) scheme, construed by Tendai esoteric discourses.²⁵ Before examining in more detail the oddly enigmatic discussion above, one aspect to note concerning the general characteristics of discussions in *Keiran* is their "condensed" quality. As previously mentioned, records by the Tendai chroniclers, or *kike*, were based on collections of the thin cut papers on which the main points under each topic were concisely written. Moreover, these *kike* transmissions were circulated not for the sake of the lay populace, but mostly for Tendai scholar-monks on Mt Hiei, who were well-versed in Tendai doctrine and practices, as well as the contemporary culture of the Tendai temple complex on Mt Hiei. Given these facts about the *kike* records, it is not so surprising to observe that *Keiran*'s overall dense writing is replete with metaphors and allegories that spare elaborate, systematic explanations. Reading *Keiran* today often challenges the reader's imagination and the ability to visualize, and requires active exegetical efforts to interactively mobilize text-external and -internal knowledge.

Returning to details in the quoted discussions about *kami*'s manifestation, first, the Three Poisons (*sandoku* 三毒) are the three defilements (Skt. *kleśā*) formulated in the early stages of Buddhist philosophy, and indicate greed, hatred and ignorance, all of which are serious hindrances to attaining enlightenment. Associated with the second of the Four Noble Truths, i.e., *samudaya* (J. *jittai* 集諦), they are the very roots of this-worldly, samsaric existence. They could be understood as the three elements of ignorance (Skt.

---

24 Teeuwen 2000, 95–116.

25 This passage contains so many concepts to be explained in order for us to appreciate what it refers to in the sense of basic Buddhist philosophy, and specifically how it is connected to Tendai esoteric teachings. However, for the sake of efficiency, I will confine my discussion to the bare minimum of information that is most relevant to the subject of this study.

avidyā; J. *mumyō* 無明), that is, the antithesis of enlightenment. According to the above passage, ordinary human beings are themselves the embodiment of these three contaminants that hinder attaining enlightenment. This is a typical Buddhist view of ordinary beings, but stating that these poisons take the form of a snake sounds like a riddle. This is a characteristic of Tendai esoteric (Taimitsu 台密) discourse, which understands realities according to six fundamental cosmic elements (*rokudai* 六大): i.e., earth (*chi* 地), water (*sui* 水), fire (*ka* 火), air (*fū* 風), space (*kū* 空) and mind/consciousness (*shiki* 識) in the cosmology of Esoteric Buddhism. Concretization or hypostatization of absolute reality and inner awakening is arguably the central interest of esoteric teachings and practices. Explaining the difference between exoteric and esoteric teachings, *Keiran* asserts that esoteric teachings establish concrete forms and objects (*keishiki* 形色) onto the essence of suchness, but exoteric teachings do not.[26] In that sense, "putting (or adding) on" a physical form to an abstract idea of the ground for the three poisons can be viewed as a typical Tendai esoteric interpretive method.

As this serpentine form of the three poisons is shared by all ordinary people, *kami* "respond" to that by appearing in the form of a snake. Also noteworthy in the quoted dialogue is the hypothetical interlocutor's question about the reason for *kami*'s manifestation in the snake form. This implies that *kami*'s appearance as a snake was at this point already an established symbolism or narrative.[27] Throughout *Keiran* the symbol of the snake plays a crucial role not only as a representation of *kami*, but more importantly, as a multilayered sign that offers a key to understanding Tendai's view of *kami* and its deep connection to the Tendai's core doctrinal notion of nonduality and original enlightenment. In any case, through *Keiran*'s statement that *kami* respond to ordinary beings, we can gather an esotericized rationale of *kami* as the *nirmaṇakāya*, the manifestation body of Buddha. One idea to note in particular in the

---

26 T.76, 2410: 746c25–26.

27 The rationale for the combination of *kami* and the snake is not clearly revealed in *Keiran*. That said, it is worthy to note that a great variety of *kami*, including Amaterasu, are indeed said to appear in the dragon-serpent deities mentioned in numerous mythic accounts and legends in Japan.

above passage is that the unconditioned and original (*musa honnu* 無作本有) form of the three poisons is the form of the snake. The idea of *musa* is crucial in the history of Mahayana philosophy. It is deeply related to two concepts that speak of the most essential nature of truth, that is, the primordial/unconditioned (Skt. *asaṃskṛta*) and the non-arising/ uncreated (Skt. *anutpada*). The word *musa* can be understood more correctly and naturally when it is considered together with the term "natural" or "such-of-itself" (J. *hōni* 法爾), which was coined within East Asian Buddhist traditions. In other words, *musa* indicates the nature of truth that is unconditioned, innate, the most "aged," and unchangeable, or in other words *tathatā* (suchness).

Thus *musa honnu* represents the core of the Mahayanist view of *tathatā* and the doctrinal teachings based on the view. In particular, the development of the idea of *tathatā* played a central role in the growth of Mahayana doctrinal philosophy and its divisions into many schools. The view of truth as the unconditioned and innate is directly connected to the discussion about the nature of enlightenment. The original enlightenment thought central to Japanese Tendai integrated the idea of *musa honnu* as an ontological principle (*ri* 理), working together with the epistemological (*chi* 智) mechanism of our consciousness.

The meaning of original enlightenment is quite straightforward: it means enlightenment that all sentient beings innately possess. The idea itself was grounded upon the *tathāgatagarbha* line of thought that had been developed throughout the history of Mahayana Buddhism. Based on this hermeneutic tradition, Japanese Tendai reformulated the concept of original enlightenment and elaborated on it as a systematic doctrinal thought by integrating the basic idea of original enlightenment in the *Awakening of Faith in the Mahāyāna* (Ch. *Dacheng qixinlun* 大乘起信論) with major philosophical problems generated from the historical debate between the Huayan 華嚴 and Tiantai 天台, as well as by incorporating various ideas embedded in esoteric teachings.[28]

---

28 Tamura and Umehara 1970, 251–3. For a detailed examination of the Tendai original enlightenment thought, see Stone 1999.

Returning to the examination of the quoted passage, it is surprising to detect two conflicting statements. One says that the snake is the essence of the three poisons; the other asserts that the snake is also the essence of original enlightenment. How should we understand this paradox? To better understand this problem, other recurring comments in *Keiran* that use the snake symbol are noteworthy.

> ....the form (體) of the unconditioned thought of all sentient beings is *the winding snake mind* (or mind winding like the snake) (蛇曲心). That is why all of them are responsive to the snake form. Thus kami appears in the form of the snake... This [form of the unconditioned thought of all sentient beings] means the original essence of all beings' Buddha nature. ... the form of the (unmoving) unconditioned, original enlightenment is the form of the snake.[29]

In this case, what has the form of the snake also is the form of our thought. Although the three poisons are related to human thoughts and consciousness, it becomes clearer here that *kami*'s manifestation is deeply connected to the human mind and consciousness. As previously noted, considering *kami*'s salvific role, *kami*'s manifestation in the snake form occurs for communication with our mind – *kami* manifest on our consciousness and thus lead us to awakening. According to *Keiran*,* an ordinary human's mind, in the form of the snake, is contaminated with the three poisons, but this is in reality the form of the unconditioned, inherent original enlightenment, which opens the door for us to attain true enlightenment. Here we see an expression of the Tendai doctrine of nonduality between enlightenment and ignorance, which is the ground for the Tendai development of the thought of original enlightenment. Nevertheless, this does not mean that we can achieve enlightenment just as we are, without practice. Then, what makes us attain enlightenment? And what is the "content" of our enlightenment? At this point, the important part in the above passage that we should ponder is the meaning of the "winding snake

---

29 T.76, 2410: 623b. For * in the text following: T.76, 2410: 517c26–7.

mind" or our mind winding like the snake, as this allegory is again found linked with *kami*'s manifestation by *wakō dōjin*.

Dance of our mind and kami's manifestation

Medieval Tendai's esoteric method of discussing abstract principles by using allegories with concrete forms is understandable, but a question remains as to why the essence of our thoughts or original enlightenment has to take the form of the snake. For this question, another allegory of the snake expressed as the winding snake mind offers a small clue. What we should pay attention to in this allegory is the symbolism of the snake as related to its winding, coiling quality. And yet *Keiran* connects this concept to our thoughts and mind, which are inherently endowed with original enlightenment. If we understand the rationale of Tendai original enlightenment thought, the meaning of the winding snake mind becomes quite clear: it is the "hypostatization" of the nonduality of origin (*hon*) and trace (*jaku*), and represents nonlinearity in the process of original enlightenment.

All in all, *hongaku* is the enlightenment that everyone possesses inherently, but whose truth ordinary people cannot realize. However, when we raise our mind toward enlightenment, practice and eventually reach our awakening, we come to realize that we were already, immanently enlightened from the beginning. So one does not achieve enlightenment or liberation after a series of sequential practices as the final result. In that sense, one's "attainment" of enlightenment is a reaffirmation of what he or she has always possessed.[30] Seen from the perspective of original enlightenment, then, realization is simultaneously the result and the cause of our practice.

However, medieval Tendai scholars viewed enlightenment not as the final destination, but something one can achieve, then lose, and attain again. Then one should go back to the initial stage of raising mind and practice, and yet even this return is not a simple

---

30 Stone 1999, 216–17.

linear process since it actually entails mind contemplation practice on complicated, multilayered levels of consciousness. Most lay people in medieval Japan misunderstood original enlightenment and believed that everyone was an enlightened Buddha as they were without any effort, and it is well known that this kind of indulgence contributed to the eventual degeneration of the Tendai school in the late medieval period. However, as Jacqueline Stone's examination of medieval Tendai's original enlightenment suggests, the core of medieval Tendai original enlightenment thought lies in the "recursive" mode. In addition, "sustainability" was the key to their doctrine of original enlightenment, as only practice could sustain the precious fruit of Buddha.[31]

The simultaneity of cause and effect, and the nonlinear, recursive nature of the mechanism of original enlightenment, guide us to unravel the allegory of the winding snake mind. Let us imagine the path – roads toward enlightenment for convenience' sake. If the road is straight and linear, from the beginning, the walker should move through changing topological locations, and thus the point at which s/he arrives should be an entirely different point from the beginning location. However, if the roads are nonlinear – winding, twisted or curled – traversing the roads should cause a continuous return to the same point. Of course, this is what happens in three-dimensional realities, and the human mind is not something that is visible in a three-dimensional manner. Rather than moving by means of a simple zigzag return, the paths toward enlightenment in our mind should operate in a far more complex, coiling and mutually intersecting recursive mode. This is, I infer, what *Keiran* symbolizes by the allegory of the winding snake.[32] Seen in this

---

31 Ibid.

32 Deeper contemplation on the constant return to the starting point leads us to realize that the "structure" of our mind, which mirrors reality, resembles a Möbius strip. Consequently, one never truly discerns the difference between the beginning and the end, cause and result, inside and outside, origin and trace, and so forth. In other words, these pairs are not really in opposition to each other, and even if the currently manifested "provisional" order between a given pair becomes reversed, there would be no change in value and structure on a fundamental level. The complex mechanism of original enlightenment well presents

light, the winding snake mind can be understood as a visualization of our mind's contemplation practice, which is central to attaining enlightenment. However, since the human mind is not something that one can see with one's own eyes, it is difficult to understand the manner in which the constantly recurring movement of original enlightenment actually works and how it can be associated with the form of the snake or the winding pattern. And *Keiran*'s compact phrases still do not provide a more detailed explanation. This is the point that requires a more or less imaginative visualization and integrated thinking based on fragmentary hints that are scattered throughout *Keiran*.

What we should bear in mind in analysing this allegory is that unlike physical movement on roads in our normal state of reality, the paths in our mind, i.e., the essence of our mind in the snake form, do not actually "move" by zigzagging from one point to another. What is the movement that can be seen constantly going back and forth without moving, without a change of location? Today's people define this concept as "vibration"; *Keiran* refers to it as "shaking/trembling dance (*shinbu* 振舞)." According to *Keiran*, all things and beings in the Dharma realm do their own shaking dance,[33] and *kami*'s manifestation by *wakō dōjin* also occurs according to the shaking dance. *Keiran* adds another esoteric metaphor to this concept: the shaking dance, which is synonymous with the identity of *wakō dōjin*, represents the appearance of the mysterious union of married couple, i.e., a sexual union.[34] There is something in common between *wakō dōjin* and this mysterious union between man and woman. It is a mutual response, or the nondual unity between two seemingly disparate realities. If this communication can be successfully performed, there is nothing that can obstruct these

---

the recursion and reversion between the origin (cause) and trace (result) and their ultimate nonduality.

33 T.76, 2410: 760b–762c.

34 T.76, 2410: 511b. A more extensive examination of the association between esoteric Buddhist symbolism of this sexual union and trembling dance is found in Yamamoto Hiroko's study of *Ijin,* strange divinities. See Yamamoto 1998, 413 in particular.

two worlds. This is the mysterious penetrating power (*jinzūriki*) that can co-respond to anything, without any hindrance, due to the ability to do the shaking dance. What Tendai esotericism sees in *kami* must be the ideal of the non-obstructive ability that can resonate with anything in various realities. That is, *kami* is the epitome of the ideal shaking dance.

Then, the moment when we vibrate our mind, that is, perform our innate shaking dance and resonate with "others," can be seen as a kairotic moment in which we reclaim our original enlightenment. Of course, unceasing efforts toward mind vibration practice are necessary. Using another allegorical expression in *Keiran*, we can realize original enlightenment only by doing the dance of the winding snake. Gathering all these esoteric discussions in *Keiran*, the rationale of *kami*'s guidance to enlightenment by *wakō dōjin* now seems very clear. Through their superior ability to effect the shaking dance, they resonate with the essence of our original enlightenment, which also does the inherently endowed shaking dance. What should be appreciated in *kami*'s manifestation on our mind is the message from *kami* that evokes in us our inherent capacity – the capacity of the shaking dance, i.e., non-obstructive communication, and nondual unity with everything in the entire Dharma world. In that sense, *Keiran*'s allegories of the winding snake and the shaking dance are excellent symbolons that invite us to the inconceivable principle of mysterious unity that forms neither one nor two.

Concluding remarks – Kami's lesson

Enlightenment for medieval Tendai scholar-monks meant nothing other than realizing the nondual, perfect unity among all realities in the Dharma realm. In that sense, their discourse, which illuminated the oneness of Kami and Buddha, can be viewed as a reflection of such awakening. At the same time, it is also possible that the study of the Kami-Buddha discourse itself would have guided one to enlightenment. One may say that various dimensions centring

Medieval Tendai Buddhist views of kami 101

on medieval Tendai's discourse of the Kami-Buddha combination, that is, the discourse itself, as well as the formulation, examination and dissemination of such discourse, can all be a type of exegetic practice through which one contributed to transmit the ultimate Tendai Buddhist truth. What those scholar-monks found in the course of their examination of the Kami and Buddha relationship was the fundamental principle of nonduality, accomplished by a mysterious mutual penetration, which they referred to as the shaking dance. The shaking dance of all realities was what made *kami* manifest, or "dimming their light and becoming like the dust" for sentient beings. The shaking dance must be the essential identity of the spirit that resides in all things, expressed in the language of medieval Tendai esotericism. *Kami*'s salvific power lies in the shaking dance and its exceptional quality of non-obstructive penetration and resonation, which presses our realization of the nondual oneness of all beings and things in the world – that is to say, the reality of non-discrimination, non-obstruction and perfect unity between self and the other. The moment when one resonates, or "dances with" *kami*, and achieves the realization of truth, is the moment of liberation and the blissful time of enlightenment rather than a nauseating moment in the Sartrean sense. It is the ecstatic moment of "contact" with the spirit in the shamanic festivity.

An important lesson that we eventually may glean through this decoding of *Keiran*'s allegorical messages, however, is that all of these communications and the ultimate awakening depend upon how we perceive and act. Without our recognition, contemplation and subsequent action, we can never greet *kami*'s *wakō dōjin* manifestation, nor receive their invitation to the grand ball along with all the "other" strangers in the world. Can we dance together with true joy of the non-obstructive, nondual equality of you and me? Further, how can we actualize such a principle in our real world? These are the questions that *kami* throws upon us with the sound of silent vibration.

Abbreviation

T: *Taishō shinshū daizōkyō* 大正新修大蔵経. 85 vols. 1924–32. Takakusu Junjirō 高楠順次郎 and Watanabe Kaigyoku 渡辺海旭 (eds.). Tokyo (Taishō Issaikyō Kankōkai).

References

PRIMARY SOURCES
The Lotus Sūtra 妙法蓮華經 translated by Kumārajīva 鳩摩羅什 (c. 344–413 CE). T.9, 262.
A Commentary on the Vimalakīrti Nirdeśa Sūtra 注維摩詰經 by Sengzhao 僧肇 (384 [alt. 374]–414). T.38, 1775.
Keiran shūyōshū 渓嵐拾葉集 by Kōshū 光宗 (1276–1350). T.76, 2410.

SECONDARY SOURCES
Deal, William, and Ruppert, Brian 2015. *A Cultural History of Japanese Buddhism.* Malden (Wiley-Blackwell).
Faure, Bernard 2015. *Gods of Medieval Japan 1: The Fluid Pantheon & Gods of Medieval Japan 2: Protectors and Predators.* Honolulu (University of Hawaii Press).
Grapard, Allan G. 1998. "Keiranshūyōshū: A Different Perspective on Mt. Hiei in the Medieval Period" in: Richard Payne (ed.), *Re-Visioning "Kamakura" Buddhism.* Honolulu (University of Hawaii Press).
Inoue Nobutaka (ed.; tr. Mark Teeuwen and John Breen) 2003. *Shinto – A Short History.* New York (RoutledgeCurzon).
https://doi.org/10.4324/9780203462881
Itō Satoshi 2012. *Shintō towa nanika: kami to hotoke no nihonshi.* Tokyo (Chūō kōron shinsha).
Park, Yeon Joo (Yeonjoo) 2016. "Shaking Dance in the Stormy Valley: Tendai Discourse on Kami-Buddha Relations in Fourteenth Century Mount Hiei." PhD dissertation, University of Illinois at Urbana-Champaign.
Park, Yeon Joo (Yeonjoo) 2017. "Ilbon jungse cheontae bulgyo eui kami damron" (Medieval Japanese Tendai Buddhist Discourse of Kami) in: *Hwan-Donghae Jiyeok Eui Oraeden Hyeonjae* (*Folk Religious Traditions of Northeast Asia*). Seoul (Kyung Hee University Press).
Rambelli, Fabio and Teeuwen, Mark 2003. *Buddhas and Kami in Japan: Honji Suijaku as a Combinatory Paradigm.* New York (RoutledgeCurzon).
Ruppert, Brian O. 2014 "Nihon chūsei no nettowaku sō to shōdō shōgyō no denpa" in: *Higashi Ajia no shūkyō bunka: ekkyō to henyō.* Tokyo (Iwata Shoin), 369–93.
Satō Hiroo 1998. *Kami/hotoke/ōken no chūsei.* Kyoto (Hōzōkan).

Stone, Jacqueline I. 1999. *Original Enlightenment and the Transformation of Medieval Japanese Buddhism.* Honolulu (University of Hawaii Press).
Sueki Fumihiko 2003. *Chūsei no kami to hotoke.* Tokyo (Yamagawa Shuppansha).
Tamura Yoshirō and Umehara Takeshi 1970. *Zettai no shinri Tendai.* Tokyo (Kadokawa Bunko).
Tanaka Takako 2003. *Keiran shūyōshū no sekai.* Nagoya (Nagoya Daigaku Shuppankai).
Teeuwen, Mark 2000. "The Kami in Esoteric Buddhist Thought and Practice" in: John Breen and Mark Teeuwen, eds., *Shinto in History: Ways of the Kami.* Honolulu (University of Hawaii Press), 95–116.
Yamamoto Hiroko 1998. *Ijin: Chūsei nihon no hikyōteki sekai.* Tokyo (Heibonsha).
Yoshida Kazuhiko 2006. "Honjaku shisō no juyō to tenkai: honji suijaku setsu no seiritsu katei" in: Hayami Tasuku (ed.), *Nihon shakai ni okeru hotoke to kami.* Tokyo (Yoshikawa Kōbunkan), 198–220.

About the author

Yeonjoo Park received a doctorate from the University of Illinois at Urbana-Champaign for her dissertation on medieval Tendai discourse on Kami-Buddha relations (2016). Now settled in Korea, she has published on topics relating to Japanese Buddhism, Shinto, and interreligious dialogue and peace. Park is currently associated with the Nanzan Institute for Religion and Culture, and has taught philosophy and Japanese Buddhism at Dongguk University in Seoul, Korea.

5

Conceptions of kami in the writings of the Tendai monk Jien

Vladlena Fedianina

Introduction

The Tendai monk Jien (1155–1225) was a famous Japanese historian and a renowned poet. His well-known writing *Gukanshō* (愚管抄 "Record of Foolish Random Thoughts" or "Miscellany of Ignorant Views") and his later poems express complex philosophical and religious concepts, including his views on deities or *kami*.

Jien, a member of the the Kujō branch of the Fujiwara family, supported his brother, the regent Kanezane (1147–1207),[1] and he also exchanged Japanese poems (*waka*) with the founder of the first Kamakura shogunate Minamoto Yoritomo (1147–99), enjoying the patronage of the ex-Emperor Go-Toba (1180–1239). Jien was appointed head-priest (*zasu* 座主) of the Tendai school in 1192, 1201, 1202 and 1213, rising to to senior high priest (*daisōjō* 大僧正).

Primary sources

The present study is based on Jien's historical work *Gukanshō* and his *waka* – cycles of Japanese poems *hōraku* 法楽 written as offerings to gods, buddhas and bodhisattvas.

His most famous writing, *Gukanshō*, is a well-researched interpretative history of Japan which appeared circa 1221.[2] This is a

[1] Fujiwara (Kujō) Kanezane was a regent *sesshō* in 1186–91 and a councillor *kampaku* in 1191–96.
[2] The authorship had long been disputed but now the author is generally recognized as the head-priest Jien. The dating had also been disputed, but now the year 1221 is recognized as the most likely.

history of Japan from ancient times, starting with the rule of the first Emperor Jinmu, to the beginning of the thirteenth century. Jien's rational interpretation of the history was based on the way of thinking which today is known as Shinto-Buddhist syncretism. In other words *Gukanshō* is a valuable primary source that enables us not only to get a closer view of the history of Japan (especially regarding the establishment of the Kamakura shogunate), but also to trace the evolution of Japanese thought in medieval times.

Jien's *waka*, numbering about 6,000 poems, were collected into the anthology *Shūgyokushū* 拾玉集 ("Collection of Precious Pearls") nearly one hundred years after his death. The *waka* were assembled in the *Shūgyokushū* in the middle of fourteenth century by Prince Son-en (1298–1356), the seventeenth high priest of Shōrenin Temple. This temple was a part of the Tendai temple complex Enryakuji and Jien had been its third high priest. These poems by Jien have been less studied[3] than his *Gukanshō*. However his later poems are of great interest, and being inspired by ideas of Japanese Buddhism, are full of references to the history of Japan and expressions of the author's original system of values.

Our research here is based on *Gukanshō* and on the cycles of one hundred poems written in the period 1213–21.[4] These so-called *hōraku hyakushu* 法楽百首 ("one hundred *hōraku* verses") were offered to various shrines and one temple, as follows:

1. *Hiyoshi hyakushu*, to Hiyoshi Shrine, 1213;
2. *Bunshu hyakushu*, to Kitano Shrine in Kyoto, about 1218;
3. *Hachiman hyakushu*, to Iwashimizu Hachiman Shrine, about 1219;
4. *Kasuga hyakushu* and
5. *Kasuga hyakushu sō*, to Kasuga Shrine, 1218–19;
6. *Kamo hyakushu*, to Kamo Shrine, 1219–20;
7. *Shikidai hyakushu*, to Ise Shrine, 1220;
8. *Naniwa hyakushu*, to Shitennōji Temple, 1219.

---

3 They have been studied by Fujiko Manaka, Munehaya Taga, Hajime Ishikawa and Hajime Yamamoto, as mentioned in works by Herbert E. Plutschow and Robert Jean-Noël.

4 Jien, *Shūgyokushū* (Ishikawa and Yamamoto 2008).

106 *Exploring Shinto*

Names of deities in the cycles of one hundred poems and Gukanshō

Name of a *kami* or a shrine	Poems	*Gukanshō*	Function of the *kami*
日吉 Hie (Hiyoshi)	+	+	Ōyamakui (Sannō) – a mountain spirit; the guardian spirit of Enryakuji. Ōnamuchi (Ōkuni-nushi) – the ruler (of Izumo Province) prior to Ninigi, the protector of the imperial court.
北野 Kitano	+	+	The spirit of Sugawara Michizane as Tenjin.
八幡（大菩薩）Hachiman (Dai Bosatsu)	+	+	Hachiman, the protector deity of the imperial family.
春日（大明神）Kasuga (Dai Myōjin)	+	+	Amenokoyane – the Fujiwara tutelary *kami*, assisted in the founding of the state. Takemikazuchi – "God of Relentless Thunder", a protector of the country, later a protector of the Fujiwara. Iwainushi (or Futsunushi). Himegami.
賀茂社 Kamo-sha	+	+ (only referring to a place or a festival *matsuri*, not *kami*)	Kamigamo jinja: Kamo Wakeikazuchi – deity of thunder and storm. Shimogamo jinja: Tamayori-hime, a mother of Kamo Wakeikazuchi; Kamo no Taketsunumi, a grandfather of Kamo Wakeikazuchi,
天照（大神宮）Amaterasu (Dai Jingū)	+	+	Amaterasu – the main protector and guardian deity of the imperial family.
平野（大明神）Hirano (Dai Myōjin)	+	+	Imaki – was prayed to for blessing of the imperial court. Kudo, Furoaki, Himegami.

大原野 (Ōharano)	+	+ (the first visit of the emperor)	Amenokoyane – the Fujiwara tutelary *kami*, assisted in the founding of the state.
松尾 Matsu-no-o	+	+ (the first visit of the emperor)	Ōyamakui – a mountain spirit.
祇園 Gion	+	+	Gozu Tennō / Susanō: Gozu Tennō – a tutelary deity who protected from epidemics / Susanō – a deity petitioned for salvation from disaster; possessed of the sword (one of the three imperial regalia).
稲荷 Inari	+	+	Inary – a tutelary deity of rice cultivation.
住吉 Sumiyoshi	+	+	Sumiyoshi sanjin (Sokotsutsu no Ō, Nakatsutsu no Ō, Uwatsutsu no Ō) and Jingū Sumiyoshi sanjin – deities of the sea and sailing.
熊野 Kumano	+	+	Deities of Kumano – Kumano gongen (at Kumano Hongū Taisha – Ketsumiko and others; Kumano Hayatama Taisha – Hayatama and others; Kumano Nachi Taisha – Ōnamuchi [Ōkuni-nushi] and others). Kumano was also conflated with Ise Shrine.
鹿島 Kashimashi	+	+	Takemikazuchi.
熱田（大明神）Atsuta (Dai Myōjin)	+	+	Atsuta shinkō (Amaterasu, Susanō, Yamato Takeru, Miyasuhime, Takeinadane).
厳島（厳嶋ノ明神）Itsukushima (Itsukushima no Myōjin)	–	+	The three daughters of Susanoo, protectors of fishermen and boats.

The names of *kami* (or any deity in this work) mentioned in the table above are given according to *An Encyclopedia of Shinto*, *Shintō jiten* and *Japan: Gods, Shrines, Rites. Encyclopedia of Shinto*.[5] We have pointed out here the deities that were worshipped in shrines in Jien's time.

Amaterasu, Hachiman and deities from Kasuga (Amenokoyane, Takemikazuchi and others) are the most frequently mentioned *kami* in *Gukanshō* and the poems. Amaterasu, Hachiman and deities from Kasuga are also dubbed with the term *sōbyōshashaku* 宗廟社稷 which in this context has the meaning "guardian ancestral deities". In the version of *Gukanshō* which we used, Hachiman, or *Dai bosatsu* (i.e., Great Bodhisattva, referring to Hachiman), appears 41 times. In 24 cases we find the deity's name in connection with its religious functions; in 17 cases the reference is to the Hachiman shrine, its precincts, the emperors' visits to the shrine and so on. Amaterasu, or *Dai jingū*, is mentioned by name 19 times and by other references 17 times, the *kami* from Kasuga (and Amenokoyane) by name 11 times and by other references 6 times, and the guardian ancestral deities are mentioned 22 times. Jien considered Amaterasu, Hachiman and deities from Kasuga not only as tutelary deities of the emperor and the Fujiwara clan, but also as protectors of Japan. However, although Hachiman has usually been thought as a protector of the Minamoto clan, he was never considered by Jien as the tutelary *kami* of the Minamoto.

There are only a few names of *kami* in the poems. Most of them are referred to, or invoked, by designating the locations of the shrines. We can be certain that we interpret these associations correctly due to the structure of cycles of poems – for example, the theme of "Shrines" or "Sacred places" (*shosha* 諸社) in *Kasuga hyakushu sō* (Jien, *Shūgyokushū* [Ishikawa and Yamamoto 2008, 359]) or "Deities" (*jingi* 神祇) and "Sacred places" (*yashiro* 社) in *Shikidai hyakushu* (Jien, *Shūgyokushū* [Ishikawa and Yamamoto 2008, 292–3, 305]).

---

5 *An Encyclopedia of Shinto* 1999; *Shintō jiten* 1999; *Japan: Gods, Shrines, Rites* 2010.

It is worth drawing attention to the shrines to which Jien's poems were offered: Hie (Hiyoshi) Shrine, Kitano Shrine in Kyoto, Iwashimizu Hachiman Shrine, the Kasuga Shrine, Kamo Shrine and Ise Shrine. All of these were included in the list of The Twenty-Two Shrines (*nijūnisha* 二十二社). The *kami* worshipped there were drawn in to clarify Jien's understanding of Buddhism.

We have already established the role and importance of Amaterasu, Hachiman and deities from Kasuga worshipped in Ise, Iwashimizu Hachiman and Kasuga Shrines. Hiyoshi Shrine with its Hie-no kami, or Sannō (Ōyamakui), took an important place in a syncretic teaching that combined Shintō beliefs with Tendai doctrine. Ōyamakui, a mountain spirit, became the guardian spirit of the Buddhist Enryakuji Temple, and Hiyoshi Shrine became a tutelary shrine, a so-called *chinjusha*, for Enryakuji. Kitano Shrine was connected with *Tenjin shinkō*, the worship of the spirit of Sugawara Michizane. Jien believed that Michizane was one of four incarnations of Bodhisattva Kannon. Two Kamo Shrines, located in the northeast corner (so-called "front demon's gates") of Kyoto, were intended to prevent misfortune from entering the capital. Rituals of both Kamo Shrines were very significant for the state.

Thus we see that the deities of shrines where Jien offered his poems were ancestor deities of the imperial family and the Fujiwara family, or guardians of these two families and the country (the country was often equated to the imperial family). This can be said about almost all deities in the poems and in *Gukanshō*. Jien claimed that in his period imperial rule required the support of Fujiwara regents and military protection, willed by ancestral *kami*.

Furthermore, *kami*, their names and their roles in the history of Japan make it abundantly clear to us that Jien shared his contemporaries' *honji suijaku* doctrine (本地垂迹, "original nature and provisional manifestation"). Jien clearly called Hachiman "Great Bodhisattva Hachiman" (*Hachiman Dai Bosatsu*) and wrote in the preface to *Hachiman hyakushu*: "Our Great Bodhisattva Hachiman is the dim radiance of Śākyamuni and Amitābha."[6] In this preface

---

6 Jien, *Shūgyokushū* (Ishikawa and Yamamoto 2008, 327).

Jien emphasizes that Hachiman has the same nature as Amaterasu[7] though there is no evidence in *Gukanshō* that Jien perceived her as a manifestation of the Buddha.

Jien referred to the deity (or deities) of Kasuga as *Kasuga Dai Myōjin* ('the Great Illuminating Kami'). This indicates that he believed that the *kami* from Kasuga was a provisional manifestation (*suijaku*) of some original nature (*honji*). However the writings of Jien that we have used have not provided us with any clues for understanding whose manifestation Amenokoyane was considered to be. Similarly, although Jien considered the deity, or deities, of Kamo Shrine to be a provisional manifestation, he nevertheless wrote "It is difficult to understand who is the original nature of Kamo Dai Myōjin."[8]

Deities and Principles (dōri)

Through a textual analysis of Jien's writings we have distinguished two main groups of deities by their relation to "Principles" (*dōri* 道理). The word *dōri* (also equivalent to *kotowari* コトハリ) has multiple meanings and refers to different phenomena in *Gukanshō* and the poems. The relationship between the deities and the Principles allows us to construct a hierarchy of deities: (1) deities which establish Principles in this world and (2) deities which act according to these Principles.

1. Deities establishing Principles in this world

The first group includes (a) Amaterasu, the ancestor goddess of the Imperial House; (b) the patron deities of the Fujiwara family and (c) Great Bodhisattva Hachiman, a guardian *kami* of the Imperial House (not the Minamoto).

Jien wrote in the afterword of the cycle of poems for the Ise Shrine: "Our country Yamato is the land of Amaterasu Ōmikami, therefore, the Principles (*kotowari*) have been fully carried out and

---

7 神宮八幡同体之本源也.
8 Jien, *Shūgyokushū* (Ishikawa and Yamamoto 2008, 312).

should be worshipped."⁹ According to Jien, the most important and dominant Principle was the deterioration of the *kalpa*, and even Amaterasu had to obey it. However she could establish her own small Principles (*dōri*) for Japan. This was a group of very powerful ancestral deities who could improve the affairs of this visible world in Japan.

The division into two worlds, the visible world (顕 *ken*) and the other, invisible world (冥 *myō*) is very clearly formulated in Jien's writings.¹⁰ Satō Hiroo pinpoints the importance of this division of worlds in medieval Japan in terms of cosmological views as follows:

> The idea that "this" world and the "other" world were separated from each other slowly began to appear in the second half of the Heian period (794–1185) on the Japanese Archipelago. Over time, the idea became perceived as a real fact. Due to these changes in cosmological beliefs, the entities perceived in ancient times as sacred, i.e. deities (i.e. kami), saints, the images of Buddha, etc. now came to be seen as local traces of the Buddha of the "other" world. More precisely, local traces were considered as manifestations of the original invisible true essence of the Buddha who had taken visible shape for salvation of all men.¹¹

It is well known that Jien depicted historical events of Japan in the context of a Buddhist vision of world history. The philosophical and ideological background of Jien's historical thought has been analysed by I. Ishida. Indian Buddhist views on time and space were complemented by thoroughly elaborated ideas of the period of The Latter Days of the Law (*mappō*) and the peripheral location of Japan.¹² The last of these found expression in the idea

---

9 Jien, *Shūgyokushū* (Ishikawa and Yamamoto 2008, 311–12).
10 Jien, *Gukanshō* (Okami and Akamatsu 1967, 325–6); *Shūgyokushū* (Ishikawa and Yamamoto 2008, 373–88).
11 Satō 2013, 217.
12 Brown and Ishida 1979, 420–51.
The next quote uncovers Jien's understanding of Buddhist cosmology:

of *sangoku* ("the three countries", i.e., India, China and Japan).[13] States of the Korean peninsula were not included in "the three countries", even though Korea was mentioned in the *Gukanshō* much more often than India. The spatial concept of *sangoku* was inseparable from the temporal concept of *mappō*, and this combination has therefore been referred to by Mark Blum as the *sangoku-mappō* approach to the writing of the history.[14] The *Gukanshō* and some of Jien's poems provide clues for his understanding of *sangoku-mappō* thought.

Jien's historical concept was based on two parts that had originated from both Buddhism and traditional indigenous ideas about *kami*. Along with his contemporaries he believed that the goddess Amaterasu had promised patronage for her rulers' dynasty for a hundred generations. It must be pointed out that in Jien's time the hundredth emperor's reign was approaching: there were only sixteen successors left. At the same time there was a widespread idea that Amaterasu had promised to protect the imperial family during these one hundred reigns. This idea was based on a Chinese poem which turned to be very popular in Japan in the late twelfth century. The original belief in the permanence of the Imperial House was transformed into the "thought of one hundred reigns" (*hyakuō*

"In sum, the Principle of deterioration and improvement of the Southern Continent (南州) – and customs of the three countries of China, India and Japan – means that deterioration alternates with improvement in this way. This Principle also means that man's life expectancy will decline to 10 years by the end of the deterioration half of this small kalpa and then increase to 80,000 years at the end (劫末) of the improving half. Within that span of time Principles operate in the same way – even with respect to Japan's one hundred reigns" (Jien, *Gukanshō* [Ishikawa and Yamamoto 2008, 148]; tr. by Brown and Ishida 1979, 36).

13 *Kasuga hyakushu sō* is divided into themes related to important Buddhist terms and categories. One of the themes is "The Three Countries" (三国). In the first *waka*, about Tenjiku 天竺 (India), Jien complains of the distance of India, where Śākyamuni Buddha preached on the Holy Eagle Peak (鷲の山). The second *waka* is about Morokoshi 唐土 (China) and is devoted to Monju (文殊, Mañjuśrī Bodhisattva, personifies Wisdom). The last of the three *waka* describes Japan (日域) as the land of Amaterasu (Jien, *Gukanshō* [Ishikawa and Yamamoto 2008, 363]).

14 Blum 2006, 31–51.

shisō 百王思想). Due to the social instability of the time this idea became closely related to the *mappō* concept.

The idea of one hundred reigns (*hyakuō shisō*) reminds us that events of Japanese history depended not only on the eternal rhythm of *kalpa*s assumed in Buddhist contexts, but also on Amaterasu. Jien believed that all forms of government in Japan came into existence at the right time according to the will of Amaterasu. Jien distinguished the following forms of government in Japan: (1) The emperor's autocratic rule. (2) The rule of emperors with the support of an assistant, which later transformed into the rule of regents (the Fujiwara). (3) The rule of the ex-emperors (retired emperors). (4) The rule of emperors with the help of shoguns and regents (both of them from the Fujiwara).

Jien said that the history of Japan was unfolding in the worsening part of the *kalpa* in accordance with Amaterasu's plan. She established Principles (*dōri*) for different stages of deterioration of the *kalpa*. Sometimes she did it in agreement with other deities, notably Hachiman and the deities of Kasuga:

> The Sun Goddess enshrined at Ise Shrine and the Great Illuminating Kami enshrined at Kasuga certainly consulted together and decided (*gijō*) [how Imperial rule was to be supported] in the distant past. And the Great Hachiman Bodhisattva and the Great Illuminating Kami of Kasuga consulted together and decided [how Imperial rule is to be supported] in the present. Thus the state was and is to be maintained. It is clear *that the decision for the present, made after the state had been buffeted* this way and that, *has been made* for these final reigns and requires that the sovereign have a guardian who has power of both learning and military might.[15]

Jien paid much attention to this divine agreement among the ancestral deities:

---

15 Jien, *Shūgyokushū* (Ishikawa and Yamamoto 2008, 347); tr. by Brown and Ishida 1979, 228.

> Long ago, the Sun Goddess made a divine agreement (*ichi-daku* [一諾]) with Ama no Koyane no Mikoto [the ancestral Kami of the Fujiwara clan; Kasuga] that the latter was to reside in and guard the imperial palace.[16]

This passage is derived from *The Age of the Gods* of *Nihon shoki* 日本書紀 ("The Chronicles of Japan" issued in 720).[17] Having sent down to the earth her grandson Ninigi-no mikoto, Amaterasu ordered Amenokoyane to help her descendants:

> You two august Kami [the other was the ancestor of the Imbe] are asked also to serve together at the imperial palace and guard it well.[18]

This *Nihon shoki* passage was repeated in a similar form in *Gukanshō*,[19] and it was also mentioned in the afterword of *Kasuga hyakushu sō*.[20] Apart from this the divine agreement was described in different words many times in *Gukanshō* and the poems (i.e., in the foreword and the *waka* of *Shikidai hyakushu*[21]). Thus, the Buddhist explanation of Japanese myths led to a Japanese interpretation of Buddhism.

Jien was convinced that Japan had a divinely inspired destiny and was guided by Amaterasu. It is a form of the *shinkoku* thought (the idea of a "divine land"'). The term *shinkoku* 神国 and its synonym at the time "the land of Amaterasu" (天照御神の御国) occurs in the following cycles of poems: *Shikidai hyakushu*, *Bunshu hyakushu* and *Kasuga hyakushu*.[22]

---

16 アマノコヤネノミコトニ、アマテルヲオン神ノ、「トノノウチニサブライテヨクフセギマモレ」ト御一諾ヲハルカニシ、… Jien, *Shūgyokushū* (Ishikawa and Yamamoto 2008, 329); tr. by Brown and Ishida 1979, 211.

17 Fujimori 2008.

18 復勅天児屋命。太玉命。惟爾二神亦同侍殿内。善為防護; *Nihon shoki* 153; tr. by Bocking 2011, 33.

19 Jien, *Gukanshō* (Okami and Akamatsu 1967, 140).

20 夫天照大神者王神也。春日明神者臣神也。若御約諾曰同侍殿内能為防護云云; Jien, *Shūgyokushū* (Ishikawa and Yamamoto 2008, 71).

21 Ibid., 292.

22 Ibid., 311, 278, 346.

2. Deities acting according to principles

These deities are acting on established principles and, by doing so, influence the affairs of this visible world. This second group of deities can be further divided into those who are benevolent to people (*zenshin* 善神) and those who are malicious (*jashin* 邪神).

Examples of *kami* who are benevolent to people are deities such as Great Illuminating Divine Beings (*daimyōjin* 大明神) and Heavenly Deities (*tenjin* 天神). They are often referred to by their names and the places of their shrines, so they are not anonymous deities. Jien gives some examples of their help. One of these benevolent *kami* is a deity from Kitano, the spirit of Sugawara Michizane (845–903). Jien believed that Michizane was an incarnation of Bodhisattva Kannon and came into this world for the salvation of people in Japan in a period of relative improvement during the deteriorating *kalpa*.[23] Jien said that there were four incarnations of Kannon (*kannon no keshin* 観音ノ化身) in Japan: Shōtoku Taishi (574?–622?), Fujiwara Kamatari (614–669), Ryōgen (912–985) and Sugawara Michizane. They came to improve the deteriorating *kalpa*. Shōtoku Taishi was greatly venerated by Jien. In the evening of his life Jien was an abbot (*bettō* 別当) of Shitennōji Temple where Shōtoku Taishi was worshipped (this faith being known as *Taishi shinkō*). Jien's *Naniwa hyakushu* was devoted to Shōtoku Taishi and offered to Shitennōji.

Malicious deities (*jashin*) on the other hand are nameless and they were thought to appear in the visible world due to the degradation of the *kalpa*.

> During this Final Age (*yo no matsu* 世ノ末) we have been moved inexorably toward the Principle that state affairs are not peaceful. And since it is the destiny of the times that we come to a point at which evil demons and bad *kami* (*akumajashin* 悪魔邪神) are purposely and definitely making things worse, even the beneficial power (*keyaku* 化益) of the Three Treasures of Buddhism, and of the good *kami* (*zenshin* 善神), is ineffective.[24]

23 Jien, *Gukanshō* (Okami and Akamatsu 1967, 154–7).
24 Ibid., 346; tr. by Brown and Ishida 1979, 227.

Some of them can be hardly called *kami*: they are innumerable evil demons and creatures, vengeful spirits (*onryō* 御霊). The cult of vengeful spirits (*onryō shinkō* 御霊信仰) was a part of the Buddhist orientation of Jien (*Gukanshō* [Okami and Akamatsu 1967, 156, 178–80, 186, 262, 290, 304, 337]). We use his term *onryō* here, vengeful spirits, which Jien did not distinguish from *goryō*, which is otherwise used for the vengeful spirits of noblemen.

The appearance of wrathful and vengeful spirits was explained by Principles (*dōri*, i.e., the laws of the universe), but the appearance of evil spirits, in turn, explained the origins of natural and social cataclysms. In the *Gukanshō* some spirits (those of Sugawara Michizane, Fujiwara Motokata, Fujiwara Akimitsu, the monk Raigo from the Mii-Dera Temple, Fujiwara Tadamichi) exacted revenge on their direct offenders and their offspring. The spirits of Emperor Sutoku and the Taira warriors brought misfortune upon the entire country. However "personal" revenge in this case is a rather relative term: ultimately, it also has an adverse impact on the whole country.

Kami in the Buddhist context

We have compared our classification of deities based on their relation to the Principles (*dōri*) with others, relying especially on research by Fabio Rambelli and Nadezhda Trubnikova. They analysed other primary sources of that period, namely *Nakatomi harae kunge* 中臣祓訓解 ("Nakatomi Purification Ritual" from the end of the twelfth century) and *Kōfukuji sōjō* 興福寺奏状 ("Kōfukuji Temple Petition," 1205).

In *Nakatomi harae kunge* the *kami* are classified by their level of enlightenment: (1) *kami* of original enlightenment (*hongakushin* 本覚神), (2) *kami* on their way to enlightenment (*shikakushin* 始覚神) and (3) unenlightened *kami* (*fukakushin* 不覚神).[25]

The division of *kami* into two main groups of "provisional *kami*" (*gongeshin* 権化神) and "real *kami*" (*jitsuruishin* 実類神)

---

25 Rambelli 2009, 245–6; Trubnikova 2011, 299.

How alternative groups of deities correlate with each other

According to Principles-*dōri* (Jien)	According to a level of enlightenment (*Nakatomi harae kunge*)	According to *honji suijaku* doctrine (*Kōfukuji sōjō*)
Deities who establish Principles	Deities of original enlightenment (two deities from Ise Shrine)	Provisional deities
Benevolent deities who are acting on established Principles	Deities in the process of actualizing of enlightenment / Deities deluded away	Provisional deities / Real kami
Malicious deities who are acting on established Principles (including evil creatures from invisible world)	Deities deluded away	Real kami

in *Kōfukuji sōjō* is based on the *honji suijaku* concept.[26] It envisioned the "provisional *kami*" as being temporary manifestations of buddhas and bodhisattvas. The "real *kami*" were deities of a more simple nature.

The table above shows how alternative groups of deities correlate with each other. Evidently, this scheme is incomplete: the identification of *kami* with buddhas and bodhisattvas was a complicated process that was partly determined by political strategy and depended on the circumstances.

Classifications are moreover different in different sources. However many medieval typologies suggest that the *kami* of Ise Shrine were increasingly defined in terms that differed from the *honji suijaku* concept and finally became envisioned as "being the very essence of Dharma-nature itself."[27] In the *Gukanshō* of Jien that we have studied we do not find evidence that Amaterasu is defined in terms of *honji suijaku*. This can be explained partly by the nature of our primary sources: they were not designed to make Buddhist teachings and doctrines clear in a direct way. Rather, the *Hachiman hyakushu* and *Kasuga hyakushu sō* were intended to express the ideas of the *Lotus Sūtra* and the main statements of

26 Trubnikova 2011, 298.
27 Rambelli 2009, 247.

Buddhism teaching in poetry. Still, one thing is beyond doubt: the supremacy of Amaterasu. Jien not only wrote that "Amaterasu is the queen of *kami* (*ōjin* 王神)"[28] but the whole structure of his philosophical thought suggests it.

This can be confirmed by other writings of Jien. For example, in the so-called *Hisei betsu* 毘逝別 ("Besides abhiṣeka," 1210) it is said that the "original nature" of Amaterasu is Buddha Mahāvairocāna (Dainichi Nyorai 大日如来).[29]

Conclusion

In Jien's writings we see reflections of the *kami* in Buddhist intellectual traditions. We have pointed out two main features of Jien's understanding of *kami*.

1. Perception of *kami* in the context of *honji suijaku* doctrine, although in most cases it is not clear what the "original nature" (*honji*) of the deities is presumed to be.
2. Hierarchy of *kami*. Amaterasu is "a queen of kami" and she establishes some Principles (*dōri*) for Japan. Other *kami*, good and evil, act in the visible world following Amaterasu's rules and the rules of the universe (Principles or *dōri*).

This second feature is deeply connected to the concept of "the divine land" and in accordance with this Jien proclaimed Amaterasu to be the creator of Japanese history.

Jien's conceptions of *kami* rested on the worldview of Indian Buddhism enriched with some specific Japanese ideas. To Indian Buddhist cosmological theory, which explained the decline of the world by the cyclic theory of the four *kalpa*s, Jien added non-Indian ideas, in particular an idea about the role of ancestral *kami*, above all of Amaterasu. This was the result of the long journey that the Tendai and Shingon monks had made in order to reconcile on a theoretical level the specificity of Japanese *kami* with the universalist views of Buddhism.

28 Jien, *Shūgyokushū* (Ishikawa and Yamamoto 2008, 371).
29 Mizukami 2005, 56.

References

An Encyclopedia of Shinto 1999. Inoue Nobutaka (ed.). Kokugakuin Digital Museum. http://k-amc.kokugakuin.ac.jp/DM/dbTop.do?class_name=col_eos

Blum, Mark 2006. "The Sangoku-Mappo Construct: Buddhism, Nationalism, and History in Medieval Japan" in: Richard K. Payne and Taigen Dan Leighton (eds.), *Discourse and Ideology in Medieval Japanese Buddhism*. London and New York (Routledge), 31–51.

Bocking, Brian 2011. *The Oracles of the Three Shrines: Windows on Japanese Religion*. London and New York (Routledge).

Brown, Delmer, and Ishida Ichiro (trans.) 1979. *The Future and the Past: A Translation and Study of the Gukanshō, An Interpretative History of Japan Written in 1219*. Oakland, CA (University of California Press).

Fujimori, Kaoru 藤森馨 2008. "Nishin yakudaku shinwa no tenkai" 二神約諾神話の展開. *Nihon ni okeru shūkyō tekusuto no soisō to sōjihō* 日本における宗教テクストの諸位相と統辞法. Nagoya Daigaku 名古屋大学 7, 236–44.

Japan: Gods, Shrines, Rites. An Encyclopedia of Shinto. 2010. I. Smirnov and A. Mescheryakov (eds.), issue XXVI. Moscow (Orientalia et Classica, Russian State University for the Humanities).

Jien, *Gukanshō* 愚管抄. In: Okami Masaso 岡見正雄 and Akamatsu Toshihide 赤松俊秀 (eds.), 1967, *Nihon koten bungaku taikei* 日本古典文学大系 86. Tokyo (Iwanami Shoten).

Jien, *Shūgyokushū* 拾玉集. In: Ishikawa Hajime 石川一 and Yamamoto Hajime 山本一 (eds.), 2008, *Waka bungaku taikei* 和歌文学大系 58. Tokyo (Meiji Shoin).

Mizukami, Fumiyoshi 水上文義 2005. "Jien no musōki to jingi shisō" 慈円の「夢想記」と神祇思想. *Tendai gakuhō* 天台学報 47, 55–64.

Nihon shoki 日本書記 ("The Chronicles of Japan"). *Nihon koten bungaku taikei* 68. Tokyo (Iwanami), 1965.

Rambelli, Fabio 2009. "Before the First Buddha: Medieval Japanese Cosmogony and the Quest for the Primeval Kami." *Monumenta Nipponica* 64/2, 235–71. https://doi.org/10.1353/mni.0.0080

Satō Hiroo 佐藤弘夫 2013. "Honji suijaku no kinsei" 本地垂迹の近世 in: Lucia Dolce ドルチェルチア and Mitsuhashi Tadashi 三橋正 (eds.), *Shinbutsu shūgō saikō* 「神仏習合」再考. Tokyo (Bensei Shuppansha), 215–42.

Shintō jiten 神道事典 1999. Inoue Nobutaka 井上順孝, Okada Shōji 岡田莊司, etc. (eds.). Tokyo (Kobundō, Kokugakuin Daigaku).

Trubnikova, Nadezhda 2011. "The Tendai School's 'Original Enlightenment' (hongaku) Tradition in Japanese Religious and Philosophical Thought in 12th–13th cc." Habilitation dissertation, Moscow (Institute of Philosophy of the Russian Academy of Sciences).

About the author

Vladlena Fedianina is Chair of the Japanese Language Department of Moscow City University. She holds a doctorate in Japanese History (of Japan) from Moscow State University (2006), translated the *Kitano Tenjin Engi* into Russian, and has published widely in the field of the history of Japanese religions.

6

Buddhist-Shinto syncretization at the medieval Suwa Shrine

Iwasawa Tomoko

Introduction

The Suwa Shrine is famous for its Great Pillar Festival (*Onbashira-sai* 御柱祭) held every six years. Some twenty thousand active participants are joined by more than one million viewer-participants in the celebration of the festival. Sixteen specially selected fir trees are cut down in the mountains and their gigantic trunks are dragged over miles of rough terrain to the villages around Lake Suwa, where they are erected in the courtyards of the four shrines that constitute the Suwa Shrine. Some scholars interpret this unique Onbashira festival as symbolizing the ancient nature worship characteristic of native Shinto thought. A historical analysis, however, shows that the meaning of *kami* enshrined there was transformed into various modes, especially under a strong influence of esoteric Buddhism in medieval times. This essay will examine such multiple faces of *kami* of Suwa that were uniquely developed through the interaction of Buddhist and Shinto traditions in the medieval period.

Overview of ancient Suwa

The origin of a Japanese shrine sometimes reflects a historical confrontation and compromise between ancient clans contesting for dominion over the region. The Suwa Shrine is an example.[1] It

---

1   We can track the history of Suwa back to the ancient Jōmon period of Japan (c. 14,500–300 BCE) the prehistoric period belonging to the Stone Age, characterized by the hunter-gatherer culture. Archaeological study shows that Suwa was one of the most populated regions in this period. The population

consists of two main sites, the Upper Shrine (*kamisha* 上社) and the Lower Shrine (*shimosha* 下社), which are located, respectively, to the southeast and the northwest of Lake Suwa (**Figure 1**). This formation of two sites actually represents the historical confrontation of two clans: the Moreya 洩矢氏 and the Kanazashi 金刺氏 in ancient Suwa. The Moreya later called Moriya 守矢氏 are the native inhabitants who had occupied the territory southeast of Lake Suwa, while the Kanazashi migrated to Suwa around the sixth century and settled in the northwest of Lake Suwa.

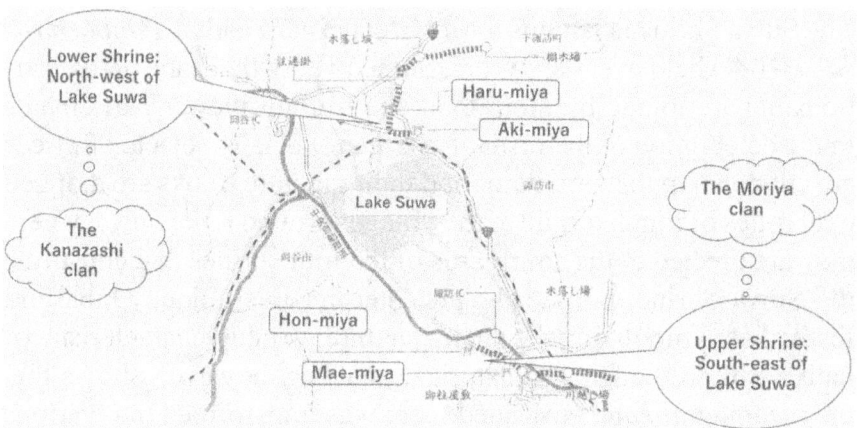

Figure 1 Location of Upper and Lower Shrines at Suwa.

---

history of the ancient Japanese is generally explained by the "dual structure model," which maintains that "the modern Japanese population was formed as a result of the mixture of the Jōmon people, who were part of the archaic Asian population, with the new Asian population, who came to the Japanese archipelago from the continent during and after the Yayoi period (c. 300 BC–200 AD)" (Junko Habu, *Ancient Jomon of Japan*, NY: Cambridge University Press, 2004, 50–1). Those Yayoi people introduced the technology of rice cultivation, as well as that of iron making, and eventually overwhelmed the indigenous Jōmon culture. In the Suwa region, too, such confrontation of Jōmon and Yayoi cultures probably took place. What is interesting about Suwa, however, is that the native Jōmon culture (the hunter-gatherer culture) was not completely eradicated by the new Yayoi culture (the farming culture), but they created a unique coexistence system, in both political and religious spheres, throughout the history of Suwa.

In the formal record, the oldest description of Suwa appears in the "Land Ceding" chapters of the *Kojiki* (古事記, 712 CE), in which Suwa is explained as the place where Takeminakata-no-kami 建御名方神 escapes after being defeated by Takemikazuchi-no-kami 建御雷神. Here Takeminakata, the second son of Ōkuninushi-no-mikoto 大国主命, symbolizes the Izumo clan, while Takemikazuchi, a messenger of Amaterasu, represents the Yamato clan. Pursued by Takemikazuchi, Takeminakata runs as far as Lake Suwa and pleads for his life, promising never to leave the place and never to disobey the commands of the heavenly deities governed by Amaterasu. It is very doubtful if Takeminakata signifies any historical figure, for there is no mention of this *kami* except for this single episode in the *Kojiki*. Scholars have detected in this mythologized account the outlines of a narrative telling of a prehistoric struggle between the Yamato immigrants, who worshipped Takemikazuchi, and members of the Izumo clan, who claimed descent from Takeminakata. Seemingly, the struggle between the Yamato and the Izumo clans continued among the groups that moved to Suwa. Historians further propose that the Izumo descendants, who were later called the Kanazashi clan, began to settle in the Suwa region around the sixth century.

Thus, around this period, confrontation occurred between this new immigrant group and the indigenous inhabitants, the Moriya clan. In Suwa, the folklore varies in narrations of this battle, which, according to history, seems to have resulted in the victory of the immigrant party. Archaeological findings support this view, indicating that the power shift took place in Suwa around the mid-sixth century, when the old type of tombs prevalent in Suwa until then were totally replaced by a new type associated with the Yamato *kofun*; the former, mainly found at the southeast of Lake Suwa, probably belonged to the indigenous Moriya clan, while the latter, found at the northwest of the lake, can be associated with the immigrant group.[2] Historians also say that, around the mid-sixth century, a clan of Suwa cultivated a favourable relationship

---

2 *Suwa-shi shi: Jōkan* 諏訪市史・上巻, ed. Suwa-shi shi hensan-iinkai (Suwa: Suwa-shi, 1988), 542–51.

with the Yamato court, was given the name "Kanazashi" after the emperor's palace called Kanazashi-no-miya 金刺宮,[3] and served as political governors (*kokuzō* 国造) of Suwa since then.[4] It is supposed that this clan named Kanazashi corresponded to the immigrant Izumo group.

The victory of the Kanazashi clan, however, did not necessarily mean that they could take complete control over Suwa; indeed, they gained political power, but had to keep competing with the strong religious influence possessed by the Moriya clan, which had dominated Suwa since ancient times. This historical background provided the Suwa Shrine with its unique dual religious system of the *ōhōri* 大祝 and the *jinchō* 神長, who, together, reigned over the Suwa religious community.

It is said that the Upper Shrine was established around 587 CE, when the Kanazashi family appointed their eight-year-old son, Otoyori, as the *ōhōri*, the head priest of the Suwa Shrine.[5] The *ōhōri* was regarded as a *kami* in human form (*arahitogami* 現人神), descended from the clan *kami* (*ujigami* 氏神), Takeminakata, to govern the Suwa county. With this *ōhōri* resided another religious leader called the *jinchō*, the shaman who alone was believed to have an ability to communicate with the *kami* of Suwa with his esoteric technique. Traditionally, the position of *ōhōri* was held in succession by members of the Kanazashi family, while that of *jinchō* was inherited by the Moriya family.[6] The founding of the Upper Shrine therefore symbolized this dual system of *ōhōri* and *jinchō* that had been established in the mid-sixth century; the *ōhōri*

---

3   The emperor at that time was Kinmei 欽明天皇, who was enthroned from 539 to 571 CE.

4   *Suwa-shi shi: Jōkan*, 551. The *ōhōri* of the Upper Shrine changed their name from "Kanazashi" to "Miwa" (神, which was also pronounced "Jin") in the early ninth century, and then to "Suwa" in the medieval period. Ibid., 712.

5   Ibid., 620.

6   The present Moriya family head no longer serves as *jinchō* but corresponds to the seventy-eighth generation according to their pedigree. While the *jingi* system was enforced by the Yamato regime around the eighth century, the local Suwa community was establishing its own unique dual regime, the politico-religious system of *ōhōri* and *jinchō*, which continued until the Meiji Restoration.

being the representative of the political, and the *jinchō* that of the religious. The Lower Shrine, on the other hand, was founded much later, around 853 CE. Located to the northwest of Lake Suwa, it first functioned as the political headquarters of the Kanazashi clan, and then turned into the place of worship that enshrined their clan *kami*.⁷

In this essay, I will focus on this unique dual system of *ōhōri* and *jinchō* of the Suwa Upper Shrine. There is no specific record that provides information about its structure in the ancient period; instead, we have rich historical materials of the medieval period, written by Moriya Mitsusane 守矢満実, the *jinchō* in the fifteenth century. Mitsusane became the *jinchō* in 1445, and contributed to developing what he called the Suwa-ryū Shintō 諏訪流神道,⁸ a radical reinterpretation and reorganization of the *kami* worship of Suwa that actively adopted the thought and practice of esoteric Buddhism. This essay will examine how *kami* worship and esoteric Buddhism were ingeniously amalgamated in medieval Suwa, and what made this fusion possible.

The development of Suwa-ryū Shintō in the medieval period

The introduction of Buddhism into Suwa probably occurred in the early ninth century, when the Buppō-ji 仏法寺 was founded as a *bettō-ji* 別当寺⁹ of the Suwa Upper Shrine.¹⁰ The Buppō-ji worshipped Dainichi as its principal object, and became one of the leading temples in Shinano 信濃 (a larger district including Suwa) to spread esoteric Buddhism.¹¹ We know little about the

---

7 *Suwa-shi shi: Jōkan*, 707–8.
8 Mitsusane Moriya, "Suwa daimyōjin shinpi gohonji daiji" 諏訪大明神神秘御本事大事, *Suwa shiryō sōsho* 諏訪史料叢書 5, 420. Regarding the Suwa-ryū Shintō, see also the essay of Hiroko Yamamoto, "Chūsei-no Suwa," *Gendai Shisō* 45/2 (2017), 130–45.
9 *Bettō-ji* is a temple attached to a shrine, being synonymous with *jingū-ji*.
10 According to the oral tradition of the Buppō-ji, the temple was founded by Sakanoue no Tamuramaro in 807 CE.
11 *Suwa-shi shi: Jōkan*, 732–4.

development of Buddhism in Suwa during the Heian Period, but, by the Kamakura Period, Buddhism seems to have taken root in the Suwa Shrine under the influence of the *honji suijaku* theory.[12] A text of the Kamakura Period, called *Suwa daimyōjin ekotoba* 諏訪大明神画詞,[13] states that the *honji* (i.e., the original form) of the *kami* of the Upper Shrine was Fugen, whereas that of the Lower Shrine was Kannon.[14] As Yūshō Miyasaka points out, this association of Fugen and Kannon seems to have been established by interpreting the topography of the Suwa basin as the central part of the Womb Mandala (i.e., *chūdai hachiyōin*, central pedestal constituted by an eight-petalled lotus). The Upper Shrine and the Lower Shrine are located, respectively, to the southeast and the northwest of Lake Suwa, and if Lake Suwa is taken as Dainichi in the Womb Mandala, the shrines correspond, respectively, to bodhisattvas Fugen and Kannon (**Figure 2**).[15] At the Upper Shrine, which was thus regarded as the realm of Fugen, the Fugendō (a temple enshrining this bodhisattva) was built in 1292, and the Jingūji complex that included the Fugendō seems to have been completed by then.

It was, however, in the Muromachi Period that a more radical reinterpretation of the *kami* of Suwa was introduced by

---

12 *Honji suijaku* 本地垂迹 "refers to the idea that the Buddhist deities provisionally appear as Shinto *kami* in order to spiritually save sentient beings in Japan. The *kami* are thus the manifestations (*suijaku*; literally 'traces'; i.e. the form appearing in the world to save sentient beings) of the Buddhist deities, and the Buddhist deities are the *honji* (literally 'original ground') of the Shinto *kami* (namely, their true form and substance). Ultimately, the two entities are seen to form an indivisible relationship." (*Encyclopedia of Shinto*, Kokugakuin University Digital Museum.)

13 *Suwa Daimyōjin Ekotoba* 諏訪大明神画詞 is a medieval text written by Suwa Enchū around 1350.

14 *Suwa Daimyōjin Ekotoba*, in *Shinto Taikei, Vol. 30 Suwa*, Tokyo: Shinto taikei hensankai, 1982, 33–4.

15 See Yūshō Miyasaka, "Kami to hotoke no yūgō" in: *Onbashira-sai to Suwa Taisha*, Tokyo: Chikuma Shobō, 1987, 151. Takami Inoue refers to Miyasaka's theory in his essay, "The Interaction between Buddhist and Shinto Traditions at Suwa Shrine" in: *Buddhas and Kami in Japan*, New York: Routledge, 2003, 291.

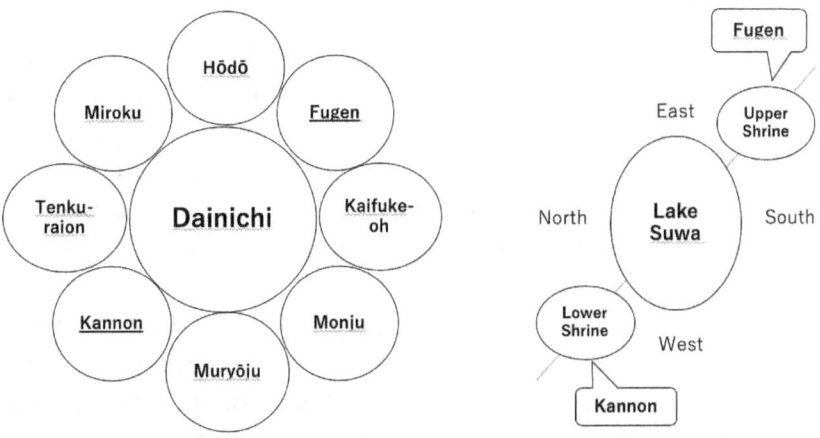

Figure 2 Upper and Lower Shrines at Suwa, corresponding to Bodhisattvas Fugen and Kannon. Reproduced from Inoue (see note 15 above).

incorporating the thought and practice of esoteric Buddhism. The person who made this reformation was the *jinchō*, Moriya Mitsusane. He wrote many texts that expounded Suwa-ryū Shintō. Among them, *Suwa daimyōjin shinpi gohonji daiji* 諏訪大明神神秘御本事大事 is regarded as the most important as presenting in detail the syncretization of Suwa-Shinto with esoteric Buddhism. Mitsusane carried out various reformations, one of which was the spatial transformation of the Upper Shrine.

The Suwa Upper Shrine consists of two main sites: the Hon-miya 本宮 and the Mae-miya 前宮. The Hon-miya has a unique structure; there is no Main Hall (*honden* 本殿)[16] but only the Hall of Worship (*haiden* 拝殿).[17] Another point to mention is that the shrine has, as an object of worship, a large rock called the

---

16 The *honden* "is the central structure of a shrine that houses the seat of the deity worshipped there" (*Encyclopedia of Shinto,* Kokugakuin University Digital Museum).

17 The *haiden* "is the building provided for the performance of ceremonies and for worshipping the shrine's *kami*. Normally located in the foreground of the shrine's sanctuary (*honden*), the *haiden* is usually built on a somewhat larger scale than the *honden* and tends to be the structure most noticed by ordinary worshippers. While the *honden* is the structure that actually encloses the seat of

Suzuri-ishi 硯石, which is located at the boundary of the precinct of the shrine and the sacred mountain behind it. This represents the presence of a rock-worshipping cult called the *iwakura shinkō* 磐座信仰, which presumably has been in existence since the neolithic Jōmon Period.[18] Historians suggest from these observations that the ancient Hon-miya had neither the Main Hall nor the Hall of Worship, but only the *iwakura* as the primal sacred object, an expression of ancient nature worship.

When was the Hall of Worship created, then? It was probably at the time of the *jinchō* Moriya Mitsusane that the Hall of Worship was added to the Hon-miya's site, and this made a drastic change of the axis of worship, not only at the Hon-miya but in the entire Upper Shrine.[19] When people used to worship the *iwakura* and the sacred mountain behind it, they were facing the southwest direction, with the four great pillars (*onbashira* 御柱) surrounding the *iwakura* as if they were protecting it. Mitsusane changed this axis by building the Hall of Worship at the centre of the shrine's site so that people could face the southeast direction. To the southeast of the Hall of Worship was the inner sanctum covered with trees and a thicket of bamboo grass. In this sanctum, Mitsusane established a small Buddhist pagoda called the Iron Pagoda (*o-tettō* お鉄塔), which he made the principal object of worship at the Hon-miya. In esoteric Buddhism, a pagoda symbolizes Dainichi;[20] in the Suwa Shrine, too, this Iron Pagoda, enshrining a stupa (the symbolic enshrinement of Buddha's relics) and the *Lotus Sūtra*, became the symbol of Dainichi. With this pagoda at its centre, the shrine's site itself was regarded as a realization of a Buddhist mandala. Furthermore, when people worshipped the pagoda from the

---

the *kami* (*shinza*), the *haiden* is the place where visitors engage in acts of worship, such as participating in various rituals and making entreaties to the *kami*" (*Encyclopedia of Shinto,* Kokugakuin University Digital Museum).

18 *Iwakura* is "a formation of rocks to which a *kami* is invited to descend for worship" (*Encyclopedia of Shinto,* Kokugakuin University Digital Museum).

19 *Suwa-shi shi: Jōkan*, 739.

20 In esoteric Shingon Buddhism, Dainichi is regarded as the World-Buddha of universal enlightenment, and Śākyamuni himself is considered to be but a temporary manifestation emanating from the *kami* Dainichi.

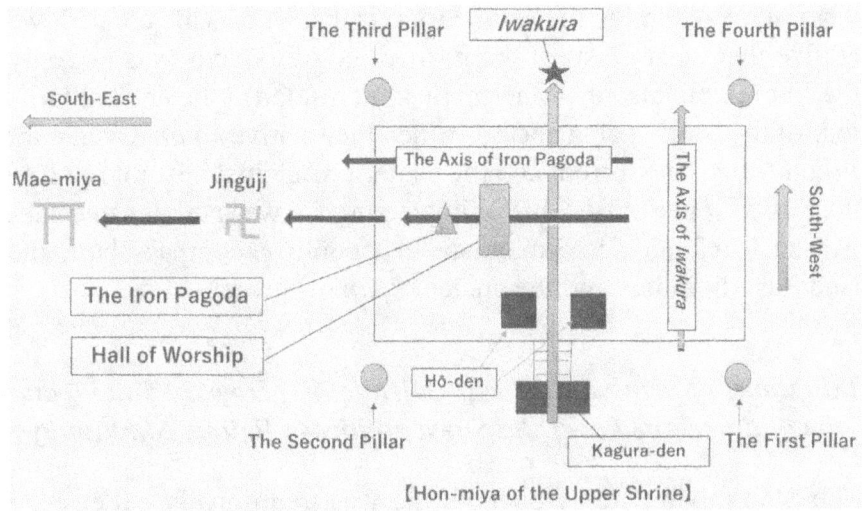

Figure 3 Position of the Iron Pagoda in the Suwa Upper Shrine.

Hall of Worship, they were actually facing not only this pagoda but also the Jingūji, which stood at a distance along the same southeast axis (**Figure 3**).

In esoteric Buddhism, after the thirteenth century, esoteric *kami* ideas and practices began to be handed down in the form of "initiations" (*kanjō* 灌頂), by which the initiate established a bond with a divinity. What was central to such *kami* initiations was the instruction of the practitioner in a secret technique enabling him to "attain union" with a certain *kami*. The initiating master taught his disciple a sequence of mudras, mantras and accompanying visualizations, so that the disciple's "body" (*shin* 身), "speech" (*ku* 口) and "mind" (*i* 意) are united in a single entity.

Such a technique of initiations seems to have been practised in the Suwa Shrine, too. In *Suwa daimyōjin shinpi gohonji daiji*, Mitsusane describes the "Suwa method of initiations" in detail by providing various mudras and mantras for the initiate. What should be emphasized is that, in the Suwa method of initiations, the ultimate *kami*, with which one should attain union, was not Dainichi or Fugen, but Mishaguji – the *kami* of Suwa that had been worshipped by the *jinchō* Moriya family since the ancient period. Now, when we re-examine the southeast axis that Mitsusane created, we realize that what exists at the farther end of the axis was not only the Jingūji, but also the Mae-miya, which stood at the ancient territory of the Moriya clan and enshrined their native *kami*, Mishaguji. When Mitsusane introduced the esoteric Buddhist cosmology into the Suwa Upper Shrine, his ultimate purpose was perhaps to establish such a large-scale mandala that could encompass both the Buddhist divinities and the ancient *kami* of Suwa.

Initiations of being united with Mishaguji – How the jinchō and the ōhōri reigned over the Suwa politico-religious community

The Mae-miya of the Upper Shrine was traditionally called "the field of *kami*" (*gōbara* 神原) and regarded as the most sacred place in the Suwa religious community. There existed the residence of the *ōhōri*, and most important rituals of the Upper Shrine were held at this place. In Suwa, the *ōhōri* was regarded as a *kami* in human form (*arahitogami*) to govern the Suwa county both religiously and politically. With this *ōhōri* resided another religious leader called the *jinchō*. Traditionally, these positions were held by members of the Kanazashi family and Moriya family, respectively. This dual system of *ōhōri* and *jinchō* continued in Suwa from ancient times to the beginning of the Meiji Period.[21]

In this dual system, it was the *jinchō* who monopolized the execution of various rituals in the Upper Shrine, for he was a shaman who alone was regarded as having an ability to communicate with the *kami* of Suwa. Even the *ōhōri* was under the governance of the *jinchō*. As such, the enthronement of the *ōhōri* was one of the most important rituals, being the initiation of a new *ōhōri* as an *arahitogami*. The *ōhōri* was supposed to be a boy of around eight years of age, chosen from the Kanazashi family. In this initiation, the Moriya *jinchō* played the central role, which let the *kami* of Suwa descend and dwell in the boy so that he could be reborn as the new *ōhōri*, a *kami* in human form. This enthronement was carried out

---

21 The last *ōhōri* was Suwa Yoritake, who was enthroned in 1841.

at the place called the Keikansha 鶏冠社 in the Mae-miya, where a large rock was situated under a holly tree. Here we find some of the essential characters of Mishaguji, which was always believed to descend on a sacred tree and a sacred rock. The boy who would become the new *ōhōri* sat by this rock and was given a series of initiation rituals. In the Muromachi Period, the *jinchō* Moriya Mitsusane added esoteric Buddhist elements to this initiation by adopting the method of *sokui kanjō*[22] (i.e., the imperial enthronement initiation developed in the medieval period, in which the imperial regent revealed to the new emperor secret mudras and mantras to be performed by him on his way to the enthronement platform on the day of his accession to the throne).[23] Interestingly, it was not Buddhist monks but the *jinchō*, the head priest, who performed all these esoteric Buddhist initiations as the master. By adopting such a method, the *jinchō* made the rituals more and more complicated, which contributed to intensifying the mythical authority of the *jinchō* in the Suwa politico-religious community.

The *kami* of Suwa were traditionally called by various names, such as "Takeminakata" in the mythic narrative, and "Suwa Daimyōjin," the manifestation of Bodhisattva Fugen, in the medieval *honji suijaku* context. Underlying these *kami*, however, there existed another one called "Mishaguji," which had been worshipped by the Moriya clan since the ancient period. In *Suwa daimyōjin shinpi gohonji daiji*, Moriya Mitsusane describes this Mishaguji as the principal *kami* of Suwa.[24] What is Mishaguji, then? We can explore it by examining another important event of the Upper Shrine – the *ō-mitatemashi-shinji* 大御立座神事.

The *ō-mitatemashi-shinji* is a sacred feast, the communion between the *kami* of Suwa (symbolized by the *ōhōri*) and its people.

---

22 *Suwa-shi shi: Jōkan*, 421. It is said that the esoteric Buddhist way of initiation was adopted, for the first time, for the enthronement of the *ōhōri* Suwa Yorinaga in 1446 (ibid., 738).

23 Mark Teeuwen analyses the structure of *sokui kanjō* in detail in "The Kami in Esoteric Buddhist Thought and Practice" in: *Shinto in History*, Honolulu: University of Hawaii Press, 2000, 105–9.

24 See "Suwa daimyōjin shinpi gohonji daiji," *Suwa Shiryō Sōsho*, 5, 426.

The people offer various sacrifices to delight the *kami* so that it may bless the land of Suwa with a rich harvest in the coming year. After this communion, the *kami*'s medium would visit all the areas of Suwa county to spread the divine blessing. This medium was called *okō* 神使, literally meaning "the messenger of the *kami*," which consisted of six boys under fifteen years old, selected every year from each district of the Suwa county.

The preparation for this event started in mid-December, when a large cave called *mimuro* 御室 was tentatively created in the semi-underground of the Mae-miya. On New Year's Eve, the *ōhōri* and the *jinchō* entered this cave, where the *jinchō* prayed that Mishaguji might descend and tell them which six villages should dedicate the *okō* that year. After this divine oracle was given, each assigned village chose a boy and started to purify, not only him, but also the entire village. First, people demarcated the village with *shimenawa*,[25] built a hut of abstinence where the boy stayed in seclusion, and in front of this hut, erected a pillar, at the top of which was hung the meat of deer and boar as the sacrifice to the *kami*.

In this hut, the boy stayed for a month, together with the *goshintai*[26] of *Mishaguji,* so that he would become pure and sacralized enough to serve as the *okō* on the very day of the *ō-mitate-mashi-shinji*. On the first day of this purification ritual, the *jinchō* attached the spirit of Mishaguji to the boy, and then performed an initiation ritual including a series of mantras and mudras like an esoteric Buddhist *kanjō*. After the very strict, month-long seclusion, the *jinchō* gave the boy final verification for having fulfilled the abstinence, and took him to the Mae-miya, as if he himself were a sacrifice dedicated to the *kami* of Suwa. Thus, the *okō* (six boys representing villages of Suwa) gathered at the Mae-miya and participated in the final feast.

---

25 *Shimenawa* is a straw rope hung around a site to demarcate sacred or pure space.

26 In Shinto, *goshintai* 御神体 means an object of worship generally housed in a shrine and believed to contain the spirit of a deity.

Buddhist-Shinto syncretization at Suwa Shrine 133

Figures 4a and b Arrangements for the festival of *ō-mitatemashi-shinji* as observed at the Suwa Shrine today. Instead of 75 real heads, three stuffed deer heads are used symbolically. Photographs © 2018, Kobayashi Kikuichi.

The *ō-mitatemashi-shinji* is held in mid-March at the hall of Mae-miya called *Jikkenrō* 十間廊. The festival is observed by the Suwa Shrine even today, but its style has been drastically changed since the Meiji Period (**Figures 4a and b**). So, we can imagine its previous style only by analysing the surviving literature.[27] The sacrifices traditionally dedicated at this feast were 75 heads of deer and such beasts and birds as rabbits and pheasants, reflective of the hunting culture. In this communion ritual, the *okō* first offered the sacrifices to the *ōhōri*, who, then, performed the ritual act of eating them, and shared them with all the participants. When the sacred communion was thus fulfilled, the *ōhōri* finally bestowed on the *okō* a crown of *tama* symbolizing their "rebirth as the children of *kami*." Now, the six boys, having been sacralized as mediums of *kami*, would visit all the areas of Suwa for several days to spread the spirit of *kami*, so that the land of Suwa would be blessed with a good harvest and happiness in the coming year. This ritual, called *mawari-tatae* 廻り湛え, simultaneously meant that the land of Suwa was now under the political control of the *ōhōri*. His divine authority, however, had to be always guaranteed by the *jinchō*, the religious leader, for the essence of the *kami* manifested in the *ōhōri* belonged to *Mishaguji*, with which the *jinchō* alone was qualified to communicate.

When we observe this *ō-mitatemashi-shinji,* we find a very complicated character of the *kami* of Suwa, *Mishaguji*. It is, on one hand, a wild divinity that devours the flesh of animals, including human beings, which reminds us of the notion that the divine prefers "blood." It is, on the other hand, a benevolent *kami* that blesses the land of Suwa with an abundant harvest. We may interpret such contradictory faces of *kami* as expressing an intricate fusion of two traditions which had conflicted with each other over the long history of Suwa – the *kami* of hunters worshipped by the Moriya

---

[27] The literature includes *Suwa Daimyōjin Ekotoba* 諏訪大明神画詞, *Okō Otō no Nikki* 神使御頭之日記, *Nennai Shinji Shidai Kuki* 年内神事次第旧記 and *Suwa Kamisha Monoimi-rei* 諏方上社物忌令. Hiroko Yamamoto analyses the meaning of *ō-mitatemashi-shinji* in "Toraware no seidō-tachi" in: *Suwa-gaku*, ed. Hiroko Yamamoto, Tokyo: Kokusho-kankō-kai, 2018, 101–30.

clan (= the *jinchō*) and that of farmers revered by the Kanazashi clan (= the *ōhōri*). In the Suwa politico-religious community, neither of these *kami*(s) was eliminated, but they were combined skilfully, by inventing a unique dual system of *jinchō* and *ōhōri*. Not only combining the *kami*(s) of different cultures, the *kami* of Suwa also absorbed the elements of esoteric Buddhism and developed a more complicated system of worship than ever, called Suwa-ryū Shintō, as we have seen in the previous section. In this fusion of *kami* and buddhas, the Suwa-ryū Shintō even inverted the prevalent *honji suijaku* theory and tried to emphasize that Mishaguji, the ancient *kami* of Suwa, was the source of the buddhas, rather than the reverse. After all, Suwa Daimyōjin, which had been the popular name for the *kami* of Suwa in the medieval period, included all these diverse faces, even contradictory elements.

This tradition of the Suwa Shrine, uniquely characterized by multiple faces of *kami*, dramatically changed when the Meiji government enforced the dissociation of *kami* and buddhas/bodhisattvas in 1868, trying to eradicate any Buddhist elements sustained by Shinto shrines. In addition, the government prohibited what they regarded as savage customs of *kami* worship. As such, the long-inherited traditions of the Suwa Shrine were drastically transformed, some of them becoming extinct. Now, people no longer remember the complexities of *kami* worship developed by the Suwa Shrine in its long history – the metamorphosis of *kami* that takes advantage of whatever is useful for its existence.

About the author

Iwasawa Tomoko is professor of Comparative Religion at Reitaku University in Chiba, Japan. She holds a doctorate in Philosophy of Religion from Boston University. Her publications include "Philosophical Implications of Shinto" in *The Oxford Handbook of Japanese Philosophy* (2019), "Transcendence and Immanence, West and East: A Case Study of Japanese Divinity" in *Existenz* (2018), and *Tama in Japanese Myth: A Hermeneutical Study of Ancient Japanese Divinity* (2011).

7

Underground Buddhism at the Ise Shrines

D. Max Moerman

The Ise Shrines (*Ise Jingū* 伊勢神宮), which venerate the tutelary deities of the imperial lineage, are today presented as sites of an enduring and immutable native tradition. Such an image of permanence, however, is of rather recent invention, and one, moreover, that erases a complex history of transformation and change. The image of Ise as the homeland of an indigenous religion untouched by Buddhism is one created by eighteenth- and nineteenth-century Nativists, promulgated by the Japanese government until the end of the Pacific War, and one that continues to be promoted by the Ise Shrines today. The promulgation of the Separation Edicts of 1868 – which segregated religious deities, clergy, institutions and images into the mutually exclusive categories of Buddhist or Shinto – was one of the most radical events in the history of Japanese religion and one that forever changed the status, structure and administration of Ise. For the previous thousand years, Buddhist practices, texts, deities and beliefs had been an integral part of Ise's religious and institutional culture. Yet the relationship between the gods and the buddhas at Ise is neither simple nor self-evident. It is a relationship with its own history, one that has been often obscured and sometimes buried. This article is an attempt to excavate one piece of that history.

Buddhist institutions, practices, discourses and representations were present at Ise since at least the eighth century. According to the *Shoku Nihongi* 続日本紀, the state history composed in 797, Takidaijingūji 多気大神宮寺, the shrine-temple (*jingūji* 神宮寺) of the imperial princess at Ise (*saigū* 斎宮), was relocated to Watarai-gun 度会郡 in 698 to better serve the shrines.[1] In 766, an imperial

---

1 *Shoku Nihongi*, Monmu 文武 2.12.29, Vol. 1, 14.

envoy was sent to "the temple of the Great Deity of Ise" with the gift of a life-size (*jōroku* 丈六) statue of a Buddha to serve as its principal icon.[2] In 767 the court issued an imperial order that Ōkasedera 鹿瀬寺 be established as the state-sponsored temple of the Ise Shrines in perpetuity. Yet the earliest records of Ise Shrine ritual, the *Protocols of the Imperial Great Shrine* (*Kōtaijingū gishikichō* 皇大神宮儀式帳) of 804, declare such basic Buddhist terms as "Buddha," "sutra," "pagoda," "monk," "temple" and "lay practitioner" as taboo (*imi* 忌).[3] The prohibitions at Ise against Buddhist vocabulary, practices and practitioners during certain ritual occasions suggest an historical tension between shrine and temple traditions yet also reveal the intimacy of the two. The isolation of *kami* and buddhas at Ise indicates that a difference was drawn between the traditions and yet it remained a difference in need of explanation.

It is this complex relationship that the Buddhist monk Mujū Ichien 無住一圓 (1227–1312) attempts to explain in the opening tale of his thirteenth-century *Collection of Sand and Pebbles* (*Shasekishū* 沙石集).

> While I was on a pilgrimage to the Great Shrine, an official explained to me why words associated with the Three Treasures of Buddhism were forbidden at the shrine, and why monks could not closely approach the sacred buildings. In antiquity, when this country did not yet exist, the deity of the Great Shrine, guided by a seal of the Great Sun Buddha (*Dai Nichi Nyorai* 大日如来) inscribed on the ocean floor, thrust down her august spear. Brine from the spear coagulated like drops of dew, and was seen from afar by Mara, the Evil One, in the Sixth Heaven of Desire. "It appears that these drops are forming into the land where Buddhism will be propagated and people will escape from the round of birth-and-death," he said, and came down to prevent it. Then the deity of the Great Shrine met with the demon king and said, "I promise not to utter the names of the Three Treasures, nor will I

---

2 *Shoku Nihongi*, Tenpyō-jingo 天平神護 2.7.23, Vol. 4, 128.
3 Teeuwen and Breen 2017, 33–4.

permit them near my person." Being thus mollified, he withdrew. ... Outwardly the deity is estranged from the Dharma, but inwardly she profoundly supports the Three Treasures. Thus, Japanese Buddhism is under the special protection of the deity of the Great Shrine. ... Since all of this arose by virtue of the seal of the Great Sun Buddha on the ocean floor, we have come to identify the deities of the Inner and Outer Shrines with the Great Sun Buddha of the Two-Part Mandala; and that which is called the Heavenly Rock Cave is the Tusita Heaven of the Buddha Maitreya.[4]

The true history of Buddhism at Ise, according to Mujū's tale of origins, is thus purposely concealed. It is a history that reaches back before the Japanese islands even existed, yet one that remains forever hidden, buried deep beneath the waves. Mujū's answer to an apparently inexplicable situation – the prohibition of Buddhist institutions, individuals, discourses, rituals and representations at the Ise Shrines – is to reformulate the classical myth of Japanese cosmogony to expose the apparent ban on Buddhism as a clever ruse concocted by the Sun Goddess to thwart the archenemy of the Dharma and establish Ise as the secret headquarters of a national Buddhist underground. What appears on the surface as a taboo is shown to have a deeper underlying meaning, inscribed on the ocean floor by the Great Sun Buddha before the Land of the Gods was even formed, representing not a prohibition but rather a promise of protection and preservation. The implication of this primordial arrangement between the Sun Goddess Amaterasu and the Great Sun Buddha reveals the sacred landscape of the Ise Shines as essentially Buddhist. The *kami* of the two Ise Shrines are really the Great Sun Buddha of the Mandala of the Two Realms (*ryōkai mandara* 両界曼荼羅): the Womb Realm (*taizōkai* 胎蔵界) and Diamond Realm (*kongōkai* 金剛界), the substrate of all forms of esoteric Buddhist thought and practice. The Heavenly Rock Cave (Ama no Iwato 天岩戸) behind which Amaterasu concealed herself in the Age of the Gods is none other than the heavenly cavern of

---

4   Mujū Ichien, *Shasekishū*, 59–61.

Tusita in which Maitreya, the Buddha of the Future, awaits the dawning of a new Buddhist age.

Mujū's account of the hidden history of Ise's sacred landscape represents an advanced stage of a Buddhist discourse on the shrines that developed from the mid-twelfth century and was produced by the priests of the Inner and Outer Shines themselves.[5] As Mujū's account suggests, it was not until the medieval period that the Ise Shrines were fully explained as a fundamental and foundational Buddhist site. This Buddhist reading of Ise, however, is presented in medieval sources less as a historical development than as an original condition, like the seal of the Great Sun Buddha inscribed at the bottom of the ocean, always already there. Scholars such as Mark Teeuwen, Abe Yasurō, Itō Satoshi and Kadoya Atsushi have traced the chronological development of this discourse through doctrinal, ritual and iconographic sources and offered a new textual history of Ise. Mark Teeuwen has noted that the late twelfth century witnessed "the beginning of a flood of writings that offered a broad array of new interpretations of the site of Ise, its shrines and its kami," which produced a "fluid body of cross-referencing texts."[6] Abe Yasurō has examined the temple archives of Shinpukuji and analysed "Shinto as written representation" and "medieval Shinto as text."[7] I would like to take a step back from this fully formed textual corpus to examine earlier practices that contributed to the conditions of its possibility: practices carried out in the late twelfth century by members of Ise's sacerdotal lineages that may help us to better understand the individual and institutional agents responsible for the transformation of the religious culture and the religious landscape of the Ise Shrines. My hope is that the archaeological evidence presented in this article might contribute in some small way to this body of scholarship and suggest how material culture might complement and complicate our history of Ise.

---

5   On the historical development of this discourse, see Teeuwen 1996.
6   Teeuwen and Breen 2017, 61.
7   Abe 2006–07.

Underground Buddhism

Compared to the underwater seal of the Great Sun Buddha and Amaterasu's undercover support of the Three Treasures, the earlier practices represented a different kind of underground activity and a different sort of textual practice. In the second half of the twelfth century, prominent members of the priestly lineages of the Ise Shrines – Watarai 度会, Arakida 荒木田, Isobe 佐伯 and Ōnakatomi 大中臣 – buried consecrated copies of Buddhist sutras, mandalas and images in the earth at sacred sites in the immediate vicinity of the Inner and Outer Shrines. The burial of sutra texts and other objects of Buddhist visual and material culture was an open secret: a public act in an age of religious crisis. For the twelfth century represented, to many Japanese, a crucial turning point in the history of Buddhism: the onset of *mappō* 末法, the final degenerate age of the Buddhist Dharma, in which both the availability of Buddhist texts and the ability of people to realize them would reach their lowest points. The ineluctable decline of the Dharma presented soteriological problems for both the tradition and the individual. The death of the Dharma challenged, of course, the very existence of Buddhism and required acts of protection and preservation to ensure its survival. But *mappō* also had implications for individual practitioners for whom personal salvation became increasingly difficult as the source of teachings receded into an inaccessible past and the spiritual capabilities of humans diminished. Although a concern with *mappō* clearly informs the practice of sutra burial, the preservationist impulse was not necessarily the sole motivating factor. Inscriptions accompanying sutra burials also express the hope that, due to this meritorious act, the donor (or other individuals to whom the merit is being transferred) will be reborn, in the interim, in Amida's Pure Land. Sutra burials illustrate the belief that the future of the Dharma and the future of the individual are linked, and that this critical juncture in the salvation of both Buddhism and Buddhists could be addressed with the same religious practice. Sutra burials offered the ritual strategies and material means whereby the end-time could be prepared for and paradise secured.

By the early twelfth century, sutra burials could be found in every province of the country from Satsuma to Dewa.[8] They were most commonly carried out at or near temples, shrines or sacred mountains, and performed either by Buddhist monks or by Buddhist laity under monastic supervision. What makes the Ise burials so notable and so surprising, given the received understanding of Ise, is that they were performed by members of the priestly lineages of the Inner and Outer Shines, commonly thought to abhor all things Buddhist, and directed toward the Buddhist salvation of Ise priests themselves. The direct involvement of Ise's sacerdotal lineages – Watarai, Arakida, Isobe and Ōnakatomi – in Buddhist practices had a long history. As early as the tenth century, the priests of the Ise Shrines built Buddhist temples to gain salvation after death, took the tonsure and became Buddhist monks in the final years of their life, and received Buddhist funerals and memorial services.[9] The excavated materials from the sutra burials at Ise, however, provide physical evidence of the depth of their Buddhist faith and a material record of the construction of Ise as a site of Buddhist texts and objects, Buddhist rituals and clergy, and Buddhist aspirations and ideals. It is a record, moreover, of great historical specificity in which the names, dates and motivations of the practices and the practitioners are inscribed in ink and clay in the hopes of outlasting the Final Age.

The sutras buried at Ise were transcribed according to strict ritual protocols and then interred to protect and preserve the Dharma until the arrival of the Buddha Maitreya some 5.67 billion years in the future. As Ise's Heavenly Rock Cave is, as Mujū explains, none other than Maitreya's Tusita Heaven, the sacred ground of the shrine's landscape is an ideal site to secure the sutras. The scriptures and related deposits were produced in a variety of materials – paper, copper, bronze, glazed and unglazed ceramic – and were buried at nine different sites over a period of thirty years, from

---

8 For the chronology and locations of these sutra mounds, see Seki 1990, 37–53.

9 On the shrine-temples of Ise, see Hagiwara 1985.

1156 to 1186.¹⁰ I will limit my discussion, however, to two examples that most clearly reveal the role of Ise's priestly lineages in such practices. One group of sutras, transcribed in ink on paper, placed into cylindrical stupa-shaped containers made of bronze or copper, and then encased in a second outer ceramic vessel, were buried at what is known as the Mount Asama Kyōgamine 朝熊山経ヶ峰 sutra mound, 542 metres above sea level, east of the Inner Shrine. Like many other examples across Japan, the Mount Asama materials were interred in small underground chambers lined and sealed with stones and marked, like a grave, with earthen mounds and stone stupas. A second group of sutras, signalling perhaps an even more explicit concern with the preservation of the Dharma, were inscribed on clay tiles that were glazed and fired and then buried at three sites in the hills just west of the Outer Shrine known as the Komachi 小町 and Bodaisan jingūji 菩提山神宮寺, and Eitaizan Kyōgamine 永代山経ヶ峰 sutra mounds.¹¹ These burials speak to more than the historical and soteriological anxieties of the age. They also specify Ise as the site where such anxieties were expressed and where, it was hoped, they could be conquered as well.

Preparing for the Pure Land

Forty-three sutra deposits, dating from 1156 to 1186, have been excavated from numerous individual burial sites at Kyōgamine within a thirty-square-metre area beside the Shingon temple of Kongōshōji 金剛証寺 near the summit of Mount Asama. In addition to the sutras and their containers excavated at Mount Asama, a wide range of other items were also included in these burials such as bronze mirrors engraved with Buddhist images, ceramic pedestals for Buddhist images, knives, scissors, flints, needles, porcelain and lacquered covered dishes, plates of various sizes, tea bowls,

10 Ceramic sutra containers with inscriptions dated 1156 and 1186 have been excavated from Mount Asama sites 5, 8 and 10c. Kodama 2008, 10.

11 For a comprehensive history of these sites and their scholarship, see Kodama 2008, 29–72.

sake decanters and cups, fans, glass beads, and coins.[12] As rich and varied as the objects themselves, the individuals responsible for the Mount Asama burials reveal a complex network of familial and institutional lineages that formed the texture of the religious communities of Ise in the late twelfth century.

Among the earliest and most revealing of the Mount Asama burials is a bronze sutra tube dated by inscription the fifteenth day of the eighth month of 1159 containing thirteen sutra scrolls, including the *Lotus Sūtra* (*Myōhō renge kyō* 妙法蓮華経), which in the East Asian tradition includes the *Sutra of Innumerable Meanings* (*Muryōgi kyō* 無量義経) and the *Sūtra of Meditation on the Bodhisattva Universal Virtue* (*Kanfugen bosatsu gyōbō kyō* 観普賢菩薩翹望教) as its opening and closing sections. The sutras had been transcribed and dated the previous day by the nuns Benkaku 弁覚, Myōi 妙意, Ryōjitsu 良実, Jōzen 定禅 and Jōi 定意 of Jōkakuji 常覚寺, a temple located in the Yamada region of Watarai District, so that members of the Ōnakatomi and Watarai lineages might "avoid rebirth in the Six Realms and all become Buddhas and attain the way."[13] The sponsor was the nun Shinmyō 真妙, from Jōshōji 常勝寺, another temple of the Watarai lineage in the same region, and the names of another ten monks who contributed to the project in the hope of "forming karmic connections (*kechien* 結縁)" are also listed. The central purpose of these pious efforts of so many Buddhist nuns and monks was to guarantee the postmortem salvation of the former Head Priest (*negi* 禰宜) of the Outer Shrine of Ise, Watarai Masahiko 度会雅彦, who had died exactly four months earlier, in the fourth month of 1159. An inscription on the back of the *Sūtra of Meditation on the Bodhisattva Universal Virtue* states that the sutra was "transcribed to assure the rebirth of Masahiko's noble spirit in Amida's Gokuraku Pure Land." A transcription of the *Bucchō sonshō daranikyō* 佛頂尊勝陀羅尼經, also buried on the same day, was similarly transcribed, according to

---

12 The contents are itemized in Seki 1999, 457–8. The citations of sutra burial inscriptions that follow all refer to those transcribed in Seki's volume.

13 The inscription, which appears at the end of the third chapter of the *Lotus Sūtra*, is transcribed in Seki 1999, 456 (#121).

an inscription, "so that the noble spirit of Masahiko becomes a Buddha and attains the Way."[14]

In addition to the sutras, three bronze mirrors included in the burial provide visual analogues to the petitioner's inscription. Two are round and the third rectangular, and all bear images of the Buddha Amida. The rectangular mirror is decorated with images of cranes, pine trees and islands of immortality on the back, and the front is incised with a welcoming descent of Amida and his attendant bodhisattvas to the shores of a mountain beside the sea. The back of one of the round mirrors is decorated with embossed images of birds, butterflies and sprigs of maple, and the front is incised with an image of a seated Amida attended by the bodhisattvas Kannon and Seishi. The other round mirror is incised on both sides with images of Amida. On one side, the Buddha of the Western Pure Land is shown seated alone on a lotus pedestal, hands held in a mudra of meditation. The other side depicts the very salvation of the Ise priest that the burial was meant to assure. Amida is shown, attended by the bodhisattvas Kannon and Seishi, in welcoming descent (*raigō* 来迎), amid clouds and flower petals, rays of light emanating from his halo toward the open doors of a pavilion where a devotee, in this case Watarai Masahiko himself, receives the light of Amida's halo as he faces the divine host.

The choice of the *Lotus Sūtra* and the goal of Pure Land rebirth was entirely in keeping with the practices of late Heian Period sutra burials. The *Lotus Sūtra* was the scripture most commonly interred. It was a text that explicitly encouraged its own transmission, enshrinement and veneration. Like a number of other early Mahayana sutras, the *Lotus Sūtra* claims that because of its status as the textual corpus of the Buddha's teachings, it supersedes the corporal relic of the Buddha himself as the true body of the Buddhadharma. Indeed, the *Lotus Sūtra* reserves the highest praise for those "who shall receive and keep, read and recite, explain, or copy in writing a single verse of the *Scripture of the Blossom of the Fine Dharma*, or who will look with veneration on a roll of this

---

14 Ibid., 456 (#122).

scripture as if it were the Buddha himself."[15] In carrying out these scriptural instructions, the sponsors of sutra burials enjoyed the combined merit of copying and protecting the sutra together with that of building a stupa in which to enshrine and venerate it. These practices were understood to be particularly timely as the Buddha of the *Lotus Sūtra* emphasizes that such methods of textual preservation and devotion are to be undertaken specifically "after my extinction, in an evil age."[16]

Rebirth in Amida's Pure Land was also a common goal in Heian religious culture and one advocated and idealized within the *Lotus Sūtra* as well. The representation of Amida's welcoming descent incised on the interred mirrors follows a standardized iconography found in countless texts and paintings of the period. Although the elements of landscape depicted on the mirrors – mountains rising precipitously from the sea, island archipelagos viewed from afar – are the sort of idealized images commonly represented in scenes of Buddhist and Daoist paradises, they also share a decidedly local flavour: they are very like the sort of landscape viewed from the summit of Mount Asama looking out toward Ise Bay. Even more local references, however, are to be found among the names of those involved in the Kyōgamine burials. The Kyōgamine burials were not exclusively for the priests of the Outer Shines. A ceramic sutra vessel dated the eleventh day of the eighth month of 1173 excavated from Mount Asama site 1 contained a copy of the *Lotus Sūtra* transcribed and offered for "peace and tranquility in the present and future life" for "the Shrine Priest Arakida Tokimori, Fourth Rank Lower Grade Priest of the Great Shrine of Ise."[17] Although often portrayed as hereditary rivals in histories of Ise, the burial side by side of sutras transcribed for the Pure Land rebirth of leading priests of the Watarai and Arakida lineages illustrates a closeness in matters of Buddhist practice. Another illustration of this is to be found within an 1145 seated image of Yakushi Nyorai, the Buddha of Healing, donated to Jōsenji 定泉寺, one of the eight temples of

---

15 *Myōhō renge kyō*, 30b.
16 Ibid., 31a.
17 Seki 1999, 457 (#128).

the sacerdotal lineages of the Ise Shrine. It was offered jointly by the Arakida Kannushi (神主) and a member of the Watarai lineage, who may have been his wife. Their names appear side-by-side inscribed on the interior of the image.[18]

A Canon in Clay

An example of even greater cooperation between priestly lineages is illustrated by tile sutras buried at the Komachi, Bodaisan and Eitaizan sites near the Inner Shrine. More than 420 inscribed ceramic tiles, each approximately 25 × 30 cm, were buried at the three sites between the fifth and seventh month of 1174. An undertaking of such a scale required the participation of many individuals, members of the Ōnakatomi, Isobe, Watarai and Arakida lineages, as well as the funds, materials and technologies necessary to produce, inscribe and transport the sutra tiles. The sutras inscribed include the *Lotus Sūtra* in 169 tiles; the *Dainichikyō* 大日經 in 122 tiles; *Kongōchōkyō* 金剛頂經 in 40 tiles; the *Soshitchikyō* 蘇悉地經 in 83 tiles; the *Rishukyō* 理趣經 in 7 tiles; the *Amidakyō* in 4 tiles; and the *Hannyashingyō* in a single tile. In addition to these sutras were also dharani texts, a Lotus mandala in Siddham characters, a Diamond Realm and Womb Realm mandala, a lotus pedestal, four mandorlas and a seated Buddha image, all made of the same light grey clay.

A concern with the preservation of the Dharma throughout the dark days of the Final Age is evident in the material used – fired clay of the sort used for roof tiles – intended to withstand the test of time. In their votive prayers, the participants refer explicitly to the Final Dharma. Inscriptions on three separate tiles and on one of the mandorlas announce the age as "the time of Śākyamuni's Final Dharma."[19] As with the Mount Asama burials, the identities of those involved reveal the interwoven lives, afterlives and aspirations of Ise's religious community. The names of two monks

---

18 Tōkyō Kokuritsu Hakubutsukan 2009, 179.
19 Seki 1999, 460 (#134), 461 (#134), 463 (#145), 466 (#160).

who played a leading role in the production and burial of the sutra tiles appear throughout the inscriptions as Shamon Seikan 沙門西観 and Kongōbushi Junsai 金剛仏子遵西. They are identified as monks from Mankakuji 万覚寺 in Irago 伊良, Atsumi District 渥美郡, Mikawa Province 三河国. Seikan and Junsai are listed in the colophons of the tile *Lotus Sūtra*, *Dainichikyō*, *Kongōchōkyō*, *Soshitchikyō* and the Diamond Realm mandala. Seikan, together with his fellow monk Ryūen, was also responsible for the seated Buddha image which was dedicated in a memorial service for their departed parents. Like the Mount Asama burials, the tile sutras were dedicated to assuring the Pure Land rebirth of a Head Priest of the Ise Outer Shrine Shrine, in this case Watarai Tsuneyuki 度会常行, who served as *negi* from 1144 until his death in 1160 at the age of seventy-four.[20] Yet as at Mount Asama, the enormous ritual production offered the opportunity for members of Ise's other sacerdotal lineages to contribute to the Buddhist salvation of additional family members as well. One of the ceramic mandorlas was offered for a nun of the Ōnakatomi lineage.[21] Another was offered by a male and female member of the Watarai lineage, together with Seikan and Junsai and six other monks, for the benefit of a member of the Isobe lineage.[22] A third mandorla was offered for a member of the Arakida lineage.[23] Three senior members of the Watarai lineage are listed among the names of those associated with the production of the *Lotus Sūtra* tiles but so too are members of the Isobe and Mononobe clans. The *Dainichikyō*, offered for the benefit of "Watarai Tsuneyuki's noble spirit," similarly includes the names of members of the Ōnakatomi and Arakida lineages.

The inscriptions suggest connections not only between and across sacerdotal lineages but also between the material resources and technologies of multiple shrine and temple institutions. Although the sutras were buried at Ise, they were not local products. They were produced, according to inscriptions on the tiles, in

20 Ibid., 461 (#135).
21 Ibid., 466 (#159).
22 Ibid., 467 (#160).
23 Ibid., 467 (#162).

Irago, Atsumi District, Mikawa Province. Irago, located at the tip of the Atsumi Peninsula directly across the Ise Bay, was a region covered with estates that supplied tribute and resources to the Ise Shrines and had long been a centre of ceramic production. Roof tiles produced for the eleventh-century restoration of Tōdaiji have been excavated from a tile kiln site in Irago as well as from eleven other kiln sites in the region.[24] Other excavated materials identify the Atsumi Peninsula as the origin for the ceramic materials buried at Ise. An outer ceramic sutra case buried elsewhere at Ise is signed by a monk who identifies himself as "a resident of the shrine land of Kachi (鍛治御園住人僧)," an estate held by the Inner Shrine on the Atsumi Peninsula. Kachi (also written 加治), the site of numerous kilns, also produced lotus-form pedestals of the kind excavated from Komachi.[25] One of the ceramic mandorlas from Komachi is inscribed by Fujii Narishige 藤井成重 as "an offering of white clay, for rebirth in the Pure Land, at the time of Śākyamuni's Final Dharma, at Mankakuji in Irago, Atsumi Province."[26] The ceramic sutra tiles, containers, mandorlas and lotus-form pedestals buried at Ise were thus produced for the Buddhist salvation of the priests of the Ise Shrines, out of the local clay from estates they controlled on the Atsumi Peninsula, manufactured and inscribed by artisans and monastic scribes at Mankakuji, fired in the kilns of Irago, and transported, like any other tribute due, by boat across the Ise Bay. This massive production of Buddhist texts, a canon cast in clay, was then buried underground at the Ise Shrines, to preserve the Dharma for the next 5.6 billion years and also, according to the donative inscription, to secure for the shrine priests "the proper state of mind at the moment of death, rebirth in Amida's Pure Land, protection of the state in all ten directions, benefit and joy to all sentient beings, presence at the advent of the Future Buddha, Maitreya, and the proper performance of all Buddhist memorial services."[27]

24 Okamoto 1965, 19.
25 Ibid.
26 Seki 1999, 466 (#160).
27 Ibid., 464 (#147).

The Buddhist texts, objects, and images buried at Ise in the twelfth century offer material evidence of a historical consciousness. For the members of the shrine's sacerdotal lineages – Watarai, Arakida, Isobe and Ōnakatomi – the sutra burials marked a crucial juncture in Buddhist history. They signalled, in the words of the inscriptions themselves, "the time of Śākyamuni's Final Dharma," a long age of religious decline, a downward descent in the perpetual cycle of Buddhist chronology until "the advent of the Future Buddha, Miroku." But the burials also mark a more personal kind crisis in the life cycles of the families themselves: the transition from life to death and from death to rebirth. The burial of sutras was a response by members of Ise's priestly lineages to this confluence of the personal and the historical, a crisis of mortality in their familial lives and in the life of Buddhism, and an attempt to address the inevitability of change.

For us today, the sutra burials at Ise call attention to a history of change obscured by claims of continuity. Such claims, legislated by the Meiji state, sought to restore Japan to a religious past it never had. This invented tradition required the erasure of Ise's religious history and the construction of a past untouched by Buddhism. Ise's sutra burials, however, reveal that beneath such recent ideological constructions lie earlier strata of religious complexity in which the priests of Ise turned to Buddhist texts, Buddhist images, Buddhist practices, Buddhist rituals and Buddhist ritualists to address a time of crisis in their personal lives and in the history of their religion. In this sense the sutra burials at Ise offer another kind of buried treasure: one that reveals the underground history of a place that we long thought we knew. Sutra burials, like so many time capsules, provide the materials for an archaeology of religious aspiration. They allow for an excavation of Ise's religious history that requires us to look deeper than modern claims of a uniform and unaltered tradition. They reveal a history of difference and a history of change; a religious landscape not isolated from Buddhist traditions but deeply grounded therein.

References

Abe Yasurō 2006–07. "Shintō as Written Representation: The Phases and Shifts in Medieval Shintō Texts." *Cahiers d'Extrême-Asie* 16, 91–117. https://doi.org/10.3406/asie.2006.1252

Hagiwara Tatsuo 萩原龍夫 1985. "*Ise jingū to Bukkyō*" 伊勢神宮と仏教 in: Hagiwara Tatsuo (ed.), *Ise shinkō* 伊勢信, Vol. 1. Tokyo (Yūzankaku), 231–9.

Kodama Michiaki 小玉道明 2008. *Ise Yamada no gakyō* 伊勢山田の瓦経. Matsusaka (Hikari shuppan).

Mujū Ichien 無住一圓. *Shasekishū* 沙石集. NKBT 85.

Myōhō renge kyō 妙法蓮華経 (Ch. *Miaofa lianfa jing*). T 262 9, 1a–62c.

Okamoto Hideo 奥村秀雄 1965. "*Ise chihō ni okeru maikyō*" 伊勢地方における埋経. *Museum* ミュジアム 167 (February), 14–22.

Seki Hideo 関秀夫 1990. *Kyōzuka to sonno ibutsu* 経塚とその遺物. *Nihon no bijutsu* 日本の美術 9/292.

Seki Hideo 関秀夫 1999. *Heian jidai no maikyō to shakyō* 平安時代の埋経と写経. Tokyo (Tōkyōdō).

Shoku Nihongi 続二本紀, 4 vols. SNKT 12–16.

Teeuwen, Mark 1996. *Watarai Shintō: An Intellectual History of the Outer Shrine in Ise*. Leiden (CNWS).

Teeuwen, Mark and Breen, John 2017. *A Social History of the Ise Shrines: Divine Capital*. London (Bloomsbury).

Tōkyō Kokuritsu Hakubutsukan 東京国立博物館 (ed.) 2009. *Ise Jingū to kamigami no bijutsu* 伊勢神宮と神々の美術. Tokyo (Kasumi Kaikan).

About the author

D. Max Moerman (PhD Stanford University, 1999) is Professor in the Department of Asian and Middle Eastern Cultures, Barnard College, Columbia University and Co-Chair of the Columbia University Seminar on Buddhist Studies. His research interests lie in the visual and material culture of premodern Japanese Buddhism. He is the author of *Localizing Paradise: Kumano Pilgrimage and the Religious Landscape of Premodern Japan* (Harvard, 2004) and the forthcoming *The Japanese Buddhist World Map: Religious Vision and the Cartographic Imagination*.

8

Shinto spaces and shinbutsu interaction in the Noh

Dunja Jelesijevic

Drawing on its religious, ritual and literary origins, Noh developed as a performance art and a literary genre with unique content, structure and aesthetic. Incorporating Shinto-related mythology and performance, Buddhist spirituality, literary sophistication of the classics, and aesthetics of mysterious beauty, intensity and depth, Noh, in an interactive and dynamic fashion, responded to the medieval Japanese worldview where boundaries between beings, entities, and visible and invisible realms were blurred, and where religious concepts and ideologies were in a vigorous dialogue. In fact, the Noh stage emerged as a particularly appropriate site for interaction between the buddhas, bodhisattvas and the *kami*, between the living and the dead, between sentient and non-sentient beings. Without relying exclusively on a single dominant religion or ideology, religious content in Noh consisted of conceptual and narrative elements from both Buddhism and Shinto, as well as other traditions. That way, Noh positioned itself prominently within the discourse of the medieval combinatory processes, by offering a performative model, both artistic and ritual, that could address simultaneously all different sides of the *shinbutsu* (*kami*/buddhas) paradigm.[1]

---

1 In Japan, the process of interaction between buddhas and the *kami* and the combinatory paradigm of their association is known as *shinbutsu shūgō* 神仏習合. It is generally understood that this process developed in Japan in stages, between the eighth and twelfth centuries. Initially, the buddhas and bodhisattvas were just viewed as foreign *kami*, then as protectors of the Dharma, the Buddhist teaching. A later phase saw the development of the doctrine *honji suijaku* 本地垂迹 (original source/trace manifestation), according to which *kami* are manifestations of buddhas and bodhisattvas. The process culminated in the final stage, *han honji suijaku* 反本地垂迹 (inverted *honji suijaku*) where the *kami*

While most Noh plays in one way or another exhibit religious content, in a number of them the narrative, protagonists and their surroundings are conceptualized in a way that engages religious traditions in various types of interplay. Focusing particularly on the symbolic language that relates to space, the following discussion will explore some instances of how this interplay is being carried out and what is accomplished by it. I argue that, in the Noh, Shinto spaces are configured in such a way that they enable and facilitate *shinbutsu* interaction, and Noh is able to achieve this precisely because it is a literary genre and performance art positioned intimately close to, yet outside of, mainstream religion. This, in turn, allows for any tensions, contradictions or ambivalences to be freely enacted, interrogated and, potentially, resolved. I will look more closely at two Noh plays, *Yamamba* and *Nonomiya*, as case studies for how performative, literary, geographical and ritual space overlap in mutual reinscriptions of Buddhist and Shinto cosmologies. These two plays are particularly useful for such inquiry as they exemplify, respectively, two most prominent ways in which Shinto space is materialized: a distinguished shrine and its surroundings, and an open natural space (a mountain) understood to be residence of *kami*, while their main protagonists in the Noh, called the *shite*,[2] are an extension and embodiment of this space, eventually themselves becoming sites for the religious interplay taking place.

Sacred space: Enchanted space, enlightened space

In his seminal discussion on the relationship between Shinto shrines and Buddhist temples, Allan Grapard points out that while Shinto may not have expounded a comprehensive doctrine, its ideology is

---

are understood as the original trace, under the influence of doctrines such as original enlightenment. For an extensive discussion on the *shinbutsu* paradigm, see Rambelli and Teeuwen 2006.

2 *Shite* is the main role and the protagonist in Noh and some other forms of traditional Japanese theatre. In Noh, *shite* frequently appear as supernatural beings (ghosts, demons etc.), who appear in the first act in a human form disguising their identity, and appear in their true form in the second act.

expressed through shrines, ritual and particular attitudes to space. He contends that premodern Japanese religiosity as a whole is, in fact, "grounded in specific sites" (Grapard 1993, 5). In other words, people experience and practice their religiosity through affiliation to a site or locale and meanings they ascribe to and behaviours they exhibit towards that locale, rather than adhering to doctrine or creed. Certain objects and natural formations when appearing together have come to signify characteristic markers of a Shinto space, such as a mountain, a body of water and, resulting from the history of Shinto/Buddhism combinatory processes, proximity of a Buddhist temple (Grapard 1982, 198). Presence of water, usually a spring, pond or river is significant, due to its association with (the ritual of) purification, one of the central concerns of Shinto beliefs and practices, while mountains, in Shinto, take on a specific significance due to a number of coinciding associations: they are sacred as residence of the *kami*, they are sometimes considered *kami* themselves, and they are traditionally understood as places where various transcendent and supernatural realms are located (Grapard 1982, 199–202; Faure 2000, 179–87). Therefore, a site thus configured is transformed from an ordinary natural spot into an enchanted realm that is a replication of Shinto cosmology, and represents a sacred space with porous boundaries between the visible and invisible worlds, between this world and the "other".

On the other hand, over the centuries and throughout the course of its geographical proliferation, Buddhism expounded exquisitely sophisticated doctrine, and concepts of space that emerge from it are derived from those doctrinal concerns. While trying to distil a "Buddhist" definition of space in a way that would account for all intricacies and diversity of Buddhist traditions would be an impossible task and well beyond the scope of this essay, it is important to take note of several key points that are relevant for the discussion at hand. First and foremost, the understanding and significance of physical space as a site of achieving buddhahood, which transforms earthly concrete space into an enlightened category, as "illusory dualities are integrated or realized as non-dual" (Grotenhuis 1998, 2), namely, where the distinctions between enlightened and non-enlightened, samsara (the world of suffering and rebirth) and nirvana (freedom from rebirth) are erased. The visual representation of such non-dual space is mandala, "a kind of cosmic ground plan or map [which] lays out a sacred territory or realm in microcosm, showing the relations among various powers active in that realm, [...] a sacred precinct where enlightenment takes place" (Grotenhuis 1998, 2). Just as space is depicted by a mandala, from the same point of view of nondualism entire geographical locations can be observed as projection of a mandala, and how this projection occurs is frequently mapped out through the established routes of ascetic pilgrimage (Grapard 1982, 207–14). Within this space, furthermore, thanks to doctrines such as *hongaku* (original enlightenment)[3] and *sōmoku-jōbutsu* (enlightenment of trees and plants),[4] a possibility was opened of enlightenment for natural elements, and even enlightenment of inanimate objects, all of which had implications for enlightenment of sentient beings who occupy those spaces, as well as those who visit them. This way, ordinary natural space is transformed into enlightened space.

Within the context of medieval combinatory processes in Japan, Shinto and Buddhist geographical and cosmological spaces intertwined. In the arts and literature this was articulated through manipulation of spatial metaphors. Performance arts with their own set of concerns regarding space added a unique dimension to how religious and sacred space could be explored, as the space conceived by the text is superimposed onto the space of the performance – the stage. In the case of Noh, due to its peculiar aesthetics the mostly barren stage becomes a playground for the mind that

---

3   The Tendai school of Buddhism in Japan developed the *hongaku* 本覚 (original enlightenment) doctrine drawing on the Mahayanist *śūnyatā* doctrine (emptiness of all phenomena) and particularly its interpretation of the all phenomena as nondual. For an extensive discussion on the doctrine of original enlightenment, see Stone 2003.

4   The *sōmoku-jōbutsu* 草木成仏 (enlightenment of trees and plants) doctrine draws on the doctrine of original enlightenment with the implication that non-sentient beings possess the original enlightenment just as sentient beings do, therefore trees and plants (and in some cases even inanimate objects) can be enlightened. For extensive discussion on this doctrine and its implications, see Rambelli 2001.

fills the empty spots, so it is possible to infuse specific meaningful spatial markers with additional symbolism. Space in the dramatic narrative is demarcated through the act of movement, by mapping it out via travel sequences, which often coincide with the aforementioned pilgrimage routes; and through engaging with varied set of boundaries by establishing, breaching, contesting and negotiating them. The Noh stage is a performative space onto which narrative spaces are projected, and the acts of demarcation are acted out. In *Yamamba* and *Nonomiya* spatial markers are formulated to present overlaps of the *shinbutsu* cosmologies. The Buddhist cosmology is inscribed into the Shinto cosmology, that is, the enlightened space is written over the enchanted space (and vice-versa). This space is not predetermined but engaged and produced by actors on the stage and in the text. In both plays the protagonist is identified with the space she inhabits and the overlaps come to be reflected in her own body.

Yamamba

Yamamba 山姥 ("Mountain Crone"), a fourteenth-century Noh play attributed to Zeami,[5] takes as the subject matter a popular creature from folklore. A performer from the capital, Hyakuma Yamamba 百ま山姥, and her retinue get lost in the mountain on the pilgrimage to Zenkōji temple, and encounter a mysterious old

---

5   There is some debate among scholars about the authorship of *Yamamba*. While there is no documentation that clearly determines the author, Royall Tyler, for example, is of the opinion that the play in many ways does not resemble Zeami's hand, and that "the vigor and themes" of *Yamamba* "richly recall Kan'ami," Zeami's father. Dōmoto Masaki, on the other hand, credits Zeami with the play's authorship. Drawing on Kōsai Tsutome and Nishino Haruo, as well as her own discussion on the overall "ideology" of the play, Harada Kaori concludes that *Yamamba* was most likely penned by Zeami, allowing for the possibility that there was a *kusemai* by Kanami it was based on. Whether he actually authored *Yamamba* or not, Zeami had written about it in his treatises, so it clearly was a significant piece to him, and if he did author it, it would be amongst his early pieces. Tyler 1992: 155; Dōmoto 1997: 187; Harada 2009: 113.

woman who turns out to be Yamamba, the she-demon of ancient lore. She asks her accidental guest to perform for her, but gradually takes over the performance herself and dances off into the mountains, "whereabouts, not to be known"[6] (*yukuhe mo shirazu* 行方も知らず) (Sanari 1931, 3184).

Just as its namesake protagonist, the play *Yamamba* is somewhat of an anomaly in the Noh canon as several conventions of the genre are disrupted, one of which has to do with the setting of the play. The setting is unusual, as all of the action takes place *en route*, whereas typically events of Noh plays are firmly associated with places that are very specific destinations. While those may be (and usually are) revealed as liminal locations in various ways, it is not common to find a setting that is so conspicuously in-between, as this random rest-stop on a journey through a mysterious mountain. However, the destination of this journey is hardly insignificant, and while it is true that none of the action takes place there, its influence and its symbolism are prominent. Zenkōji is a significant locale both historically and as a part of the folk tradition, and it is featured in *setsuwa* Buddhist anecdotes, and in *emaki* picture-scrolls throughout the medieval and early modern periods. It was (and still is) run both by Tendai and Pure Land schools, but as a prominent site of worship it was so popular that it practically developed its own base of believers (Abe 1998, 194–6). For *Yamamba*'s pilgrims, Zenkōji, the "Temple of the Good Light" (善光寺), which awaits them at the end of the treacherous passage through the mountain, signifies the enlightenment at the end of the Path.

Throughout the play, physical, natural and geographical space is used metaphorically to convey religious meaning. Hyakuma's journey is most transparently a metaphor for a lifetime of suffering, as much as it is a religious pilgrimage, and she is traversing the symbolic sacred geography as she moves through the physical space. This is depicted through her *michiyki*, the travel sequence,

---

6   All translations in this discussion are mine. For the most recent English translation of *Yamamba*, see Brazell 1999. For the most recent English translation of *Nonomiya*, see Shirane 2007.

in which sacred space is configured through establishing its buddhological confines.

> 梢波立つ汐越の、梢波立つ汐越の、安宅の松の夕煙消えぬ
> 憂き身の、罪を斬る彌陀の劍の礪波山。雲路うながす三越
> 路の國の末なる里問へば、いとど都は遠ざかる境川にも着
> きにけり、境川にも着きにけり (Sanari 1931, 3167–8)
> *Kozuenami tatsu shiokoshi no, kozuenami tatsu shiokoshi no, ataka no matsu no yūkemuri kienu uki mi no, tsumi wo kiru mida no tsurugi no tonamiyama. Kumoji unagasu mikoji no kuni no sue naru sato toeba, itodo miyako ha tōzakaru sakai kawa ni mot suki ni keri, sakai kawa ni mot suki ni keri.*
> Tidal waves as high as treetops, tidal waves as high as treetops of the Ataka pines. As persistent as the evening mists gathering in them are the sins of our own selves adrift in the realm of suffering, cut down by the sword of Amida, whose shape the Tonami peak borrows. Passing along the cloudy road province after province, three in all, we ask for directions in the remote village, far from the capital. We arrive at the Sakai river, we arrive at the Boundary river.

The party makes its way through mists and obstacles of the temptations and sins of the suffering world, province after province, lifetime after lifetime, with the sword of Amida aiding them along the Path, and the Good Light of the Buddhist enlightenment as their destination. Their journey is about to make a significant detour, as they cross the Boundary river, a boundary in both literal and metaphorical sense. Here they enter the mountains, the realm of Yamamba. By this point, Yamamba's abode has been established by all the aforementioned major markers of a Shinto space: a supernatural mountain, a body of water, and the proximity of the Buddhist temple. The Buddhist space of the Path is inscribed within Shinto sacred space, and proceeding up the mountain, Hyakuma and her retinue enter the ancient spiritual world, transgressing into a space of a different kind. Simultaneously, they are encroaching on a sacred territory belonging to *kami*, and following Amida Buddha's path. And it is Amida's path that takes them into the heart of the realm of Yamamba, hinting at special association or even conflation between Yamamba and Amida Buddha. This is perfectly consistent with the philosophy of nondualism that permeates the play, and is a basis for a complex and multilayered network of overlaps and identifications, following the logic of *shinbutsu* associations.

The path leads Hyakuma and her retinue through a magnificent landscape saturated with religious and poetic symbolism. Earlier, when they ask for directions, the party is informed that there are different ways to reach their destination; one of the paths is bound to grant them karmic merit, but that path is, unsurprisingly, the most difficult one and fraught with danger, and this is the path that Hyakuma chooses. As a literary strategy, this choice highlights how with moving away from the capital Hyakuma's identity shifts; leaving her carriage behind and continuing on foot, like a pilgrim, she is a step away from the Centre, and moving closer to a liminal space.

As soon as the company moves into the mountain the sun sets suddenly in the middle of the day. This fantastic occurrence immediately establishes the extra-ordinary character of the space, while darkness here also stands for attachment and delusion – the clouds of delusion that prevent enlightenment. It becomes clear that the real reason for going into the mountains is because it is inevitable for the two Yamambas to face each other.

Deep in the woods, the party encounters the real Yamamba, who appears to them in the form of an old woman. She says she is offering them lodging because she wants to hear the famous Hyakuma perform "Yamamba" song and dance, and this is "why [she] had the sun set" (*sono tame no koso hi wo kurashi* そのためにこそ日を暮らし) (Sanari 1931, 3172). She has come to satisfy her curiosity, but also to express her resentment. Yamamba, the mountain crone, is known for making rounds across the mountains – her *yamameguri* 山廻り. The dance that Hyakuma performs, and has built her reputation on, is specifically this *yamameguri*. Yamamba irascibly suggests that the dancer is ignorant of the very thing that makes her who she is – the dance that earned her renown and gave her her name. Despite reprimanding her, though, Yamamba continues to insist on seeing Hyakuma's performance. She is drawn to Hyakuma:

although Hyakuma has chosen to venture into Yamamba's abode, Yamamba has lured the woman in for her own purpose – she needs Hyakuma's help.

Yamamba thus frames the dance – what would conventionally be seen as entertainment – as a religious ritual and Hyakuma is the ritualist who performs it. Yamamba pleads: "Please, sing your song and thus dispel my illusory attachments" (*waga mōshū wo harashi tamae* わが妄執を晴らし給へ) (Sanari 1931, 3172). At a first glance it seems clear that she is asking for Buddhist service, which is visually additionally fortified by describing the site of the ritual as illuminated by the moonlight – a common reference to Buddhist enlightenment. At the same time, given the nature of Hyakuma's profession, the nature of Yamamba as a mountain-dwelling supernatural creature and her association with the *kami*-worshipping folk tradition, and the fact that the moonlit space is symbolically established as a Shinto site, Hyakuma's service can be interpreted as a ritual of *kami* placation. This way, Shinto and Buddhist ritual overlap under the aegis of nondualism.

However, this familiar Noh plot point, where the wandering Hyakuma is asked to pacify the demoness Yamamba and aid her in achieving enlightenment, conceals a twist. Not daring to refuse Yamamba's request, Hyakuma begins her performance with a song:

> 松風ともにふく笛の、松風ともにふく笛、聲澄み渡る谷川に手まづ遮る曲水の月に聲澄む深山かな、月に聲澄む深山かな (Sanari 1931, 3176)
> *Matsukaze to mo ni fuku fue, matsukaze to mo ni fuku fue, koe sumi wataru tanigawa ni te mazu saegiru kyokusui no tsuki ni koe sumu miyama kana*
> The purest sound of the flute joined by wind in the pines, the purest sound of the flute joined by wind in the pines echoes through the valley; the poets' hands interrupt the river's meandering stream with their cups. Oh, the crystal clear voices deep in the moonlit mountain! Oh, the crystal clear voices deep in the moonlit mountain…

Yamamba approaches along the stage bridgeway and interrupts Hyakuma:

> あら物凄の深谷やな、あら物凄の深谷やな寒林に骨を打つ、靈鬼泣く泣く前生の業を恨む。深野に供ずる天人返す返すも幾生の善を喜ぶ。(Sanari 1931, 3177)
>
> *Ara monosugo no shinkoku ya na, ara monosugo no shinkoku ya na, kanrin ni hone wo utsu, reiki nakunaku zenjō wo uramu. Shinya ni hana wo kuzuru tennin kaesugaesu mo kisho no zen wo yorokobu.*
>
> Ah, how amazing these deep valleys, how amazing these deep valleys! In cold and dark graveyards, the furious restless spirits beat on their bones, crying in regret over the misdeeds of their former lives. On peaceful gravesites, the celestial spirits return ever again to bring offerings to their tombs, rejoicing in the good acts of their many lifetimes.

Hyakuma's invocation of the poetic pastoral scene, celebrating this-worldly beauties of the scenery and human relations, recalling the sensory enjoyment of nature, poetry, companionship and mundane excursions is countered and contrasted by Yamamba's harsh reminder of this-worldly life's impermanence and the consequences of human actions. Yamamba seems to once again rebuke Hyakuma on her lack of understanding of these existential truths. However, she then moves on to categorically counter her own statement:

> いや。善悪不二。何をか恨む。何を喜ばんや。(Sanari 1931, 3177)
>
> *Iya. Zenaku funi. Nani wo ka uramu. Nani wo ka yorokobanya.*
>
> No! Good and evil are not two! What is there to regret? What to rejoice in?

This line opens Yamamba's counter-performance and draws the main idea of the play into focus. It is clear that nondualist presuppositions infuse the *Yamamba* narrative. Numerous statements of identifications point to this, culminating in the adage "good and evil are not two" (*zenaku funi* 善悪不二).

The Noh *Yamamba* is regarded as a literary work that is an example *par excellence* of medieval Japanese religiosity (Abe 1998, 192; Harada 2009, 115). Abe Yasurō (1998, 192–6) identifies *Yamamba* as an expression of principles of the Buddhist doctrines of emptiness, nondualism and original enlightenment, while Harada Kaori (2009, 115), acknowledging the significance of nondualism, privileges emphasis on Zen aesthetics and attitudes towards language. Both scholars concur that along with the Buddhist philosophy, we also find strong representation of *kami* worship, female performers as ritualists, and the *shinbutsu* paradigm in *Yamamba* (Abe 1998, 192–6; Harada 2009, 115). Abe suspects that Hyakuma is a *miko* from the imperial shrine or a *nenbutsu* dancer who became a *shirabyōshi*: in other words, a performing woman with a ritual association (1998, 190). Female performers frequently and significantly performed various types of ritual functions, while an image of a performing woman vested with a ritual authority or religious power was a popular literary construct. Wakita Haruko (2001, 13, 31) agrees with Harada that a significant part of the overall religious framework of the play is developed under the influence of Zen philosophy, adding that the *shinbutsu* paradigm is nestled within this framework, along with the influence of the philosophy of nondualism, strongly connected to the Tendai's concept of original enlightenment. There is clearly an overall consensus amongst scholars as to which religious orientations and concepts are present in *Yamamba*, and the discrepancies are mainly in the specific emphasis. Through incorporating a panoply of ideas and concepts related to both Buddhist and non-Buddhist orientations, *Yamamba* reflects the richness of the Japanese medieval religiosity. Noh as a genre made this possible, as it embraced disparate discourses to be harmonized as a part of a shared structure.

Nonomiya

Authorship of *Nonomiya* 野々宮 ("Shrine in the Field") has long been a subject of speculation, but is nowadays mostly attributed to Zenchiku (Atkins 2006). Source material for the play is the complicated love story from the eleventh-century novel *Genji monogatari* ("The Tale of Genji"), between the protagonist, Prince Genji, and the late crown prince's widow, the proud aristocratic Lady Rokujō. The first act recalls the *Sakaki* chapter, in which Genji visits Lady Rokujō after she has, in an unprecedented move, followed her daughter, the incumbent Ise priestess, to the Nonomiya shrine where she needs to purify and prepare herself for her lofty appointment. The opening scene of the play takes place centuries later, when an itinerant monk (the *waki*,[7] counterpart/deuteragonist of the play), finds himself at the seemingly abandoned Nonomiya shrine on the outskirts of the capital. There he encounters a young maiden who is eventually revealed to be the spirit of Lady Rokujō, hopelessly bound to keep returning to Nonomiya, the place of her last encounter with Prince Genji. While the tone of the first act is one of nostalgic melancholy, in the second act where Rokujō returns in her ghostly form, her attachment is one of anger and resentment as she recalls the humiliating episode of the carriage fight with Genji's principal wife Aoi no Ue. The play culminates in the striking image of a straw carriage carrying Rokujō, going back and forth through the shrine's *torii* gate.

In a more conventional Noh fashion, the plot of *Nonomiya* is firmly set in the play's eponymous shrine. Similarly to *Yamamba*, the play features a *shite* who is intrinsically connected with the space she occupies and, it seems, organically united with it. While, unlike *Yamamba*, couched in the august literary tradition, *Nonomiya* still presents an almost mythical setting, thanks to, as Paul Atkins (2006, 197) points out, its status as "pure fiction" being a "Genji" play. This status stems from both the source material's fictionality, as well as the way it had been disseminated throughout the Muromachi Period (1336–1573) and found its way onto the Noh stage. Namely, rather than being read directly, shared knowledge about the events of *Genji monogatari* was created through a series of "handbooks," poetic commentaries and digests, and it was this knowledge that "Genji" plays were based on (Goff 2014). This manner of dissemination created a certain lore around *Genji* and gave the quality of an oral tradition to its retelling, infusing it with

---

7   The *shite*'s interlocutor and foil. Frequently the *waki* is a religious figure who is asked to perform religious service to appease the restless spirit of the *shite*.

a mythical aura that made layering of actual mythical narratives onto the main threads in dramatizations of *Genji* quite appropriate.

The play opens to the *waki* introducing himself as a travelling Buddhist monk, stating his desire to visit Sagano having spent some time in the capital. His monologue invokes motifs of impermanence and transience, as he is visiting relics of the past in an autumn excursion. This imagery is then contrasted with the outlook of the shrine:

> 我この森に来て見れば。黒木の鳥居小柴垣。昔に変はらぬ有様なり。こはそも何と云ひたる事やらん。(Sanari 1931, 2407–8)
>
> *Ware kono mori ni kitemireba, kurogi no torii koshibagaki, mukashi ni kawaranu arisama nari, kowa somo nani to iitaru koto yaran.*
>
> As I enter the wood I see an unbarked-wooden *torii* and a brushwood fence; everything is unchanged since olden times – how can this be, I wonder.

While Nonomiya is an actual place, the appearance of the locale suggests that the grounds of the shrine are not quite an ordinary space. The shrine seems abandoned, but in curiously good condition, and the *waki* wonders why time has spared it, which suggests to the audience that this particular place is somehow extraordinary, and the "reality" of it is questionable. As the *waki* enters he passes double boundary markers. The shrine enclosure is hidden within a wooded area, and is at the same time accessible (through the *torii*) and confined (by the wood and the fence). The implied spatial liminality is supplemented by temporal liminality, as the visitor arrives at this destination in the "evening as clear as can be" (*kokoro mo sumeru yūbe* 心も澄める夕べ) (Sanari 1931, 2408), the time of transition from the day to night. Through these rhetorical moves, it is established that the *waki* has entered an "other," enchanted space.

Wishing to dispel any potential doubt that, as a Buddhist monk, he may be out of place in these surroundings, he notes that the Great Shrine at Ise (and, by association, Nonomiya) excludes no one, thus immediately placing the events of the play within the *shinbutsu* framework:

> 伊勢の神垣隔てなく。法の教への道直ぐに。ここに尋ねて宮所。(Sanari 1931, 2408)
> *Ise no kamigaki hedate naku, nori no oshie no michi sugu ni, koko ni tazunete miyadokoro.*
> The sacred fence of Ise Shrine makes no distinctions; it is the Path of the Buddhist teaching straight and true, that leads me to this shrine.

The Ise shrine makes no distinctions between the Gods and the Buddhas, and this time it is the Shrine of the Sun Goddess and *her* "good light" that lies at the end of the path.

Enter the *shite*, lamenting how autumn has come to the shrine where she "has grown used to flowers" (*hana ni nare koshi* 花に馴れ来し) (Sanari 1931, 2408). Her monologue draws parallels between the flowers bound to die in autumn and her own heart, as her love with Genji blossomed and withered like autumn flowers. Her sleeves "wither in a dew of tears" (*nao shiori yuku sode no tsuyu* 猶しをり行く袖の) (Sanari 1931, 2408) and her heart changes colour with the autumn that echoes her betrayed love. All these references again invoke impermanence, but now also highlight strong connection between the young maiden and her environs. A number of studies have been dedicated to exploring how descriptions of the shrine and its setting resonate with the *shite*'s personhood. Suzuki Sayaka (2014, 4–7) analyses motif of the "wood" (*mori* 森) in the two acts of the play, and suggests that its transforming appearance is a metaphor for the *shite*'s state of mind, as it reflects the shift in how she remembers her lost love with Genji. In addition to these connections, Atkins (2006, 219–30) argues that the shrine and its surroundings with its lush vegetation, in the course of the play, become identified with the female *shite* in a very physical way. It is clear that this *shite* is strongly identified with the space she occupies both spiritually and physically.

One of the central images in the first act is the *sakaki* branch, which functions as a multilayered signifier. It is the motif that links the play to the novel, as it evokes Rokujōs's emotional and erotic attachment to Genji. Originally a ritual symbol of purification, in the novel the branch carries on a connotation of love and erotic connection, and even assumes phallic symbolism in the manner it is given to Rokujō by Genji (Bargen 1997, 97). However, in the play the latter connotation becomes secondary, as the *sakaki* branch is reappropriated for its original, ritual use. The *shite* appears on the stage with the *sakaki* branch in her hand, explaining that she comes to the shrine every year, unbeknownst to anyone, to perform ritual services (*gojinji wo nasu* 御神事を為す) (Sanari 1931, 2409). Furthermore, the branch is, at this point, basically an extension of her body and thus becomes metonymically related to her. The branch in the *shite*'s hand designates her as a Shinto ritualist, but also the object of ritual as she gets identified with her ritual implement, and as the *sakaki* tree casts its shade over the scenery the entire landscape is subsumed in *sakaki* imagery:

昔に変はらぬ色ぞとは。榊のみこそ常盤の陰の。森の下道秋暮れて。紅葉かつ散り。(Sanari 1931, 2410–11)
Mukashi ni kawaranu iro zo to wa, sakaki nomi koso tokiwa no kage no, mori no shita michi aki kurete, momiji katsu chiri.
As the autumn grows deeper along the path through the wood covered by the evergreen shade of the *sakaki* tree, it is only the *sakaki* that retains its colour, unchanged since olden times, while the crimson maple leaves wither and fall.

In her monologue the girl attributes to the *sakaki* branch a quality that posits it counter to the Buddhist understanding of the world; the marker and symbol of Shinto endures in the face of impermanence.

While it is typical in Noh for the *shite* to hide an identity beneath the one initially presented, in the dreamscape that is the scenery surrounding Nonomiya shrine and the *shinbutsu* religious framing, the encounter between the monk and the maiden presents multiple possibilities as to which identities are embodied by each character. The beginning of their conversation evokes the exchange between Lady Rokujō and Genji – she chastises and rebukes him and then turns him away: "your presence here is unwanted; please leave right away!" (*onkoto naru ga, kitari tamō wa habakari ari* 御事るが来り給ふは憚りあり。とくとく帰り給へとよ)   (Sanari

1931, 3177). This encounter with the *waki* is replicating Genji's ill-conceived visit, where he is rebuffed by Lady Rokujō, and in both cases the men symbolically violate sacred boundaries. These circumstances of the encounters and the rebukes that follow also recall the notable mythical encounter that resulted in breeching and re-establishing boundaries between the world of the living and the underworld: Izanagi's journey to bring Izanami back from the land of the dead.[8]

Discussing mythical episodes depicting this and other such encounters, Grapard (1991, 21) defines early Japanese cosmography as "spatial projection of experiences of violence and transgression." According to this view, Shinto cosmology is established through a series of instances where female seclusion and ocular taboos are violated. This establishes the separation between cosmological units and maps out the boundaries of the universe humans occupy. These boundaries, however, remained porous and permeable, leaving the possibility for them to be challenged. Genji does that when he ignores Rokujō's status at Nonomiya shrine requiring her to remain purified, and the *waki* does it, all *shinbutsu* proclamations notwithstanding, through his intrusion into the enchanted Shinto realm that by all accounts did its best to remain hidden. However, these acts of transgression in both cases carry kernels of appeasement and reconciliation. While Genji certainly was driven by his desire for his wronged lover, that was not his only motivation to visit Nonomiya. In the novel, Rokujō's seclusion followed

---

8 In the mythology section of the eighth-century mythohistory *Kojiki* ("Records of Ancient Matters"), the brother/sister divine couple Izanagi and Izanami create the Japanese isles and birth numerous deities. Upon birthing the Fire God, Izanami is burnt and has to go to the land of the dead, Yomi no Kuni. Griefstricken Izanagi follows her to the underworld with intention to retrieve her. She cannot accompany him back, as she has already been defiled by eating the food made there. Eventually she relents, under the proviso that Izanagi does not look at her as they leave the land of the dead. He is unable to restrain himself, and turns to look at her, only to see a rotting corpse. Frightened, he starts running away, as Izanami gives chase, until he finally escapes successfully, sealing the entrance to the land of the dead. For the most recent English translation see Borgen and Ury 1990.

two instances of deaths caused by her jealousy materializing and possessing one of Genji's early lovers, Yūgao, and his wife Aoi no Ue. Genji's visit to Nonomiya, in part, was an attempt to get into Rokujō's good graces and thus avoid any potential future possessions (Bargen 1997, 96). That way, Genji's visit symbolically functions as a rite of pacification. In the play, the spirit keeps coming back, and it is now incumbent upon the *waki*, the Buddhist monk, to complete this task. The first act ends in the image of the *torii* illuminated by the moonlight – a perfect visual *shinbutsu* symbol.

The latter part of the play is contrasted to the first half in tone and motifs that are emphasized. Still relying on the *Genji monogatari* as the source material, the *shite* re-enacts the "carriage fight," the infamous incident between Lady Rokujō and Genji's principal wife, Aoi no Ue, in which the former is humiliated. The juxtaposition of the two storylines, the *Sakaki* chapter (depicting Genji's visit), and the *Aoi* chapter (depicting the carriage fight and Aoi's subsequent fatal possession) provides for a dramatic shift in the backdrop for the second act, as it delves back into the depth of Rokujō's attachment, and brings into clearer focus Buddhist motifs and imagery.

The second act sees the *shite* return, now in her true form as Rokujō's ghost, as she recalls and re-enacts the carriage fight. In the way the *sakaki* branch is identified with the shite in the first act, now a different symbol, the carriage, assumes this connotation.[9] The way Rokujō talks about the two carriages is likened to their occupants:

物見車の様々に殊に時めく葵の上の、御車とて　[...]　身は小車のやる方も、なし (Sanari 1931, 2417)
Monomi guruma no samazama ni, koto ni tokimeku Aoinoue no, onkuruma tote [...] mi wa oguruma no yaru kata mo nashi to.

---

9 Kuramochi Nagako (2017: 71) notes that in the early days of performance it is likely that an actual carriage prop would appear on the stage, but this practice was phased out over time, and the brushwood fence with the *torii* came to signify both its primary meaning as well as that of the carriage as the *shite* moves through the *torii* on the stage.

> Amongst many different viewing carriages, Aoi no Ue's was particularly splendorous […] I had no choice in my own small carriage.

Rokujō's carriage is lovely but unassuming and fragile, the feelings Rokujō struggles with, as she herself is neither of those things but is relegated to them. The other carriage is splendorous and magnificent, as is becoming for a high-ranking princess and the principal wife.

However, just as the *sakaki* branch is a metonymy for the Shinto space meticulously constructed in the first act, this function is here transferred to the imagery of the carriages. This becomes clearer with the final proclamation of Rokujō (given this time by the chorus), where she invokes the Parable of the Burning House from the *Lotus Sūtra*:

> ここはもとより忝なくも。神風や。伊勢の内外の鳥居に出で入る姿は生死の道を。神は受けずや思ふらんと。又車にうち乗りて家宅の門をや。出でぬらん家宅の門。(Sanari 1931, 2419)
>
> *Koko wa moto yori katajikenaku mo kamikaze ya, Ise no uchi to no torii ni ide iru, sugata wa shōji no michi wo kami wa ukezu ya omōran to, mata kuruma ni uchi norite, kataku no kado wo ya ide ni nu ran, kataku no kado.*
>
> Here, gratitude has always been offered to the divine winds; I step back and forth through the *torii* of the Inner and Outer Shrines, just as I do on the path of lives and deaths, all the while thinking that the *kami* will probably not receive me. I climb into the carriage again, I will probably not pass through the gate of the Burning House, the gate of the Burning House.

The appearance of carriages transforms the entire religious framework and the nature of the space, as they transpose the entire space into the Buddhist realm of the Burning House of suffering and the vehicles of the Buddhist teaching leading to Enlightenment. In the Parable of the Burning House invoked in the play, Father, who represents the Buddha, uses expedient means to get his children to leave the house that is on fire. He does this by promising the children three kinds of carriages, all representing the "lesser" vehicle, but eventually gifts his children one big, resplendent and luxurious carriage of the Mahayana – the Great Vehicle of Buddhism.[10] By re-enacting the carriage fight from the *Genji monogatari* and placing this re-enactment in the framework of the *Lotus Sūtra*, the small carriage of Rokujō and the luxurious carriage of Aoi assume additional meanings. Furthermore, the whole scene still takes place enclosed within the brushwood fence with the unbarked-wooden *torii*. Once again, as we saw earlier in *Yamamba*, the Buddhist cosmology is inscribed into Shinto cosmology. In the way the Nonomiya's surroundings are described in the two acts of the play, the imagery and symbolism are juxtaposed, contrasted and conflated. The enchanted Shinto space that defies impermanence, from the first act, becomes the stage on which the Buddhist drama of suffering and enlightenment is enacted, not just for the *shite*, but for all sentient beings, and, of course, the audience. The *torii* gate becomes the gate of death and life, the transitional point in samsara – the cycle of rebirth.

While the play takes place entirely on the Nonomiya shrine grounds, throughout the text, Shinto and Buddhist imagery intertwine to create a discursive and performative space in which all constituents of this space (the shrine constructions, natural elements, and even protagonists themselves) are shifting signifiers interchangeably occupied by Buddhist and Shinto identities. Ritual activities and their outcomes taking place are also shifting, as the play ends in an ambiguous open-ended denouement.

Concluding discussion

Writing about esotericism in the works of Zenchiku, Susan Blakeley Klein (2006, 229) noted that "A grounding assumption of the medieval episteme was that the linguistic/symbolic relation of signifier and signified is not arbitrary, as we believe today, but motivated (ultimately non-dual)" adding that "…for all of these

---

10 For a complete English translation of the *Lotus Sūtra*, see Burton Watson 1993.

texts, both religious and artistic, the notion of the ultimate non-duality of signifier and signified transformed the material world into a virtually unlimited field of semiotic play." The close readings of plays *Yamamba* and *Nonomiya* demonstrate how Noh used the poetic and geographical references to situate the protagonists within a specific religio-ritual framework – namely *shinbutsu* framework – and how from there the protagonists could move to prompt the interaction between the mutually superimposed cosmological signifiers. Locked in this framework, the protagonists, themselves signifiers, interact with their environment in a number of ways (stasis and movement, action and inaction, questioning and reiterating, denying and confirming) that would not necessarily be amenable (at least in a straightforward way) to a mainstream ritual. The space is configured in the two plays in such a way that it establishes an organic and systematic relationship between the physical/geographical space, and things that populate/inhabit it – constructions, natural elements or beings. In a way, they all grow out of one another, and through a system or network of identifications become interchangeable. The central figure in this process is the *shite*, who is presented as a metonymical extension of the place she occupies. At the same time, the space itself becomes embodied in the *shite*, thus personified, and such a *shite* is herself a religious ritualist – and (with the help of the *waki*) is performing a rite for the audience. Thanks to the nature of Noh as a uniquely multi-faceted performative structure, these moves all become productive ways of association with the religious codes.

Noh takes various religious symbols and reconstitutes them in new, constructive ways. In other words, we can look at Noh as a way to organize symbols belonging to disparate traditions and make them work together more or less cohesively. Noh is not just a reflection of religion but an arena in which religious traditions can interact, through their respective symbolic languages. In Noh, various religious elements are being harmonized by enacting the tensions and conflicts that underlie their relationship. What is particularly interesting about Noh is that it uses spatial codes to bring about this dialogue between disparate traditions. I believe that by enacting this ambiguity, the ritual of Noh both resolved and reinforced the tensions that characterized medieval Japanese worldviews and the relationships between religious traditions.

References

Abe, Y. 1998. *Yuya no kōgō: chūsei no sei to seinaru mono*. Nagoya-shi (Nagoya Daigaku Shuppankai).
Atkins, P. S. 2006. *Revealed Identity: The Noh Plays of Komparu Zenchiku*. Michigan monograph series in Japanese studies. Ann Arbor (Center for Japanese Studies, University of Michigan).
Baba, M. 2007. "Yamanba kō." *Nihon kayō kenkyū* 47, 35–47. https://doi.org/10.1080/03060497.2007.11083968
Bargen, D. G. 1997. *A Woman's Weapon: Spirit Possession in the Tale of Genji*. Honolulu (University of Hawaii Press).
Bethe, M. 1976. "Nonomiya." *Kobe College Studies* 22, 237–73. https://doi.org/10.1080/09670877609412377
Brazell, K. (ed.) 1999. *Traditional Japanese Theater*, revised edition. New York (Columbia University Press).
Borgen, R. and Ury, M. 1990. "Readable Japanese Mythology: Selections from *Nihon shoki* and *Kojiki*." *The Journal of the Association of Teachers of Japanese* 24/1, 61–97. https://doi.org/10.2307/489230
Dōmoto, M. 1997. *Zeami no nō*. Tokyo (Shinchōsha).
Faure, B. 2000. *Visions of Power: Imagining Medieval Japanese Buddhism*, second edition. Princeton, NJ (Princeton University Press).
Goff, J. E. 2014. *Noh Drama and "The Tale of the Genji": The Art of Allusion in Fifteen Classical Plays*. Princeton, NJ (Princeton University Press).
Grapard, A. G. 1982. "Flying Mountains and Walkers of Emptiness: Toward a Definition of Sacred Space in Japanese Religions." *History of Religions* 21, 195–221. https://doi.org/10.1086/462897
Grapard, A. G. 1991. "Visions of Excess and Excesses of Vision: Women and Transgression in Japanese Myth." *Japanese Journal of Religious Studies* 18, 3–23. https://doi.org/10.18874/jjrs.18.1.1991.3-22
Grapard, A. G. 1993. *The Protocol of the Gods: A Study of the Kasuga Cult in Japanese History*. Berkeley (University of California Press).
Grotenhuis, E. 1998. *Japanese Mandalas: Representations of Sacred Geography*, first edition. Honolulu (University of Hawaii Press).
Harada, K. 2009. "Yoshiashibiki no yamauba – sakuhin kenkyū yamanba." *Bungaku ronsō* 83, 112–30.
Harada, K. 2010. "Jisei henka – yōkyoku yamanba nochiba no shisō." *Bungaku ronsō* 84, 82–100.
Kitahara, K. 2018. "Aoi sasaki maki no hikaru genji to rokujo miyasudokoro: Nonomiya ni okeru futakumi no zoto uta wo chushin ni." *Tokyo daigaku kokubungaku ronshu*, 1–17.

Klein, S. B. 2006. "Esotericism in Noh Commentaries and Plays: Konparu Zenchiku's *Meishuku shū* and *Kakitsubata*" in: B. Scheid and M. Teeuwen (eds.), *The Culture of Secrecy in Japanese Religion*, first edition. New York (Routledge).

Kuramochi, N. 2017. "Nonomiya no kuruma to tsuki: Meisei daigaku kenkyu kiyo." *Jinbungakubu Nihon bungaku gakka*, 69–79.

Rambelli, F. 2001. *Vegetal Buddhas: Ideological Effects of Japanese Buddhist Doctrines on the Salvation Of Inanimate Beings*. Kyoto (Cheng & Tsui).

Rambelli, F. and Teeuwen, M. (eds.) 2006. *Buddhas and Kami in Japan: Honji Suijaku as a Combinatory Paradigm*. New York (Routledge).

Sanari, K. 1931. *Yōkyoku taikan: A Comprehensive Study of Nō Texts*. Tokyo (Meiji Shoin).

Sharma, A. 1994. *Religion and Women*, McGill Studies in the History of Religions. Albany (SUNY Press).

Shirane, H. 2007. *Traditional Japanese Literature: An Anthology, Beginnings to 1600*. New York (Columbia University Press).

Stone, J. I. 2003. *Original Enlightenment and the Transformation of Medieval Japanese Buddhism*. Honolulu (University of Hawaii Press).

Suzuki, S. 2014. "Nonomiya ko: mori to kokoro to no henyo, yomigaeri wo megutte." *Kokusai kankei hikaku bunka kenkyu* 12/2, 1–23.

Tyler, R. 1992. *Granny Mountains: A Cycle of Nō Plays*. Cornell East Asia Series 18. Ithaca: Cornell University Press.

Wakita, H. 2001. *Josei Geinō No Genryū: Kugutsu Kusemai Shirabyōshi*. Shohan. Kadokawa Sensho 326. Tokyo (Kadokawa Shoten).

Wakita, H. 2005. *Nōgaku no naka no onnatachi: onnamai no fūshi*. Tokyo (Iwanami Shoten).

Watson, B. 1993. *The Lotus Sutra*. New York (Columbia University Press).

About the author

Dunja Jelesijevic is Assistant Professor of Comparative Study of Religions and Asian Studies at Northern Arizona University. She holds a PhD in Japanese religion from the University of Illinois at Urbana-Champaign. She studied at Nagoya University as a Japan Foundation Fellow. Her research interests include premodern Japanese religion, literature and performance arts, with a specific focus on religious aspects of Noh theatre. Her broader interests include East Asian Buddhism and East Asian folk religions, as well as Chinese religion, philosophy and literature. Dr Jelesijevic has written and presented on the topics of religion and ritual in a number of Noh plays.

9

Buddhist-style pilgrimage with Shinto meanings

Michael Pye

Introduction

As is well known, the idea of circulatory pilgrimage to multiple sites (*o-meguri* お巡り) was first developed in Japan in the context of devotion to the Bodhisattva Kannon at thirty-three widespread sites in western Japan and with the equally famous route around the island of Shikoku including eighty-eight sites. While researching the contemporary state of these and numerous related pilgrimages, I learned not only that the procedure of *o-meguri* was quite widespread in the world of Shinto, but also that this apparently imitative extension was not such a recent development as first appeared. Consequently, in my book *Japanese Buddhist Pilgrimage* (2015), I decided to include a lengthy chapter entitled "Going Round to Other Divinities," illustrating there how the idea of *o-meguri* came to be transferred from Buddhism to the context of Shinto.[1] This process evidently happened at least in part due to the popularity of the circuits for visiting the much-loved Seven Gods of Good Fortune (the Shichifukujin 七福神), short circuits which include Buddhist and vaguely Shinto-related divinities in combination.

But for Shinto shrines the idea did not stop there. There are various groups of shrines which invite people to visit them in sequence. For example, in Tokyo: Hassha fukumairi 八社福参り; in Kyoto: Jūrokusha shuin meguri 十六社朱印めぐり and Kyōraku hassha

---

1 Pye 2015, 141–80 (Chapter Five). The topic was earlier treated in a booklet which appeared in 2004. A basic version of the present paper was given at a symposium of the International Shinto Studies Association in 2017. Previous titles such as: "Single and Multiple Pilgrimage in Shintō" or "Imitating Buddhism but Being Shintō" or "Multiple-goal and Single-goal Pilgrimages" simply refer to the same work in progress.

京洛八社; and in Tochigi Prefecture: Shimotsuke Hassha Mairi 下野八社参り.[2] Apart from these typical examples, there are others with patriotic themes such as the Tokyo Ten Shrines Pilgrimage (Tokyo Jussha Mairi 十社めぐり), founded in 1975 to commemorate the fiftieth anniversary of the commencement of the reign of Emperor Hirohito. Moreover, it transpires that in prewar times it had been common to collect the commemorative calligraphy and seal (*shuin* 朱印)[3] of important shrines such as those listed as *kanpeisha* 官幣社, including some of national and some of regional importance. Another focus of attention was provided by the numerous mausolea of the Japanese emperors.

These commemorative *shuin* were assembled on a hanging scroll (*kakejiku*) or in a folding notebook (*shuinchō*), just as in the case of Buddhist circulatory pilgrimages (*reijō meguri*). However, while the original meaning of this documentation in Buddhism was as a receipt for a merit-making donation of money, theoretically to sponsor the copying of a Buddhist sutra, this was no longer relevant for the Shinto practice, for which there is no corresponding concept of merit. From this simple example we can see that the "meaning" of pilgrimage in Buddhism and the "meaning" of pilgrimage in Shinto is not necessarily the same. When we study religions it is up to us to explore these divergent meanings. While recognizing the strength of sheer rites, often unexplained by those who perform them, I do not share the view that rites are altogether without meanings. Indeed, it is desirable when studying rites, to find out what meanings, with varying degrees of explicitness, they may bear.

In what follows, two further, rather prominent examples of Shinto-related circulatory pilgrimage (*o-meguri*) will be considered with a view to reflecting further on the precise characteristics

---

2   For these and the following cases see Pye 2004, 159–80. Shimotsuke (or Shimozuke) is an ancient province name, its use here suggesting antiquity.

3   Distinguish between *shuin* 朱印, referring to the cinnabar colour of the imprinted seal, and *shūin* 集印, meaning the assembling of seals (sometimes confused during a typesetting process). The latter is more frequent in Buddhist contexts.

of pilgrimage in the context of Shinto. The first case is that of twenty-five places connected with Sugawara Michizane, starting and ending in Kyōto. The second case is that of the 125 shrines of Ise. The important shrine of Ise is of course well known for its traditional *o-Ise-mairi*,[4] but what has *o-meguri* got to do with it? We will see below. There are two underlying questions to keep in mind. The first thing to ask ourselves is, how does such a conception of pilgrimage in Shinto fit in with wider theory of pilgrimage in religion? And the second question is, how should we understand the "meaning" of pilgrimage in Shinto, given that it is not the same as the meaning of pilgrimage in Buddhism?[5]

A general definition of pilgrimage has been formulated as follows: *Pilgrimage is the deliberate traversing of a route to a sacred place which lies outside one's normal habitat.*[6] This definition sounds simple, but it is meaningful. On this definition, pilgrimage does not just mean visiting a holy place such as a local shrine or a church in the vicinity, there and back. In Japanese that would be *o-mairi*. In the case of *a pilgrimage*, the pilgrim goes away from the normal home area, to another place or places. This means that the nature of pilgrimage is determined as much by the *way* as by the goal.

On the basis of this definition, we then come to an important distinction within the concept of "pilgrimage" as found in Japan. If the pilgrims are "going round" a number of places, for example thirty-three sites where Kannon-sama is revered, this is a circulatory pilgrimage (*o-meguri*) and there is no one single goal of greatest importance. The goal is the completion of the way; so the way *is* the goal. But if pilgrims are travelling to one place of paramount importance such as the Buddhist temple Zenkōji, the Grand

---

4 Cf. Nishigaki 1983; Teeuwen and Breen 2017.

5 For the first of these questions see a longer discussion in Pye 2015, Chapter One (Introduction) and for the second see especially Chapter Seven ("The Meaning of Japanese Buddhist Pilgrimage").

6 Pye 2015, 16. This and the related general observations about the nature of pilgrimage go back to a dictionary entry by the present writer for the *Macmillan Dictionary of Religion* (London 1993).

Shrine of Izumo, or the Jiba at Tenri, just to name three important Japanese examples at random, then that place is indeed the goal. The "way" is still important. But the fact that there is one major destination means that we should think of this as a "single-goal pilgrimage." It might seem that this does not really matter. However it is of great interest in the study of religions because the existence of circulatory pilgrimages, notably in Japan, tells us that in pilgrimage, it is the way which is important, even including the way back, with proofs of completion. There is of course more to the theory of pilgrimage than just that. Yet it is an important point, and one that is relevant to the two examples considered below.

Visiting the god of learning

First then, let us consider the idea of visiting twenty-five places associated with Sugawara Michizane, the god of learning. These places are referred to collectively as *Sugawara kō seiseki nijūgohai* 菅公聖蹟二十五拝, meaning "Twenty-five Sacred Places for Worshipping Prince Sugawara." It is of course possible to visit just one such place to worship him, for example Kitano Tenmangū in Kyoto, or indeed any other local Tenmangū shrine, of which there are thousands across the country. However, since modern times it has been proposed that visitors could aim to visit twenty-five specified places which all have something to do with the great poet and calligrapher. Kitano Tenmangū is the concluding shrine in that list, number twenty-five. Number one is Michizane's place of birth, originally in the aristocratic residential area of the former Kyoto Imperial Palace grounds, and now marked by a shrine called Sugawara-in Tenmangū Jinja just to the west of those grounds. Rather important are the Nagaoka Tenjin Shrine, a place to the southwest of the ancient capital where Michizane stopped on his journey into exile; and of course his place of exile marked by Dazaifu Tenmangū itself, at Dazaifu in Kyushu. Of the twenty-five, five are in Kyoto itself, one is at Nagaokakyō (Kyōto-fu), two are in Nara Prefecture, six are in Ōsaka-fu (one at Fujiidera City, one at Takatsuki City and four in Ōsaka City), five in Hyogo

Prefecture, one in Kagawa Prefecture, two in Hiroshima Prefecture, one in Yamaguchi Prefecture, and two in Fukuoka Prefecture (of which one is at Dazaifu).[7] It would be rather impractical to visit all twenty-five sacred sites in one journey, and it would not matter very much about the sequence. Nevertheless, the places are numbered, and they begin with Michizane's presumed birthplace and end at Kitano Tenmangū. The latter shrine was originally built to assuage his spirit, presumed to have been raging all round Kyoto causing terrible storms because of the injustice he had suffered. The fact that the shrines are numbered as a sequence implies that this arrangement is in principle a *circulatory* pilgrimage. It is not focused only on Dazaifu or only on Kitano in Kyoto. The goal is not just Kitano Tenmangū, number twenty-five, but the completion of the whole sequence.

One can indeed visit Kitano Tenmangū just by itself, and many people do so, in order to pray for advancement in their studies, whether as children, as older students or as academic research staff. It is not at all unusual for a scholar who is otherwise very rational in outlook, and considers himself or herself to be "not religious," to carry an *o-mamori* (amulet) from Kitano Tenmangū on their person. After all, Michizane is described at the Nishiki Tenmangū in Kyoto as the "god of the head," i.e. the "god of brains" (*atama no kami-sama*). However, the point of the circulatory option is that one may decide to try and visit all twenty-five shrines, this being considered more likely to bring about academic prowess, especially if undertaken on behalf of another person.

In other parts of the country there are further examples of twenty-five Tenmangū shrines being grouped in this way. In their names, the alternative expression *nijūgosha junpai* may also be found and this includes the element *jun*, which is also found in the phrase *junrei*. Both *junpai* and *junrei* are common expressions for pilgrimage which include the idea of a sequence or circulation. Thus within Kyoto itself there is a smaller list of shrines to visit, known as

---

7   Full details of these shrines and their addresses, with the numbering, are shown on various Japanese websites such as http://www.tenmangu.com/25hai.htm which means that pilgrimage enthusiasts countrywide can easily find them.

Rakuyō Tenmangū nijūsha junpai. On the other hand a similar list in Tokyo is known simply as *Edo Nijūgo Tenjin*. The reasons for the existence and the location of these shrines are very varied and reflect the tangled history of Japanese religious institutions. The number for these sequences is however always twenty-five, and this is probably because the alternatives are imitative, just as one can have thirty-three sites to visit Kannon-sama in any region of Japan, but there are always thirty-three.[8] This is another indication that the Shinto lists are imitative. For the Tenmangū shrines, if one cannot perform the standard twenty-five, then a more local alternative will do, but for completion it will still be twenty-five.

In spite of the parallel to Buddhist routes, the reason for "going round" is specific. It is not for Buddhist devotions. Pilgrims who cherish special devotion towards Michizane for reasons connected with study, learning or calligraphy, or who wish their children or grandchildren to "do well" at school or university, may decide to visit all of these shrines. Therein lies the "meaning" which is specific to this type of shrine. The usual Shinto symbols such as the *torii* are present, although the Tenmangū buildings have a certain villa-like quality about them, suggesting that they are home to a human *kami* rather than a more ethereal spirit. At Tenmangū shrines, the usual forms of behaviour relating to concepts of purity and transaction with the deities are in evidence, and other this-worldly benefits may also be sought. However, the main point of interest is in the promotion of success in studies. In other Shinto shrines, some other meaning will be uppermost depending on the shrine, for example the ever-popular *en-musubi* (for tying the knot), or again patriotic loyalty.

Local information suggests that this Michizane pilgrimage was initiated by a person named Matsuura Takeshirō 松浦武四郎 (1818–88), an educator who made a point of visiting the twenty-five shrines and leaving a stone monument (*ishibumi*) at each

---

8   See various examples in Pye 2015 (Chapter Two: "Going Round to Visit Kannon-sama").

one.⁹ A divine mirror (*shinkyō*) at Kitano Tenmangū, which he also donated, has a picture of Hokkaido on it, because the Kitano Tenmangū was involved in the opening up of that great northern island which was in full swing at that time. Matsuura is also known for having devised a board game (a version of *sugoroku*) in which the players seek to proceed with a number of stops towards the final position on the board which represents Kitano Tenmangū. His overall intention was evidently in a general sense educational, namely to heighten the sense of motivation towards writing and learning among young people.

In the case of this pilgrimage the precise sequence of visiting is not important, and transport arrangements need to be taken into account. However, the fact that the shrines are numbered shows that they are linked in accordance with the concept of *o-meguri*, and therefore that together they form a single *circulatory* pilgrimage.

Pilgrimage at Ise Jingū

We turn now to the second main case to be considered. At Ise there is a very interesting relationship between *o-mairi* and *o-meguri*, The popularity of *o-Ise-mairi* from Edo times onward is well known, and privately I enjoy looking at a wood-block print which shows pilgrims excitedly crossing the Miyakawa and being showered by happiness – bringing *taima* from the sky. It is only recently however that I have noticed that a journey circulating around a very large number of shrines in the Ise area is suggested in travel brochures. The Kintetsu Railway proposes a package journey from the major centres, Osaka, Kyoto or Nagoya, with a bus and rail pass (*furi-kippu*) to take one all around the Ise-Shima area. I therefore paid a fieldwork visit there in 2014 to look into these matters in detail. I had previous knowledge of the Ise shrines, having

---

9   This has not been corroborated with reference to other historical sources, but there is no reason to believe that it is untrue, or that the origin of the pilgrimage is either older or later. The imitations mentioned above may be presumed to be later unless there is information to the contrary.

visited to collect teaching materials, to visit the Kōgakkan (university), and also for other enquiries including visits in 1973 and 1993, when the *shikinen sengū*[10] was being prepared.

In a recent pamphlet issued by the railway company, while the central focus is on visiting the Naikū and the Gekū, four *bekkan* are also listed with photographs: Tsukiyomi no miya, about half way between Gekū and Naikū, another Tsukiyomi no miya (written differently) at Gekū, Izawa no miya which is at Isobe machi in Shima-shi, and Yamato hime no miya which is reached from Ujiyamada Station. The very beautiful Izawa no miya is located in quiet woodland, and is associated with nearby rice paddies for the ritual planting and harvesting of rice (*gotaueshiki* on June 26 each year). The pamphlet also lists seven shrines at which it is possible to obtain a commemorative *shuin*. These include the two main shrines, the four *bekkan* just mentioned and also Takihara no miya, which is a *bekkan* of Naikū (the "Inner Shrine"). Takihara no miya is the most distant and can only be reached by a JR railway line. Nevertheless, since the three last-named *bekkan* are all at some distance from the main Jingū complexes, the encouragement to take along a *shuinchō* is also a general encouragement to travel around. The pamphlet refers to this as *go shuin meguri*, thus introducing the term typical of circulatory pilgrimage, though inexactly. It is significant that these shrines are not sequentially numbered.

Of notable interest for the present study is the fact that Yamato hime no miya was founded as recently as Taishō 12 (1923), the *chinza* having been on November 5. This is said to have occurred because of "enthusiasm" on the part of the Jingū authorities and the local population, and evidently contributed in some way to the ongoing national policy of strengthening the political profile of Shinto for the benefit of the Japanese state, here hinted at by the element Yamato in the name Yamato no hime (Princess Yamato).

As specialists will be aware, though apparently none have studied the mater in detail, there is a formal concept of 125 shrines referred to with the neutral term *sha* 社 which are linked to Ise

---

10 The *shikinen sengū* is the regular rebuilding of the Ise shrines which under normal circumstances takes place once every twenty years.

Jingū. In some contexts the term *o-meguri* is brought into play. With this in mind, what is the situation on the ground? Although I have only visited a limited number of the 125 shrines so far, the situation seems to be quite interesting.

The idea of visiting all of these 125 shrines is not quite new. It was certainly current in prewar times, in the Shōwa Period, and possibly earlier. However, the number 125 seems to be very stable. It is therefore relevant that, as noted above, one of the shrines was not founded until 1923. It is therefore possible that it was after that date that the "enthusiasts" began to count how many associated shrines there were altogether.

In two undated but recent booklets published by the Shinto Sūkeikai (Association for Shinto Devotions), the 125 shrines are listed and briefly explained in full. First let us look at them from the point of view of *o-meguri*. The shrines are grouped together geographically for ease of visiting, and maps provided accordingly. However there is no overall numbered sequence from one to 125. This is a first indication that we are not dealing here with a straightforward transfer of the idea of circulatory pilgrimage from the Buddhist model. The shrines are distributed into twelve groups, pride of place being given to the Naikū group and the Gekū group. The two booklets, as might be expected since they emanate from the same source, are consistent in their nomenclature of the twelve groups. However, after Naikū and Gekū, they are not at all consistent in the sequence of the shrine groupings. This further strengthens the observation that there is no significant numbered sequence here, but only the overall number of 125. Obviously people will visit the Gekū and the Naikū first,[11] with some of their associated shrines, and then simply look around to see what else they can visit. Travellers, whether pilgrims or tourists or both, are likely to visit Sarutahiko Jinja which is on the bus route between the two main complexes. Further afield they may visit the famous Meotoiwa ("wife and husband rocks"), two rocks in the sea which

---

11 It is sometimes said that one should visit the Gekū first and then the Naikū, which implies a progression from the junior to the senior shrine.

are linked with a sanctifying rope (*shimenawa*). These rocks have their own shrine which is nothing to do with Ise Jingū.

Both booklets refer to each separate group of shrines as a circulation, a *meguri*. In one case the sum total of 125 shrines is referred to as *Ise no Jingū Hyakunijūgosha meguri*, thus making a single *meguri*, at least notionally, out of all the shrines. The second booklet is entitled *Jingū 125 sha junpai annai*. Here the term *junpai* also suggests circulatory pilgrimage. However, I think we are confronted with rather casual usage here, and the term *o-meguri* is probably being used in a neutral, practical sense, to make these visits seem interesting. We recall that the shrines are not numbered sequentially.

Recently I acquired two prewar booklets for young people which promoted devotion towards Ise Shrine. In one of these, dated Shōwa 10 (1935) there is a clear reference to the 125 shrines, while in the other, dating from Shōwa 11 (1936), though it is more substantial, there is no such reference.[12] This suggests that at that period the concept still had a somewhat uncertain status.

In the first booklet, entitled *Ise sangū shiori*, we find a simple table which sets out the numbers of the smaller shrines connected with Ise Jingū, with an indication of their different types. Surprisingly, this is found immediately, on page 1, under the heading *Jingū no enkaku* 神宮の沿革 ("The history of [Ise] Shrine"). This is an extremely short "history" for it covers only one page! Perhaps it would be better described as a *yurai* 由来, a tale of origin. It states that the Naikū was founded in the year 657 of Kigensetsu and the Gekū in the year 1138 of Kigensetsu.[13]

However, in the 81-page textbook, entitled *Sangū dokuhon*,[14] there is not the same clarity. The last section refers to various places, mainly buildings, under the heading *shinkyō meguri*

---

12 Nakayama 1936.

13 Kigensetsu is the foundational year of calendrical time, referring to the accession of Jinmu Tennō. The specific date, February 11, was initially abolished after the Second World War, but was later reinstated under the designation *Kenkoku kinen no hi* (National Foundation Day).

14 Nakayama 1936.

神境めぐり (p. 74.) The term *shinkyō* refers in a very broad sense to shrine precincts. The places listed include a wide range of institutions and places such as the Kōgakkan, a Shinto training college with a close connection to Ise Jingū, but also the famous twin rocks, the Meotoiwa mentioned above, which have nothing to do with the Jingū. So here we are simply in the field of tourism and *meisho* (famous places).

Returning to the first booklet, the types and numbers of the associated shrines are set out as follows.

Kōtai Jingū (Naikū):
  10 *bekkan*   33 *sessha*   16 *massha*

Toyouke Daijingū (Gekū):
  4 *bekkan*   17 *sessha*   8 *massha*

Others (not differentiated between Naikū and Gekū): 37 shrines (*sha*)

Total: 125 shrines

The number and the types of shrine remain unchanged today, so in this respect there is stability. It is striking that the text indicates that these shrines are not really to be thought of as separate shrines at all! This is important. Moreover it states that there is no relative status between the various shrines and their various enshrined divinities, as there is (i.e. was) among the various *kanpei taisha*, a systematic list which graded shrines hierarchically. It must be remembered that in those days the concept of *kanpei taisha* was more prominent than it is today, and it also invited circulatory pilgrimage around the various shrines. All of the 125 Ise shrines named here, the booklet says, can be referred to together as a single Jingū (...*tada, jingū to mōshiageru no de aru*). This idea is reinforced in various ways on the spot today, through verbal information and public notices.

Conclusions

From these examples, some conclusions may be drawn. First, a pilgrimage to the Michizane shrines illustrates, once again, that the Buddhist concept of circulatory pilgrimage is easily transferred to Shinto shrines. In this as in some other cases the completion of the way becomes more prominent than the goal. The case of Ise should however be regarded in a certain sense as a *contrary* example. Although the term *meguri* is used here in some contexts, to stimulate visits, and although there are many more shrines to visit than just one, this does not really amount to a *circulatory* pilgrimage in the analytical sense. Rather, it is just one, complex, single-goal pilgrimage, to Ise Jingū. Even though times and styles have changed, the idea of *o-Ise-mairi* remains relevant insofar as it refers to one single goal consisting of 125 shrines in total.

Second, there is of course no Buddhist element of meaning whatever in either of the two cases considered here. The meaning of visiting the Michizane shrines lies in the religious focusing and assurance of scholastic or academic aspiration or ambition. Rather differently, the meaning of visiting the various sub-shrines at Ise is entirely in harmony with the meaning of visiting the Naikū and/or the Gekū. Here the main point lies in the purification of the individual's heart or mind, and in the strengthening of one's personal identity as part of a shared national orientation. The sub-shrines simply support this meaning, and do not offer any major alternatives. This implies not only that it is possible to distinguish between Buddhist and Shinto meanings in Japanese pilgrimage, but that it is also possible to see considerable diversity of meanings within the overall family of Shinto.

References

Nakayama, Asanosuke 中山朝之助 1936. *Sangū dokuhon* 參宮読本. Ujiyamashi (Keishin Kyōikukai).

Nishigaki, Seiji 西垣晴次 1983. *O-Isemairi* お伊勢参り. Tokyo (Iwanami Bunsho).

Pye, Michael 2004. *The Structure of Religious Systems in Contemporary Japan: Shinto Variations on Buddhist Pilgrimage.* Marburg (Centre for Japanese Studies, Occasional Papers 30).
Pye, Michael 2015. *Japanese Buddhist Pilgrimage.* Sheffield (Equinox Publications).
Teeuwen, Mark and Breen, John 2017. *A Social History of the Ise Shrines: Divine Capital.* London (Bloomsbury).

About the author

Michael Pye (born 1939) first resided in Japan from 1961 onwards. From 1968 he taught Religious Studies in England and in 1982 became professor for the Study of Religions at Marburg University, Germany. He was president of the International Association for the History of Religions from 1995 to 2000. On retirement he returned to Japan for several years, being associated with Otani University, Kyoto. Publications include *Strategies in the Study of Religions* (2013) and *Japanese Buddhist Pilgrimage* (2015).

10

Why does Shin Buddhism reject the worship of the kami?

Robert F. Rhodes

Introduction

It is well known that the vast majority of the Japanese people possess multiple religious identities, stereotypically praying at Shinto shrines on New Year's Day, getting married at a Christian church and conducting funerals at Buddhist temples. But several Japanese religions have developed and maintained a discourse rejecting this pluralistic stance, most notably Shin Buddhism. In this paper, I will focus on Shin Buddhism and first discuss the reasons for its rejection of *kami* worship, a position known in Shin Buddhist discourse as *jingi fuhai* 神祇不拝. Then, in the second part of the paper, I will consider how, with the growth of the Shin Buddhist school, Zonkaku 存覺 (1290–1373) and Rennyo 蓮如 (1415–99) created a Shin Buddhist discourse taking a more conciliatory position towards the Japanese *kami*. Finally, in the third part of the paper, I will focus on two stories from Gōzei's 仰誓 (1721–94) *Myōkōnin-den* 妙好人傳 ("Biographies of the Myōkōnin") from the late Edo Period to see how he sought to promote the normative Shin Buddhist position towards the *kami*, even while presenting evidence that it was not always strictly observed in practice.

Shinran's argument for rejecting the worship of kami

Shinran 親鸞 (1173–1262), the founder of Shin Buddhism, famously declared that those who have sincerely entrusted themselves to the saving power of Amida Buddha's vows must not worship any other buddha or deity. As I have argued elsewhere (Rhodes 1994), he was especially adamant in rejecting the worship of the so-called "heavenly gods and earthy spirits" (*tenjin chigi* 天神地祇). These supernatural beings included not only the Indian deities that appear in Buddhist scriptures but also the native Japanese *kami*. (In the pages below, I will use the term "gods" when referring to these supernatural beings in general, and the word "*kami*" when speaking specifically about the gods of Japan.)

This stance rejecting the worship of the gods is still a prominent feature in Shin Buddhist discourse. To give one example, Hoshino Genpō, in his *Kōge Kyōgyōshinshō* (a multivolume commentary on Shinran's *Kyōgyōshinshō*, published between 1977 and 1983), writes that,

> as long as one takes refuge in the Buddha, one must never take refuge in heavenly beings and gods other than the Buddha. This is the fundamental prerequisite of religion. When people are simply following the customary religious practices (*tannaru kanshūteki na sūhai ni oiteha* 単なる慣習的な崇拝においては), there are frequently cases where they worship a variety of heavenly beings and gods, especially in Japan. But in a genuine religion, it is impossible to take refuge in one god and simultaneously take refuge in a different god. (Hoshino 1983, 2010–11)

Similarly, although empirical data is conspicuously lacking, it appears from my admittedly limited observations that, on the practical level, the *kami*-rejecting ethos is still quite strong within the Shin Buddhist community, especially among its elites, specifically the temple priests and their family members.

Shinran's admonition not to worship the *kami* derives from his insistence on relying exclusively on Amida Buddha.[1] He stressed that humans are so heavily burdened with karmic evil that they are incapable of undertaking any practice whatsoever to gain release from the cycle of rebirths. In order to be liberated from the cycle of rebirths, he argued, it is necessary to entrust oneself in Amida Buddha's promise, set forth in the eighteenth of his forty-eight

---

1 On Shinran's Buddhist thought, see Bloom 1968.

vows, to bring all who would recite the *nenbutsu* ("Namu Amida Butsu") to his Pure Land. Moreover, Shinran emphasized that the faith required to attain birth in the Pure Land must be genuine faith, which he called "true and real faith" (*shinjitsu shinjin* 眞實信心). He maintained that, because of their karmic evil, humans are incapable of arousing genuine faith that is free of self-serving egotistical attachments. Genuine faith can only be "turned over" (*ekō* 回向) to humans from Amida Buddha himself. Such genuine faith, Shinran believed, is necessarily characterized by complete and undivided reliance on Amida. Hence, he maintained that all who would truly entrust themselves to Amida must not venerate any other buddhas or supernatural beings, including the native Japanese *kami*.

Shinran's position against worshipping the gods is stated most clearly in his major doctrinal work, the *Kyōgyōshinshō* 教行信證 ("Teaching, Practice, Faith and Realization"). In fact, the second half of the "Chapter on the Transformed Buddha and Land" (*Keshindo no maki* 化身土卷), the last and longest chapter of the *Kyōgyōshinshō*, is taken up by a number of lengthy quotations from Buddhist texts dealing with the gods. Taken together, these passages drive home Shinran's message that these gods should not be made the object of one's veneration. Let me cite the first two of these passages.

> The *Nirvāṇa Sūtra* states, "If one has taken refuge in the Buddha, one must not further take refuge in various heavenly gods (*tenjin* 天神)."
>
> The *Śūraṅgama Sūtra* states, "Those among lay women who hear this *samādhi* and seek to learn it: ... Take refuge in the Buddha yourself, take refuge in the Dharma, take refuge in the Sangha. Do not serve other teachings, do not worship heavenly beings (*ten* 天), do not enshrine spirits (*kijin* 鬼神), do not heed any days considered lucky." Further it states: "Lay women who wish to learn this *samādhi*...must not worship heavenly beings or enshrine spirits." (CWS: Vol. 1, 255, slightly amended)

Shin Buddhism and the worship of kami 189

In these quotations, the terms "heavenly gods," "heavenly beings" and "spirits" (*tenjin* 天神, *ten* 天 and *kijin* 鬼神 respectively) refer to the gods of India, but Shinran extends their meaning to include the Japanese *kami* as well.

After introducing these two scriptural passages, Shinran goes on to cite numerous other passages dealing with the gods from the Buddhist texts, and then, as a way of conclusion, introduces the following quotation from the *Analects*.

> The *Analects* says, "Jilu 季路 asked, "Should we serve the spirits (*kijin* 鬼神)?" Confucius said, "You should not serve spirits. Why should people serve spirits?" (CWS: Vol. 1, 289)

This is perhaps the most famous passages in the *Kyōgyōshinshō* denouncing the worship of the gods. However, it is important to note that Shinran has deliberately misquoted the *Analects* here. The original passage reads: "Jilu asked, 'Should we serve the spirits?' The master said, 'Unless you have learned to serve people, how can you serve the spirits?'"[2] As is well known, Shinran frequently provides idiosyncratic readings of textual passages to express what he considers to their true meanings, and this is one example of such readings.

Closely related to this prohibition concerning the worship of the gods is the injunction not to put one's faith in various forms of divination. This is clearly found in the following verse from Shinran's *Shōzōmatsu wasan* 正像末和讚 ("Hymns on the Dharma Ages").

> How lamentable it is that monks and laypeople
> Select "fortunate times" and "auspicious days,"
> And paying homage to heavenly gods and earthy spirits,
> Engage in divination and rituals of worship.
> (CWS: Vol. 1. 422, slightly amended)

Shinran links the preoccupation with divining one's fortune and choosing auspicious times ("fortunate times" and "auspicious

---

2   This passage is found in Book 11, section 12 of the *Analects*. For an alternative translation, see Lau 1979, 107.

days" in the verse above) to acts of devotion to the "heavenly gods and earthy spirits." As this verse shows, Shinran saw the worship of these gods and spirits as attempts to manipulate them for the worshipper's egotistical purposes, such as gaining good fortune and warding off disasters. However, Shinran saw this as an indication of the believer's lack of faith in Amida. In Shinran's view, people who have sincerely entrusted themselves to Amida have no need to engage in divinations to foresee and control their future since, through their faith, they can accept whatever may come their way with equanimity, being fully assured of their future birth in the Pure Land.

Yet, it is important to note that Shinran did not deny the existence of the gods. In fact, he even maintained that the gods will protect and serve Pure Land practitioners. Shinran makes this point throughout his writings. For example, in the "Chapter on Faith" (*Shin no maki* 信巻), the third chapter of the *Kyōgyōshinshō*, he enumerates ten benefits enjoyed by *nenbutsu* practitioners, the first of which is that they are "protected and sustained by unseen powers" (*myōshū* 冥衆 i e., by the gods, CWS 1: 112).[3] Similarly, he quotes several sutra passages in the second half of the "Chapter on the Transformed Buddha and Land" to make the same point. From the *Abhiṣeka Sūtra* ("Sutra of Ritual Sprinkling"), he quotes the following words.

> Without revealing themselves, the thirty-six spirit-kings, together with their followings of spirits as numerous as the sands of the Ganges ten billionfold, will take turns protecting those who receive the three refuges. (CWS: Vol. 1, 273)

Finally, in his *Jōdo wasan* 淨土和讚 ("Hymns on the Pure Land"), we find the following verse.

---

3 Incidentally, the fourth and fifth benefits are "the benefit of being protected and cared for by all the buddhas" and "the benefit of being praised by all the buddhas." This shows that, although Shinran admonished his readers not to entrust themselves to buddhas other than Amida, he believed that they too would protect and look after *nenbutsu* practitioners.

> The heavenly gods and earthy spirits
> Are all to be called good spirits,
> For together these good gods
> Protect the person of the *nenbutsu*.
> (CWS: Vol. 1, 354, slightly amended)

All of these passages reveal that Shinran believed that the gods protect and look after *nenbutsu* practitioners. This shows that Shinran did not deny the existence of the gods; he simply maintained that they were not to be worshipped by *nenbutsu* practitioners.

Let me summarize my arguments so far. Shinran, like all other Japanese monks of the medieval period, recognized that the universe was populated by a number of spiritually powerful buddhas, gods and spirits. However, he was also convinced that the only possible way to achieve release from the cycle of birth-and-death and gain buddhahood available to such evil persons as himself was to entrust themselves in Amida Buddha's unconditional vow to bring all who would recite the *nenbutsu* in faith to the Pure Land. It is for this reason that Shinran advocated sole reliance on Amida Buddha – not because there are no other buddhas or deities in the world, but because Amida is the only one who can guarantee the salvation of an evil person like himself. Simply put, since the sole reliable source of salvation is Amida Buddha's vows, one must entrust oneself exclusively and wholeheartedly to his vows. And this, in turn, means that there is no need to rely on any other buddha or deity in the quest for buddhahood.

Developments after Shinran

In the way outlined above, Shinran emphasized that *nenbutsu* practitioners must rely absolutely on Amida Buddha and refrain from venerating any other buddhas or gods, including the native Japanese *kami*. However, a major change in the Shin Buddhist approach to the *kami* occurred between the time of Kakunyo 覺如 (1270–1351), the third abbot of Shin Buddhism, and Rennyo, the eighth abbot. A major reason for this shift was the increase in the number of Shin Buddhist adherents during this period. The number of Shin Buddhist adherents gradually expanded for about a century and a half after Shinran's death and finally increased exponentially under Rennyo's leadership. This growth demanded the creation of a more conciliatory approach towards the *kami* since many of the people who joined Shin Buddhism found it hard to discard the *kami* that they had previously worshipped (Akamatsu and Kasahara 1963, 117). As a result, a new Shin Buddhist discourse concerning the *kami* was created utilizing the *honji-suijaku* 本地垂迹 theory, which holds that native Japanese *kami* are "traces" (*suijaku* 垂迹) of the original (*honji* 本地) Indian buddhas and bodhisattvas.

The classic expression of this new discourse is found in Zonkaku's *Shojin hongaishū* 諸神本懐集 ("Collection on the Original Intent of the Kami"). Zonkaku, who was Kakunyo's son, is known as the author of the *Rokuyōshō* 六要抄 ("Essentials from the Six [Chapters of the *Kyōgyōshinshō*]"), the first commentary on the *Kyōgyōshinshō*, and is credited with being the first person to systematize Shin Buddhist doctrines. On the basis of the *honji-suijaku* theory, Zonkaku argued that all Japanese *kami* are manifestations of the buddhas and bodhisattvas, and that these buddhas and bodhisattvas are, in turn, manifestations of Amida Buddha. Hence, this means that the *kami* are all ultimately manifestations of Amida Buddha. For this reason, Zonkaku explains, if one would simply worship Amida, it is simultaneously possible to pay reverence to all the *kami*. Or, to put it differently, since the worship of Amida automatically implies the worship of this Buddha's *suijaku kami*, it is only necessary to worship the former and not the latter. Zonkaku further argues that the *kami* appeared in this world to lead all beings to the Buddhist teachings.

This new rhetoric was effectively employed by Rennyo, who created a large and formidable Shin Buddhist organization under his leadership. In his *Ofumi* 御ふみ ("Pastoral Letters"), Rennyo commanded his followers to "cast off all thoughts of courting favor with the *kami* and other buddhas" (Rogers and Rogers 1991, 172) declaring that "we simply do not rely on any of the other buddhas and bodhisattvas or on the various kami…" (Rogers and Rogers 1991, 175). However, Rennyo also enjoins his readers to refrain from belittling the *kami*, both because they are manifestations of

Amida and because they work to lead all beings to the Buddhist teachings and protect *nenbutsu* practitioners (Rogers and Rogers 1991, 175–6). In this way, Rennyo incorporated the *kami* into Shin Buddhism, seeing them as manifestations of Amida Buddha's compassionate desire to lead all beings to release from the cycle of rebirth. At the same time, however, Rennyo taught Shin Buddhist believers not to worship the *kami*, even while treating them with respect.

Examples from Gōzei's Myōkōnin-den

In the remaining part of my paper, I would like to consider several interesting stories found in Gōzei's *Myōkōnin-den*, to see how he sought to disseminate Rennyo's teachings concerning the *kami*. It is hoped that this will help shed light on the worship of *kami* among Shin Buddhists "on the ground" so to speak.

The *myōkōnin* 妙好人 (literally "wonderfully excellent people") are exemplary Shin Buddhist *nenbutsu* practitioners. The *Myōkōnin-den* is a collection of stories about such people complied in the late Edo Period (1600–1868). It was originally written by Gōzei in 1753. Initially, Gōzei's collection circulated in manuscript form but was finally published by Sōjun 僧純 (1791–1872) in 1842. In addition, between 1842 and 1858, Sōjun compiled and published four sequels to Gōzei's collection. Around the same time, Zōō 象王 (dates unknown) also gathered similar *myōkōnin* stories and published them in 1850. Hence, the *Myōkōnin-den* as we now have it is a composite work, consisting of six parts: part one by Gōzei, parts two to five by Sōjun and part six by Zōō.[4]

A few words about Gōzei and his age may be useful here.[5] Gōzei was born in Kyoto as a son of a Nishi Honganji temple priest.

---

4 On the composition of the *Myōkōnin-den*, see Kikufuji 2003, 10–37. Hisao Inagaki's translation of Gōzei's portion of the *Myōkōnin-den* can be found in the homepage of the Shin Buddhist Fellowship of West Hartford (http://shin-westhartford.tripod.com/id18.html).

5 A short biography of Gōzei is found in Ryūkoku daigaku 1972–74, Vol. 1, 1205–6.

In 1761, he was dispatched to Iwami 石見 province (now part of Shimane prefecture) to combat the heretical teachings that were being disseminated there by Enkū 圓空 of Nagato 長門. From then on, Gōzei lived in Iwami and wrote numerous commentaries on Shin Buddhist texts as well as other works on the Shin Buddhist teachings, including the *Hekinan taiben* 僻難對辨 ("Replies to Jaundiced Criticisms") treating the Shin Buddhist attitude towards *kami* worship, and the *Jisai nikujiki benwaku-hen* 持妻肉食辨惑編 ("Defence of Clerical Marriage and Meat Eating") defending the Shin Buddhist custom of married clergy. By the late Edo Period, when Gōzei was active, the head Shin Buddhist temples in Kyoto (the Nishi and Higashi Honganjis) were assiduously working to strengthen their authority by stamping out heresies and imposing doctrinal orthodoxy throughout Japan. As noted above, Gōzei himself was sent to Iwami from Kyoto to deal with a perceived heresy. Gōzei's *Myōkōnin-den*, although not concerned with doctrinal matters, was compiled with a similar motive: to create an ideal image of a *nenbutsu* practitioner that would serve as the norm of conduct for the Shin Buddhist community as a whole.

Among the twenty-one stories of *nenbutsu* practitioners found in Gōzei's original *Myōkōnin-den*, there are conspicuous references to the *kami* in two of them. The first is found in the entry concerning Chūzaemon 忠左ェ門 of Kashima 鹿島 county in Hitachi 常陸 province (now Ibaraki prefecture). This is one of the longer stories found in the *Myōkōnin-den* but it can be briefly summarized as follows. Chūzaemon originally belonged to the Zen school but after his wife died, he became aware of the impermanence of all things and wished to prepare himself for his eventual death. Since he was not sure as to which Buddhist teaching he should follow, he prayed for guidance to both the local *ujigami* 氏神 (tutelary *kami* of a particular locality) and the *kami* of Kashima Shrine 鹿島 located three *li* 里 (about 12 km) from his home. However, Chūzaemon failed to elicit any response from them. Hence, he practised *zazen*, Shingon esoteric teachings and Pure Land *nenbutsu* recitation one after another, but none of these practices provided him with the peace of mind he sought. Finally, after he turned sixty, he became a follower of Nichiren Buddhism.

Around this time, Chūzaemon resolved to remarry and after praying at the shrine of the local *ujigami*, he was able to find a suitable wife. However, the wife refused to recite the *daimoku* 題目 (the phrase "Namu Myōhō Rengekyō" ["Hail to the Sūtra of the Lotus Blossom of the Wonderful Dharma"], the recitation of which is the central practice of the Nichiren school). As a result, Chūzaemon came to resent the *ujigami*. One day, after two years had passed, Chūzaemon discovered his wife praying in front of a dresser and inquired what she was doing. She replied that she was reciting the *nenbutsu* before a *honzon* 本尊 (object of worship; in Shin Buddhism, it is frequently a hanging scroll inscribed with the phrase "*Namu Amida Butsu*") hidden in the dresser and confessed that she was a Shin Buddhist believer. After being instructed in the Shin Buddhist teachings from his wife, Chūzaemon realized that this was what he was looking for and joyfully took refuge in it. Later when he read Rennyo's *Ofumi*, Chūzaemon came across Rennyo's words that the *kami* all strive to lead people to faith in Amida Buddha and was overjoyed, finally realizing that the *kami* had been trying to direct his attention to the Shin Buddhist teachings all along. Gōzei concludes his account by noting that he had actually heard this story from the priest of Seirenji 青蓮寺 in the city of Mito 水戸 in Hitachi province (Kashiwahara and Fujii 1973, 180–3). This story refers explicitly to Rennyo's *Ofumi* and was obviously recounted to underscore its teaching that the *kami* are the provisional manifestation of Amida Buddha, sent to the world out of this Buddha's compassionate desire to liberate all beings from the cycle of birth-and-death.

The second story in the *Myōkōnin-den* referring to the *kami* concerns that of Gentarō 源太郎, the *shōya* 庄屋 (village headman) of Asuna 阿須那 village of Ōchi 邑智 county and a parishioner of the Sairenji 西蓮寺, a Nishi Honganji temple. Although his family had been Shin Buddhist believers for generations, Gentarō maintained a *kamidana* 神棚 (household altar for the *kami*) in his home. On one occasion, the learned Nishi Honganji priest Taigan 泰巖 (1711–63) was visiting the Sairenji. During his visit, Taigan told Gentarō that, in order to properly carry out the duties as village headman, it was necessary to follow the Shin Buddhist teachings scrupulously, including the teaching not to venerate the *kami*. As a result, Gentarō and his wife decided to remove the *kamidana* from their house. But thinking it improper to remove it all at once and attract unnecessary attention, they decided to get rid of it gradually. First, they stopped lighting candles in front of the *kamidana*. Then they ceased to present an offering of sake to it. Finally, they removed the *mamori fuda* 守札 (the talisman enshrined in the *kamidana*) and, taking care not to treat it disrespectfully, presented the *kamidana* to the local shrine to be disposed of properly (Kashiwahara and Fujii 1973, 187).

Gōzei's point in recounting this story is clear: devout Shin Buddhist believers should not pay reverence to the *kami* by keeping a *kamidana* in their homes. However, as Kodama Shiki has pointed out, Gōzei is also cautioning his readers not to treat the *kami* irreverently (Kodama 1975, 40). In the story, the *kamidana* is not destroyed with vengeance but is gradually discarded and the sacred objects in it are handled with respect to the end. Again, this accords with Rennyo's admonition not to belittle the *kami* and to treat them with due courtesy.

However, if we look at this account with a critical eye, another important point emerges. The fact that Gōzei highlights the act of removing the *kamidana* as an exemplary sign of a pious *nenbutsu* practitioner, also suggests that not a few Shin Buddhist parishioners did actually have a *kamidana* in their homes. If so, it would mean that the injunction against venerating the *kami* was not uniformly followed by all Shin believers. Although little research has been conducted on this topic, there are some important studies showing that this was indeed the case. For example, Kashiwahara Yūsen has shown that a surprising number of Shin Buddhist temples have Shinto shrines in their grounds (Kashiwahara 1969, 135–60). Markus Ruesch's paper in this volume also discusses this point, using the example of the Kinshokuji 錦織寺, the head temple of the Kibe 木辺 branch of Shin Buddhism. Similarly, Kodama Shiki has demonstrated that the Sumiya 隅屋 family of Aki 安芸 province (now Hiroshima prefecture), the owner of a major iron mining enterprise and a *danka* 檀家 (parishioner) of the Shin Buddhist temple Kōfukuji 光福寺, also patronized, not only other

Shin Buddhist temples, but Shinto shrines and Zen and Shingon temples throughout Aki (Kodama 1975, 192–214).

Finally, I have heard from my colleague, a professor at Otani University and a priest of a Shin Buddhist temple in Ishikawa prefecture, that it is still common for the parishioners of his temple to have a *kamidana* in their homes.[6] This was surprising because Ishikawa prefecture has long been considered to be one of the strongholds of Shin Buddhism. These examples indicate that the Shin Buddhist attitude towards the *kami* was not, and is not, monolithic. The mainstream Shin Buddhist discourse against venerating the *kami* notwithstanding, it must be said that Shin Buddhists actually held a wide range of attitudes on this topic.

Conclusion

In conclusion, it may be said that Shinran was strongly opposed to the worship of the native Japanese *kami*, maintaining that Amida Buddha should be venerated as the sole source of salvation. However, with the growth of the Shin Buddhist school, a more conciliatory approach to the *kami* became necessary. To respond to this demand, Zonkaku and Rennyo created a new discourse concerning the *kami* based on the *honji-suijaku* theory, arguing, first, that the native Japanese *kami* were manifestation of Amida Buddha; second, that the mission of the *kami* is to lead people to the Buddhist teachings (specifically the teachings of Shin Buddhism); and finally that, for these reasons, the *kami* must be respected (though not worshipped). During the late Edo Period, this interpretation of the *kami* was incorporated into Gōzei's *Myōkōnin-den*, which sought to create and disseminate an ideal image of a devout Shin Buddhist *nenbutsu* practitioner. However, contrary to the professed aim of Gōzei's *Myōkōnin-den*, we can discern signs in this text suggesting that the admonition to refrain from worshipping the *kami* was not always faithfully followed throughout the Shin Buddhist community.

6   In a private conversation with Fujihara Masatoshi 藤原正寿 on July 18, 2018.

Abbreviation

CWS: Hirota, Dennis et al. (trans.) 1997, *The Collected Works of Shinran*. 2 vols. Kyoto: Jodo Shinshu Hongwanji-ha.

References

Akamatsu Toshihide 赤松俊秀 and Kasahara Kazuo 笠原一男 (eds.) 1963. *Shinshushi gaisetsu* 真宗史概説. Kyoto (Hōzōkan).
Bloom, Alfred, 1968. *Shinran's Gospel of Pure Grace*. Tuscon (University of Arizona Press).
Hisao Inagaki n.d. "Gosei's Myokonin Stories," homepage of the Shin Buddhist Fellowship of West Hartford [http://shin-westhartford.tripod.com/id18.html].
Hoshino Genpō 星野元豊 1983. *Kōge Kyōgyōshinshō, Keshindo no maki 2* 講解教行信証—化身土の巻末. Kyoto (Hōzōkan).
Kashiwahara Yūsen 柏原祐泉 1969. *Nihon kinsei kindai Bukkyōshi no kenkyū* 日本近世近代仏教史の研究. Kyoto (Heirakuji).
Kashiwahara Yūsen 柏原祐泉 and Fujii Manabu 藤井学 (eds.) 1973. *Kinsei Bukkyō no shisō* 近代佛教の思想, *Nihon shisō taikei* 日本思想体系 57. Tokyo (Iwanami Shoten).
Kikufuji Akimichi 菊藤明道 2003. *Myōkōnin-den no kenkyū* 妙好人伝の研究. Kyoto (Hōzōkan).
Kodama Shiki 児玉識 1975. *Kinsei Shinshū no tenkai katei* 近世真宗の展開過程. Tokyo (Yoshikawa Kōbunkan).
Lau, D. C. 1979. *The Analects (Lun yü)*. London (Penguin Books).
Rhodes, Robert F. 1994. "Shin Buddhist Attitudes towards the Kami," *The Eastern Buddhist* 27/2, 53–80.
Rogers, Minor L. and Rogers, Ann T. 1991. *Rennyo: The Second Founder of Shin Buddhism*. Berkeley, CA (Asian Humanities Press).
Ryūkoku Daigaku 龍谷大学 (ed.) 1972–1974. *Bukkyō daijii* 仏教大辞彙. 7 vols. Tokyo (Fusanbō).

About the author

Robert F. Rhodes, emeritus professor of Otani University, is the general editor of *The Eastern Buddhist*. His research is centred on the Pure Land and Tiantai/Tendai teachings of China and Japan. He is the author of *Genshin's Ōjōyōshū and the Construction of Pure Land Discourse in Heian Japan* (University of Hawaii Press, 2017).

11

Multiple divinities in Shin Buddhist temples

Markus Ruesch

Introduction: The typical attitude of Shin Buddhism towards Shinto and Shinto towards Shin Buddhism

In Japanese Buddhism, sects deal with divinities in very different ways. Many of them even include Shinto shrines in their precincts. Buddhist theories of the past have even argued for the unity of Shinto and Buddhism. Although such a relationship with Shinto can be called the main characteristic of Japanese Buddhism, the Shin Buddhist sect (Jōdo Shinshū 淨土眞宗) is a special case. Shin Buddhism normally rejects not only Shinto but also other figures from the Buddhist pantheon. However, if we have a closer look at local temples, we find that under certain circumstances this macro perspective is not applicable to all so-called Shin Buddhist temples. Therefore, a study of such "unusual" cases can help us understand the strong local boundaries of temples and the rhetoric surrounding their individual as well as sectarian nature.

The complicated relationship between the Shin Buddhist sect and Shinto is grounded in the explicit rejection of *kami* worship by its founder, Shinran 親鸞 (1173–1262).[1] This is also reflected in the tendency of the Shin Buddhist followers to not provide an altar for *kami* in their homes.[2] This relationship has even become an essential narrative in biographies and in architecture. Interestingly, there is a negative attitude on both sides. One example of the Shin Buddhist

---

1 See especially the following hymn by Shinran: "How lamentable it is that monks and laypeople / Select 'fortunate times' and 'auspicious days,' / And paying homage to gods of the heavens and earth, / Engage in divination and rituals of worship" (Hirota et al. 1997, p. 422; *Teihon Shinran shōnin zenshū* 1969, Vol. 2, 211).

2 See also Robert Rhodes' article in this book.

attitude is the most well-known biography of Shinran, written by his great-grandson Kakunyo 覺如 (1270–1351): *Honganji Shōnin (Shinran) den'ne* (本願寺聖人（親鸞）傳繪, "An Illustrated Biography of Honganji's Saint Shinran," in short: *Godenshō* 御傳鈔, "Scripture about the Biography [of the Saint Shinran]," 1295). Kakunyo emphasizes that Shinran provided the true concept of salvation. Shinran is in this context not only approved of by a Shinto priest, but also by a *kami* itself.[3] Other biographies even speak about Shinran visiting the Ise Shrine and getting access to parts of the shrine that were customarily prohibited.[4] We must consider here that this contact between Shin Buddhism and Shinto cannot be characterized as harmonious, or even inclusive. The authors of such biographies want to say that Shinran shared the *true* meaning of religious practice and that Shinto is *false*.

Opposite cases can be found. One example is Hakone Shrine 箱根神社. Although a statue of Shinran is part of its inner precincts, there is not any hint of it on the present shrine's map or in the shrine's architectural structure. Instead, one may argue that the shrine tries to avoid any consciousness of the statue of Shinran at all. The statue itself is only referred to as "patriotic martyrdom students' cenotaph" (*junkoku gakuto ireihi* 殉国学徒慰霊碑). This attitude also reflects the historical changes after the Meiji restoration and the separation of Shintō from Buddhism. Before these events, the shrine was the responsibility of a Buddhist temple. However, after the separation, this temple was removed, and statues of the Buddha Amida 阿彌陀 and Shinran, and several manuscripts handwritten by Shinran, had to be moved to a Shin Buddhist temple (Manpukuji 萬福寺) on the other side of the village. Until the separation, the Hakone "Shrine" also contained a so-called Shinran Hall.[5] Besides the abolition of the Shin Buddhist parts within the district, it is an exciting fact that other aspects of Buddhism have only changed slightly. One example is the Buddhist deity, Benzaiten 辨財天, that is now enshrined in a Benzaitensha; which

3   *Teihon Shinran shōnin zenshū*, Vol. 4, esp. 38–39, 44.
4   Shunjo and Ekan 1801, Vol. 2, fols. 12b–14a.
5   See also Ryōtei 1803–09, Vol. 10, fol. [20b].

in this case is not surprising, as Benzaiten has a connection to water, which is a central aspect of the Hakone Shrine.

But to what extent can such a relationship be called "typical" for Shin Buddhism and Shinto? In my opinion, it reflects the relationship in a macro perspective. In this paper, I want to show that we should rely rather on a more complex range of sources to become aware of the plurality of Japanese religion even *within* one denomination. This does *not* mean that an approach through doctrinaire texts (Shinran's standpoint) or political decisions (the separation of Shinto and Buddhism) leads us in a wrong direction. However, these texts cannot explain *all* developments within Buddhism or Shinto. I want to state that the concrete places of praxis – e.g. the temples and shrines – are more in dialogue with their *local circumstances* than with the doctrine. Therefore, doctrine must fit local peculiarities, rather than local peculiarities fitting doctrine. Since locality plays such a decisive role, we can observe in Japan a complex reality of various religious identities.

Hence, I will focus on the narrative and material developments of one Shin Buddhist temple that is highly influenced by its locality. Here, I will rely on origin-tales and the development of the precincts. Based on this analysis, I want to discuss the temple's rhetoric of emphasizing its originality *and* orthodoxy. This approach may be one good example to consider the interwovenness of the material and philological side of religions. Therefore, this concrete case will provide new insight into the relationship of Shin Buddhism and Shinto. This also leads – in a broader sense – to an essential aspect of the dialogues between Shinto and Buddhism. Namely, I want to claim the existence of continuity of inclusive dialogues that does not end with the separation in the Meiji Period.

Kinshokuji's historical context and the temple's importance[6]

The temple I want to focus on is called Kinshokuji 錦織寺. Today it is affiliated with the Shin Buddhist branch Shinshū Kibeha 眞

---

6   For the following historical summary see Kinshokuji 1996, 67–89.

宗木邊派 and located in Shiga 滋賀 Prefecture, near Kyoto 京都. It is said to have been erected in 858 (Ten'an 天安 2) by the third abbot of the Tendaishū 天台宗 Ennin 圓仁, who built a hall named "Ten'an Hall." The object of worship was the protector deity Bishamon 毘沙門. Tales state that this statue was originally carved by the founder of the Tendai sect Saichō 最澄, who installed it at the head temple Enryakuji 延暦寺. According to origin stories, Ennin brought this statue to the place that would become Kinshokuji after having a dream. Its first contact with "Shin Buddhism" goes back to the year 1235, when Shinran was returning from east Japan to Kyoto. When he reached Bishamon's hall it was late and he rested inside. Bishamon appeared in his dream and told him to instal a statue of Amida instead. Shinran carried a wooden statue of Amida – the central Buddha in Shin Buddhism – as a "portable Buddha (*jibutsu* 持佛)" on his shoulders since his time in east Japan. Following this manifestation, Shinran installed the Amida statue in the centre of the hall and the Bishamon statue on an altar beside it. Therefore, at this very place, the "portable Buddha," a symbol for Shinran's unique quality as an eminent monk, became stationary. This stationary aspect relates not only to the Amida statue as an object but also to Shinran's seeking for a permanent place that could represent his teachings. This installation presents one of Kinshokuji's arguments for its outstanding position within the various Shin Buddhist sects. One part of the argument consists of this permanent Amida statue. The other central part to argue for Kinshokuji's unique character is the point that its place never changed during the history of the temple.

The installation of the Amida statue marks the beginning of the Shin Buddhist history of the temple, which then became Kinshokuji. The origin of the name goes back to an event of the year 1238, in which two little boys appeared at the inner part of the hall. The boys spun threads out of lotus flowers, and two heavenly maidens wove (*shoku* 織) these into a brocade (*kin* 錦). Shinran showed this brocade to the Shijō Tennō 四條天皇. The Tennō – at that time about three or four years old – was very moved by this piece and therefore decided to dedicate an imperially-authorized name to the temple: "The temple of woven brocade and heavenly gods protecting the dharma" (*tenjin gohō Kinshoku no tera* 天神護法錦織之寺). After Shinran's death, Kinshokuji became strongly tied to Zonkaku 存覺 (1290–1373), the son of Kakunyo. The Kibe branch was to an extent an influential group until the rise of Rennyo 蓮如 (1415–99), the eighth head-priest of Honganji. This development had a strong influence on a significant number of local Shin Buddhist groups and resulted finally in the leading role of the two great Honganji branches until today. Kinshokuji also experienced a two-sects period, where priests from Shin Buddhism as well as Jōdoshū 淨土宗 were responsible for the temple. Hence, in the eighteenth century, Kinshokuji was reconnected solely to Shin Buddhism.

This short historical orientation makes clear that Kinshokuji's development can be characterized as one of a positive and open approach to its multisectarian history, especially its roots in Tendai Buddhism. This is a great difference from other Shin Buddhist branches, who see their founding origins in most cases in Shinran himself. Therefore, Kinshokuji's conditions can be called suited to be in a friendly relationship not only against other Buddhist sects but also against Shinto. From a rhetoric standpoint, it is remarkable that, apparently, all branches interpret their founding history as the reason for their outstanding position within the different Shin Buddhist branches. One group of branches emphasizes the point that Shinran himself erected the head temple. The other group, which includes Kinshokuji, highlights the temple's long history and the influence of Shinran on this multisectarian character.[7]

Kinshokuji in literature: The main narrative

Kinshokuji became the subject of different tales in a Shin Buddhist context. These representations in literature give us an important insight into its local identity. In most cases, Kinshokuji is mentioned in biographies about Shinran, but in one case, it is also mentioned

---

7   See also, for an overview about the history of the main branches in Shin Buddhism, Dobbins 1989, 112–31.

in a compilation of tales about the disciples of Shinran.⁸ I want to refer to the founding tale of Kinshokuji and later Shin Buddhist tales.

The founding tale consists of two parts: a picture scroll and a written text which is attributed to Zonkaku.⁹ The narrative begins with Shinran's separation from his teacher Hōnen 法然 (1133–1212) and continues with his time in exile and post-exile in east Japan. This long period of Shinran's life (about sixty per cent) covers only twenty per cent of the two scrolls. The reason lies in the narrative's intent to focus on the history of the temple's principal object of worship. In this sense, the main function of Shinran is to bring this statue of Amida to its final place. Therefore, the first line of the text states, "The primary object of worship is [Amida] Nyorai that the founder Shinran the holy had installed and worshipped."¹⁰

This main motive, as well as more detailed parts of the tale, apparently refer to another Amida-temple in central-east Japan, called Zenkōji 善光寺. The narrative of this temple was comparatively well known, as literature from the late Heian Period (twelfth century) already mentions it, and Zonkaku names it explicitly in the text.¹¹ The reference to Zenkōji is an essential hint regarding Kinshokuji's multisectarian and popular characteristics. Zenkōji is also characterized by a highly pluralistic structure, with regard to architecture and ritual, and even the inner structure of the temple-hall reveals the popular aspect of Zenkōji. It is also apparent that various Shinran-biographies (including the Kinshokuji

---

8   Kinshokuji is also mentioned in the collection of famous places in Ōmi Province (present Shiga Prefecture) *Ōmi meisho zue* 近江名所圖會. However, this is not a completely new publication but only a reprint of other tales.

9   See Kinshokuji 1996. The biography *Kinshokuji den'neki* 錦織寺傳繪記 written by Zonkaku is published in Sasaki 1910, 86–93. Here, Sasaki refers to Zonkaku as Jōrakudai Shaku-Zonkaku 常樂臺釋存覺.

10   Ibid., 86.

11   Even Shinran himself refers to the narrative of Zenkōji, namely, in his hymns. The first of the five hymns on Zenkōji talks about the discovery of the Amida statue: "The TATHAGATA of Zenkō-ji temple, / Taking pity on us, / Came to Naniwa Bay [in the form of a statue] [sic]. / At that time Moriya, not knowing the word 'Buddha,' […]" (Hirota et al. 1997, 425; *Teihon Shinran shōnin zenshū*, Vol. 2, 217).

Multiple divinities in Shin Buddhist temples 205

Figure 1 Shinran goes to recover the statue of Amida.

Figure 2 Recovering the statue of Amida in the tale of Zenkōji.

version) directly refer to the Zenkōji narrative, as the illustrations on the previous page demonstrate. The illustrations show Shinran, who recovers an Amida statue (**Figure 1**), and the scene of recovering it, in the founding tale of Zenkōji (**Figure 2**).[12] One other very similar scene is, for example, the carrying of the portable Buddha by Shinran and the founder of Zenkōji.[13]

Zenkōji was also an essential reference for the Shinshū Takadaha branch 眞宗髙田派. However, in contrast to Kinshokuji, which shows parallels only to the narrative, the Takada branch emphasizes the direct contact with Zenkōji by Shinran. In this version, Shinran erects the head temple of the Takada branch in east Japan, and then visits Zenkōji after having a dream. The primary object of worship in this temple appears in his dream and tells him that he should come to take it to the new temple. In the same night, the priests of Zenkōji had a dream that an eminent priest would come and they should give him the famous Amida statue of Zenkōji. Therefore, the new head temple, founded by Shinran, came to hold one of the most well-known symbols of popular Buddhism at that time, which stands for the idea of all people's salvation. Besides the connection with Zenkōji, the narratives of the Takada branch and the Kibe branch are also similar in their emphasis of connections to the court.

From Amida's appearance in Kakunyo's biography onwards, the narrative focuses on Amida's way to its most appropriate place with Shinran as a medium, and ends with the erection of Kinshokuji. The interesting point lies in the fact that the Kibe branch uses this scroll during the most crucial event in Shin Buddhism: Hōonkō 報恩講, the memorial of the founder, Shinran. This usage means that the figure "Shinran" as an object of the ritual is in almost every respect connected with the head temple. In contrast, the scripture scrolls and texts by Kakunyo used by the Hongan-ji branches contain almost the whole range of Shinran's biography beginning

---

12 Shunjo and Ekan 1801, Vol. 2, fols. 60b/61a (above); Hakue 1692, Vol. 3, fol. 13b (below) (both property of the Waseda University Library, Kotenseki Sogo Database).

13 Shunjo and Ekan 1801, Vol. 2, fol. 68a; Hakue 1692, Vol. 4, fol. 12a.

with his ordination and ending with his funeral and building of a mausoleum. This erection may be a similarity in the narrative's ending since this mausoleum is said to be the beginning of Honganji. However, at least two points differ strikingly from the Kinshokuji narrative. One is the fact that no statue of Amida is mentioned at all. The narrative focuses solely on Shinran. The second point is the reference to other divinities or Shinto. In the case of Kinshokuji, we see that Shinran enables Amida to enter into a kind of dialogue with a divinity. In Zonkaku's tale, Bishamon says: "If you instal the [statue of A]mida and Buddha-dharma flourishes, I will protect the spreading [of the teachings] well."[14] In contrast to this narrative, the Hongan-ji branch emphasizes Shinran's outstanding position relative to Shintō shrines and their representatives; shrines' divinities and manifestations (*gongen* 權現) included. Furthermore, Shinran's contact with the court in general, and the appearance of the Tennō in particular, is an exciting and significant difference.

Shinran-biographies written in the early and mid nineteenth century[15] adopted this narrative in most cases with only slight changes. In these cases, the Kinshokuji part is only a short section compared to the whole biography or tale. One reason for this minor position in the story lies in the fact that they are supporting another branch or refer to a hierarchy of Shin Buddhist branches, where Kinshokuji is in the lower ranks.[16] One biography of Shinran (Ichizen, *Shinran shōnin goichidaiki zue*), as well as a tale about famous Shin Buddhist temples (Ryōtei, *Nijūyohai junpai zue*), state that the statue of Bishamon (here: Tamonten 多聞天) was carved by Saichō and installed by Ennin.[17] The biography

14 Sasaki 1910, 90.
15 Shunjo and Ekan 1801; Ryōtei 1803–09; Ichizen [1859].
16 The biography by Shunjo and Ekan follows the narrative of Takada branch with its head temple Senjuji 專修寺. The Takada-narrative focuses on Shinran's time in east Japan. The Ryōtei biography is connected to the narrative of Honganji. Therefore, this biography shows the two Honganji in the beginning. Ichizen's biography is chronologically structured and combines different traditions of Shinran-biographies.
17 Here mentioned with the posthumous names Dengyō Daishi 傳教大師 (Saichō) and Jikaku Daishi 慈覺大師 (Ennin) (Ichizen [1858], Vol. 4, fol. 10b).

calls the hall built by Ennin not "Ten'an Hall" but "Deity Hall" (*ten'ōdō* 天王堂).[18] The two works also emphasize the temple's connection to Zonkaku and its high rank in a directory from the first half of the nineteenth century called *Unjō [meiran]* 雲上[閲覧].[19] In this directory, Kinshokuji appears as the smallest of six Shin Buddhist temples with abbots of imperial lineage (*monzeki* 門跡).[20] The *Unjō meiran* mentions Zonkaku as the first abbot of Kinshokuji after Kakunyo.

A last remarkable point is mentioned in the tale about famous Shin Buddhist temples. Here, the narrator describes the heavenly boys and maidens as "*kami* from sky and earth" (*tenjin chigi* 天神地祇).[21] Their appearance is explicitly connected with the actions of *kami*. Thus we can summarize the narrative of Kinshokuji as follows:

- The origin of the temples goes back to two main figures in *Tendai* Buddhism.
- *Shinran* came to Kinshokuji due to the Amida *Buddha*.
- He settled there for a time due to the *deity* Bishamon.
- The temple's name goes back to the actions by three manifestations of *kami*.
- The temple gets officially recognized by the court / the *Tennō*.

The development of Kinshokuji's precincts

In the following, I want to analyse the temple's precincts, both as they exist today and as found in descriptions and illustrations in tales. This shall enable us to add an architectural aspect to the narrative aspect. I want to compare six stages: (1) the precinct before

---

18 The alternative name of the hall is only mentioned in Ichizen [1859], Vol. 4, fol. 9b.

19 Ryōtei 1803–09, Vol. 1, fol. [58a], Ichizen [1859], Vol. 4, fol. 12b.

20 In the case of most temples, the directory mentions also the value of the territory: Honganji (300 *koku* 石), Higashi Honganji 東本願寺 (not indicated), Kōshōji 興正寺 (150 *koku*), Bukkōji 佛光寺 (6.8 *koku*), Senjuji (350 *koku*) and Kinshokuji (20 *koku*). *Unjō meiran taizen* 1849 [1837], Vol. I, fols. 63a–69a.

21 Ryōtei 1803–09, Vol. 1, fol. [60a].

Multiple divinities in Shin Buddhist temples 209

Shinran's arrival, (2) after the changes caused by Shinran, (3) after its completion by Shinran's disciples, (4) its later stage in premodern Japan, (5) its stage in modern Japan and (6) its present stage.

(1) Before the arrival of Shinran, "Kinshokuji" contained only one hall with Bishamon as the primary object of worship (**Figure 3**).[22] (2) Concerning Shinran's appearance and installation of Amida as the primary worship, two slightly differing narratives exist (**Figure 4**). In the first case, Amida was installed at the centre and Bishamon moved to the side.[23] In the second case, Amida became the only object of worship in the main hall, and Bishamon got installed in another hall beside this.[24] (3) The aforementioned scroll about the origin of Kinshokuji shows one remarkable difference.[25] This difference concerns the temple's structure after the completion by Shinran's disciples. Beside the Amida and Bishamon halls, we see a Shinto shrine located *within* the temple precinct (**Figure 5**). On the one hand, this characteristic of Kinshokuji has existed through to today but, on the other, the shrine itself appears in various forms.

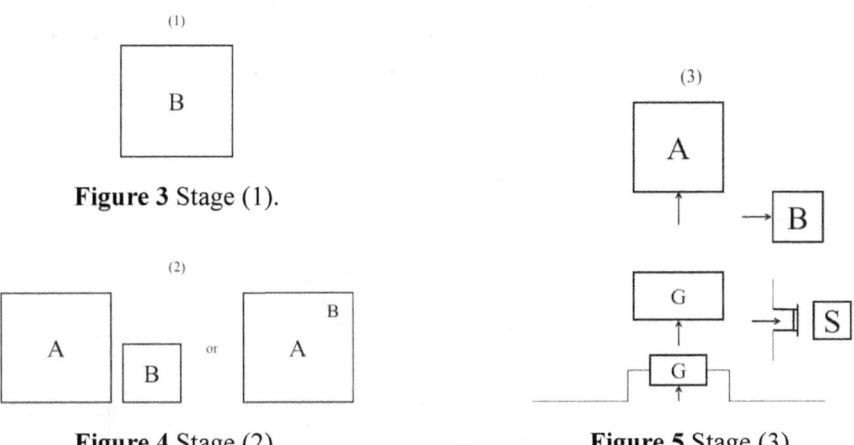

Figure 3 Stage (1).

Figure 4 Stage (2).

Figure 5 Stage (3).

22 According to the *Bishamon engi* 毘沙門縁起 as referred to in Kinshokuji 1996, 67/68.
23 Sasaki 1910, 91.
24 Shunjo and Ekan 1801, Vol. 2, fol. 69a (*betsuden* 別殿), Ichizen (1859), Vol. 4, fol. 10a (*betsudō* 別堂).
25 The scroll is published in Kinshokuji (1996), 54–8, see the precincts on p. 58.

210 *Exploring Shinto*

The final stage as illustrated in the picture scroll can be called the beginning of Kinshokuji's Shinto-history.[26]

(4) The two texts from the eighteenth century show the "Main Hall" and "Deity Hall" or "Bishamon Hall"[27] and a Shinto shrine – that is the same structure as before (**Figures 6 and 7**). But in

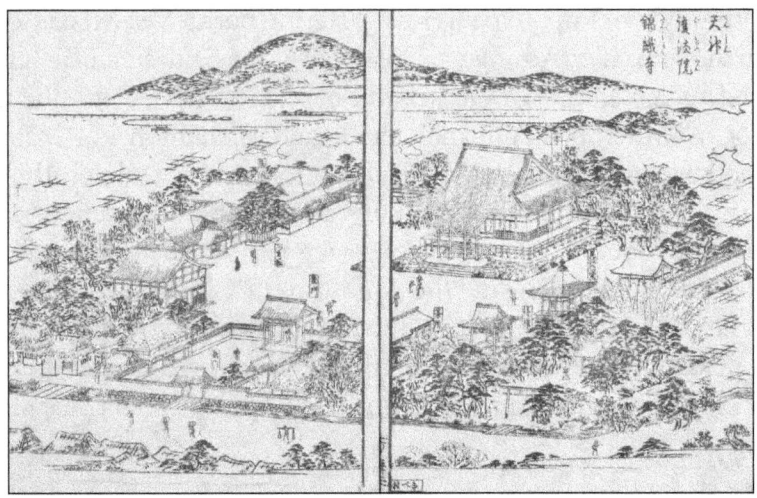

Figure 6 Kinshokuji at stage (4).

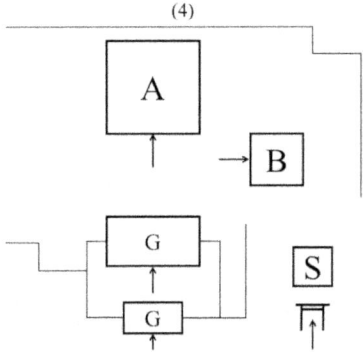

Figure 7 Stage (4).

26 **Figures 3–5 and 7–9** are slightly simplified schematizations. The abbreviations indicate the following buildings: A: Amida Hall, B: Bishamon Hall, G: Gate, M: Founder Hall (Mieidō 御影堂), Ma: Mausoleum of Shinran, S: Shrine.

27 Ryōtei 1803–09, Vol. 1, fol. [57b].

contrast to the previous example, the shrine's entrance leads directly to the outer part of the temple's precincts. Although the appearance of the shrine itself is remarkable, the new context is also important. Especially in the older tale, we can also observe the detail that the temple's wall seems even to exclude the shrine. This interpretation is supported by the fact that the shrine itself is the only conspicuous building not described by a name panel.[28]

Therefore, temple and shrine are in a difficult relationship between inclusion and exclusion. It is worth adding that the combination of the temple, Kinshokuji, with a shrine is a singularity within the whole Shin Buddhist tale, which consists of ten volumes and nearly 250 temples described. The other few exceptions are nearly all temples that are usually connected to other Buddhist sects.[29] Hence, it cannot be claimed the shrine is only a simple landscape feature in the illustration. The existence of Kinshokuji is strongly connected with the shrine.

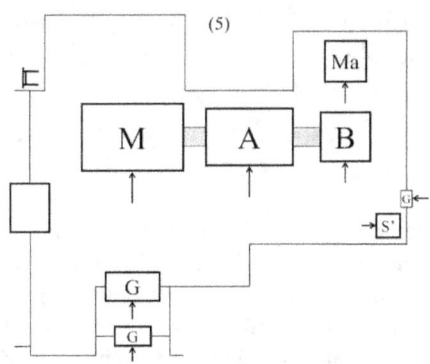

Figure 8 Stage (5).

28 Ibid. (property of the Waseda University Library, Kotenseki Sogo Database).

29 The other Tendaishū- and Jōdoshū-exceptions are Rokkakudō 六角堂 (Ryōtei 1803–09, Vol. 1, fols. [20b/21a]), Tsukinowadera 月輪寺 (ibid., Vol. 1, fol. [30b]), Chion'in 知恩院 (ibid., vol. 1, fol. [36a]) and Zenkōji (ibid., Vol. 5, fols. [9b-12a]). The Shin Buddhist exceptions are Saihōji 西方寺 (ibid., Vol. 4, fols. [26b/27a]), Kōjunji 孝順寺 (ibid., Vol. 4, fols. [44b/45a]), An'yōji 安養寺 (ibid., Vol. 9, fols. [48b/49a]) and Kansenji 勸專寺 (ibid.).

(5) In a postcard from the end of the nineteenth century[30] we see remarkable differences (schematized in **Figure 8**). I want to highlight three points. First: The number of halls has significantly changed. In the centre, we find three halls connected through a bridge. This architectural point became a highly typical characteristic of Shin Buddhist temples, and all the more magnificent temples share this point. The added – and largest – hall is supposedly the Founder Hall. Hence, we can conclude that Kinshokuji began with the modern times to stress its connection to Shinran more than before. The newly erected mausoleum of the founder also symbolizes this standpoint. Second: The displayed range of the precinct has become very wide. But in contrast, the old shrine has been deleted.

This, in turn, relates to the third point: A new shrine appears in the inner precinct of Kinshokuji. This shrine even gets a name panel which reads: Sannō Gongen 山王権現, that is, "Sannō manifestation." The shrine that has been deleted from the map may be the local Kibe Shrine 木部神社 (formerly Akuōji Shrine 惡王子神社). Here is not the place to refer to the architecture of Enryakuji and the Sannō Shrine's 山王社 function within it.[31] At this point, it is essential to know that the Sannō Shrine is one prototype of the theory of *honji suijaku* 本地垂跡,[32] and therefore, an ideal object

30 *Shigaken Yasugun Shinshū Kibeha honzan Kinshokuji no kei* 1896.
31 Referring to a map of Enryakuji from 1767 (Take 2013), we can observe various Sannō Shrines at prominent places. Within the Sannō structure, the so-called "Seven Shrines of Sannō" (*Sannō shichisha* 山王七社) are most important. The seven *kami* are associated with seven Buddhist deities, i.e. the Buddha Śākyamuni, Yakushi 藥師 and Amida, and Bodhisattvas Senjukanzeon 千手觀世音, Jūichimenkanzeon 十一面觀世音, Jizō 地藏 and Fugen 普賢. Except for that of Fugen, all six Sannō shrines are located in front of halls that have as the primary object of worship one of these deities (and one shrine is not in front of a hall with Jūichimenkanzeon but Shōkannon 聖觀音). The exception is located in the area Imurodani 飯室谷 and front of a hall with Fudō Myōō 不動明王. However, a reference to the connection of Fugen and Fudō could harmonize even this exception. Therefore, we can already see due to this structure that Kinshokuji also uses this function of Sannō Shrine but only in a different way. One more important point is the connection to Bishamon.
32 Alicia Matsunaga provides a fascinating reading of a Shin Buddhist *honji suijaku* theory. She connects Shinran's emphasis on the accommodated body

for Kinshokuji and its Tendai-roots. Moreover, the Sannō Shrine in Kinshokuji's precinct is in front of Bishamon Hall. The result is a line of halls with the following primary objects of worship and increasing size: Sannō Gongen, Bishamon, Amida Buddha and Shinran. Due to the abolition of the Kibe Shrine from the map and the new focus on Shinran, we can say that the temple has loosened its local connection in favour of a closer relationship to a somewhat "Buddhist" element.

(6) Today, the temple has almost the same structure as it did in the late nineteenth century (**Figures 9 and 10**). The separation of Kinshokuji and the shrine of Kibe is also reflected in the shrine's entrance having been rotated 90 degrees from its former direction. Its architectural rhetoric emphasizes a clear distinction between temple and shrine. Further, we can see that the objects of worship within the Sannō Shrine are statues of Buddhas. Although we cannot make any statements about the objects in previous times, the present situation clearly reflects the view that Shinto is *one aspect* of Buddhism.

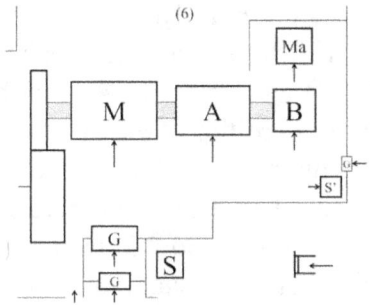

Figure 9 Stage (6).

Figure 10 Kinshokuji temple today.

(*ōjin* 應身, also transformed body [*keshin* 化身]) of Amida with the idea of *honji* as "the reality of 'oneness-as-it-is'" and *suijaku* as "the Original Vow of Hōzō Bosatsu" (Matsunaga 1969, 278). Matsunaga also refers to the similar use of the terms "transformed body" and "*suijaku*" by Kakunyo in the *Godenshō* (ibid., 280). However, she stresses a tendency to understand *honji suijaku* rather as a means to reach "a more idealistic Buddhist interpretation" than to get into contact with Shintō (ibid., 282).

That is, this shrine in a corner of the temple's precincts shows new developments in Japanese religion (the separation of Buddhism and Shinto) as well as its tradition. It is strongly bound to both directions. The remarkable point is that Kinshokuji, as part of a branch of Shin Buddhism, had ideal conditions to get fully rid of any Shinto elements. But the temple decided to keep these roots to some extent and, therefore, remains somewhere between its locality and a sectarian boundary. This led Kinshokuji to its outstanding Shinto element among other Shin Buddhist temples. Although it is apparently difficult to suggest about the present situation of all Shin Buddhist temples, Kinshokuji is at least outstanding in being a Shin Buddhist *head temple* with a Shinto shrine in contrast to all other head temples of the so-called "Ten Branches of Shin Buddhism" (*Shinshū jippa* 眞宗十派).

The rhetoric of inclusion: Materials in dialogue with texts

To conclude, I want to highlight three points we can gain from my analysis of Kinshokuji. First: We saw that a temple's local conditions are highly important. Although Tendai Buddhism and the deity Bishamon stand in contrast to Shinran and his teachings, Kinshokuji found a way to include them and not break with its local tradition. It is important to note here that its association to Shin Buddhism is not only a contemporary attribution, but a self-description we find already in premodern times. Therefore, we are not anachronistically arguing if we think about Kinshokuji distinctly being a Shin Buddhist temple. But at the same time, sectarian attributes are only useful to a certain extent when trying to understand the rhetoric of a certain temple. My analysis of materials from literature and architecture gives us a quite more appropriate understanding of the actual Kinshokuji. It shows that keeping local tradition might be more important than macro-level sectarian ties. The case of Kinshokuji made clear that this does include not only other denominations of Buddhism, but also the so-called "alien" parts like Shinto. This rhetoric of inclusion can be characterized as the *changing of relationships* rather than deleting former aspects.

Multiple divinities in Shin Buddhist temples 215

Going back to the conclusion of the narrative of Kinshokuji, we can describe these relationships as follows:

Bishamon *protects* ...	
The Tennō officially *recognizes* (and therefore *protects*) ...	Shin Buddhism
Shintō is an *expression of* ...	

Therefore, we can speak of multiple divinities while one and the same term can play a considerable variety of different roles. These terms (Bishamon, Shintō etc.) are as mere labels only the *basis* for a process that connects them with concrete, individual contexts.

This leads to the second point: Nonetheless, one should not think that I am arguing *against* a macro perspective. I want to stress that this macro perspective should be understood as the just-mentioned "basis" for a more concrete interpretation. The macro or the so-called "orthodox" interpretation is always present. Therefore, it represents an essential reference for defining its own standpoint. Aspects of religions as tales or architecture are means to harmonize the local situation with the global understanding of, e.g., a sect. My analysis of Kinshokuji made clear that we should not understand it as an exception, but rather that we should understand Japanese Buddhism itself as an amalgam of exceptions. It is not entirely individual but at the same time not merely bound to a sect. Although these cases can be called exceptions, the notion of "exception" itself requires the rule. Therefore, Kinshokuji is one example of a Buddhist temple that stands on the border between rule and autarchy. This way of being an exception is, however, the most satisfactory way for a temple to guarantee its twofold integrity. The present-day precincts of Kinshokuji and especially its connection of Bishamon Hall[33] with Amida Hall and Shinran Hall

---

33 Today, the Kibe branch even performs services at the Bishamon Hall three times per year: January 16, May 16 and September 16. These days address the Related days (*ennichi* 縁日) of Bishamon, that is, the first day of the tiger in January, May and September. The hall with Bishamon is now called Ten'an Hall, and it holds the services in honour of the founding of the hall, the arrival of Shinran and the founding of Kinshokuji.

highlight that they are the result of the local Kinshokuji narrative which was in a struggle with the existing Shin Buddhist narrative as well as Shintō narrative. Therefore, we need the *macro as well as the micro perspective.*

Finally: This approach has shown us one remarkable point concerning Shinto. Shinto is seen as being strongly bound to its distinct location. But we have seen that Buddhism also possesses a local aspect – a temple's identity is in most cases closely connected with the local situation. Therefore, *theories* about the compatibility of Buddhism and Shinto (like *honji suijaku*) are important *aspects* of a greater discourse about their compatibility. In addition, these aspects also fundamentally include local tales and material aspects. Hence, we can conclude that Shinto is also strongly influenced by "Buddhist" tales. These are all different tools for bringing different approaches to one local place together. The interwovenness of Buddhism and Shinto is not only characterized by the Buddhist viewpoint of "including something" but also the viewpoint of Shinto, namely the task of "being included". In turn, their complementary nature allows them to rely on (e.g.) theoretical strengths of the so-called "other". Hence, we should understand the process of the contact of Buddhism with Shinto as not only integration or harmonization of the first. It is to some extent even more critical to recognize the new qualities to which Shinto got access. Theories like *honji suijaku* may seem like discourses for Buddhism to avoid contradictions with Shinto. However, this field of interest also influences in the opposite direction. Through Shinto's connections with Buddhism, Shinto got access to entirely new areas of, what I tentatively want to call, the religious practice of people. In this sense, the sphere of influence of Buddhism *as well as* Shinto became wider through their new interconnection.

The case of Kinshokuji has shown us that Japanese Buddhist temples, as well as Shinto shrines, must always be understood as interwoven entities struggling for their local integrity.

References

Dobbins, James C. 1989. *Jōdo Shinshū: Shin Buddhism in Medieval Japan*. Bloomington, Indianapolis (Indiana University Press).
Hakue 白慧 1692. *Zenkōji engi* 善光寺縁起. 5 vols. Kyoto (Hishiyamagobee 菱屋孫兵衛).
Hirota, Dennis et al. 1997. *The Collected Works of Shinran*. Vol. I, The Writings. Kyoto (Jōdo Shinshū Hongwanji-ha).
[Ichizen 一禪 1859]. *Shinran shōnin goichidaiki zue* 親鸞聖人御一代記圖繪. 5 vols. Kyoto (Kōto Shorin 皇都書林).
Kinshokuji 錦織寺 1996. *Shinran shōnin gosokuseki no honzan: Kinshokuji* 親鸞聖人御足跡の本山：錦織寺. Kyoto (Seigensha 青幻舎).
Matsunaga, Alicia 1969. *The Buddhist Philosophy of Assimilation: The Historical Development of the Honji-Suijaku Theory*. Tokyo (Sophia University).
Ryōtei 了貞 1803–09. *Nijūyohai junpai zue* 二十四輩巡拜圖會. 10 vols. Osaka (Kawachiya Tasuke 河内屋太助).
Sasaki Gesshō 佐々木月樵 (ed.) 1910. *Shinranden sōsho* 親鸞傳叢書. Tokyo (Muga Sanbō 無我山房), 86–93.
Shigaken Yasugun Shinshū Kibeha honzan Kinshokuji no kei 滋賀縣野洲郡真宗木邉派本山錦織寺之景 1896. Postcard.
Shunjo 舜恕 and Ekan 慧觀 1801. *Shinran shōnin eshiden* 親鸞聖人繪詞傳. Kyoto (Kōto Shorin 皇都書林).
Take Kakuchō 武覚超 2013. *Hieizan shodōshi no kenkyū* 比叡山諸堂史の研究. Kyoto (Hōzōkan 法藏館).
Teihon Shinran shōnin zenshū 定本親鸞聖人全集 1969. 9 vols. Kyoto (Hōzōkan 法藏館).
Unjō meiran taizen 雲上眲覽大全 1849 [1837]. 2 vols. Older versions of this directory were titled *(Bansei) Unjō meikan* (萬世) 雲上明鑑. Kyoto (Takehara Yoshibee 竹原好兵衞).

About the author

Markus Ruesch is currently a JSPS International Research Fellow at Ryukoku University. He has studied Japanese Studies and Philosophy and holds a doctorate in Japanese Studies from Freie Universität Berlin (2018). Ruesch has published on Shin Buddhism and Buddhist Literature. In his monograph *Argumente des Heiligen* (2019) he writes on hagiographies with a focus on Shinran.

12

Responsive reflections on Buddhism and Shinto

Katja Triplett

This paper focuses on the complex relations between Buddhism and Shinto and how they manifest in intellectual conceptualizations as well as in the shaping of religious sites, taking into account all of the eight preceding contributions in Part 2 of the present volume entitled "Exploring Borderlands of Shinto."[1] These contributions are by: Yeonjoo Park (Medieval Tendai Buddhist views of *kami*), Vladlena Fedianina (Conceptions of *kami* in the writings of the Tendai monk Jien), Iwasawa Tomoko (Buddhist-Shinto syncretization at the medieval Suwa Shrine), D. Max Moerman (Underground Buddhism at the Ise Shrines), Dunja Jelesijevic (Shinto spaces and *shinbutsu* interaction in the Noh), Michael Pye (Buddhist-style pilgrimage with Shinto meanings), Robert Rhodes (Why does Shin Buddhism reject the worship of the *kami*?) and Markus Ruesch (Multiple divinities in Shin Buddhist temples).

On entering the "Borderlands of Shinto" hypothetical visitors will notice a change of landscape and recognize markers set up by inhabitants of these lands to inform the visitors of their whereabouts. Some visitors may be astutely aware that they traverse borderlands of Shinto. Some feel like trespassers. Others would see the visit as a homecoming. But many cross the borderlands because they posses multiple religious identities and then simply choose one of many options in the religious landscape of Japan to which the borderlands of Shinto belong.

---

1 The author thanks the International Shinto Studies Association (ISSA) and the ISSA team for making possible her contribution to the two-part panel "Multiple religious identities in Japan", organized and chaired by Michael Pye at the 2018 annual conference of the European Association for the Study of Religions (EASR) in Bern.

To possess multiple religious identities as the normal way of life comes as a surprise to those who are used to working with religious landscapes that emphasize an exclusivist approach. How can you be a member of one religion and, in addition, practise another? And indeed, in contemporary Japan the religious sites are usually marked as separate from each other. If you want to fulfil the Shinto side of your identity, you visit the Shinto shrine. If you want to do something Buddhist, you go to the Buddhist temple. The name of the site is an additional identity marker because it uses either the word for Shinto shrine or Buddhist temple in it. One glance at the name and you know where you are: in the Shinto world or the Buddhist world. Of course, this is in reality more complicated. Today's religious landscape is the result of a not entirely peaceful process instigated by the state at the end of the nineteenth century. The state policies were designed to clarify and separate Shinto and Buddhism in a precise manner.

The eight papers being considered here as "Borderlands of Shinto" addressed what may come as an even greater surprise than having a multiple religious identity as the normal way of life. Not only were Buddhism and Shinto practised side-by-side but they were also practised at one and the same site. Religious practice in premodern Japan included visits to shared sacred spaces that usually had the form of temple-shrine complexes. The eight authors discuss the relationship between what in a simplified way could be called "Shinto" and what could be called "Buddhism". They look at historical sources roughly from the medieval and early modern periods, with important excursions to developments in the nineteenth century to the present. They use several key terms to describe the transformation processes they encountered in their sources: reinterpretation, reorganization, fusion, amalgamation and syncretization. Other key terms to describe the phenomena and the relations between Buddhism and Shinto they encountered in their sources were: that the two religions overlap, interact; that they are syncretic, entangled and intertwined; and that there is interplay between the two.

I find especially noteworthy that the position in the history of Japanese religions of some of the new religions emerging as the result of such transformation processes were termed "unique" as in the case of Suwa-ryū Shintō 諏訪流神道 in the chapter by Iwasawa Tomoko, and also perhaps Shin Buddhism (Jōdo Shinshū 浄土真宗) in the time of Shinran 親鸞 (1173–1263) expressed in the chapter by Robert Rhodes. The break of these religions from tradition can also appear as "radical." Markus Ruesch addresses this aspect of exceptionality in his chapter when he states that singularity or uniqueness can be interpreted simply as an indication of a great variety in the relationship between Shinto and Buddhism. In other words: what is so unique is the enormous plurality of religions. One of the fascinating outcomes of these contributions in Part 2 is that we are being made aware of finding a much greater variety of religious forms in medieval Japan than previously thought.

The contributors have explored a wide range of sources that allow an assessment of the daily life and work at these shared sacred spaces, and how these spaces were conceptualized in ritual and art. They look at architectural structures and materials such as bronze containers for texts and inscribed clay tiles that were once buried on purpose. Other sources explored include foundation narratives and origin tales, maps, commemorative papers and other materials of a pilgrimage, learned treatises and encyclopedias, noh theatre scripts and props, and poetry. I see as one further overall result of the eight explorations that local conditions in the various regions of the Japanese archipelago played a much more significant role than the conceptual distinctions made in doctrinal texts.

Two principal outcomes of the research presented here will have in my view an impact on future research in Shinto Studies. These are: (1) the variations of the *honji suijaku* paradigm and, connected to it, (2) the range of identity markers distinguished by the eight authors in their sources.

Variations of the honji suijaku paradigm

The fact that multiple religious identities are a salient feature of Japanese religiosity derives not least from the influential *honji suijaku* 本地垂跡 ("original ground and traces left") doctrine that took on paradigmatic significance. As outlined by the authors in Part 2, this doctrine is the base for the view that the buddhas are the original form of Indian or Japanese deities. Yeonjoo Park contributes with original insight on this well-known doctrine by zooming in on the Tendai monk Kōshū's 光宗 (1276–1350) monumental encyclopedia *Keiran shūyō shū* 溪嵐拾葉集 ("Collection of Leaves Gathered in Tempestuous Brooks"). In this tradition the *kami* of Japan manifest outwardly in the world, taking various shapes including that of a writhing snake, but on an absolute level they are identical with the buddhas and, by implication, with the human mind. The point of departure is the esoteric Buddhist doctrine of nonduality and the Tendai teaching of original awakening. Despite the postulation of nonduality, the relationship between Buddhist and Shinto deities remains hierarchical: the "original ground" are the buddhas manifesting as *kami* to aid practitioners in their arduous practice. The meaning of the *kami* here appears as being thoroughly Buddhistic. Much of the discussion in the *Keiran shūyō shū* and other works cover the relationship between a certain Buddha with a particular *kami*, often the principal divinities of a specific locale.

This doctrine of *honji suijaku* in a Buddhist key was reversed not long after the appearance of works such as the *Keiran shūyō shū*, for example by the influential Yoshida Kanetomo 吉田兼倶 (1435–1511) with his *Yuiitsu Shintō* 唯一神道, the "One and Only Shinto". Now, the *kami* range higher than the buddhas, but the doctrine essentially remains the same: there is an origin and a manifestation of this origin on earth, i.e. in Japan.

With the idea that the origin is a universal, ultimate principal or entity, an idea derived from esoteric Buddhism, two additional variations occurred: the Suwa-ryū Shintō of Moriya Mitsusane 守矢満実 (fl. 1471–86) not only supposed that the various *kami* are the origin but that they all originate from one ultimate *kami*, Mishaguji ミシャグジ. I see the interpretation by Zonkaku 存覺 (1290–1373), one of the principal authorities in Shin Buddhism in the medieval period, to be somewhat parallel to what Moriya stated. Zonkaku not only postulated that the buddhas are the origin and the *kami* their manifestations – a traditional stance – but that all buddhas come from one Buddha, Amida.

Finally, I see yet another reformulation of the paradigm: it was proposed that in mythical times the *kami* and the buddhas together made a secret plan to protect Japan and guide the Empire through the crisis of *mappō* 末法, the period of the final Dharma. Vladlena Fedianina has detailed this in her presentation on the Tendai Buddhist monk and poet Jien 慈圓 (1155–1225) who was from the powerful Fujiwara family. And Max Moerman elaborates on it when he mentions the opening tale of the thirteenth-century collection of Buddhist tales *Shasekishū* 沙石集 ("Sand and Pebbles"). While there is still a hierarchy apparent in the relationship between the *kami* and the buddhas in these two examples, *kami* and buddhas cooperate on the same level, and the unfolding events in history were thought to be part of their joint action.

It seems clear to me that Jien wished to legitimize the prominent role of the imperial and the Fujiwara families as protectors of Japan as well as the authority of the shogunate in Kamakura because he profited from it both as a Fujiwara and a high priest. He had to position himself in a new political environment and it was important for him to depict the tutelary *kami* of the imperial and the Fujiwara families as being on a par with the buddhas and to classify some deities as threatening evil influences that needed to be exorcised.

Hundreds of years of shifting mutual identification of buddhas and *kami*, and narratives embedded in written and oral culture, provided a rich ground for the formulation of plots in noh. Noh is a form of high-culture theatre developed in the fourteenth century, to which Dunja Jelesijevic turns in her contribution to this volume. She explores the plots of two pieces, *Yamamba* 山姥 ("Mountain Crone") and *Nonomiya* 野々宮 ("Shrine in the Field") and highlights aspects of the play's scripted performance in relation with the *honji suijaku* paradigm and the Buddhist teaching of nonduality. Compared to the other examples in Part 2 of the volume, the sources here remain highly ambiguous in what they say about *shinbutsu* 神仏 (*kami*-buddha) relationship. The plays are intentionally ambiguous in order to create and maintain the suspense of the audience.

I see in Dunja Jelesijevic's presentation on noh a fruitful link with Yeonjoo Park's chapter in that we recognize here an artistic but also ritualistic reworking of Buddhist speculations on the human mind with the result of a highly stylized psychodrama. For example the image of the "winding snake" as a symbol for the convoluted but inherently awakened nature of the mind as described in Kōshū's *Keiran shūyō shū* finds in my view an expression in the play *Yamamba* when the dancer and her fellows take a dangerous serpentine mountain path in order to reach their final destination.

The starting point of Michael Pye's discussion of Shinto pilgrimage is his wider definition of pilgrimage as "the deliberate traversing of a route to a sacred place which lies outside one's normal habitat," so formulated to include circulatory pilgrimages as well as journeys to one special site. While most twentieth-century pilgrimages in Shinto imitate the pilgrimage to sites of the Seven Gods of Fortune (Shichifukujin 七福神) the circulatory pilgrimage to a group of twenty-five shrines dedicated to the deified Heian Period scholar Sugawara no Michizane 菅原道真 (845–903), the god of learning, appears to significantly depart from it. This popular pilgrimage to the god of learning goes back to the personal initiative of a nineteenth-century educator who laid the focus on visiting the shrines dedicated to the god for attaining academic success, which can be said to be a rather concentrated aim. In contrast, the Seven Gods of Fortune pilgrimages found in various cities are in my view a relic of the pre-Meiji Period ambiguity of *shinbutsu* relations: The Seven Gods of Fortune are cherished without the pressure of having to sort them into categories of Buddhist and "other" divinities. Here, ambiguous *shinbutsu* relationship is celebrated. Compared to the enjoyment of noh that deals with troubling themes of evanescence and death, pilgrimages to shrines and temples housing these seven gods are done in a light-hearted way focused on this-worldly benefits.

Yet a different matter is another Shinto pilgrimage that Michael Pye introduces and analyses. The visit to no less than 125 shrines of different types belonging to the Ise Shrine brings the pilgrim in principle to different divinities that exist in no particular hierarchical order. Various sources indicate that the pilgrim is in fact visiting one single entity in its multiple appearance. This concept is in my view reminiscent of the idea of nonduality expressed in Buddhist texts, for example as "mutual identity" (*sōsoku* 相即) or "neither one nor two" (*funi* 不二).

Identity markers

Apart from the often very complex classification schemes of *kami*, *deva*, spirits, demons, heavenly kings, bodhisattvas, buddhas and so on, the sources analysed by the eight authors of Part 2 in the present volume speak of how the social actors further marked the boundaries of what they held to be Buddhist or Shinto. Max Moerman mentions that during Ise Shrine rituals the use of Buddhist terms was taboo. Considering this prohibition of things Buddhist, it seems surprising that Ise Shrine priests privately built Buddhist temples and paid for sutra burials to ensure a good birth in the next life.

That Shinto abhors death and blood because both are polluting was elevated to a defining feature for all phenomena roughly identifiable as Shinto. However, is the ritual practice at Suwa Shrine that included blood sacrifice then Buddhist and not Shinto? I think it is a local variation that defies such labelling which apparently did not bother anyone in premodern times. It is telling, and Iwasawa Tomoko points this out, that the practice of blood sacrifice was eradicated in the Meiji Period. The strict application of this defining marker led to a transformation, and indeed to the disappearance, of this local ritual tradition.

An officially celibate lifestyle and dealing with objects identified as coming from Indian or Chinese religions such as the sutras and incense seem to have been significant markers of Buddhism. Besides language (technical terms, names of deities, taboo words) and embodied action (dressing, sexuality, rituals, pilgrimage) the attention to space seems to have been and still to be of utmost importance in marking boundaries.

"Shinto spaces" are not only the Shinto shrine and places in the wild – a mountain, rock-formation or waterfall – but also the modest, small altars for the *kami* (*kamidana* 神棚) usually hanging on the wall inside homes or shops. As Robert Rhodes relates in his chapter, parishioners and priests in Shin Buddhism negotiated how to remove and abstain from using such altars while, in reality, many families seem to have revered the *kami* in their homes or were even patrons of village Shinto shrines, not following the strictly orthodox guidelines laid out by Shin Buddhist authorities.

That shrines and temples coexisted at the same site is a well known phenomenon, but Markus Ruesch highlights a centuries-old institution of a *kami* shrine at a Shin Buddhist temple site that has survived since medieval times, i.e. at a site that formally speaking should be devoid of *kami*-related architecture and worship according to Shin Buddhist orthodoxy. However, the temple Kinshokuji 錦織寺, the site in Shiga Prefecture that he investigated using illustrations in picture scrolls and maps, shows that a *kami* shrine was always present at the site although appearing in different architectural layouts over the centuries. These changes indicate negotiation patterns in regard to the inclusion of Shinto at Kinshokuji, an attitude that seems also to have been more prevalent in other parts of Japan than heretofore thought in academic research.

Finally, chapters addressing the notion of travel to Shinto sites further explore topics of orthodoxy and transgression. A more abstract "Shinto space" is created in noh as an artistic form outside of institutionalized religion but in close relation to it, as noh was often performed on stages at shrine-temple sites. Noh plays focus on the permeability of the realms of the Shinto-Buddhist cosmology, the natural landscape and the sacred sites. The figures of the plays wander between the seen and unseen worlds that ultimately are one. Dunja Jelesijevic emphasizes the liminality of the realms the protagonists traverse during the play. This would preclude the idea of transgression. However, when a Buddhist priest enters the precincts of the seemingly abandoned Shinto "shrine in the field" (Nonomiya), a shrine maiden scolds him that he has committed a transgression into a purified space. The event in the play mirrors Genji's transgression upon approaching his lover at the very same shrine a long time past. Similarly, the human dancer in *Yamamba* enters the abode of the mountain crone uninvited and thus trespasses in the spirit's realm. The visits to these Shinto spaces and the ensuing encounters with spirits or ghosts appear highly transfigured in these noh plays; nevertheless the narratives point to an actually lived religiosity of travel and pilgrimage to remote and less remote sacred sites that were familiar to the audience of the plays.

From the Meiji Period onward, linkages of several Shinto shrines formed circuits, often in urban centres. Michael Pye stresses that while such Shinto shrine circuits were clearly modelled on Buddhist circulatory pilgrimage, they offer specific Shinto interpretations combining the celebration of the nation with wishes for the prosperity of one's family. The visit to multiple shrines linked by associations founded for this purpose is also thought to multiply the benefits. Obtaining this-worldly benefits in Shinto is a meaning akin but not identical to the purpose of meritorious action in Buddhism. The proponents of pilgrimage in Shinto need to negotiate a Shinto orthodoxy within a ritual structure and understanding of this-worldly benefits. Buddhist temples have dominated these ideas and practices but as they used to be sites combining Buddhist and Shinto worship and ritual transaction, obtaining benefits through circulatory *Shinto* pilgrimage was felt to be a plausible venture. The set-up of pilgrimages to shrines of the god of learning and to 125 shrines linked to the great Ise Shrine can be interpreted as a move further toward the exclusion of meanings marked as Buddhist and the inclusion of meanings thought to represent Shinto. The most important identity marker in the Ise Shrine pilgrimage to 125 shrines is upholding an exclusive relation to the imperial family. Perhaps we are here leaving the borderlands and approach another topic: the not undisputed claim of Ise as the "heartland" of Shinto.

***

In closing, let me briefly address an important question raised in our discussion at the conference in Bern: If premodern Japanese did not have a concept of religion, then what does it mean to talk about their "religious identity"?

Perhaps there was no concept of religion, not even a term for "religion" as we have in modernity, but this does not mean that social actors in premodern Japan did not consciously have a "religious identity." The case studies show that the various persons could clearly identify what they saw as pertaining to religion and to a particular religion, too. They conducted rituals they saw as traditional and, more importantly, they created new rituals, ceremonies and sites. They constructed novel classifications of deities based on a powerful paradigm. They endlessly played with variations of this paradigm and the ambiguities resulting from mutual identification of *kami* and buddhas. They shaped new lifestyles and engaged in institutional politics. The result is a plural landscape of local religions that have in common a preoccupation with relating *kami* and buddhas to each other in ever more creative ways, often to combat what they felt to be the crises of their times.

If borders are heavily disputed or established to confine those within or keep others out, borderlands can be minefields – to stay with the image evoked by the title of this group of contributions. In Japan, the borderlands of Shinto seem, in contrast, for the most part of history at least, a dynamic but rather fortunate place.

About the author

Katja Triplett was Professor of the Study of Religions at Göttingen and is currently based at the Humanities Centre for Advanced Studies "Multiple Secularities – Beyond the West, Beyond Modernities" at the University of Leipzig. Her doctorate in the Study of Religions from Marburg University, where she also studied Japanese Linguistics and Anthropology, was published as *Menschenopfer und Selbstopfer in den japanischen Legenden* (2004). She has since published widely on Japanese religions.

Part 3
The Puzzle and Fascination of Sect Shintō

13

Sect Shintō and the case of Ooyashirokyō

Michael Pye

Introductory considerations

It is often remarked that Shinto has no formalized teaching, and the existence of several Shinto "teaching sects" with a total following of millions of believers may therefore seem surprising. These sects are referred to collectively as *kyōha shintō* 教派神道, a term usually translated into English as "Sect Shintō" or in earlier days also as "Sectarian Shintō" (see further below). Literally, the term *kyōha* implies a "teaching (*kyō*) subgroup (*ha*)." An alternative term is *shūha shintō* 宗派神道, in which *shūha* has the meaning of "religious sect" but this is less commonly used by representatives of the leading groups in question. The element *shū*- also forms part of *shūkyō*, the standard term for "religion" (see also further below). In English writing it has been usual to speak of Sect Shintō, to distinguish it from "Shrine Shintō" (*jinja shintō* 神社神道), the latter referring to the majority of Shinto shrines throughout the country. It must be admitted that the word "sect" has recently become difficult because popular media use it to refer to small religious groups with a sensational news value of some kind. To avoid such associations we might refer to "Teaching Shinto Groups" or, for the convenience of brevity, just Teaching Shinto, that is, a variant of Shinto which offers a particular form of guidance or teaching which goes beyond everyday shrine visits.

Simplified accounts of Japanese religions frequently include the ideas that "Shinto is the ethnic religion of the Japanese," "Shinto does not have any teaching or doctrine" and "Japanese people are just not very religious anyway." The combined effect of these ideas, if true, would indeed amount to the exclusion of the possibility of there being any kind of "sects" within Shinto. How can an ethnic group have a sect? How can a religion with no teaching have subgroups which differ in their teaching? How could a non-religious population maintain special-interest religious groups? However, each of the previous statements is false, or at any rate only amounts to a half truth, or less. Let us consider briefly the weaknesses of these widespread assumptions.

The first statement, that Shinto is "the" ethnic religion of "the" Japanese, and that means by implication of all Japanese, is false because many Japanese people, at least in modern times, in fact have little to do with Shinto shrines or rites. As a total population of more than 125 million they fail to coalesce solely around Shinto as "the" ethnic religion of the nation. Admittedly, supposedly secular segments of population are quite likely to visit Shinto shrines on various occasions for what may be regarded as more or less customary reasons. For example, a natural scientist might well carry an amulet from the shrine of the god of learning, Tenjin-sama. But conversely, there are many other *non*-Shinto focuses of ideological, cultural, religious or spiritual attention, especially in the field of Buddhism and among popular new religions. What can be stated is the lesser claim that Shinto is a specifically Japanese religion and that it does not normally extend its range beyond Japanese populations.

The second questionable assertion, that Shinto has no teaching, only arises insofar as a model of "doctrine" as being an essential feature of religious systems is erroneously projected onto a religion in which ritual practice is predominant. The ritual aspect of Shinto is not without conceptual accompaniment (as ritual can scarcely ever be), even though this is not highly structured in a doctrinal format. Moreover, Shinto is not at all the only religion of this kind. Traditional Hinduism, i.e. Brahmanism, is certainly another. Traditional Judaism is yet another. In these cases, ideas of various kinds may flourish but they are typically not formally promulgated by a centralized ecclesiastical authority or defined as "doctrine." This does not mean that there are no concomitant ideas at all, and indeed in complex mythological narratives ideas are rampant. Religion always includes a conceptual component of some kind, even if it is only secondary or preparatory to spiritual perspectives, as in the deepest forms of apophatic mysticism or in position-less Buddhist experience. In the case of Shinto there are plenty of mythological allusions and other concepts which are regularly expressed during ritual acts and in various kinds of occasional explanations.

The third dubious assertion also turns on a definition, namely on what counts as "being religious." Without going too far here into this frequently contested subject, what is important to note is that while secularization has certainly occurred in significant respects in Japan,[1] large numbers of Japanese people even today *voluntarily* participate in religious activities of some kind and, significantly, make a financial contribution for the privilege. When people pay, it implies that they place a value on what they pay for, and that they expect to benefit from it in material but often also in spiritual terms. It is a matter of fact that some of the organizations supported by active voluntary participation fall into the category of Teaching Shinto Groups.

In sum, it is quite essential to qualify these unwarranted, oversimplified assumptions, whether presupposed by observers or put forward by insiders to the tradition. Nevertheless, to the extent that "Shinto" is a specifically Japanese religion, with at least a *claim* on the loyalty of the population in general, it is fair to consider how far it makes sense to speak of subdivisions which have been referred to as sects. This may be regarded, at least *prima facie*, as something of a puzzle. To put it bluntly, if a Shinto priest is earnestly wishing to encourage people in any one local area to hold Shinto in high esteem, why not simply encourage them to visit and support their local shrine? Surely, as "clan children" (*ujiko* 氏子) they should above all revere their "clan divinity" (*ujigami* 氏神). Indeed, at New Year the Association of Shinto Shrines (Jinja

---

[1] Insofar as "secularization" means a loss of power on the part of leading religious institutions, the two main events were the rejection of Buddhism during the modern state-building programme of the nineteenth century and the disestablishment of Shinto following World War II. Cf. Pye 1995. The hollowing out of spiritual sensitivity as a cultural process, for example in recent decades, is a somewhat different matter and could be quite variously assessed.

Honchō) encourages people always to visit the *ujigami* first.² At the summer festivals of local shrines, residents and visitors alike are nowadays gathered in to be regarded as *ujiko*, regardless of their demographic history. There is no room for sectarian division here.

In the title of this paper we use the expression "Sect Shintō" in order to flag the field of contention in well-known terms, and indeed it is difficult to avoid. As mentioned earlier, "Sectarian Shinto" will also be found and may have the advantage of getting away from recent pejorative associations of the word "sect" in western media. Yet here too care is needed. In English the expression "sectarian" does usually bear the implication of an aggressive wish to be distinctive that is typically not appropriate in this context. It might suggest that the groups concerned actively seek to distance themselves from the general field of "Shinto" but in real life this is not usually the case.

If we leave foreign terms aside, the most appropriate term is the emic designation *kyōha shintō*, already introduced above, the preferred self-designation of a group of thirteen Shinto-oriented religious bodies. This appears both as a general category and as the proper noun used in the name of the Kyōha Shintō Rengōkai, which for want of a better solution has been translated as "Sect Shintō Federation." The term "federation" here has the implication of an alliance. These groups are allied in seeking to safeguard their independent identities in terms of religious freedom under the law and protection against interference by larger Shinto organizations. This need arose because of the political developments in modern Japan up to the end of the second world war, during which time religious bodies of various kinds were dragooned into supporting the ideological programme of the central government, or else repressed. A full literal translation of *kyōha shintō* would be "teaching subgroups of Shinto," for while the element *kyō* simply means teaching, the appended element *-ha* does further imply

---

2   It is well known that on account of massive demographic changes the concepts of *ujigami* and *ujiko* can now only be used metaphorically. On the other hand, their use in the contexts mentioned amounts to a certain kind of religious imperative.

a group which asserts some independence within a wider field, a specific branch of some description. In sum, the basic, older meaning of the English word "sect" is not entirely inappropriate.[3]

The word "sect" has also been used to translate the Japanese term *shūha* as found in a further expression used in the present context, namely *shūha shintō*. We find here the element *ha*, explained above, and also the element *shū* which, unpacked, means respect for an authoritative lineage. This term also appears in the modern Japanese word for religion, namely *shūkyō* which, though contested in some quarters, effectively refers to "religion" or "religions" in a broad sense, as they appear all over the world. In modern Japanese it is perfectly normal to refer to, say, Hinduism or Jainism as being "a religion." The expression can be and is used by specialists studying religions without regard to the greater or lesser degree of doctrinal content as compared with ritual behaviour. Although the term *shūha shintō* is quite innocuous, the representatives of the groups in question generally prefer *kyōha shintō*. The groups do almost always identify themselves through showing respect for a specific authoritative lineage, typically starting with a founder-figure or *kyōso* 教祖. By contrast, although many priestly families are presumed to be descended from their ancestral *kami*, Shinto in general, as a religion, has no dominant founder-figure. The Shinto sects on the other hand usually identify the date of the foundation, something which is not possible for Shinto in general. The preferred term *kyōha* throws the emphasis on the "teaching" (*kyō* 教) which had been promulgated and is now being passed on. The common character for *kyō* (derived originally from Chinese *jiào*) can also be read in Japanese pronunciation as *oshie*, a widely used verbal noun from *oshieru*, to teach. It is in this sense that it occurs in the names of leading groups such as Kurozumi-kyō or Konkō-kyō. These names are usually written without hyphens, but they are added here to show the construction.

---

3 See my article "Elements of a General Theory of Innovation" in Pye 2013, Vol. II, 130–51.

The puzzle and fascination of "Sect Shintō"

After these preliminaries we turn, centrally, to the puzzle of the very existence of "Sect Shintō." The phenomenon arises because, within the wider field of Shinto in which ritual activities admittedly take precedence over their conceptual accompaniment, the emergence to prominence of some distinctive teaching (a *kyō* or *oshie*) led on occasion to the development of loyal, special-interest groups, i.e. sects. In any religion, even when emphasis is laid on a distinctive ritual practice, there is always some equally distinctive conceptual accompaniment to it. This may seem theoretically unproblematic. On the other hand, if the relative lack of interest in "teaching" is one of the general features of Shinto while at the same time there is a claim on the attention of an overall population and not just of a limited group, then the representatives of a specialized interest group may fairly be called upon to explain how it is that it is still a "*Shinto* sect" rather than just any new religion. What is "Shinto" about it? In cases where the distinctiveness is less a matter of a newly promulgated teaching, but rather a matter of specialized, non-typical ritual activities as in the mountain cults Fusōkyō 扶桑教 and Ontakekyō 御嶽教, the question may seem less acute. However, even then the question does not disappear entirely because there is a voluntary membership which is not demographically related to a local natural community or to the Japanese ethnos in general.

For the observer, where does the fascination lie? It arises precisely because so many leaders in the general field of "Shinto" decided at some point that they did have something special to teach, that they had an *oshie* to offer, which could not be found in just any village shrine. The clue to the puzzle lies in the term -*kyō*, meaning *oshie*. We note that the general term is not just *shintō-ha* but *shintō kyōha*. The resultant pattern of shrine organizations and religious activity is a rich and fascinating field for research, especially as each group has its own relationship to the wider field of "Shinto." This may be illustrated by the briefest consideration of just two examples: Kurozumikyō and Jikkōkyō, both of which go back to pre-Meiji times before the state intervened to insist on centralized definitions of what Shinto is about.

Kurozumikyō 黒住教 is named literally after its founder Kurozumi Munetada (1789–1850), the chief priest of a Shinto shrine in Okayama who advanced his own positively delineated understanding of devotion towards the sun-goddess Amaterasu, of whom human beings are part spirits. This included the teaching that human life is fundamentally tending towards the good, and that this tendency could be reinforced through a special practice or form of "prayer" known as *nippai* 日拝, literally "sun-worship", which involves facing the rising sun to breathe it in through a contrived convulsion of the abdomen. The claim of Kurozumikyō to be "the oldest religion founded by a Japanese person"[4] accentuates the central role of its founder, which sets it off against the simple idea that every Japanese community has its local shrine which has been there from time immemorial. The conceptualized teaching was formulated by Munetada in terms of seven "warnings" against failure to observe key points in one's daily life. Positively put, his followers were enjoined to develop a sense of *marukoto* (a simple neologism written only in phonetic script), which means roundedness. Apart from the distinctive practice of *nippai* mentioned above, there is impressively simple ritual activity in a broadly Shinto style at the Kurozumi Shrine in Kyoto (near the Yoshida Shrine). This is the third important centre of the religion after the original shrine and the new buildings at the sacred site (*reichi* 霊地) known as the Shintōzan 神道山 in Okayama. Even with these few introductory hints it can be seen how a distinctive, sectarian pattern of teaching and practice can arise through devotion to Amaterasu, who was after all a major divinity in ancient Shinto mythology and one elevated to centrality in modern times.[5]

4   Official website, most recently accessed December 2018.
5   The writer's field observations of Kurozumikyō took place on various occasions dating from 1979. For a valuable overall study see Hardacre 1986. For earlier information see Holtom 1938, who presents it among "faith-healing sects" along with Konkōkyō and Tenrikyō. Holtom has a lengthy and valuable section on "Sect Shintō" but it was reprinted after the war without any updating. It includes a fine portrait of Yoshimura Masamochi, the founder of Shinshūkyō.

As a second, and rather different example of "Sect Shintō" we may in all brevity consider Jikkōkyō 實行教, the name of which means "Teaching of Actual Practice." It differs from Kurozumikyō in having a complex derivation rather than one single originator. Like Fusōkyō, this sect, as it came to be, is based on a much older movement called Fujidō, the "Way of Fuji," a name which includes a significant pun. Fuji refers indeed to Mount Fuji (富士山 Fuji-san), a central object of devotion for the pioneer Hasegawa Kakugyō 長谷川角行 (1541–1646), who travelled the length and breadth of Japan encouraging the performance of austerities with reference to the famous mountain. However, the characters used to write the name "Fuji" in this case are not the normal ones (shown above) but 不二, a combination that means "not two," with the implication of nondualism as current in Buddhist thought. In the late Edo Period the leadership got into trouble with the authorities for demanding reforms in advance of the expected appearance of the future Buddha Miroku (Skt. Maitreya), and the movement was temporarily forbidden. Following the Meiji Restoration, however, reverence for the mountain was recalibrated to emphasize the new patriotism. Many followers of the Way of Fuji were drawn into a movement founded by Shibata Hanamori (1809–90). In 1879 the name Jikkōsha 実行社 was adopted, in which the ending -*sha* should be noted as being the term for shrine. This name was later changed again however to Shintō Jikkōkyō so that it would be recognized as a form of "teaching" Shinto rather than a movement competing with the wider shrine system.[6] The other main movement arising out of the Way of Fuji, Fusōkyō, is introduced by Shishino Fumio in the next paper of this volume.

Listing Shinto sects

The nature of Sect Shintō has frequently been indicated by the straightforward citation of a list of the Shinto sects. However, care must be taken in this respect because this apparently important list

---

6 For more information on Jikkōkyō see Holtom 1938, 216–23.

has been adjusted in changing circumstances. Initially the setting up of such a list was an administrative act by government. In postwar times however, because of the newly defined freedom of religion, the concept of *kyōha shintō* was relaxed. Some were able to leave this category, while others joined it. It is therefore appropriate to distinguish and compare the historically fixed official listing of the groups and a more recent informal version representing the free association of various groups in postwar and contemporary times. The formal prewar government list included thirteen bodies, as shown in the A list below, while the current Kyōha Shintō Rengōkai list includes twelve, as shown in the B list below. The sequence is alphabetical for the first list, while the second list diverges slightly to show the correspondences.

A	B
Fusōkyō	Shintō Fusōkyō
Jikkōkyō	Jikkōkyō
Konkōkyō	Konkōkyō
Kurozumikyō	Kurozumikyō
Misogikyō	Misogikyō
Mitakekyō	Ontakekyō
- -	Ōmoto
Shintō Honkyoku	Shintōtaikyō
Shinrikyō	Shinrikyō
Shinshūkyō	Shinshūkyō
Shūseiha	Shintōshūseiha
Taiseikyō	(now withdrawn)
Taishakyō	Izumo Ooyashirokyō
Tenrikyō	(now withdrawn)
Total: 13	Total: 12

It will be noted that Taiseikyō and Tenrikyō dropped out of the list. The departure of Tenrikyō, a well-known major religious movement, is particularly significant. It is occasionally suggested that a factor in this decision was that the postwar international mission of Tenrikyō, especially in Korea, was inhibited through its earlier association with Shinto in colonial times. However, the reason given in Tenrikyō quarters is that Tenrikyō is simply a distinctive religion with its own revelation and its own soteriology. In other words, it just is not a sect of Shinto. This seems to be quite a natural point of view. The argument is that the revelations vouchsafed to its foundress are held to be of universal validity and that it therefore cannot be that Tenrikyō is a sect or subdivision of a religion normally restricted to one ethnos. In this way Tenrikyō escapes from the puzzle of how there can conceivably be "Sect Shintō," and it may be added that viewed independently the line of thought is quite plausible in that the main elements of this religion are indeed distinctive.

An important group which *joined* the free *renmei* is Ōmoto (also known as Oomotokyō). It is striking that Ōmoto (meaning "Great Source") is now associated with "Sect Shintō"; after all, in earlier times it was harassed and oppressed for expressing very distinctive ideas which seemed to rival those of government-sponsored Shinto. Although in this sense Ōmoto has come in out of the cold, as the saying goes, and although its main buildings (once razed to the ground at governmental behest) are certainly broadly shrine-like in style, it continues to be quite distinctive in its traditions and current activities. Moreover, Ōmoto has itself been the source of various new movements that do not find their way into this list. An example is the group known as Jinsei tengan gakkai 神声天眼学会 ("Study Group for the Voice of God and the Celestial Eye") founded by Kurata Chikyū 倉田地久 and currently headed by his second son Kurata Usan 倉田宇山.

But how important are these lists anyway? The Kyōha Shintō Rengōkai self-consciously consolidates a set of organizations which have a common interest in their current social and legal status. In the annual government-sponsored publication *Shūkyō nenkan*, however, there are many more organizations which are assigned to the category of *shintōkei* 神道系 that is, the "Shinto line of tradition." This whole plethora of new religions is occasionally claimed for "Sect Shintō" with the dramatic argument that since Shinto is *the* Japanese religion par excellence *all* religions initiated in Japan are a form of Shinto. However, such a statement cannot be accepted because it is obviously not the case. Most new religions in Japan draw in various ways on the wider religious culture of the country, including Shinto, but are by no means beholden to the latter's dominant features. The archetypical case is that of Tenrikyō which, though founded in Japan and featuring divine dance movements of Shinto heritage, rejects the ethnic perspective in favour of universality.

Two religions which might somehow be assigned to the *shintōkei* are Ennōkyō 円応教 ("The Perfectly Adapted Teaching") and Byakkō Shinkō Kai 白光真宏会 (the "White Light Association"). The founder of Ennōkyō, Fukata Chiyoko 深田千代子 (1887–1925), certainly learned from her local Shinto shrine (for example how to read and write), but also from a nearby Buddhist temple. An important feature of Ennōkyō is the emphasis on ancestor veneration which is rooted both in Shinto and in (Japanese) Buddhism. The founder of Byakkō Shinkō Kai, "Master Goi," i.e. Goi Masahisa 五井昌久 (1916–80), was a spiritual medium believed to have received messages directly from the spirit world.[7] However, having observed the activities of these two groups in some detail, it would not occur to me to regard them as pertaining to "Shinto" and they certainly did not split off in a sectarian manner from any wider body of Shinto.

Izumo Ooyashirokyō and Shintō diversity

In the cases just mentioned, diversity points outside the widely perceived realm of "Shinto" but it is equally pertinent to note the diversity which somehow remains within that realm. Some notes are therefore offered here on Izumo Ooyashirokyō 出雲大社教, the religion based on the Grand Shrine of Izumo (Izumo Taisha) which is so important as the locus for significant narratives in the early mythology of Shinto.[8] Of the divinities revered here, let us

---

7 On Byakkō Shinkō Kai see Pye 1986. There have been significant developments since then: an updated study has been prepared but is not yet published.

8 For a substantial and authoritative account of Izumo Taisha in general see Senge 1980, and more recently in English, Zhong 2016. A brief, but authoritative

recall that Ōkuninushi is regarded as the founder and developer of the country, that is, the land as led by Izumo, while Susano-o was the disruptive brother of Amaterasu who broke down the edges of the rice paddies until he was restrained. The religion now to be considered is a modern foundation that was formerly known as Taishakyō (after Izumo Taisha) and only later (and currently) as Ooyashirokyō, written with the same characters. Even though it apparently has the greatest number of followers among all the Shinto sects, Ooyashirokyō has been little studied, apparently only receiving attention in general overviews.

Taishakyō 大社教 was set up as an independent sect in 1882 (Meiji 15) by Senge Michihiko 千家尊福 (1845–1918), the eightieth chief priest (*gūji*) of Izumo Shrine itself, who became the new religion's first administrative head (*kanchō* 菅長). This followed a nationwide organization of Izumo Shrine supporters, in 1873, in the form of a fraternity (*kō* 講) known as the Izumo Taisha Keishinkō 出雲大社敬神講.[9] Note that Senge Michihiko is not designated as a "founder" or *kyōso* 教祖, as in some other cases, for here the "teaching" is presumed to have been that of Izumo Taisha since time immemorial, guarded by the Senge family of priests. This initiative was a direct response to the governmental policy of forbidding the propagation of any teachings as "Shinto" which diverged from official directives. The general stance of Izumo Taisha is to regard itself as being distinct from, and in terms of myth-narrative, as senior to Ise Jingū, the home of Amaterasu with the all-important link to the imperial line and the imperial household. In this way, at a time when political uniformity was being strongly demanded, Taishakyō (later Izumo Ooyashirokyō, also abbreviated as Ooyashirokyō) played a major role in maintaining the diversity of Shinto traditions. It provided a mode for the development of a network of loyalties across the country and significantly, at least for some, a cemetery at Izumo itself for the receipt

---

statement about Ooyashirokyō may be found on pages 78–82 in the substantial booklet *Izumo Taisha yusho ryakki* 出雲大社由緒略記 published by the shrine itself in 1929.

9 Senge 1980, 197.

of believers' ashes. According to the official yearbook of religions (*Shūkyo nenkan*, Bunkachō ed.) of 2016, the group counted 168 "churches" (*kyōkai* 教会)[10] of which about two-thirds were registered as religious corporations. Qualified teachers (*kyōshi* 教師) of the group numbered 8,149, of whom 6,026 were male and 2,123 were female. The total number of believers was calculated as 1,262,503, making it a relatively large group.

The local centres of Ooyashirokyō share some characteristics with the usual form of Shinto shrines but have a stronger tendency to provide congregational space for followers to enter. Take for example the Izumo Taisha Tokyo Bunshi 出雲大社東京分祠 located at fashionable Roppongi in Tokyo and hemmed in by a high-speed road and various crowded buildings. This is a shrine of steel and concrete, a far cry from the glorious wooden structure of Izumo Grand Shrine in distant Shimane Prefecture with its peaceful rural surroundings. But here too the great god Ookuninushi no Oomikami 大国主大神 is revered. People travel here from all over the wider Tokyo area by train, bus or car. Even foreign tourists arrive, simply because this shrine is on one of the lists of things to be seen. Perhaps they are disappointed that it is not like the ancient wooden structure of Izumo Taisha itself, which they are unlikely to get to on account of its remoteness. But there are rituals and other practices to be carried out here. Never mind that one needs to go up a flight of steps into the second floor of a building!

The writer visited this shrine on March 17, 2018 and this was just the season for a special calligraphy activity for children known as the *shingohōshojōshokai* 神語奉書浄書会 (**Figure 1**). This practice was founded in 2010 (Heisei 22). In 2018 (Heisei 30) it took place on March 15, March 17, March 18 (a Sunday), March 21 (being the calendrically significant *shunbun no hi* 春分の日) and April 1. The children are invited to bring their own calligraphy brush (*o-fude*), or failing that a modern style *fude*-pen, in order to write a special purificatory calligraphy (*jōsho* 浄書). Their calligraphy is then offered to the divinity as a *hōsho* 奉書, a "writing offering."

---

10 This term is used indiscriminately for Christian churches and the local meeting places of any religious groups.

244 *Exploring Shinto*

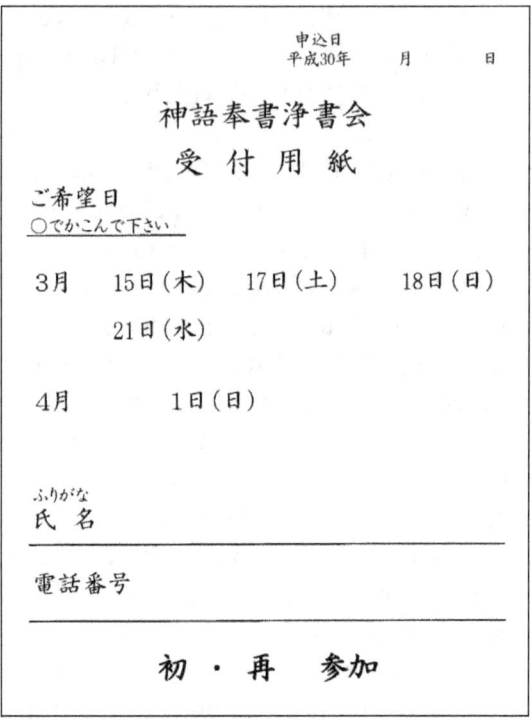

Figure 1 Application form for attendance at calligraphy offering.

The prescribed text of the calligraphy is referred to as a *shingo* 神語, a "divine word." This text consists of eight characters which run as follows:

> 幸魂 奇魂 *sachimitama kushimitama*
> 守給 幸給 *mamoritamai sachihae tamae*
> Bountiful spirit, mysterious spirit
> Grant protection, grant us bounty[11]

An explanatory comment asserts "This prayer has been passed down at the Grand Shrine of Izumo since ancient times." It is further explained as "a prayer for purifying the heart, for giving

11 Writer's translation.

internal strength, and for enabling us to pass our days in a joyful manner." This is no doubt very Shinto-like.

Apart from this, the shrine offers the opportunity to pray for most of the usual things such as good partnerships (*enmusubi* for which Izumo Taisha itself is famous), safety of the home (*kanai anzen*), flourishing business (*shōbai hanjō*), warding off evil (*yakuyoke*) and safety in traffic (*kōtsū anzen*). Others mentioned in brief are safe travel (*ryokō anzen*), fulfilment of heart's desire (*shingan jōju*), prayer for qualifications (*gōkaku kigan*), health in mind and body (*shinshin kenzen*) and healing of sickness (*byōki heiyu*).[12] In addition to such very typical petitions the shrine offers prayer ceremonies for personal life rites such as first shrine visit (*hatsu-miya-mairi*), seven/five/three shrine visit (*shichigosan*) (when children aged three, five or seven are taken to a shrine to pray for their health and good development) and weddings. Again, these rites are all very typical of many Shinto shrines.

A special ritual is regularly performed by the priests of this group, namely the *Izumo yashiki jichinsai* 出雲屋敷地鎮祭. In this ritual, Ookuninushi, also known by the popular name of Daikoku-sama, is invited to dwell in the same dwelling (*yashiki* 屋) as the people, thereby protecting them from unruly directional influences (*hōi no kyōsō* 方位の凶相). Through the alternative pronunciation of his name this divinity is brought very close to the people, for as Daikoku he is also very popular as one of the Seven Gods of Good fortune (*shichifukujin* 七福神).[13] It is especially interesting that, unlike an ordinary *jichinsai* which is carried out once only, this *jichinsai* can be repeated, for example each year. In this way the followers are kept together as a widespread religious community scattered throughout Japanese society and by no means restricted to the Izumo region.

---

12 For documentation and discussion of such lists of prayerful requests, see Pye and Triplett 2007, 90–3.
13 In this connection he is usually portrayed or sculpted holding a mallet to indicate his role in sound construction and linked with a partner, Ebisu, who holds a large fish indicating success in commercial enterprises.

Renewal, innovation and pluralism in the Shinto world

With this and the various preceding examples in mind, we may conclude with a few reflections on renewal, innovation and pluralism in the Shinto world. Although this is not the place for a general discussion of "newness" or "innovation" in religion,[14] we cannot altogether avoid the questions about what, in Shinto, counts as "new" and as "reform" and how these are related to each other. When is a new religion "new"? And when is it the same religion as before?

There is an interesting paper by Stanley Weinstein entitled "The Concept of Reformation in Japanese Buddhism" (1973). The subject so posed might seem a little out of fashion these days, but it does not really go away. Weinstein refers to a widely used distinction between *kyū-bukkyō* and *shin-bukkyō*, i.e. "old" and "new" Buddhism, which refer to Nara-Heian and Kamakura Buddhism respectively; but he argues that he prefers to think of the *shin-bukkyō* sects as an example of "Reformation" because they seek to restore and redevelop existing traditions.[15] This view is broadly speaking to be recommended. It is most appropriate in respect of the Buddhism of Nichiren (1222–82), secondly so for the Zen traditions, and less so for the Pure Land teachings. The latter also had ancient roots, but these were arguably not so central to earlier phases of Buddhism. In any case, both Nichiren for his part, as well as the leaders of Zen Buddhist schools in other ways, all claimed to be restoring essential features of the central Buddhist tradition which in their view had been overlaid with extraneous material.

The analogous question may be posed whether there is any such thing as "reform" in Shinto. In brief the answer must be a mixture of yes and no. Are the *kyōha*, like other initiatives within the thought-world of Shinto, some kind of "reform" movements? Are the "teachers" trying to tell us about a real or deeper meaning of Shinto? Tentatively, I venture to suggest that Kurozumikyō falls

---

14 See "Elements of a General Theory of Innovation in Religion" in: Pye 2013, Vol II, 130–51.

15 Weinstein 1973, p.77.

initially into the type of a reform movement. A renewed emphasis on Amaterasu was ushered in by its Shinto priest founder, and his movement then morphed into a new religion with Shinto features but with an untypical emphasis on the personal subjectivity of faith. Konkōkyō by contrast was founded outside the context of Shinto shrines, initially as a religiously oriented counselling ministry, but it acquired some features of Shinto practice in the process of its development and establishment. It is therefore not a "reform" movement within the Shinto pattern. The religion Shinshūkyō, again, with its founder Yoshimura Masamochi 芳村正秉 (1839–1915) might well be considered as a Shinto reform movement, analogous to the case of Kurozumikyō. This teaching led to the development of a chain of affiliated shrines all over the country which to the casual visitor are no different from any other Shinto shrines. The special teaching (cf. the paper by Yoshimura Masanori, the third head [kanchō 館長] of this group, in the present volume) is embedded within the life of these shrines. Even this variegated categorization collapses however when we come to the mountain cults listed as belonging to *kyōha shintō*, for these are, rather, an expression of the composite religious culture of the country; they were eventually drawn into the purview of Shinto for convenience when Buddhist and Shugendō elements were forced away from the country's ideological centre. On this process see further the article by Shishino Fumio, the sixth head (*kanchō*) of Shintō Fusōkyō, published below in the present volume.

The very setting up of a "sect" usually implies some lack of satisfaction with the main body. In that case, if Shinto in general makes a claim on the loyalty of all Japanese people (whatever the justification for that may be), then how can there be any kind of Shinto "sect"? It seems puzzling that what is supposed to be common to all Japanese people could need to have any separate, special organizations. Of course, the current situation of religious pluralism and freedom means that the claim of Shinto to be *the* religion of the Japanese people cannot be maintained, either legally or plausibly. But even if we leave that on one side there are some pertinent questions to be posed to representatives of *kyōha shintō*. This is the basic puzzle. If Shinto can be referred to as the religion of the Japanese people, how can it be divided into "sects"? Tentative answers are given above, but it is also of interest to ask representatives of various Shintō "sects" to respond to two sets of interconnected questions. The first is: (a) Can your religious organization be referred to as belonging to "Shintō"? Is it a "Shintō" organization? What is "Shintō" about it? The second set of questions is: (b) If Shintō is in some sense the national or common ethnic religion of Japanese people, why and how do you separate off as a "sect"? Why does the religion need to be a *kyōha*? It appears likely that the answers will not all be the same. The observer's conclusion must be therefore that "Shintō" is considerably more diverse than is sometimes suggested by representative priests. This conclusion, though apparently simple, has important implications for our understanding of the religious culture of Japan and for our tentative answers to the question: What is Shinto?

References

Bunkachō 文化庁 (ed.) 2016. *Shūkyo nenkan* 宗教年艦. Tokyo (Bunkachō).

Hardacre, Helen 1986. *Kurozumikyō and the New Religions of Japan.* Princeton NJ (Princeton University Press).

Holtom, D. C. 1938. *The National Faith of Japan: A Study in Modern Shintō.* London (Kegan Paul, Trench, Hubner).

Izumo Taisha (ed.) 1929/1981. *Izumo Taisha yusho ryakki* 出雲大社由緒略記. Izumo (Izumo Taisha).

Pye, Michael 1986. "National and International Identity in a Japanese Religion: Byakkoshinkokai" in: Victor C. Hayes (ed.), *Identity Issues and World Religions, Selected Proceedings of the International Association for the History of Religions*. Netley, Australia (The Australian Association for the Study of Religions).

Pye, Michael 1995. "Säkularisierung in Japan?" *Dialog der Religionen* 5/2, 140–6.

Pye, Michael 2013. *Strategies in the Study of Religions*. 2 vols. Berlin/Boston (de Gruyter).

Pye, Michael and Triplett, Katja 2007. *Streben nach Glück. Schicksalsdeutung und Lebensgestaltung in japanischen Religionen. Mit Beiträgen von Monika Schrimpf.* Berlin (LIT-Verlag).

Senge, Takatoshi 千家尊祀 1980. *Izumo Taisha* 出雲大社. Tokyo (Kodansha).

Weinstein, Stanley 1973. "The Concept of Reformation in Japanese Buddhism" in: Japan P.E.N. Club (ed.), *Studies on Japanese Culture Vol. II*. Tokyo (Japan P.E.N. Club), 75–86.

Zhong, Yijiang 2016. *The Origin of Modern Shinto in Japan*. London (Bloomsbury).

About the author

Michael Pye (born 1939) first resided in Japan from 1961 onwards. From 1968 he taught Religious Studies in England and in 1982 became professor for the Study of Religions at Marburg University, Germany. He was president of the International Association for the History of Religions from 1995 to 2000. On retirement he returned to Japan for several years, being associated with Otani University, Kyoto. Publications include *Strategies in the Study of Religions* (2013) and *Japanese Buddhist Pilgrimage* (2015).

14

Meiji government policy, Sect Shintō and Fusōkyō

Shishino Fumio

I write this paper as the current head of Shintō Fusōkyō 神道扶桑教, being the sixth in line since the first generation of the leadership initiated by Shishino Nakaba 宍野半 (1844–84). Shintō Fusōkyō was recognized as a separately established sect in Meiji 15 (1882) by decree of the [governmental] Office for Shinto Affairs (Shintō Jimukyoku 神道事務局). It originally derived from Fujidō 富士道 [Way of Fuji].[1] The foundation of Fujidō occurred when Fujiwara Kakugyō Tōkaku 藤原角行東覚 (1541–1646) stood at the summit of Mount Fuji on June 3, 1572 (Genki 3) and discerned the divine will. If counting from Kakugyō as the founder, I myself am the twelfth in line.[2]

Sect Shintō as referred to in the title of today's seminar "The Puzzle and Fascination of Sect Shinto" includes thirteen different groups that may be simply classified in four categories as follows: (1) those which have a founding figure and are based on

---

1   **Translator's note.** The name "Way of Fuji" includes a significant pun. Fuji refers indeed to Mount Fuji (富士山 Fuji-san); however, other characters used to write the name "Fuji" in this context were 不二, a combination that means "not two," with the implication of nondualism as current in Buddhist thought.

2   **Translator's note.** The original title of the paper in Japanese would be translated in full as "The meaning of 'Sect Shintō' as it arose out of Meiji government policy." However, special reference is made in the paper to the religion known as Shintō Fusōkyō 神道扶桑教, a popular, long-established religious movement focused on pilgrimage to the summit of Mount Fuji, and so the title has been adjusted to indicate this. The author of the paper is the current head (*kanchō* 管長) of Shintō Fusōkyō, and at the ISSA international seminar in 2017 his paper was preceded by an informative DVD about the group. The present translation was prepared by the volume editor, with a few explanatory additions being given in square brackets or as footnotes.

the doctrine or teaching of the founder; (2) those which arose in the context of mountain-related religious faith (*sangakushinkō* 山岳信仰) and became settled as a religious group (*kyōha* 教派); (3) those which came into being in connection with Shinto shrines referred to in the ancient texts; and (4) those founded on the basis of a teaching about morality. Broadly speaking, these distinctions seem to work. To the first category, in which there is a founding figure to whom a doctrine is ascribed and whose leadership is thought to be enabled through the strength of a divine being, belong Kurozumikyō 黒住教, Shinshūkyō 神習教, Misogikyō 禊教, Shinrikyō 神理教, Shintōtaiseikyō 神道大成教, Tenrikyō 天理教[3] and Konkōkyō 金光教. To the second category, mountain-related religious faiths, belong my own group Fusōkyō, another group known as Jikkōkyō 實行教 which similarly sees Mount Fuji as its basic location of religious practice, and Ontakekyō (as mentioned in the paper by Michael Pye immediately before this). To the third category belong religious groups which arose in the context of classical shrines[4] to promulgate specific teachings. This was against the background of the Meiji government's policy of regarding such shrines as "not religious" and therefore not themselves able to promote a "teaching" (*oshie* 教え). Groups arising in this way are the Ooyashirokyō 大社教 which arose at Izumo Grand Shrine (though in what sense this is a "classical shrine" might be questioned) and the Jingūkyō 神宮教 which was born in the context of the Jingū of Ise. With the fourth category I propose to refer to groups based on "morality" [*dōtoku* 道徳] or, to use the words of the administrative head of Shintōshūseiha 神道修成派, "the basis, rather than religion, is a kind of moral education."

Considering the previously raised question "whether these groups are Shinto" I would answer that our own Fusōkyō *is* a

3   **Ed.** Though listed for a while among the thirteen "Shinto" sects, for political and administrative reasons, Tenrikyō withdrew shortly after the end of the war, arguing that it was based on an independent revelation. Its missionary work in Korea was thus able to continue.
4   **Ed.** The general expression *kotenteki jinja* 古典的神社 used here sidesteps the usual formal categories to indicate shrines of great importance referred to in classical writings such as the *Nihonshoki*.

Shinto group, but that Fujidō, the precursor group from the early the Edo Period, was strongly coloured by Buddhism. As to why Fujidō took up the path of involvement in Kyōha Shintō, this is something in which Shishino Nakaba 宍野半 (mentioned above) was greatly involved. Nakaba was born in Kagoshima and was known popularly as a "Satsuma boy." In his youth he studied National Learning in the Hirata tradition in Kyoto. At that time Hirata Atsutane 平田篤胤 (1776–1843) had already died and so he studied National Learning under Hirata Kanetane 平田鐵胤 (1799–1880). Thereafter, in the wake of the Meiji Restoration he came to Tokyo in the company of his highness Arisugawa no Miya Takahito 有栖川宮幟仁. Here I follow the *Kyōha Shintō Rengōkai Hyakunenshi* ("One Hundred Year History of the Association of Sect Shinto") but for further details reference may also be made to the website of the Kyōha Shintō Rengōkai 教派神道連合会 website. In Meiji 5 (1872) the [new] Ministry of Education (Kyōbushō 教部省) was set up, and Shishino was appointed to the bureaucracy, became the accounting secretary of the Daikyōin 大教院 [a government agency for promoting religious teachings in a patriotic spirit], a post equivalent to a financial discernment officer. Later on he was appointed to be the first chief priest of Fuji Sengen Grand Shrine (Fuji Sengen Taisha 富士浅間大社) in Suruga Province (now Shizuoka Prefecture) when this was designated as a *kanpeisha* 官弊社.[5] It was here that he encountered Fujidō ("Way of Fuji"). The Fuji Fraternities (*fujikō* 富士講), consisting of organized teams from among the Fujidō faithful, were so popular in the city of Edo that it was said that in its 808 districts there were 808 fraternities, and that their members numbered 80,000 people. In 1742 (Kanpō 2) however, they had been prohibited by the Edo Bakufu from spreading their teaching. Shishino Nakaba was requested by members of the Fujikō (i.e. at that time followers of Fujidō) to try to get this ban lifted, and accordingly he made efforts to get the movement established as an independent group. Just at that same time the campaign of "destroy Buddhism and

---

5 **Ed.** Nationally and regionally listed shrines which revered the Emperor and were thereby granted special status.

kill Shaka" [i.e. Śākyamuni, the Buddha] was started off with the decree for the separation of Shinto and Buddhism, and the conservative wing within the government was seeking to set up Shinto as the state religion. Followers of the Fujikō or Fujidō, therefore, seeking to get the ban on propagation lifted in the new context of the Meiji government's policy on religion, sought to rely on Shishino Nakaba who had just been appointed by the government to the Fuji Sengen Taisha.

This is the answer to the question posed earlier as to why, if a group is "Shinto," it can at the same time be a sect. The Fujidō which had been suppressed by the Bakufu had been strongly coloured by Buddhism, and under Shishino's guidance was refigured as a Shinto sect influenced by the National Learning of the Hirata school. As a result, it seems appropriate for the category of "sect" (*kyōha*) to be applied. While Shishino was engaged in the administration of the Daikyōin as an organ of the religious policy of the Meiji government, he followed the path of promoting the fortunes of a particular religious group, and in this way he reflected the religious situation of the country as a whole.

The Meiji government, in order to assert its own governmental standing, began by rejecting the policies of the previous Bakufu government. At the same time, even while the Meiji government was using the slogan "Revere the Emperor and expel the barbarians" to denigrate the Bakufu, it nevertheless had no alternative but to open the country up. As the country was opened, one of the government's most serious concerns was the expansion of the influence of Christianity. This was a widespread fear. In 1867 (Keiō 3), during the suppression of the Kirishitan [Christians descended from the first generation of Catholic converts] at Uragami (the fourth Uragami collapse), residents of Uragami, being self-avowed Kirishitan who rejected Buddhist style funerals, were rounded up and tortured. The Meiji government followed up the Edo Bakufu policy of suppressing the Kirishitan by banishing more than 3,000 Christian believers of whom 662 lost their lives. The combined western reaction to this was so strong that in 1873 the third item of the "five proclamations" (the one prohibiting "the Kirishitan heresy") was taken down, believers were released, and the Christian faith was publicly permitted. The conservative faction within the Meiji government strongly rejected the decriminalization of Christianity and expressed opinions such as "even if the ban is dropped the treaty demands of the West should not immediately be accepted" and that account should be taken of "the widespread fear of Christianity among the general population." However the pressure from the western side continued, and being bound by the unequal treaties the relaxation of the prohibition was upheld. It is in this context that we should consider the policy on religion advanced by the Meiji government.

In the Edo Period it had become a matter of course that under the Bakufu government Buddhism was effectively the state religion. The temples had become organs of political administration insofar as the family registration system lay under their jurisdiction. Moreover, since only Buddhist funerals were recognized for the population throughout the country, it could be said that the people were broadly speaking followers of Buddhism. The "state religion" (*kokkyō* 国教) under the Bakufu was therefore, so to speak, Buddhism. The new government on the other hand could not afford to recognize this state of affairs because of its close association with the Bakufu. Neo-Confucianism might have seemed to be an option, but it would have been a rather weak one. Accordingly, since the purpose was to set up a new government based on reverence for the Emperor, there was a move to make Shinto into a state religion and this Shinto was to centre on the great goddess Amaterasu as the divine ancestor of the Imperial House. This flourished through the setting up of the Jingi-in, the concept of the unity of polity and rites (*saisei itchi*) and the promotion of the three principles of the "Great Teaching" [namely: reverence for *kami* and love of country; clarification of the will of heaven and the way of humanity; respect for the reigning Emperor].[6] Hand in hand with the shift towards making Shinto the state religion, the first year of Meiji (1868) saw the promulgation on March 27 of the ordinance on the separation of Shinto and Buddhism known as the *shinbutsuhanzenrei* 神仏判然令. A series of decrees was issued in the same year relating to

6 敬神愛国、天理人道を明らかにする、皇上の奉載.

this separation of Shinto and Buddhism, and it may be added that the appearance of the movement known as "destroy Buddhism and kill Shaka" led to very large attacks against the Buddhist side and strengthened a sense of crisis about the very survival of Buddhism.

What did the Buddhist side do in search of a restoration of its fortunes? It seems to me that, rather than taking the path of battling against the Meiji government, the Buddhist side preferred to work hard to cooperate with it in a skilful manner. The Jingi-in was set up on the basis of "*saisei itchi*" and "restore the monarchy" but the Buddhist party centred on Shimaji Mokurai 島地黙雷 (most of them were followers of the Honganji-ha)[7] criticized the policy of making Shinto the state religion on the grounds that Shinto alone would not be sufficient to defend Japan from the combined pressure of the western powers and from Christianity. They urged tirelessly that the country could be protected more effectively with the additional cooperation of Buddhism. Shimaji, stemming from Chōshū [a feudal realm in western Japan], made skilful use of his connections to Kido Takayoshi 木戸孝允 who, as is well known, was a pupil in the Shōkason-juku (松下村塾).[8] Moreover the Buddhist priest Gesshō 月性 (1817–58),[9] who was close to Yoshida Shōin 吉田松陰, while urging the defence of Japan by naval means for the repulsion of foreigners, strongly promoted the idea of "protecting the country with the Buddha-Dharma." Bearing in mind that the Honganji [i.e. Nishi Honganji] received financial support for its role in the toppling of the Bakufu, it may be asked if there were not those in the Chōshū faction in government circles who suggested that it would be wise to take account of opinions coming from the Buddhist side.

7 **Ed.** This is the largest of the Shin Buddhist denominations, based on the Western Honganji, closely followed by the Ōtani-ha, based on the Eastern Honganji, both in Kyoto.

8 **Ed.** A late Edo Period private school at Hagi, in what is now Yamaguchi Prefecture.

9 **Ed.** Gesshō, referred to only by this name, was based at a temple of the Honganji-ha of Shin Buddhism named Myōenji 妙円寺 located at Uda City in Nara Prefecture.

Some may consider it more appropriate to think of Shishino as having kept himself rather distant from these matters, and this should always be borne in mind. At the same time I suspect that taking account of the interpersonal connections and the finances will clarify the truth. Indeed, the Kyōbushō was set up at the suggestion of Shimaji Mokurai and others. But when Shimaji departed for investigations overseas with the Iwakura Mission group the Kyōbushō did not function very well. The idea was that Buddhism and Shinto should join forces to put the propagation of the "Great Teaching" into effect, using "morals" as a concretization of Shinto, and in this sense six Buddhist groups had united to support the Daikyōin. However, this Daikyōin too, when we look at it in detail, did not really develop a joint propagation programme; four Shin Buddhist groups left it, and after about two years it ended in failure.

To put it bluntly, the religious policy of the new Meiji government issued a very large number of directives. It seems to me that the policy of setting up Shinto as the state religion of Japan did not really work out as intended. Going around from one thing to another simply led to confusion. The intention was to set up Shinto as the state religion in accordance with the principle of *saisei itchi* 祭政一致 ("unity of rites and politics") but it was clumsily approached. Moreover, on the basis of their observations overseas, Shimaji Mokurai and Prince Iwakura Tomomi 岩倉具視公 concluded their work with the crisis-laden message that overseas civilization was very advanced, that Japan was lagging behind and that it was no good for the country to continue with its current set of values. It appears that, with leaders flustered by this, while entertaining various political considerations, they were resigned to the necessity of the policy of setting up a state religion. Shimaji Mokurai left many writings in which he said that the current state of the nation, as compared with that of foreign countries, was simply no good, and it seems that this must have struck a chord with key persons in government. Accordingly, since all were resigned to the policy of having some kind of state religion, a process was initiated in which Shinto was officially divided into Shinto as faith (*shinkō* 信仰) or "religion" (*shūkyō* 宗教), i.e. Sect Shintō, and shrines as organs of the state [defined as being] without a religious character.

This solution was later documented in the Shinto Directive issued by the Supreme Commander of the Allied Powers in the following terms:

> By the term State Shinto within the meaning of this directive we refer to that branch of Shinto (Kokka Shinto or Jinja Shinto) which by official acts of the Japanese Government has been differentiated from the religion of Sect Shinto (Shuha Shinto or Kyoha Shinto) and has been classified as a non-religious cult commonly known as State Shinto, National Shinto, or Shrine Shinto.
>
> The term Sect Shinto (Shuha Shinto or Kyoha Shinto) will refer to that branch of Shinto (composed of 13 recognized sects) which by popular belief, legal commentary, and the official acts of the Japanese Government has been recognized to be a religion.[10]

To sum up, the Meiji government, on the basis of the people's devotion to the divinities of heaven and earth, moved the functions of administering family registration, and of dealing with the Kirishitan, away from Buddhism and its temples over to Shinto, henceforth controlling these matters through the Jingikan 神祇官 [i.e. the Divinities Office]. Shinto-style funerals became more widespread across the country, while imperial mausolea were removed from the aegis of Buddhism and brought under state control. These shifts were presumably part of the policy to make Shinto the state religion. However, this policy was knocked off course by various political circumstances, and as a result the Meiji government put into effect a policy of dividing Shinto into two types. The shrines of state Shinto were put under state administration and presented as being without religious character; they were regarded as organs of the state based upon ritual and morals. They were administered under the Shinto Office of the Ministry of the Interior. Kyōha Shintō on the other hand was given the responsibility, as a Shinto of faith or religion, both for promoting the spirit of imperial decrees

---

10 *Translations and official documents: The Shinto Directive.* General Headquarters, Supreme Commander for the Allied Powers.

through the spread of the Great Teaching, and at the same time for providing funeral practices, the latter being a symbol of practically lived religion which could be seen to be based on freedom of faith. It consisted of people-based organizations with the function of spreading Shinto as a people's faith, and was administered as such by the Religious Affairs office of the Ministry of Education. This is the reason why permission was given for the establishment of Shinto sects by decree of Meiji Tennō, and explains why Fusōkyō can be described as "Shinto" and "a sect" at one and the same time.

Additional note on the "Heart Fuji"[11]

A long-standing custom in Fusōkyō is for pilgrims to write the character for "heart" (心) with a calligraphic frame or flourish suggestive of the shape of Mount Fuji. Variations result depending on the individual's preference of just how to incorporate the character into the summit of the mountain. In the example shown here (**Figure 1**), with brushwork by Shishino Fumio, two slogans are included in the body of the mountain which are repeated many times during the climb. These are *rokkon shōjō* 六根清浄 ("purify the six roots"), a standard, Buddhist-inspired phrase chanted by various kinds of pilgrims across Japan, and *onyama seiten* 御山晴天 ("holy mountain, clear sky"). Even when there are mist and clouds covering the lower reaches of the mountain, the air around the upper part is often clear and uplifting. The chant of *rokkon shōjō, onyama seiten* thus illustrates and indeed induces the pilgrims' religious progress brought about by the ascent. Through this severe practice the pilgrims achieve full clarity of vision.

The mystical meaning of the mountain is also expressed in other ways. For example, the inner funnel of the volcano, currently dormant, links the depths of the earth with the highest point in the whole of Japan, with only "heaven" above it. Another important phrase

---

11 This section was added by the Editor following an interview with Shishino Fumio at the Shintō Fusōkyō headquarters in Setagaya-ku, Tokyo, on October 30, 2019.

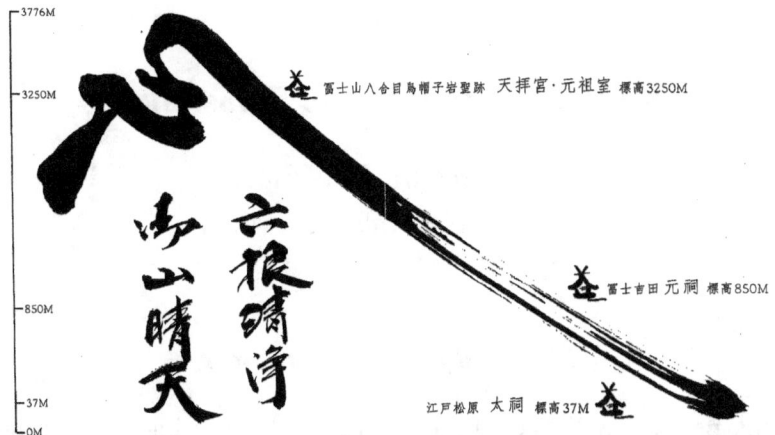

Figure 1 Calligraphic "Heart Fuji" with the two phrases *rokkon shōjō* and *onyama seiten*, brushwork by Shishino Fumio, and indications of the heights to be scaled from base to summit.

linking two groups of four characters was coined by Kakugyō, the first founder-organizer of Fujidō, and runs *tenchi heian, mannin anpuku* 天地平安 萬人安福, meaning "peace in heaven and on earth, peace and happiness for all people." Although this refers literally to ten thousand people, the round figure is all-inclusive, and so the phrase is now interpreted as a call to world peace.

About the Author

Shishino Fumio 宍野史 was born in 1962 and is the sixth administrative head (*kanchō*) of the religious denomination Shintō Fusōkyō 神道扶桑教. He is a trustee of the Sect Shinto Association, member of the committee on religious corporations in the governmental Cultural Affairs Department, and Executive Secretary of the Japanese League of Religions (Nihon Shūkyō Renmei). He also serves as a trustee of the World Federation Culture and Education Promotion Council.

15

Introducing the faith of Shinshūkyō

Yoshimura Masanori
Translated by Yamauchi Ayako

Shinshūkyō as a Shinto sect

In this paper I will take the opportunity to provide a brief introduction to the faith of Shinshūkyō 神習教,[1] with reference both to its current state and its perspective for the future. I am writing as the current head of Shinshūkyō, and am grateful for the opportunity to contribute to this forum, the ISSA seminar on "The Puzzle and Fascination of Sect Shinto." I will also address the questions posed to various groups at the beginning of the seminar by Michael Pye, namely "Is your group Shinto?" and if so "Why is it a Shinto Sect?"

Shinshūkyō understands itself to be a pure form of Shinto, because we worship nothing but the deities that appear in Japanese classics like the *Kojiki* ("Records of Ancient Matters", 710) and the *Nihon shoki* ("The Chronicles of Japan", 720). Additionally, most of the rituals we practise originate in Shrine Shintō (Jinja Shintō), with just a few alterations.[2] At the same time it is not easy to give a simple explanation of exactly how Sect Shintō, known in Japanese as Kyōha Shintō, began. In his contribution to this volume entitled "Meiji Government Policy, Sect Shintō and Fusōkyō" Shishino Fumio has offered a plausible explanation, namely that it was reactions to the various changes to Shinto made during the Meiji Era that inevitably led to the emergence of Sect Shintō.

---

1   The name of this group, written with the characters shown in the main text, should not be confused with the modern term *shinshūkyō* 新宗教 which simply means "new religions."
2   The presentation at the seminar began with an informative slideshow.

Shinto has been categorized as a polytheistic, ritualistic religion, and various forms of Shinto, both Sect Shintō and Jinja Shintō, have been accepted. For example, some Shinto rituals are found, although rarely, in the practice of the Shugendō faith. Moreover, Jinja Shintō shrines such as Suwa Taisha, Inari Jinja, Hachiman Jinja, Konpira Jinja and Sumiyoshi Jinja, which are located throughout Japan, each support a kind of "sect" of Shinto, because at each, slightly different rituals are practised. We take it for granted that Shinto varies depending on the exact objects of faith involved, and the locations of practice, and it seems unnatural to force them to be grouped and sorted.

Kurozumi Munetada 黒住宗忠 (1780–1850), the founder of Kurozumikyō, made a remark that I found very interesting (as previously mentioned by Dr Helen Hardacre[3]), namely that he did not consider himself to be anything other than a Shinto priest. I believe that in just the same way, before the Meiji Era began, Yoshimura Masamochi 芳村昌秉 (1839–1915), the founder of Shinshūkyō, also did not consider himself to be a Shintoist in any very particular way; it was in the Meiji Era that people began to develop a clear awareness of their faith – either Shinto or Buddhist, against the background of rising numbers of Christian missionaries and Japanese Christians.

In distinction from Buddhism, the word *Shintō* first appeared in the *Nihon shoki*, where it was credited to a speaker under the rule of Emperor Kinmei in the mid-sixth century, at the time when Buddhism was officially first introduced in Japan. During the Meiji Restoration, the new government sought to find a way to control the country by using methods that were different from those of the previously ruling Tokugawa Shogunate. Therefore, the government adopted a robust anti-Buddhist attitude and brought Shinto to ascendancy by reinstating the Jingikan; this was modelled after the historic *ritsuryō* system (of administrative law) and promoted missionary work. In these circumstances, Shinto received a great

---

3   This was adduced in a paper on Kurozumikyō contributed by Helen Hardacre to the ISSA seminar, which is however not published here.

262 *Exploring Shinto*

increase in attention, which finally led to the distinction and the separation of Shrine Shintō and Sect Shintō.

Yoshimura Masamochi and the foundation of Shinshūkyō

It should be noted. first of all, that Yoshimura Masamochi (**Figure 1**) was critical of shrines as such. While he believed

Figure 1 Yoshimura Masamochi.

that the connection between the deities and the priests should be highly valued, he considered that the worship at the shrines tended to focus on rituals and festivals, and therefore was in his view neglecting the true meaning of Shinto. Masamochi began to regard himself as a Shintoist in the sense that he devoted himself to the spiritual connection with the deities. This is what led to the foundation of Shinshūkyō.

In this connection it is important to take note of Masamochi's background. He was born into the Yoshimura family, a family that had been Shinto priests for a long period, although that vocation had been abandoned some time before his birth. He was born as the second son of a medical doctor, Yoshimura Taiji 芳村泰治. Although his family was no longer engaged in Shinto, Masamochi showed a keen interest in it. He also had an ambitious interest in upward mobility which led him to study *kokugaku* ("national learning") in Kyoto, the capital, during those troubled times.

As a descendant of the Ōnakatomi 大中臣 and an imperial loyalist, Masamochi fled the power of the Tokugawa Shogunate during the Ansei Purge (1858–59) and escaped to the Yuki Shrine (Yuki Jinja 由岐神社) in the extensive mountain grounds of Kurama Temple (Kuramadera 鞍馬寺, just to the north of Kyoto), remaining there for one month. There, lamenting the deaths of his comrades and praying for the future of the country, he recalled his grandfather's instructions to reconstruct and to promulgate the Shinto of the Ōnakatomi.

Ten years after the Ansei Purge, the Meiji Restoration took place, beginning with "the return of sovereignty" (*taisei hōkan* 大政奉還) in 1868. In 1873 Masamochi was appointed as a *negi* (senior priest) at the Grand Shrine at Ise. After the relocation of the capital to Tokyo during the *taisei hōkan* information of all kinds had to pass through Tokyo, and this led to the establishment of the Tokyo office of the Ise Shrine, later called Tōkyō Daijingū. Masamochi became the head of the Tokyo office of the shrine and later served as a head priest at the Tōkyō Daijingū. Later, he moved on, choosing to cloister himself on sacred mountains in different locations. During this time, he finally established his own version of Shinto, while at the same time being enthusiastically engaged in missionary work.

Up until the law of 1881, which prohibited Shinto priests from concurrently serving as religious teachers, he worked to gain followers. Beginning from Ise, Masamochi proselytized over the Hokuriku region, including Aichi, Nagano and Niigata Prefectures, and through the Tōhoku region, where he finally reached Mount Osore, in the centre of the remote Shimokita Peninsula in Aomori Prefecture. His missionary work there was very successful and this well-known mountain came to be strongly influenced by Shinshūkyō. Mount Osore is famous for the presence of spiritual mediums, and these mediums also joined Shinshūkyō. In addition, Masamochi successfully won over followers from among the mediums of Mount Ontake in Nagano Prefecture (in central Japan), which swelled the numbers of Shinshūkyō in good time, before the law of 1881 prohibited proselytization.

The name Shinshū + kyō (the literal meaning of which is "the teaching of divine training") came from an oracle from the *kami* Yamatohime-no-mikoto, which Masamochi received during the monthly festival at the Aramatsurigū 荒祭宮, the inner shrine of the Grand Shrine at Ise. The oracle suggested that *kaminagara* 惟神 (meaning "living in accordance with the *kami*") be the foundation of the sect's doctrine. During his lifetime, Masamochi wrote several books. Among the most noteworthy is his *Uchū no seishin* 宇宙の精神 ("The Spirit of the Universe") dating from 1906. Along with the *Kojiki* and the *Nihon shoki*, this work serves as scripture for Shinshūkyō, and traditional Shinto values play a significant part in our teaching.

At around the same period, Prince Asahiko Kuni, the Chief Priest of the Grand Shrine at Ise, concentrated part of the spirit of Amaterasu into a mirror and gave it to Masamochi. The mirror has been an object of worship for Shinshūkyō from that time on. It had been lodged in the *Shinmeigū* 神明宮 which was closed down due to the *taisei hōkan*, and was returned to Ise, where it attracted the attention of Prince Asahiko Kuni.

There is an anecdote that is told about Masamochi. At the request of Yoshiko Nakayama, the mother of Emperor Meiji, Masamochi prayed for the emperor's health for more than three years, even though official documents say that it was only for three hundred days.

In 1891 Masamochi was introduced to an American astronomer, Percival Lowell, a member of a wealthy Boston family who was well known for his observatory in Arizona, which is where Pluto was discovered. Mutsu Munemitsu, the Minister of Foreign Affairs, brought them together. Masamochi taught Lowell the beliefs of Shinshūkyō; however, the devout Christian declined to accept any Shinto teaching and asked rude questions such as "Why are its followers protected with charms sold at shrines and temples?" Not offended at all, Masamochi patiently and kindly answered his questions for days, finally helping Lowell to understand Shinto. On one occasion, Masamochi got Lowell to hold a *gohei* 御幣, that is, a wand surmounted by strips of white paper, normally used in purification rituals. He then inserted a deity into it using a *kiai* 気合い shout, at which the *gohei* suddenly ran wild! Lowell was shocked at the sight and desperately tried to discover how it had been done, taking the *gohei* home and scrutinizing it, all in vain. On Lowell's second visit to Japan in 1893, he expressed his desire to offer prayers at the Grand Shrine at Ise. Masamochi arranged for an official visit, and Lowell became the first foreigner to dedicate *kagura* to the shrine.

Shinshūkyō in recent times

At present, the headquarters of Shinshūkyō is in the Setagaya area of Tokyo, and teachers are trained there. These teachers play the role both of teacher and missionary, and some are heads of their own churches and associations, where they interact with their followers and engage in missionary work. Most of the other Shinto sects operate with a similar form of organization, except for Tenrikyō, which is a *sōshōshūkyō* 創唱宗教 (i.e. a founded religion) One weakness of this form of organization is that once the headquarters comes to be disconnected from a local church, due to the absence of a teacher, it is also disconnected from the followers of that church as well.

The major annual events of Shinshūkyō are as follows. The *Tai-sai* 大祭 or Great Festival is held in April, celebrating our principal deities. The *Chū-sai* 中祭 or Middle Festival is a festival for the deities of Mount Ontake, together with our own principal deities. The *Kyōso-sai* 教祖祭, which honors Masamochi as the founder of the sect, takes place on January 21, and the *Kyōrei-sai* 教霊祭 takes place in early July, celebrating the spirits of our ancestors. During these festivals, rituals such as *narukama-shinji* 鳴釜神事 (a ritual in which the sound of a boiling kettle is used for divining the future), *hiwatari-shinji* 火渡り神事 (a fire-walking ritual) and *kugatachi-shiki* 探湯式 (a ritual using boiling water) are performed. Rituals that were once conducted but are now no longer part of the worship, include *hikime* 蟇目 and *meigen* 鳴弦. In these rites evil spirits are driven out, respectively, by the sound of an arrow being shot, or of a bowstring without an arrow being plucked.

It must be admitted that Shinshūkyō went into some decline following the promulgation of the Shinto Directive in 1945, which abolished imperial support for Shinto. Due to this powerful order Shinshūkyō was downgraded to being just one more religious organization among others. Another reason for decline is that the position of head has been passed from grandfather to grandson, not from father to son. Our sect will be 160 years old this year; however, during this entire period, we have had three heads only. I myself (the writer) am the third head of the sect. The second was Yoshimura Tadaaki 芳村忠明 (1897–1985), my grandfather, and the first was Masamochi, Tadaaki's grandfather. Interestingly, the position has been passed from grandfather to grandson. Masamochi died as soon as his grandson, my grandfather, became twenty – the legal age of adulthood in Japan – so that his position as the head of the sect could be passed on. Similarly, and oddly, because my father, who was at the time the vice-head of the sect, passed away, my own grandfather, the then head of the sect, managed to live until I turned twenty and then accordingly handed over his position. Westerners may find this sequencing rather difficult to understand; perhaps it is some kind of karma, but it is difficult for me to explain it exactly.

Presently, our activities include training teachers and conducting missions to outlying regions beyond the Setagaya area. We have been making use of the internet for nineteen years, distributing monthly mail magazines to more than a thousand subscribers. One of the strengths of Shinshūkyō is its tradition of *kamigakari* 神憑り (i.e. being spiritually possessed by a *kami*), which makes it unique, distinguishing it from other kinds of Sect Shintō. *Kamigakari* is a state of trance during which one cannot control oneself. However, what Percival Lowell witnessed with the *gohei* is also an aspect of *kamigakari*. As I mentioned earlier, various forms of Shinto exist and are well accepted. In his books on Shinto Lowell particularly stressed *kamigakari*. This shows how powerful it is. I firmly believe that our strength lies in *kamigakari* and that training for *kamigakari* is a key pillar for the future development of our organization. To be able to attain *kamigakari*, training is necessary. In those early days, trainees received long-term training over a period of several weeks to a month. However, these days, most followers have other work and can practise on weekends only, which makes it hard to produce results in a short period of time. In sum, our challenges for the future include how to focus on effective training and on missionary work.

About the author

Yoshimura Masanori 芳村正徳 was born in Tokyo in 1964. He graduated in law at Meiji University and in literature at Kokugakuin University (the leading Japanese university specializing in Shinto studies). He is now the head priest (*gūji*) of Sakura Jingū in Tokyo. In 1985 he was appointed administrative head (*kanchō*) of the religious denomination Shinshūkyō 神習教, and after regulatory adjustments as its patriarch (*kyōshu*). He is chairman of the trustees of the Sect Shinto Association, and a member of the committee on religious corporations in the governmental Cultural Affairs Department.

16

Tenrikyō and Ōmoto in the context of Kyōha Shintō

Avery Morrow

Introduction

In Japanese religious studies, the Ōmoto and Tenrikyō groups are considered to be archetypical *minshū shūkyō*, "mass religions." In turbulent mid-twentieth-century Japan, it was thought that because Ōmoto and Tenrikyō began their histories with charismatic leaders receiving revelations from unknown sources, researchers might return to the original teachings of these leaders to discover a substantially different vision of society than the liberal-capitalist course of the Japanese state. Most notably, Yasumaru Yoshio invoked the term "cosmology" as an aspect of one's worldview which can provide absolute authority entirely outside of a political regime.

This idea of "mass religions," initially developed in the postwar intellectual climate, has come under closer scrutiny in the past three decades (Nagaoka 2017). It is now recognized that neither Tenrikyō nor Ōmoto can be spoken of apart from the climate that produced them. The founders of these groups negotiated their existence with contemporary authorities while maintaining independent authority for themselves. Most notable is the two groups' relationships to the concepts of religion (*shūkyō* 宗教) on one hand, and Shinto on the other. In pre-1945 Japan, Tenrikyō sought out recognition as a religion, and affiliated with several Sect Shintō (*kyōha shintō* 教派神道) groups in order to gain such legal recognition. Ōmoto also affiliated with such groups but was never legally recognized as religion, and indeed its leaders rejected the concept of religion at several points. In the post-1945 period, Tenrikyō left Sect Shintō in order to assert a more independent religious identity, while Ōmoto registered as a religion and joined the Sect Shintō association.

An in-depth analysis of why these groups made the decisions that they did can help us understand what the word "religion" means in Japanese society and how it relates to the concept of Shinto. In this paper I will focus on developments in Tenrikyō and Ōmoto between 1865 and 1925. The word *shūkyō* was not yet in common use by 1865, and indeed we will see that during the period studied here, *shūkyō* was not quite what English speakers think of in our modern usages of "religion." I will also show how the ideas of Shinto and Sect Shintō existed in a state of tension, being not quite religion and not quite secular either.

State authority and the Tenrikyō community

It is generally believed by religious scholars that Tenrikyō did not begin as an evangelical mission, but as a community of practitioners centred around Nakayama Miki and her possession abilities. There was certainly no formal missionary work in its early years. Nagaoka Takashi refers to the original sense of common belonging as the "Oyagami community," calling it a "gathering of living gods" which originally featured multiple people with frequent possession experiences (Nagaoka 2015, 63). This community shifted rapidly through its interactions with the state.

Tenrikyō's interactions with state-authorized authorities on *kami* actually began before the Meiji Restoration. This started with an accidental disruption of a Yoshida Shinto service at Ōyamato Jinja, followed by harassment by local *yamabushi*. But the most important interactions that they had with the state were positive: the local magistrate protected them from the rampaging *yamabushi*, and in 1865 the Yoshida Shintō priest in charge of the disrupted service came to inspect Nakayama Miki's activities and was mostly positive about them, recommending that her son Shūji train at their head shrine in Tokyo. In 1867, Shūji became an accredited Yoshida Shintō priest himself and received promises of legal protection from Yoshida officials (Forbes 2005, 56–7).

Here we can see that the pre-Meiji attitude of the "Oyagami community" towards affiliation with the state was one of pragmatic cooperation, in which there was an understanding that existing institutions provided authorization and protection from persecution. The state was not yet demanding any specific form that Tenrikyō should take as a community, and seemed to be mostly tolerant. The danger came not from the state, but from other religious authorities such as *yamabushi* who were eager to suppress upstart rival movements.

While the official biography of Miki (Tenrikyō 1956b) says that she was dubious of the authority held by Yoshida Shintō and claimed they would soon disappear, Shimada Hiromi, in his critical history of Tenrikyō's early years (2008, 203), argues that this is a postwar fabrication that does not appear in any of the earliest sources. He suggests that, quite to the contrary, the positive interactions between Miki and Yoshida Shintō priests provided the basis for the use of classical *kami* in Tenrikyō myth. In effect, Tenrikyō was constructed in the early years by its positive attitude towards specialist authority. A close look at the transformation of Tenrikyō from Oyagami community to institution will reveal some subtleties not found in Shimada's polemic.

The Meiji Restoration overlooked the Oyagami community at first. In 1870, Yoshida Shintō was disbanded. By 1874, the Great Promulgation Campaign was underway, and the local Ōyamato Jinja which had once been central to Yoshida Shintō was now under new management and teaching locals the official programme for National Learning (*kokugaku* 国学). Possession practices had been banned in January 1873, and in June 1874 this was supplemented with a general ban on faith-healing (Josephson 2012, 178–81).

In December 1874, Miki asked two of her fellow practitioners to go to Ōyamato Jinja and find out what *kami* they were worshipping now. This is a rather unusual instruction, demonstrating an odd strategy towards Shinto authority that is hard to interpret on its own. I quote Roy Forbes' translation of the resulting interaction:

> The priests of Ōyamato Jinja responded that the shrine was dedicated to kami from the *Nihongi* and the *Kojiki*. Nakata

and Matsuo further asked questions concerning the types of blessings and protections that were bestowed by these kami, and the priests were at a loss as to how to answer. The silence of the priests encouraged Nakata and Matsuo to articulate that their kami Tenri-Ō-no-Mikoto, was *moto no kami, jitsu no kami* – the true and original kami – and showed them parts three and four of the *Ofudesaki*. Realizing that Nakata and Matsuo were followers of Miki, the priests mocked them and suggested it would be best for them to concentrate on farming. Then one of the priests retorted,

> To assume the name of a god not found anywhere in the ancient chronicles is inexcusable and liable to censure. The Isonokami Shrine itself is not exempt from censure, for it has allowed its own parishioners to advocate such a heresy (*isetsu* 異説) due to its inadequate supervision. At any rate, I give you fair warning that we shall visit your place one of these days. (Forbes 2005, 60)

Here we can see a sharp self-awareness on both sides. Ōyamato Jinja's new National Learning priests, representing the power of the state, understood that Nakayama Miki's community, even if it was not a "religion" or *shūkyō*, was an independent source of spiritual authority that could cause people to doubt their claim to absolute knowledge. Miki's representatives, for their part, clearly understood that the use of the *Nihongi* and *Kojiki* was nothing more than a feint, claiming mere institutional authority with no apparent justification in terms of blessings or salvation. The previous Yoshida Shintō priests had been much more sincere in their belief in the *kami*.

After this incident, Ōyamato Jinja alerted the authorities to the presence of an unauthorized faith-healing group in rural Nara, and the entire community was subject to harsh persecutions. In 1876, it was made illegal to use one's house to hold prayers. In response, Shūji registered his house as an inn, but this trick was soon uncovered when the police inspected his ledger and found that multiple parties were lodging in the same room at once (Nagaoka 2015, 74).

In 1880, Miki's son Shūji made another attempt at appeasing the police, despite these initial failures. This time he did not fail to incur Miki's wrath, and the official Tenrikyō account has her warning him that "if you go, Kami will retreat," among other harsh admonitions. Here, once again, Shimada Hiromi observes that this story first appeared in post-1945 hagiographies compiled by Miki's great-grandson Nakayama Shōzen, and claims it was invented to make Miki sound independent. However, the context in which the story appears makes this account highly unlikely to have been fabricated. Namely, the official account suggests that Shūji went *out of selfless love towards his mother* and concern over the fragility of her body. The non-believer Aochi Shin (1969, 169–70) doubts the official account for precisely the opposite reason as Shimada: Miki's harsh words seem to imply to him, as they have done for many subsequent scholars and commentators, that Shūji was unfaithful and far more concerned about the threat of police violence than obedience to his mother.

In his agnostic Biblical studies, the popular American scholar Bart Ehrman adopts the rule that if a story would have been inconvenient to the believers who wrote it, then it is likely to be true, because there is no reason to fabricate inconvenient material in a hagiography. As a rule of thumb, this applies quite well to the story of Shūji. Aochi notes that Shūji, as Miki's son, was a key source of family authority and historical continuity, and yet he seems faithless and is hardly a role model; later Tenrikyō writers have criticized him for precisely this reason. It is hard to think of a reason why Nakayama Shōzen, who devoted considerable energy to consolidating authority in the Nakayama household (Nagaoka 2015, 142ff), would have fabricated such an interaction between Nakayama Miki, the vessel of God, and a member of her own household. Even Shimada's attempt to paint Shūji as a propagator of the faith (2008, 191) is based in his cynical assumption that Shūji saw Miki as a madwoman whose madness had to be concealed.

We may assume, then, that Miki had some qualms with institutional authority. But the incident where believers were sent to Ōyamato Jinja shows that this was not a simple rejection or disinterest in other *kami*- and Buddha-related institutions. Indeed, although Miki was unhappy with Shūji for his interactions with institutional authority, she did not prevent him from registering her prayer group as Tenrin-Ō-Kōsha under the authority of a Buddhist temple. A believer's memories of this time include Shingon Buddhist *goma* ceremonies held at Miki's home in the presence of her and other early believers, presided over by a Buddhist monk, and in no way resembling later types of Tenrikyō practice (Kajimoto 1946, 47).

There is much ambiguity in these early interactions, showing that there was no standardized institution to manage "religion" or "faith" in the decade 1870–80. Tenrikyō does not show a pattern either of direct objection to Tokyo-sponsored changes to Shinto, or of wholehearted embracement of the new projects being promulgated from the top.

Attempt at affiliation as Shingaku

In Kyoto and Osaka, local Oyagami community groups attempted to organize themselves under the banner of Shingaku. Shingaku was an Edo Period popular educational institution, operating throughout the country but centred in Tokyo and Kansai, that hosted lectures on moral improvement based on a synthesis of Buddhist, Shinto and Confucian values. During the Great Promulgation Campaign, the government pushed Shingaku lecturers to reorganize themselves along Shinto lines and conduct rituals in Kokugaku style; they politely declined, pointing out that they were not Shinto specialists and had no faith or believers, but were simply a band of lecturers. The government was puzzled by this and eventually classified them as Shinto anyway. In the mid-1880s they became affiliates of Taiseikyō (Sawada 2004, 114–17, 205)

The Kyoto Oyagami community organized itself as "Tenrinsha Meisei-gumi" 天倫社明誠組 in 1881, borrowing members from a local Shingaku group, Meirinsha 明倫舎, which was still thriving at the time. Within the Osaka group, there was an argument over whether their appeal to authorities should be based on a claim to conduct Shingaku lectures, or instead on faith-healing, or else the Tenrikyō teachings. Unable to decide, the three disputers visited Nakayama Miki, who offered them a divine revelation that "the narrow path leads to a seedbed." This message was interpreted as permitting organization as a Shingaku group. The community thus petitioned the Osaka governor in 1884 to allow them to organize as the "Shingaku Lecture Space Tenrin-Ō-Sha" (*Shingaku dōwa kōkyūjo Tenrin-Ō-Sha* 心学道話講究所 天輪王社) (Kaneko 2017, 14–15).

As Kaneko (2017) observes, the authorization to organize as Shingaku is telling in its utter lack of resistance to other cosmological narratives or state authority. The close relationship with Meirinsha should have been enough to inform the Oyagami community that mainstream Shingaku contained quite different teachings from their own group. Instead, the form of Shingaku was adopted, in an attempt to convince the Kyoto and Osaka authorities that Tenrikyō had some continuity with established types of preaching and moral education.

Successful affiliation with Shintō Honkyoku

Following Shūji's death, the next affiliation sought out was with Shintō Honkyoku, the leaders of which recommended that the community organize as an independent sect. However, Osaka rejected the application to become an independent sect, in July 1885. This set in motion a very long pattern of setbacks and failed negotiations with the state (Tenrikyō 1956a, 106).

As part of the application to organize underneath Shintō Honkyoku in 1886, Tenrikyō leaders submitted a document to the sect that attempted to define Tenrikyō as a specific "religious" movement. Entitled "Initial Origin," it describes a specific day in 1838 when "the Heavenly General" chose Miki as his earthly shrine and descended into her. Shimada Hiromi (2008, 59–71) again suggests that this document was a fabrication: there are multiple contradictory accounts of this 1838 episode, and in any case, Miki's 1881 testimony to the police does not mention any particular incident that caused her to be chosen.

But there is no need to go so far as to question the account to recognize how Tenrikyō's *choice* of strategy towards institutional authority was already, during Miki's lifetime, influencing the religion's self-definition. Even Tenrikyō's own sources report that this is the earliest written description of any aspect of Miki's life, and that it forms the basis for the church's official biography of her. They also acknowledge and have reprinted some of its contradictory variants. This story was later sanctified in Tenrikyō theology, but it is not part of the Ofudesaki or Osashizu. It is safe to say that Tenrikyō's 1838 foundation story was constructed for the first time in the 1880s, as part of a *conscious strategy*.

Looking more closely at the content of the "Initial Origin" as reported to Shintō Honkyoku (reprinted in the postwar journal *Fukugen*) is revealing, both in how it arranges the narrative, and what is left unarranged. It opens with the line, "The reason for the name Tenri-Ō-no-Mikoto is said to be Miki, the wife of Nakayama Zenbei of the former Shoyashiki village in Yamabe district, Yamato province" (Kōda et al. 1957). In other words, the purpose of the document is slightly different from what we might expect. Rather than explaining the origins of an organization and its teaching, it introduces a *kami* named Tenri-Ō-no-Mikoto. The proof of Tenri-Ō's intervention in worldly affairs will be justification in and of itself for authorizing his believers to affiliate with Shintō Honkyoku. This is not, therefore, about introducing a "religion" but about establishing the existence of the *kami*! This was possibly a response to the assertion by Shinto authorities that no such *kami* existed (Katsurajima 2015, 261).

We also possess an earlier version of this text, submitted to the Osaka Amida shrine Wakōji 和光寺 in 1883 (although Shimada doubts the dating), in which the *kami* is called Tenrin-Ō 天輪王, which sounds more Buddhist. Yet in this version, like that of 1886, the draft explains that the name Tenrin-Ō comes from Miki's heart being aligned with *Tenri* 天理, the "heavenly pattern." The draft's author thus would rather be calling the *kami* Tenri, but continues the use of Tenrin as part of its appeal to temple-based affiliation. The 1886 revision shows an awareness that Shintō Honkyoku is not a temple and a non-Buddhist name like "Tenri" is acceptable. However, the 1886 text continues to employ Buddhist terms like "the Heavenly General" (*ten no shōgun* 天の将軍) and "the three thousand worlds" (*sanzensekai* 三千世界). These Buddhist terms would later be erased from Tenrikyō literature.

What we see in this stage, then, is an "Oyagami community" that does not yet think of itself in terms of a "religious organization," and has only a partial consciousness of the violent "separation of kami and buddhas" (*shinbutsu bunri*) occurring at that time in temples and shrines. The chief focus is emphasizing the existence and reality of Tenri-Ō-no-Mikoto.

Further integration into Shintō Honkyoku

After Miki's death in 1887, Tenrikyō integrated itself into Sect Shintō more fully, before, during as well as after the movement for independence from the Shintō Honkyoku sect. This was a point of criticism by more radical charismatic leaders (including Onisaburō and Tenrikyō breakaway groups), as well as postwar writers. I follow Nagaoka Takashi in seeing postwar criticisms as part of a mid-twentieth-century modernist narrative, imposed by the 1947 Occupation redefinition of *shūkyō* more than anything else. In more recent studies it has been recognized that such integration into Sect Shintō became fairly desirable for many groups after 1886 (Katsurajima 1991).

For example, very early on during the Shintō Honkyoku affiliation, Shinnosuke visited Ise Jingū on his way back from Tokyo. This is ruthlessly attacked by Aochi (1969, 204), who is not a Tenrikyō believer himself, as akin to a Christian praying at a mosque; he even goes so far as to put words in Miki's mouth, saying she would have called it an "act of heresy".

What Aochi misses is that Meiji Japan did not inherit a western conception of religion. Instead, it inherited a polytheistic, syncretic system of affiliation from the Edo Period, which had applied even to the Oyagami community in its earliest stages. Miki's curiosity about changes to the nearby former Yoshida shrine shows that this was not a matter of rigid "heresy" but rather about learning how to interact with a wider world of *kami*, buddhas, and distant state authorities that were themselves trying to figure out whether to be "religious" or "secular."

In fact, what is evident from the Ise visit is that Tenrikyō existed in an odd space between clear coercion by its institutional affiliate, and what we would today call "religion." As opposed to past decades where violence could be unleashed on Miki's rural village by any kind of authority, the state was now coming to have a monopoly on violence. Paying respects at Ise would have been seen by Sect Shintō authorities as a way to acknowledge subordination to state authority. Aochi calls it an act of "colonization" (1969, 208). But how did Miki's believers see the action?

Within Tenrikyō, the term ōbō 応法, meaning "adhering to laws," is used in a negative sense, referring to those who would simply follow the rules of the Japanese state. Here, the term "law" is used in a sense that should be seen as secular and separate from the will of Oyagami. The consistent attitude of Oyagami, according to Izō Iburi who was acting as Oyagami's mouthpiece throughout this period, was that institutional affiliation was an expedient, "this-worldly" means which had nothing to do with Oyagami's ultimate plan (Forbes 2005, 79).

In the build-up to the first annual memorial of Miki's passing/disappearance, a Sect Shintō priest based in an institution called Ōmiwa Kyōkai was angered that his group had not been invited to hold the memorial, and called the police, who were apologetic but legally obliged to break up the unauthorized gathering. This incident caused believers to consider for the first time the need to open up *kyōkai* for themselves, prompting Nakayama Shinnosuke to seek approval for this from Shintō Honkyoku. Here, again, Izō Iburi did not recognize state authority as valid until the state in return validated that Tenrikyō's headquarters was located at the Jiba. Even then, Izō issued a divine order that believers must wait to found branch *kyōkai* until the position of the headquarters was "settled," which meant waiting after the legal change for several months, until a new order came from Oyagami (via Izō) (Forbes 2005, 78–82; Tenrikyō 1956a, 105).

This compromise set a precedent within Tenrikyō. At no point did Tenrikyō merely "allow" the state to decide how it should be organized, where its headquarters would be located, and so on, as this would be considered ōbō. But Oyagami in fact permitted the faithful to make changes to doctrines in order to appeal to the state: divine messages from Izō Iburi directly tell believers, in the context of affiliation with Shintō Honkyoku, that "it is good to keep the straight line of Kami in your chest and bear the burdens of the world" (Osashizu of Meiji 21, June 23). Because these orders were coming from Oyagami, affiliation could be interpreted as following the divine will rather than the will of the state.

In May of 1889, Tenrikyō was upgraded from a sixth-order Shintō Honkyoku *kyōkai* to a third-order *kyōkai*. This afforded it new legal protections, and in February 1891 the police offered a round-the-clock watch for Miki's memorial. Shortly thereafter, Tenrikyō became a first-order *kyōkai*. At the same time, however, the organization began moving for complete independence from Shintō Honkyoku, which it was forced to support financially as its largest affiliate (Uemura 1959, 12, 16–17, 26)

Aiming to become "religion"

Tenrikyō's move for independence stretched over nearly two decades. The story of the changes that the state demanded from the Oyagami community, and the persecution that members underwent while earnestly aiming for recognition, have been well-documented in other sources. To summarize, for roughly a decade from 1889 to 1900, Tokyo authorities considered the Oyagami faith an embarrassment; in response, the community offered carefully considered documents that constructed themselves as a church with a Foundress, orthodox history and single doctrine. When this was rejected, they called on Sect Shintō authorities to help them reconstruct their teachings into something Tokyo would find appropriate. The result of this was submitted in 1900 as a second formal application, but it was indicated that it would be rejected, so that application was rescinded in 1903 (Tenrikyō 1990, 26–8).

The involvement of Sect Shintō experts may seem to indicate continued subordination to the interests of Kokugaku, but this was not the case. In fact, with the Great Promulgation Campaign long over and "anti-superstition" policies firmly in place, the Meiji state had no need for Tenrikyō; at one point, Tenrikyō leaders were even told that the government was considering a complete suppression of their entire community (Tenrikyō 1990, 26–8). Where Kokugaku relied heavily on Japan's "official histories" and the precedent of past rituals, Tenrikyō considered itself to have its own rituals and teachings which did not need to be copied from other sources, and increasingly, it was able to imagine itself as a member of a very different group of teachings.

A script for evangelism dating to 1900 shows how the faith was constructing itself during this time. This script, presumably meant to be read aloud to interested listeners on a public street, surprisingly opens with short biographies of Jesus and Muhammad. The preacher explains to the public:

> In lands East and West, among peoples yellow and white, among men and women, there are people who are not ordinary, to those who if even for a short time look up to them as the founders of a sect [*isshū*]. Among these are three great saints, the most wondrous of all wondrous people: Jesus, founder of Christianity; Muhammad, founder of Islam; and Mamichiyahiro-kotoshirume-no-mikoto [a Shinto-style "divine name" used for a short time to refer to Nakayama Miki], founder of our Tenri teaching [*Tenrikyō*].
> Jesus was the son of a carpenter, and one may dare say that he never received high education. Until age 30 he labored alongside his father, but one day he rose and spoke of Heaven's blessings, so that his followers worshipped him as the Christ and showed God's blessings to the world.
> Muhammad was an unlucky child and lost his parents, becoming a merchant in the house of his grandfather. Of course, he could neither read nor write, and until the age of 40 he passed his life as an unlettered townsman. Then suddenly he declared himself God's messenger, and gave the world *Al-Koran*, a divine book from Heaven, and told Humanity of a sacred covenant.
> As for the founder of our Tenrikyō, Mamichiyahiro-kotoshirume-no-mikoto, until age 40 she was a good wife and wise mother, then in one night by a communication between human and God, she was given a great faith for her new life.
> […]

> The life of our founder is mysterious. Truly it ranks alongside Jesus and Muhammad, the [other] two great saints. Or, there are no differences with the [other] two great saints. And just as some cursed Jesus as a demon or ridiculed Muhammad as a madman, just as there were those who judged their teachings as the dreams of idiots, there are those who slander our founder as mad, and call her teachings a type of superstition [*meishin*]. (Udagawa 1958, 4–7)

This is a fairly remarkable document in how it presents Tenrikyō, not only as a message of salvation, but as a particular way in which communication with God operates in relationship with other types of authority. Rather than trying to prove that Tenri-Ō-no-Mikoto *actually exists* as a deity, a question increasingly irrelevant to the secular state, it confronts the *political* question of how we know that a group of believers in Tenri-Ō-no-Mikoto will be a positive influence on the "nation" and "world," two concepts which are given epistemological and ontological priority. It offers a proof by analogy: great sages who communicate with God are known to exist and provide positive values.

This proposition is very much in discord with the journalist Aochi's insistence (above) that Tenrikyō has a particular dogma which necessarily views other dogmas as heretical, and that Tenrikyō's own leaders failed to live up to this standard. It may even be at odds with Yasumaru Yoshio's concept of "cosmology" as independent space. For in this preacher's account, Christianity and Islam are the results of *real communication with the divine*! The ridicule of Jesus and Muhammad are used to illustrate, not a correct attitude to have towards "false" teachings, but an *incorrect* attitude held by the state and sceptical outsiders, which denies the possibility that God from time to time offers real instruction to otherwise ordinary individuals.

The two teachings being cited as parallels to Tenrikyō carry hidden political meaning as well. Christianity, of course, was still being viewed as a threat by some Japanese intellectuals, just nine years after Uchimura Kanzō's *lèse-majesté* incident which led to widespread denunciation of Christianity. The citation of Islam, though, shows the true meaning of these parallels. At the time, Japanese authorities grudgingly allowed Christian missionaries the right to spread their teachings, due to European and American diplomatic pressure, but they refused to grant similar privileges to Tenrikyō, based on their viewpoint that "Japanese religions" were a fixed and limited number of traditional teachings. This script rejects Japan's attempt to limit the number of recognized religions and appeals to an imagined global concept of "world religions" which had only just been introduced to Japanese readers.

One might even read this script in postcolonial terms as an instance of the subaltern talking back to Inoue Enryō, Anesaki Masaharu and other intellectuals responsible for introducing the "world religions" concept to Japan in the 1890s (as described in Isomae 2014, 68–83). If these liberal intellectuals can accept the argument that God occasionally picks prophets like Muhammad and Christ and that "religion" exists prior to state intervention, then, says this argument, they must admit Tenrikyō as well.

While this argument may seem like common sense, and indeed was also adopted by a contemporary Korean educational movement (Jang 2013, 60–1), it represents a "latitudinarian" approach (American-style granting of equal rights to all approved religions) that was unfamiliar to the Japanese state at the time. In 1900, there was much confusion over what sort of religions the Japanese government was presently recognizing, and how to approach the concept of recognition in the future (Thomas 2016, 56). It was further unclear what the standards for being a "religion" *were*. Although the 1889 constitution permitted a limited freedom of religion, Tenrikyō's faith-healing and raucous services caused it to fall under much suspicion from civil authorities. When it was finally recognized as an independent sect in 1908, it was only after five applications and a heavy amount of redaction to its teachings, including rewriting the songs of the daily service and emphasizing the centrality of the Emperor (Tenrikyō 1990, 21).

The rewards of the Taishō Period

The Taishō Period (1912–26) should be properly remembered as a period of surprisingly liberal attitudes towards spiritual teaching on the Japanese archipelago, when charismatic leaders became more and more open to abandoning the system of affiliation and adopting unorthodox attitudes towards the state. Spiritual behaviours that were not always possible in the Meiji Period became possible in the Taishō Period. The change in mood seems to have been distinctly felt by Tenrikyō ministers. Sakakura Tomoo writes in the official history of Tenrikyō's youth arm that "from the end of Meiji and throughout Taishō, as rough waves of new thought rolled in from the West, the measures against modes of thought which had been facing inward turned abruptly outward, and the religion oversight policies that had existed up until then became policies of affirmative use for the heightening of national consciousness" (Sakakura 1970, 72).

Tenrikyō's first experience with this policy of "affirmative use" was the "rural improvement movement" (*chihō kairyō undō* 地方改良運動) of 1909. In sharp contrast to the Great Promulgation Campaign of the 1870s, the rural improvement movement did not rely on Shinto specialists or recipients of specialized education in any way. Instead, it was an unprecedented mobilization of all levels of Japanese society. The intent was to help non-urban Japanese define the nation in long-lasting terms familiar to them, most importantly local shrines and national holidays, and teach them about the antiquity of the imperial line. Through such manufacture of symbolic connections, individual patriotism could be maintained for the future needs of the state. (Kōmoto 1981)

It can certainly be argued that "mass religions" were considered useful by the state principally for their ability to assist in these mass education campaigns. The Three Religions Conference of 1912 is often cited as a chief example of this. It was convened in direct response to the 1910 High Treason Incident (*taigyaku jiken*) and the 105 Persons Incident in Korea, which involved (false) accusations of treason against Christian ministers (McKenzie 2003, 159, 229). Concerns grew in Japan that some varieties of "teaching" could become dangerous to the state. The appearance of socialist and labour movements, workers' strikes, and class issues caused a desire to get to the "root" of these material problems using "religious" teachings (Kim 2010, 458).

Tenrikyō considered the Three Religions Conference a major opportunity to prove the value of their religion for all of Japanese society. The organization printed 10,000 booklets for distribution throughout the country, in which it pledged to "make clear the Great Principle of respect for the Emperor and love of country." Tenrikyō ministers were instructed to reach out to their local communities and convince them that Tenrikyō was a legitimate and equal "world religion" with well-informed, patriotic teachings. A coalition of ministers assembled talks, which were taught to Tenrikyō missionaries across the country, about how Tenrikyō as a "world-class religion" could lend its teachings of stability and morality to the state (Kim 2010; McKenzie 2003, 375ff).

In May of 1919, Home Minister Sokoji again invited the three religious groups to a conference, this time to discuss recent "problems of thought"; this inaugurated the "national strength fostering movement," a similar nationwide instructional programme in which young Tenrikyō believers participated. Tenrikyō was appreciated by wider society for joining the Home Minister's initiative, and within the group, the young men who participated were credited with raising Tenrikyō's social position and allowing its Ofudesaki to be published. Tenrikyō's interests were thus drawn even closer to the ambitions of the state, a pattern that would continue into the following decades (Sakakura 1970, 63–70; McKenzie 2003, 399).

The hidden origins of Ōmoto

Kawazura Bonji's rejection of Sect Shintō

In distinct contrast to Tenrikyō, the Ōmoto movement never sought to meet the needs of state institutions. It rather became one of the chief "heresies" of imperial era Japan, gaining the support of many within the state for its patriotic ambitions, but also forcing a state crackdown. This attitude towards institutional authority is chiefly derived from one of Ōmoto's founders Deguchi Nao, who demanded that the state subordinate itself to her. However, I would like to argue here that Ōmoto had another source for its attitude towards authority, which was never explicitly stated by the group: Kawazura Bonji (川面凡児, 1862–1929).

Kawazura was a Shintoist who was also a close reader of Buddhist and Indian philosophy and propounded global religious unity, a concept that he referred to freely as the "teaching of all gods" (*zenshinkyō* 全神教) and "Worldism" or "World Teaching" (*sekaikyō* 世界教). He was a highly original thinker and completely uninterested in having his group recognized in the *shūkyō* system. He would often tell his followers, "The Miizukai is not a church [*kyōkai*, the term used for recognized Sect Shinto organizations as well as Christian churches]. It is a coterie club for enlightening the world with the *miizu* [pure authority] of His Majesty the Emperor." In his understanding, there was no contradiction between the Emperor and internationalism. Rather than starting an international organization, he imagined that each country could found its own, unique style of "World Teaching" which would propound its own "national spirit" (Miyazaki 2011, 104).

Thus it was entirely in accord with Kawazura's intentions that the Miizukai never sought recognition under the banner of Sect Shintō. He practised *misogi* water purification and other Shinto rituals, and wrote countless essays and books about "ancient Shinto," all while explicitly rejecting cooperation with the state and espousing unorthodox political beliefs. During the Meiji Period he was not particularly influential, but in the Taishō Period his philosophy study groups and *misogi* rituals were widely attended, with no apparent legal consequences. Maruyama Toshiaki (2016, 12) suggests that the reason for the benign neglect of his Miizukai was that "the age was looking for a man like him."

It has not yet been recognized in religious studies scholarship that Kawazura was simultaneously founding a "teaching" and objecting to the state's categories of *shūkyō* and *kyōkai*. Furthermore, as far as the historical record attests, this objection met with *no resistance whatsoever*, even as Kawazura's teachings grew in popularity. We will see that Kawazura's strategy towards the state had a massively understated influence on the Taishō Period situation, so at this point it is worth analysing how he remained above the law.

An unusual feature of Kawazura's "Worldism" was that he completely rejected the special authority of possession or *kamigakari* (Miyazaki 2011, 101). He was therefore denying the authority of the state to regulate his doctrines and practices, not based on the sort of epistemological access to higher truth that made state authorities nervous, but rather on the strength of his blameless character, as his behaviours were totally in alignment with state Shinto hierarchy, and he did not conduct faith-healing or other such "superstitious" activities, as well as on the purely philosophical grounds that his teaching unified all creeds and nations and stood firmly above them without objecting to any of them. Let us examine these two strategies in greater detail.

First, Kawazura professed that the newly accepted hierarchy of Shinto *kami* was the "national spirit of Japan," which could be united with the national spirits of all the other nations in the world to create the "World Teaching." This is therefore a remarkably political religion: it suggests that the truest expression of religion comes through the geographical and political forms of the nation-state, which were being "taught" to western colonies and colonized people throughout the world at that time. Furthermore, these nation-states are believed to contain a national essence, which when properly expressed will be able to unite into the "World Teaching" (Kawazura 1906, Vol. II, 236). Kawazura's initial declaration explains the absolute value of the state, source of all teachings: it provides for "the comfort of the mind and the health of the body," and issues forth from "the independent authority of the lives of its *ethnos*" (Kawazura 1906, Vol. I, 13).

Second, Kawazura's philosophical strategy of "polytheist unity," "worldism" or "teaching of all gods" consists of a mixture of Restorationism and Indian philosophy. In the context of late Meiji, Restorationism had recently lost out in the battle for ideological control of the government system, producing many dissatisfied intellectuals. One western biographer of Deguchi Onisaburō remarks that these intellectuals continued to search for an alternative to modernity well into the Taishō Period, which led to the success of Ōmoto (Stalker 2008, 48–9).

As Yasumaru observes, the teaching of "unity of Confucianism, Buddhism, and Shinto" which made up an influential part of Edo Period thought, including the basis of Shingaku lectures, contained within it the basis for intense criticism of the government and "heretical" anti-authority positions. This Edo Period cosmology was rapidly eclipsed in Meiji by western-style dualism: subject and object were firmly divided against each other and the "spiritual" was rendered invisible (Yasumaru 2013, 302, 322–3). Kawazura's work is quite clearly attempt to revive this cosmology of unity. The following proclamation, originally written in *kanbun*, is representative:

> Human beings are not the sole subjects and objects. Everything that exists, all existence, is subject and object. The men of Old resembled all things. Every subject is an object and every object a subject. They are mutually united in appearance and what is beneath. They mutually create *Miizu*. (Kawazura 1940, 25)

The mysterious invocation of "the men of Old" is Daoist: a similar statement is found in the *Zhuangzi*, namely, "the myriad things and I are one" (萬物與我為一). Since *Miizu* is in Kawazura's work the mystical authority of the Emperor, the import of this passage is that western teachings cannot properly articulate the source of this authority: only the lost Edo Period thought, if revived, can properly explain it.

It was obviously Kawazura's intent to reactivate Edo-style monism in modern public life, both in content and in style. Even the style and printing of his work reflects this ideal: some of his publications were handwritten with calligraphy or bound in Japanese-style paper, and his writing includes plenty of Sino-Japanese compositions like this. Indeed, this was a return to the "heretical" early modern worldview described by Yasumaru. Why, then, was it not recognized that this "cosmology of unity" was inherently political, and trespassing on the separation of religion from politics?

According to Ashizu Uzuhiko (1987, 165), who was intimately involved in the prewar Shinto nationalist movement, the Home

Office did indeed interpret Kawazura's work as a direct criticism of the government. In response, they held him at arm's length as a "private religionist" whose teachings "imitated Sect Shinto." If this is true, Kawazura's direct criticisms were respected as "religion," despite the fact that they were recognizably political in nature and that he was not affiliated with any Shinto branch. He certainly received much better treatment than Tenrikyō!

It seems that Kawazura's beliefs and practices summoned such an aura of authority that they had immediate and uncontroversial appeal. Fujimaki Kazuho (2009, 236) notes the centrality and primacy of the "spirit of the Emperor" (*miizu*) in Kawazura's system, and describes him as linking traditional, sacred rituals like *misogi* water purification into a "theology of the emperor" in a way that originates from "none other than the orthodox branch" of Restoration Shinto. Perhaps his teachings were valuable through the claim he made to base his internationalism and ultranationalism in legitimate orthodoxy.

Spread of Kawazura's mission into Ontakekyō and Ōmoto

According to Kawazura's semi-official biography, published after his death by one of his followers (Kanaya 1929, 100–1), shortly after Kawazura founded the Miizukai and issued its first manifesto in 1906 (Meiji 39), Jingū Takahisa 神宮嵩壽, *kanchō* (chief) of the Sect Shintō organization Ontakekyō, approached him and, expressing a firm agreement with his sense of global mission, offered to transfer leadership of Ontakekyō to him. This, of course, would have entailed bureaucratic management of the various schools of Ontakekyō and negotiations with the government over eliminating "superstition." Kawazura declined the offer.

Most of the materials about Jingū-*kanchō* and his life are now missing, so we cannot verify that he actually made such an offer, but there is in fact circumstantial evidence that he could have benefited from such an offer. Deguchi Yasuaki (1994) and Nakayama Kaoru (2007, 170ff) describe him as a Kokugaku scholar and reform-minded Shintoist who bitterly disputed with other Ontakekyō priests who were more interested in fortune-telling, asceticism and selling charms. Jingū-*kanchō* desired to modernize his sect and proposed a charity movement modelled after the Salvation Army, but around the time of this supposed meeting with Kawazura in 1906 Jingū-*kanchō* was already on the losing side of his argument against his own vice-chief (*fukukanchō*) who had the support of the mountain ascetics. Therefore, ceding control of Ontakekyō to Kawazura could have actually been to his benefit.

The following year, Onisaburō became general superintendent of Jingū-*kanchō*'s branch of Ontakekyō. At the time, Deguchi Nao and her entire family were unemployed and bankrupt in Ayabe, and Onisaburō had promised them all that he would send them remittances so that they could eat. In fact he did not send them anything but excuses, and for roughly a year they were starving almost every day, at one point eating handfuls of rotten rice several years old. Nao's daughter reports that at one stage she was peeing blood in her urine. Among Nao's few followers, this did not boost Onisaburō's popularity. He was described as a "demon" or as one of the "foreign spirits" that Nao believed were coming to destroy Japan (Deguchi 1995, 646–52).

Onisaburō was receiving letters from the Deguchis and must have been aware of what he was doing. Jingū-*kanchō* was certainly aware, because we have testimony that he called Onisaburō into his office and told him to go back to Ayabe, saying: "If you want to be in the position of Nakayama Shinjirō [first administrative leader] of Tenrikyō, you should go back and rescue Nao from her poverty" (Murakami 1978, 89). Hence Jingū-*kanchō* had a formative influence on Onisaburō's leadership in Ōmoto. This is oddly missing from Ōmoto's official histories, although Onisaburō does mention Jingū-*kanchō* in the text of his epic *Reikai monogatari*.

Kawazura's biographer suggests that Onisaburō must have heard about Kawazura at this time. Here, again, we have no direct evidence for this, but plenty of circumstantial evidence: after his return to Ayabe in 1909, Onisaburō immediately started spreading the word that he had founded a group which was a teaching of the shrines and imperial ancestors superior to all "artificial" religions, using language quite reminiscent of Kawazura (Kawamura 2017, 192). There is enough information here to conclude that, even if

Kawazura did not influence Ōmoto directly, Onisaburō actually gained an understanding of Japan's religious scene, and the disputes within it over superstition, autonomy and universalism, from his interactions with the romantic reformist Jingū-*kanchō*.

Stresses over institutional affiliation

At the very end of the Meiji Period, Onisaburō had rebuilt Ōmoto in Ayabe and was busy trying to switch its affiliation from Taiseikyō to yet another sect, Izumo Ōyashirokyō, which he felt might be more protective of Ōmoto's central deity Ushitora-no-Konjin, whom he identified with Izumo's creator god Kuninotokotachi-no-mikoto. Even as Onisaburō pushed for a more favourable affiliation, though, he would have been reading in Sect Shintō publications about the outcome of a recent legal case over the faith-healing group Renmonkyō, in which affiliation ended in a disastrous loss of property and legal rights.

Renmonkyō grew explosively up until 1894, when it was harshly criticized in the popular press for its faith-healing practices, and collapsed thereafter. The continued existence of Renmonkyō became an embarrassment to its the Sect Shintō organization Taiseikyō which legally managed it. In May 1911, a large number of Renmonkyō priests were dismissed from their positions by Taiseikyō. Taiseikyō then sued the priests to seize their assets and capital, initially losing this suit, but then winning on appeal. One Sect Shintō organization, the Shinpūkai 神風会, was outraged by Taiseikyō's use of the legal system to interfere with religious activities, and the June 15, 1911 edition of their official organ ran the melodramatic headline, "Why must we submit to a law that violates our constitutional rights?! Unconstitutional!! Unconstitutional!! Unconstitutional!!" (Takeda 1991, 28).

Shinpūkai was a Tokyo-based group of Shinto intellectuals. Its founder Miyai Kanejirō 宮井鐘次郎 began to form the group in 1903 when he founded the Great Japan Charitable Association (*Dainippon Jizen Kyōkai* 大日本慈善協会), which managed a reformatory based on "Shinto principles" of "pure love." Andō Reiji has identified the chief supporters of the Shinpūkai as including the influential Hirata-ha *kannushi*, a director of Kokugakuin, the chief priest of Shintō Honkyoku, the chief priest of Kurozumikyō, the director of Jingū Hōsaikai, and the Tokyo branch chief of Izumo Taishakyō (Andō 2014, 45–6, 51n5).

As one can guess from the activities and name of the Great Japan Charitable Association, some members of the Shinpūkai were of the opinion that Shinto needed to develop itself as a religion through the development of morality and good acts. However, there was a constant ambiguity between this ideal model for "religion" and the insistence that Shinto was not merely religion but was the basis of common morality in Japan. Shinpūkai essentially served as an interest group attempting to use the ambiguity to push for greater rights for Shinto sects. It may have been interesting to Onisaburō that the Shinpūkai embraced not only officially legitimated groups like Jingū Hōsaikai, but also widely slandered groups like Renmonkyō in their quest for collective admission of rights from the state.

Andō Reiji writes of this group that they "aimed for a Shinto reform movement to parallel the Buddhist reform movement" (2014, 332). Some articles paralleled the political criticisms of the New Buddhist Movement: for example, in their June 25, 1908 issue, a writer calling himself Kinsui Gyoshi 錦水漁史 argued that the Meiji Constitution did not guarantee full religious freedom because of the qualifying statement about "disturbing public order," and lamented that this had prevented his fellow Shintoists from effectively combating "foreign teachings and heretical sects" (in other words, Christianity).

Onisaburō remained an avid reader of the Shinpūkai newsletter even after returning to Ayabe, and in 1912 he became a branch chief of the organization (ONH 1964, 321). In the 1911 editions of their newsletter, he would have learned about the Shinpūkai's take on the widely discussed Renmonkyō case. The Shinpūkai considered the affiliation system to be a betrayal of the constitutional right to freedom of belief, and the fate of Renmonkyō to be a chief example of this.

As we saw, from 1909, Onisaburō began to claim that Ōmoto superseded all religions. In the Taishō Period, this eventually evolved into in a manifesto completely rejecting the term "religion" which will be dealt with below. We have seen in this section that this was not his original observation, but an opinion that he would have heard from his participation in Ontakekyō and the Shinpūkai. In short, Onisaburō's association with Sect Shintō helped him understand the limitations of the system by which the state recognized faith communities and offered them legal protection.

The hidden origins of the First Ōmoto Incident

In 1921, the Ōmoto group was disbanded by the Japanese government, in an investigation and trial called the "First Ōmoto Incident" to distinguish it from a much different event in the 1930s. At a simplistic level, this could be portrayed as "government interference with religion." Scholars of Ōmoto understand that there is some nuance to the incident. But it is not broadly recognized that Ōmoto was not even describing itself as a religion in 1921. Rather, it adopted a contradictory, multipronged strategy of demanding independence as a "teaching" while aiming to become the "national teaching" of the state, and at one point actually portrayed itself as a conspiracy against the government.

Superficially, Ōmoto employed the rhetoric of "world religions" in the same way that Tenrikyō had been doing since the Meiji Period. Onisaburō claimed that Ōmoto was akin to Christianity in its ability to perform miracles, driving the point home by reminding his readers that many Tokyo intellectuals who criticized Ōmoto had themselves converted to Christianity. However, this comparison was supplemented by Kawazura's vision of the national power of religions: Onisaburō insisted that Ōmoto was a Japanese force that could manifest the highest ambitions of the Japanese spirit, and further that it was more than just "religion" but would be able to encompass and unify political science, diplomacy, economics and philosophy under its belt. When Ōmoto came to trial in 1921, this was the self-description of the movement that he gave to the prosecutors (Yasumaru 1977, 95; Stalker 2008, 86–8).

Onisaburō's chief collaborator, Asano Wasaburō stated at his pretrial hearing that Ōmoto "is not a religion," but has no difference from "Shinto" in its practices (Ikeda 1982, Vol. III, 25). It should be noted that the prosecutor is not very interested in this line of questioning, since the trial is not about whether Ōmoto has overstepped the bounds of what "religions" are permitted to preach, but rather about whether it presents a danger to the government. More than the comparison to "world religions," then, this comparison to Shinto and total rejection of the word "religion" is probably closer to Asano's actual intentions and deserves closer attention.

The full meaning of the rejection of the term "religion" and preference for "Shinto" can be found in a 1920 Ōmoto pamphlet included in Ikeda Akira's *Ōmoto shiryō shūsei* (1982, Vol. II, 195–210). Discussing a manuscript of the *Protocols of the Elders of Zion*, which he describes as secret documents attesting to a grand conspiracy by a "secret mason society" (*masson himitsu kessha*), Asano introduces an analysis by a student of his named Inoue, who demonstrates to readers how the conspiracy was prophesied in Deguchi Nao's Ofudesaki. In his concluding section, Asano's disciple shows that Ōmoto is the one, true movement that will be able to counteract the conspiracy:

> You readers who have sensed that the Imperial Way Ōmoto is the Mason Society of the true kami realm (*seishinkai* 正神界), and the Mason Society is the Imperial Way Ōmoto of the corrupted kami realm (*jashinkai* 邪神界), must at the same time realize that the Imperial Way Ōmoto *is not a religion.* For our Ōmoto is not a narrow, powerless thing like a religion, but is *truly the center enacting the reform of the world.* And again, like the Mason Society, there are many points of resemblance between the two which can be seen above. We aim to unify the world, as do they, and where they state their administration principles, we are again similar. *We have the true, they have the corrupt (character); we have the divine power, they have the learning-power (in execution and applications); besides such differences, there is no difference between the two of us.* [...] ***If you do not wish to become slaves of the JEWS, then come and assemble beneath the Imperial Way Ōmoto!*** (Ikeda 1982, Vol. II, 209–10, emphasis in original)

In short, just like the "masons" or "Jews" of the *Protocols*, Ōmoto is engaged in a conspiracy against all the governments of the world. Between these two conspiracies, only one will be permitted to win; naturally, this will be the "true" conspiracy of Ōmoto, which alone has the power to unite the world under the true gods and the true Emperor. Asano, insofar as he agreed with this logic, must have been compelled to reject the term "religion" for a movement which is about to become the one-world government, both privately and at trial.

Although Asano referred to Ōmoto as a "Shinto" movement at trial, he possessed little concrete knowledge of Shinto and Buddhism, probably much like the countless thousands he was converting through his public and private lectures (Hardacre 1998, 150). He likely saw Ōmoto as a function with an end goal: not a "religion" which had a fixed relationship with government, but a "conspiracy against the world" which, through its doctrinal independence and its special access to divine power, possessed limitless capacity for change.

Onisaburō did not describe his own movement as a conspiracy in such explicit terms, and by the mid-Taishō Period he had ceased to associate it with "Shinto" in the sense of existing sects. In his 1920 essay "The Evils of Religion" (*Shūkyō no gaidoku*), he makes some statements reminiscent of Kawazura about the unity of all religions and how each religion must adapt to its "national spirit." But he then goes off in a rather different direction, claiming that any religion that fails to affirm the "five virtues" of Confucianism will never be able to unite Japan. With Confucianism being an import from China, this was certainly far from an affirmation of Japanese uniqueness (Ikeda 1982, Vol. II, 375ff).

In fact, when Ōmoto's leaders went abroad, it was not to affirm the values of Shinto-based "national teaching" or ritual but rather to *subvert* them. In December 1919, Asano Wasaburō and two other Ōmoto members took a trip to Taiwan. Ōmoto was now at the height of its power, and the sight of religious dignitaries praying at overseas *jinja* must have made an impression on Taiwanese. But here, Asano upset their expectations. Rather than preaching to them about the need for assimilation, he championed the

Taiwanese cause, saying that Japanese mainlanders were the "idiots of the world" and needed to "reform" themselves before they could dare talk to the Taiwanese. In March 1920, despite growing public criticism of Ōmoto, Asano went *back* to Taiwan, this time prophesying to the Taiwanese that great hardships were coming. (Kano 1973, 77)

This disturbed the Japanese colonial administrators. In early 1920, the matter was discussed at the highest level of administration, and in July, Ōmoto materials were completely banned in Taiwan. The timing of this is key: as Ōmoto's official history acknowledges, Ōmoto books had not yet been censored on the Japanese mainland, and it was only on August 5, 1920 that Deguchi Nao's *Ōmoto shin'yu* was banned throughout Japan (ONH 1964, 458–61).

Ōmoto's manifesto

As noted by Nancy Stalker, in 1920 Deguchi Onisaburō published an essay rejecting affiliation entirely. She summarizes it as observing that members of "independent" religious sects like Tenrikyō were actually more restricted in their activities than "unapproved teachings" like Ōmoto. The purpose of Onisaburō's publication of this essay, she writes, was to affirm his stance that "officially approved status would restrict the very essence of Ōmoto's belief in the unity of governance and religion" (Stalker 2008, 53).

This essay is characteristic of Onisaburō's ability to mix all sorts of unspoken or overlooked popular currents of the Taishō Period and offer them political weight. Onisaburō aims to appeal to ideas that Japanese readers of the time might have found credible, and through his creative bricolage we learn of a variety of credible sounding reasons for avoiding official recognition available at the time. Most notably:

> If I am asked why Kōdō Ōmoto is not an official teaching, my reason is thusly: if we were to become an official teaching, we would not be able to serve God. God is absolute and unlimited. Although it is said that man is in God's image, no

> matter how wise a man is, he can only be a drop in the grand ocean of the Divine Mind. Worldly men cannot claim to direct or supervise the teachings of God through their legislation. Because Ōmoto is a legally unrecognized teaching, we cannot be forced to revise our teachings like the official teachings do... (Ikeda 1982, Vol. II, 373)

It cannot be missed that in order to prove his point about the need for total freedom, Onisaburō temporarily adopts the guise of an objecting Christian; very nearly that of Uchimura himself, who famously failed to bow properly before a photo of the Emperor in 1891. This is a very good fit to Yasumaru Yoshio's concept of "cosmology" as the basis for heresy against the prewar emperor system. But for Onisaburō, cosmology seems to be a highly Christian concept. He takes a gamble that the Japanese public of 1920 would be willing to accept the legitimacy of this Christian concept, in a way that they were mostly unwilling to do in 1891.

Several different tactics are attempted in this article, and another is constitutionalism:

> According to the spirit of Article 28 of the constitution, freedom of religion is guaranteed. Ōmoto is an independent teaching founded on this basis. It is a so-called unauthorized teaching by law, but in terms of its actual power it is an independent teaching. In other words, Kōdō Ōmoto is an independent teaching in practice. The independent teachings attached to the religions office – Tenrikyō, Konkōkyō, Kurozumikyō, Ontakekyō and so forth, 13 in all – all of these things are under the supervision of the Culture Ministry's Religions Department, their presidents suffer the indignity of being treated as if they were appointed [by the government], and in that way all the messaging of their doctrine is restricted. They are restricted in many ways, such as being told that religionists must not interfere in politics.

This is a slightly contradictory strategy, as we also learn from this same essay that Ōmoto itself is aiming to become the "national teaching" encompassing "education, business, medicine, calendrics, heavenly and earthly literature, science, religion, philosophy, and all other things" – presumably including law. Ōmoto is not trying to become a "mere" religion, no matter how independent: Onisaburō observes that the Pope of Roman Catholicism was unable to stop World War I as the world's most powerful religious leader, and he emphasizes that Ōmoto requires more power than this. So this appeal to legalism can only serve its purpose rhetorically if it is interpreted as a kind of "expedient means" to bring readers closer to Ōmoto's actual message.

Onisaburō's approach to the religious-secular binary seems to have followed the Japanese artistic pattern of *shu-ha-ri* (守破離): following the norm, going against it, then breaking it entirely. His claims at first closely resembled those of Kawazura and other Sect Shintō leaders. In the Taishō Period, he departed from strictly claiming like Tenrikyō that he possessed the "national teaching" that the Kokugaku scholars were aiming for, and began to come up with his own mission and message. Finally, he completely transcended the religious-secular binary and openly challenged it.

His "break" from the binary makes for fascinating reading by later generations of scholars, but did it actually assist him when Ōmoto was actually accused of high crimes against the state? The answer to this question is "maybe not" – since, having refused to accept the normal category of "religion" for his behaviours, Onisaburō was forced to make an even bigger gamble about the legitimacy of his writing.

Strategies used at trial during the First Ōmoto Incident

According to Ōmoto's own historical narrative, the First Ōmoto Incident was caused entirely by the attitudes of the Japanese state, and Ōmoto's involvement in the proceedings did little to change the outcome. The background was a suspicion towards "superstition" and "misleading teachings," which were frequently prosecuted and slammed in the papers. The state's argument was aided by psychologists like Nakamura Kokyō who claimed that they could debunk the possession experiences of *chinkon-kishin*. Trumped-up charges of *lèse-majesté* served merely as the legal means to get a conviction (Deguchi 1970).

What this narrative leaves out is that Onisaburō's own teachings, including his defence against the charges against him, can be seen as a direct assault on the Japanese state. As seen above, he denounced the Religions Law and proclaimed that it was better to ignore all systems for the regulation of teachings. Furthermore, he also claimed that he and Nao could not be held responsible for works produced under the influence of spirit possession. He used both of these arguments as his legal defence in 1921.

Onisaburō's posture at trial was that all of his statements, from the most abstract to the most concrete and radical political proposals, were part of the same system of "Imperial Way" and "Taishō restoration," and could not be separated into religious and non-religious. He not only denied the category "religion," but had also created a somewhat odd shell company. For him, *Kōdō Ōmoto* (The Original Imperial Way, i.e. Ōmoto) was, properly speaking, the name of the Way itself, which humans did not invent but only participated in. The actual organization that existed in Japan's legal realm was his Dai-Nihon Shūsaikai, which was affiliated neither with a religion nor a corporate body, but was simply an association that he used for publishing his remarks about the Way (Ikeda 1982, Vol. III, 24).

For Onisaburō, the Way was all-encompassing, and could not be confined to the term "religion." Religion was something now legally barred from participation in Japanese education, while the Way included "politics, that is to say, (divine) political education and so on." He therefore stood behind two legal barriers: that Ōmoto was a vision he was describing and was not itself an organization, and that what organization he did have was not confined to the administrative category of *shūkyō*. To show his seriousness in this, he avoided words like "religion," "kanchō" and "founder" in his official language, opting to come up with his own invented terms instead (Ikeda 1982, Vol. III, 17).

Hyōdo Akiko (2007, 163) observes that Ōmoto's attempt to overcome the framework of religion, and the use of terms like "national teaching," made him appear to be putting himself at the same level as the Emperor, and was probably viewed as a direct threat. During the trial, large amounts of evidence were presented by the prosecutor that showed that Ōmoto was concealing incendiary, revolutionary rhetoric within its doctrine.

Katsurajima (2015, 266) remarks that this insistence on overstepping the boundaries of the religious category must have caused deep concern to the authorities, but they did not push Onisaburō on his definition of religion, probably for fear of diluting the power of their administrative categories. Instead, they questioned the sort of administration Ōmoto *was* conducting: who had legal responsibility for distributing the funds? What were they being used for? Were people besides Onisaburō involved in planning how funds were used? (Ikeda 1982, Vol. III, 38f).

In other words, the prosecutors at the First Ōmoto Incident were willing to surrender the point that *shūkyō* was, legally speaking, an administrative category, rather than a label that could be applied based on family resemblances. For them, regardless of what category Ōmoto fell under, the private nature of the group was obvious: it had specific agents who published its books and handled its money. The question was how liable these agents were for the dangerous sentiments contained in the books.

For this, Onisaburō fell back on a unique and rather outlandish strategy: he claimed that everything he had written was the product of possession by either divine beings or else "wicked deities" (*jashin* 邪神), so he had no control over what sort of messages appeared in the books he published. In his biography of Onisaburō, Kawamura (2017, 249–55) considers some of his answers at trial "fairly disingenuous," but concludes that Onisaburō's entire defence earnestly rested on the novel legal idea that the deities possessing him were different persons.

The state called psychotherapists to determine whether Onisaburō was "actually" in a state of possession, but this response got mixed results. One declared that rather than being in a state of "abnormality," Onisaburō merely was capable of, "innately and constitutionally, a genius for mental change." But another determined that the possession experiences were real, and the state admitted that possession was at the very least a valid category of "mental illness," leading Kawamura to conclude that this strategy was "slightly successful" (2017, 249–55).

Jason Josephson observes that a religious believer "can say no to vaccination as a member of the Church of Christ, Scientist, but if you object on the grounds that…demons told you it was bad, your petition would be rejected" (Josephson 2012, 235). "Religion," as an administrative category, essentially serves as a necessary buffer for the state between the moral absolutes provided by otherworldly being(s) and the finality of the law. Having removed the veil of "religion," Clifford Geertz's "cultural system" that systematizes divine interaction, Onisaburō exposed the impossibility of total religious freedom in any regime.

At this trial, in any case, the prosecutors were aware of the difficulties of charging Onisaburō or Ōmoto of intentionally insulting the Emperor, and so added the charges of violating the newspaper censorship laws (Watanabe 1979, 225). However, as their legal basis for the forced demolition of Ōmoto's headquarters in Ayabe, the government completely ignored Onisaburō's rejection of "religion," and ruled that the headquarters was an "unauthorized temple" – based, it would seem, on resemblances in appearance (Stalker 2008, 99).

Concluding remarks on the meaning of "religion" and "Shinto"

Today, we think of "Shinto" as one of the religions of Japan, and of "religion" as a handy designator for anything that looks like Shinto or Buddhism. However, we have seen from these two examples that before 1945, the definitions of religion and Shinto were actively being debated throughout Japan, and some would separate the two or build boundaries within them. Tenrikyō appealed to the concept of "religion" so that it could be partially freed from being regulated as "Shinto." Ōmoto used the concept of "Shinto" in a political and subversive way pioneered by Kawazura Bonji, to escape the limitations of the concept of "religion."

That being the case, when did Shinto become the "Japanese religion" that we are familiar with today, and when did Japan accept the liberal idea of "religion" that was gaining in prominence in twentieth-century America? One writer has pointed to 1929, when the head of the Religions Office, Shimomura Juichi stated that if a new bill to regulate religion were passed, "there is not the least thought in the Ministry of Culture that something becomes a religion when it receives the designation of religion...all groups with religious behaviors are religions" (Makinouchi 2003, 27). In other words, he was claiming that "religion" was already something recognizable on sight and not the result of government administration.

But it should be noted that despite Shimomura's attempt to deny "the least thought" of the term "religion" being essentially administrative in character, that "least thought" was clearly quite conceivable. In fact, we have good evidence that exceptions would be made: Uchimura Kanzō received direct assurance from the Ministry that his Bible study group and other organized parts of his Mukyōkai movement would not be treated as religion under the proposed 1929 bill. This was despite the fact that Uchimura himself recognized that some of his fellow Mukyōkai students were acting as if they were a church (Uchimura 1939, 780, 870).

The legal concept of "religion" is a government attempt to privatize certain behaviours, and as such, a change in regime brings changes to ideas of religiousness. During the American Occupation, the Shinto Directive and a new religious corporations law re-secularized the country, eliminating the old Kawazura idea of universal, superreligious Shinto and making "religion" a much more egalitarian legal concept which includes all forms of Shinto. This is the ultimate cause of Ōmoto becoming a member of Sect Shintō as well as Tenrikyō leaving it.

References

Andō Reiji. 2014. *Orikuchi Shinobu*. Tokyo (Kodansha).
Aochi Shin. 1969. *Tenrikyō*. Tokyo (Kōbundō Shinsha).
Ashizu Uzuhiko. 1987. *Kokka Shintō to wa nan datta ka*. Tokyo (Jinja Shinpo-sha).
Deguchi Eiji. 1970. *Ōmotokyō jiken*. Tokyo (San'ichi Shobō).

Deguchi Yasuaki. 1994. *Daichi no haha*, Vol. 9 (revised edition). Kameoka (Aizen Shuppan).
Deguchi Yasuaki. 1995. *Irimame no hana*. Tokyo (Hachiman Shoten).
Forbes, Roy. 2005. "Schism, Orthodoxy and Heresy in the History of Tenrikyō: Three Case Studies." Master's thesis, University of Hawaii.
Fujimaki Kazuho. 2009. *Tennō no hikyō*. Tokyo (Gakken).
Hardacre, Helen. 1998. "Asano Wasaburō and Japanese Spiritualism in Early Twentieth Century Japan" in: Sharon Minichello (ed.), *Japan's Competing Modernities: Issues in Culture and Democracy 1900–1930*. Honolulu (University of Hawaii Press).
Hyōdo Akiko. 2007. "Hyōi ga seishinbyō ni sareru toki: jinkaku henkan, shūkyō dan'atsu, seishin kantei" in: Kawamura Kunimitsu (ed.), *Hyōi no kindai to politics*. Tokyo (Seikyūsha).
Ikeda Amira. 1982. *Ōmoto shiryō shūsei*. 3 vols. Tokyo (San'ichi Shobō).
Isomae Jun'ichi. 2014. *Religious Discourse in Modern Japan: Religion, State, and Shintō*. Boston (Brill). https://doi.org/10.1163/9789004272682
Jang Seokman. 2013. "Nihon teikoku jidai ni okeru shūkyō gainen no hensei: shūkyō gainen no seidoka to naimenka" in: Isomae Jun'ichi and Yun Haedong (eds.), *Shokuminchi Chōsen to shūkyō: teikokushi, kokka shintō, koyū shinkō*. Tokyo (Sangensha).
Josephson, Jason Ananda. 2012. *The Invention of Religion in Japan*. Chicago (University of Chicago Press).
Kajimoto Narajirō. 1946. "Kyōsōsama no omoide." *Fukugen* 1, 40–52. Tenri Central Library.
Kanaya Makoto. 1929. *Kawazura Bonji-sensei den*. Tokyo (Misogi Zasshi-sha).
Kaneko Akira. 2017. "Shingaku shisō to Tenrikyō ni kan suru minshū shisō shiteki ichikōsatsu: ryōsha ga kyōyū suru 'kokoro no shisō' no kanyō kanōsei ni tsuite." *Tenri Daigaku Oyasato kenkyūjo nenpō* 23.
Kano Masanao, 1973. *Taishō democracy no teiryū: "dozoku"teki seishin e no kaiki*. Tokyo (NHK Books).
Katsurajima Nobuhiro. 1991. "Meiji 20-nendai no minshū shūkyō" in: Mahara Tetsuo and Kakeya Sahei (eds.), *Kindai tennōsei kokka no shakai tōgō*. Kyoto (Bunrikaku).
Katsurajima Nobuhiro. 2015. "Meishin/inshi/jakyō" in: Shimazono Susumu (ed.), *Series Nihonjin to Shūkyō*, Vol. 6. Tokyo (Shunjūsha).
Kawazura Bonji. 1906. *Dai-Nihon sekaikyō senmeisho*. In two independently paginated sections. Tokyo (Miizukai Shuppanjo).
Kawazura Bonji. 1940. *Kawazura Bonji zenshū*, Vol. 4. Tokyo (Kawazura Bonji-sensei 10-Shūnen Kinenkai).
Kawamura Kunimitsu. 2017. *Deguchi Nao, Onisaburō: sekai o suishō no yo ni itasu zo yo*. Kyoto (Minerva Shobō).
Kim Tae-hoon. 2010. "Ideology to kibō: Tenrikyō no sankyō kaidō." *Nihon kenkyū* (Global Institute for Japanese Studies at Korea University) 14.

Kōda Chūsaburō, et al. 1957. "Saisho no yurai." *Fukugen* 31. Tenri Central Library.
Kōmoto Mitsugi. 1981. "Kokka Shintōka seisaku to minshū" in: Ikeda Eishun et al. (eds.), *Nihonjin no shūkyō no ayumi*. Tokyo (Daigaku Kyōikusha).
Makinouchi Yū. 2003. "Senzenki ni okeru bunkashō no shūkyō seisaku: 'ruiji shūkyō' ga 'shūkyō kessha' to naru made." *Hokudai shigaku* 43.
Maruyama Toshiaki. 2016. "Maruyama Toshio to Kawatsura Bonji." *Rinri kenkyūsho kiyō* 25.
McKenzie, Timothy S. 2003. "Spiritual Restoration and Religious Reinvention in Late Meiji Japan: The Three Religions Conference and Religious Nationalism." PhD thesis, Lutheran School of Theology at Chicago.
Miyazaki Sadayuki 2011. *Uchū no daidō o ayumu: Kawazura Bonji to sono jidai*. Tokyo (Tokyo Zusho Shuppan).
Murakami Shigeyoshi. 1978. *Hyōden Deguchi Onisaburō*. Tokyo (Sanseido).
Nakayama Kaoru. 2007. *Shugen to shintō no aida: Kiso Ontake shinkō no kinsei, kindai*. Tokyo (Kōbundō).
Nagaoka Takashi. 2015. *Shinshūkyō to sōryokusen: kyōso igo o ikiru*. Nagoya (Nagoya Daigaku Shuppankai).
Nagaoka Takashi. 2017. "Minshū shūkyō kenkyū no genzai." *Nihon shisō shigaku* 49.
ONH = Ōmoto Nanajūnen-shi Hensankai. 1964. *Ōmoto nanajūnen-shi*, Vol. 1. Kameoka (Ōmoto).
Sakakura Tomoo, ed. 1970. *Tenrikyō Seinenkai-shi*, Vol. 1. Tenri, Nara (Tenrikyō Seinenkai Honbu / Tenri Central Library).
Sawada, Janine Tasca. 2004. *Practical Pursuits: Religion, Politics, and Personal Cultivation in Nineteenth-Century Japan*. Honolulu (University of Hawaii Press).
Shimada Hiromi. 2009. *Tenrikyō*. Tokyo (Hachiman Shoten).
Shinpūkai. Tōkyō Daigaku Meiji Shinbun Zasshi Bunkō.
Stalker, Nancy. 2008. *Prophet Motive: Deguchi Onisaburō, Oomoto, and the Rise of New Religions in Imperial Japan*. Honolulu (University of Hawaii Press).
Suzuki Sadami. 1996. *"Seimei" de yomu Nihon kindai: Taishō seimeishugi no tanjō to tenkai*. Tokyo (NHK Books).
Takeda Michio. 1991. "Meiji-ki no shinshūkyō to hō." *Shūkyō hō* 10.
Tenrikyō. 1956a. *The short history of Tenrikyō*. Tenri, Nara (Headquarters of Tenrikyō Church).
Tenrikyō. 1956b. *Kōhon Tenrikyō kyōso-den*. Tenri, Nara (Tenri Dōyūsha).
Tenrikyō. 1990. *A Historical Sketch of Tenrikyō*. Tenri, Nara (Tenri Overseas Mission Department).
Thomas, Jolyon Baraka. 2016. "Varieties of Religious Freedom in Japanese Buddhist Responses to the 1899 Religions Bill." *Asian Journal of Law and Society* 3. https://doi.org/10.1017/als.2016.1

Uchimura Kanzō. 1939. *Uchimura Kanzō zenshū*, Vol. 18. Tokyo (Iwanami Shoten).
Udagawa Bunkai. 1958. "Tenrikyō kyōso goryakuden." *Fukugen* 35. Tenri Central Library.
Uemura Fukutarō. 1959. *Ushio no gotoku: Tenrikyō kyōkai ryakushi*. Tenri, Nara (Tenrikyō Dōyūsha).
Watanabe Osamu. 1979. "Tennōsei kokka chitsujo no rekishiteki kenkyū josetsu: taigyakuzai/fukeizai o sozai to shite." *Shakai kagaku kenkyū* 30/5.
Watsuji Tetsurō. 1938. *Kōshi*. Tokyo (Iwanami Shoten).
Yasumaru Yoshio. 1977. *Nihon nationalism no zenya*. Tokyo (Asahi Shinbun-sha).
Yasumaru Yoshio. 2013. *Yasumaru Yoshio-shū*, Vol. 3. Tokyo (Iwanami Shoten).

About the author

Avery Morrow is a doctoral candidate in Japanese religions at Brown University, Rhode Island, USA. From 2015 to 2018 he was a MEXT Scholar in the Department of Religious Studies at the University of Tokyo. His published research includes "The Power of Writing in Deguchi Nao's Ofudesaki" (2017) and "Boundary Work in Japanese Religious Studies" (2018).

17

A postcript on Shinto diversity

Michael Pye

I take the opportunity of this postscript to offer a few concluding reflections on the whole volume. I believe that each one of the contributions offered by colleagues above is eminently worthy of being studied as it stands. The background of the seminars in various situations was already acknowledged in the preface. It should be made clear however, that invitations to participate were not tied to specific topics, except to some extent in the section on sectarian Shinto. The plan for the contents of this book was therefore not systematically preconceived, but instead arose from the individual interests which emerged among a broad international group of scholars. It is therefore very interesting to see what transpired. A preconceived encyclopedic account of Shinto, by contrast, would have to be more systematic and include more topics not covered even in this rather large group of papers.

But in any case, what would be the contours of such a systematic presentation? Shinto is often presented, especially but not only by its exponents, as a single coherent religion with distinct and regular characteristics. But whether we probe into its complex history or attempt to make a synchronic cross-section at any one period, including the present, such coherence is very difficult to pin down. The central section of our book illustrates this very well. The difficulty arises partly because the various schools of Japanese Buddhism, not all considered above, had differing modes of interaction with Shinto shrines, Shinto divinities and the many other forms of religious activity which simply crossed boundaries. Another major complication is provided by the popularity of mountain cults and the activities of the mountain ascetics (*yamabushi* 山伏), whose traditions and teachings frequently crossed any putative borders between major traditions.

Now one might have expected that successive attempts to assert a central authority in what may very loosely be called the Shinto world, whether based on Ise Shrine or on the Yoshida Shrine in Kyoto, would have created greater coherence. But the magnetic pull of other major shrines such as Izumo, Kasuga, Suwa, Atsuta, Konpira, Sumiyoshi and so on, and the development of sub-shrines which could be revered away from their main holy sites worked against this. Moreover, networks or chains of special shrine cults developed for particularly popular divinities such as Hachiman, Tenjin (Michizane), Inari or Ebisu, and these followed dynamics of their own, with important regional centres flourishing down to the present day.

One might also imagine that when Shinto was heavily politicized and ideologized in the wake of the Meiji Restoration, central authority would create new unity. To some extent this was true, but at the same time this very intention led to the splitting away of several enthusiastic groups that were defined as "religious" in a sense supposedly current in the western world. This was, broadly speaking, the genesis of Sect Shintō, as seen in the third part of this volume, and its effects have remained down to the present. The leaders of Shinto sects are quite clear today, as earlier, that their groups are mostly intended to be Shinto-oriented in character, which is certainly not the case for all of Japan's numerous new religious movements. Following the disestablishment of Shinto as a state religion at the end of World War II, a good proportion of shrines are associated under the Jinja Honchō 神社本庁 (usual English name: The Association of Shinto Shrines), and there is regular evidence of central guidance and policy signposting at shrines. In wide evidence is an instruction on precisely how to pray when visiting a shrine, a matter about which casual visitors are not always clear. Yet, overall, the diversity among the shrines and their various networks persists. There is even some recognized diversity of practice over the forms of prayer just mentioned, for example regarding the number of handclaps. It may therefore be said that Shinto is "particularistic" in two senses. First it is mainly located within one ethnic perspective, the Japanese, even if not all Japanese people are beholden to it. It is not a "universal" or "world" religion. Second, however, it is particularistic in its plurality even within that ethnos itself. This is in fact what lends it such great variety and its own special fascination. Diversity in the world of Shinto gives it a rather wide attraction among the populace of Japan and contributes to its social resilience.

About the author

Michael Pye (born 1939) first resided in Japan from 1961 onwards. From 1968 he taught Religious Studies in England and in 1982 became professor for the Study of Religions at Marburg University, Germany. He was president of the International Association for the History of Religions from 1995 to 2000. On retirement he returned to Japan for several years, being associated with Otani University, Kyoto. Publications include *Strategies in the Study of Religions* (2013) and *Japanese Buddhist Pilgrimage* (2015).

Index

Japanese names are shown family name first, with no comma.

abbot/s (Buddhist) 115, 191, 202
   in imperial lineage 208
abdomen convulsion 237
Abe Yasurō 139, 150, 156, 160–1, 171
abhiṣeka 118
Abhiṣeka Sūtra 190
ablutions 25
absolute (e.g. truth, reality) 85, 89, 94, 221, 268, 271, 285, 294, 299
abstinence (hut of) 132
abundant harvest 134
Abundant Treasure Buddha 86
accession (rites) 16, 131, 182
accommodated body 212
adaptation 38, 293
adapted primal religion 30, 89
Adapted Teaching 241
adumbration 16, 22
aesthetics 151, 154, 161
afar (worshipping from) 17–18, 27
affinity day (*ennichi*) 13
afterlives (Ise) 146
Aichi Prefecture 264
Akamatsu, Toshihide 111, 114–16, 119, 192, 198
Aki Province 196–7
akumajashin 115
Akuōji Shrine 212
Al-Koran 279
allegory/allegorical 89–90, 92–3, 97–101
Allied Powers 6, 33, 257
altar/s 195, 199, 202, 225
Ama no Iwato 138
amalgamation 80, 82–3, 125, 219

Amaterasu 6, 23, 27, 29–30, 87–9, 94, 106–14, 117–18, 123, 138, 140, 237, 242, 247, 254, 264
amatsukami 10
ambiguity 70–1, 169–70, 222–3, 227, 273, 290
ambivalences 152
Amenokoyane 106–8, 110, 114
America/n 16, 39, 67, 265, 272, 281, 300
Amida 140–1, 143–5, 148, 157, 186–8, 190–5, 197, 200, 202, 204–10, 212–13, 215, 222, 275
Amidakyō 146
Amitābha 109
amulet/s 25, 27, 177, 232
anachronism 4, 12, 63–4, 214
Analects 189, 198
anarchist 37
ancestor/s 18, 29, 266
   divine 23, 88, 108–11, 113–14, 118, 235, 254, 288
   veneration 241
ancestral religion 70
Andō Reiji 289–90, 300
Anesaki Masaharu 281
anime 18–19
animism 36, 79, 81
annual events, memorial 266, 277
Ansei Purge 263
anti-
   authority 286
   Buddhist 261
   colonialism 70
   communism 46, 48
   fascism 40
   Revolution 41
   semitism 40, 292
   superstition 278
   syncretic 72

Antoni, Klaus 24, 31
anutpada 95
anzen 245
Aochi Shin 272, 276–7, 280, 300
Aoi no Ue 162, 167–9
apologetic/s 4, 277
apologists 9, 15
appearance (supernatural) 43, 89, 92, 94, 99, 115–16, 126, 152, 164, 192, 202, 208, 226, 238, 286, 298–9
arahitogami 124, 130
Arakida (priestly lineage) 140–1, 145–7, 149
Arakida Tokimori 145
Aramatsurigū 264
archaeology 121, 123, 139, 149
archetype/s 70, 79
archetypical 241, 268
archipelago 111, 122, 145, 220, 282
architecture/al
  Buddhist and mixed 199, 200, 204, 208, 212–15, 220, 225
  shrines 25, 62, 200
Arisugawa no Miya 252
arrow (against evil) 266
arts/artistic 11, 151–2, 154, 170, 172, 220, 223, 225, 296
Asahiko Kuni (Prince) 264
Asama (Mount) 142–3, 145–7
asamskṛta 95
Asano Wasaburō 291–4, 301
ascetic/ism 83, 154, 287–8, 395
Ashizu Uzuhiko 286, 300
assimilation 35, 217, 293
Association of Shinto Shrines 7, 16, 20, 28–9, 233
Aston, William George 35–6, 52
Atkins, Paul 161–2, 164, 171
Atsumi District 147–8
Atsuta Jingū 14, 19, 23, 107, 306
attainment (enlightenment, unity with *kami*, etc.) 93–5, 96–7, 99, 129, 143–4, 188, 223, 258, 267
auspicious days 189, 199
austerities 238
authentic/ity 16, 21, 58, 60, 68, 86
avidyā 94
awe 82
axis of worship 128–30

Ayabe 288–90, 299

Baba, M. 171
Baird, Robert D. 9, 31
Bakufu (Edo government) 252–5
Ban Isoshirō 47, 52
ban (prohibition) 138, 252–4, 270, 294
Bandhyopadhyay, Bhabanicaran 69
Bargen, D. G. 165, 167, 171
beings
  deluded 83
  human/sentient 79–80, 83, 89–90, 92, 94–6, 99, 101, 126, 148, 154, 169, 187–9, 192–3, 195
  supernatural 115, 152, 237, 298–9
benefits
  Buddhist, spiritual 90, 147–8, 190, 223
  this-worldly 13, 29, 223
Benesch, Oleg 45, 52
benevolent (*kami*) 30, 115, 117, 134
Benkaku 143
Benzaiten 12–13, 200–1
Berthon, Jean-Pierre 36, 52
Bethe, Monica 171
Bettō (Jien) 115
bettōji 125
birth
  future 114
  in Pure Land 188, 190
  of divinities 166
birth-and-death 137, 191, 195
Bishamon 202, 207–10, 212–15
blessing/s 134, 279
  by *kami* 106, 132, 271
blood sacrifice 5, 134, 224
Bloom, Alfred 187, 198
Blum, Mark 112, 119
boar sacrifice 132
Bock, Felicia Gressitt 11, 31
Bocking, Brian 114, 119
Bodaisan 142, 146
bodhisattva/s (*bosatsu*) 13, 84, 90, 108–10, 113, 117, 135, 151, 192, 212, 224
  Bodhisattva Fugen 126–7, 131, 143
  Bodhisattva Kannon 109, 115, 117, 126–7, 144, 173
  Bodhisattva Mañjuśrī 112
  Bodhisattva Seishi 144

310 *Exploring Shinto*

Hachiman Daibosatsu/Great
   Bodhisattva Hachiman 106, 108–10,
   113
Hōzō Bosatsu 213
Miroku Bosatsu 149, 238
body/ies
   kami in snake 92, 96–7, 99–100, 221,
      223
   of Buddhas 86, 90, 92, 94, 144, 213
   of disciple, performer 129, 155, 165
Bohner, Hermann 36, 48–9
Borgen, R. 166, 171
bosatsu, see bodhisattva
boy/s 130–2, 134, 202, 208
Brahman/ism 31, 67, 232
Brazell, K. 156, 171
breathing (*nippai*) 237
Breen, John 8, 24, 31, 54, 60, 73–5,
   102–3, 137, 139, 150, 175, 185
Brown, Delmer 111–15, 119
Brownlee, John 37, 39–41, 47, 52
Bucchō sonshō daranikyō 143
Buddha/buddha/s, *passim*
   Amida Buddha 140–1, 143–5, 157,
      186–8, 190–5, 197, 200, 202, 207–8,
      212–13, 222
   at Ise 137–9
   Buddha of Healing 145
   Dainichi Buddha 128
   Great Sun Buddha 137–40
   Kami/Buddha 80–7, 89, 100–3, 117,
      221–2, 227, 276
   Maitreya as Buddha 138–9, 141,
      148–9, 238
   portable buddha 202, 206
   Śākyamuni Buddha 212, 253
   Vairocana(Mahavairocana) Buddha
      118
   World Buddha 63, 128
buddha nature 96, 98
Buddhadharma 144, 255
buddhahood 153, 191
Buddhism/Buddhists, *passim*
Bukkōji 208
bukkyō (*kyū-*, *shin-*) 246
Buppōji 125
burial (of sutras etc.) 140–9, 220, 224
Burke, Edmund 41
burning house parable 168

Bushido, 44–5, 47, 52–3
butsu 11
Byakkō Shinkō Kai 241
byōkiheiyu 245

calendar, calendrics 21, 45, 182, 243, 295
calligraphy/ic 7, 174, 176, 178, 243–4,
   258–9, 286
campaign 23, 252, 282
   Campaign (Great Promulgation) 270,
      273, 278, 282
categorization
   Buddhism 112
   Buddhist/Shinto/other 136, 223, 284,
      296–9
   historical/theoretical 2, 9, 11–12, 31,
      57, 62, 64–8, 70–1, 296–9
   Shinto internal 16, 112, 233–4, 239–40,
      247, 250–1, 253, 261
Catholicism 253, 296
cause and effect 97–9
cave 132, 138, 141
Celestial Eye 240
celestial spirits 160
censorship 294, 299
Chamberlain, Basil H. 36
charges (legal) 296–7, 299
charismatic 268, 276, 282
charity (organization) 73, 288–90
charms 265, 288
chi
   earth 94
   knowledge 95
Chichibu Shrine 4
chief priest 4, 237, 242, 252, 264, 290
chigi, see *tenjinchigi*
Chikubushima 12
children 23, 134, 168–9, 177–8, 233, 243,
   245, 279
China 43, 61, 65, 89, 112, 293
chinjusha 109
chinkon-kishin 296
chinza 180
Chōen 92
Chōshū 255
chōshūkyō 71
Christ 279, 281
Christian/s 71, 253, 261, 265, 281–2, 295
   (adjective) 45, 67, 186, 276, 284

Christianity 5, 69–70, 253–5, 279–80, 290–1
chroniclers (Tendai) 82, 86–7, 90, 92–3
chronicles (Japanese) 52, 114, 119, 260, 271
church (concept) 243, 284
  Christian 175, 300
  various 243, 265–6, 275, 278, 284, 299, 302
Chūzaemon 194–5
circulatory pilgrimage 173–7, 179–4, 223, 226
civil 23, 281
clan/s 108, 114, 121–5, 130–1, 135, 233
  children (*ujiko*) 23, 233
  divinity (*ujigami*) 23, 125, 233
classification/s 18, 62, 116–17, 222, 224, 227, 250, 257, 273
cognitive 80, 90
colonialism
  Japanese 240, 277, 294
  Western 42, 70, 68–9, 75, 285
combinatory (discourse/system) 45, 80–7, 94, 101–2, 112, 135, 151, 153–4, 173, 221, 226
communism 45–6, 48
Como, Michael 65, 74
comparison 4, 32–3, 34, 36, 49, 57, 66, 74–5, 79, 140, 223, 235, 256, 291–2
Confucian/ism 36, 59, 71–2, 273, 286, 293
Confucius 189
consciousness (religious) 94–6, 98
constitution/al 281, 290, 295
cosmic
  Buddha 85–6
  elements 94
cosmogony 119, 138
cosmography 154, 166
cosmology 94, 111, 118, 130, 152–5, 166, 169–70, 225, 268, 274, 280, 286, 295
court cult 60–1, 65–6, 72, 82, 106, 124, 137
  Shin connection 206–8
creation (mythic) 18, 118, 166, 286, 289
Creemers, W. H. M. 6, 31
Croce, Benedetto 40, 43
cult/s 65–6, 68, 73, 306
  associations 20
  kojiki cult 7

kokutai cult 6
mountain cults 236, 247, 305
of vengeful spirits 116
political 257
rock-worshipping 128
state-sponsored 47, 60
Tennō cult 28
see also court cult
customs 5, 50, 112, 135, 232
cycle of rebirth 169, 187, 191, 193, 195
  life cycle 149
cyclic/al 118, 149

Dacheng qixinlun 95
Dai Bosatsu 106–9
Dai Myōjin 106–7, 110
Daikoku/ten 12, 245
Daikyōin 252–3, 256
daimoku 195
daimyōjin 115
  Inari 7, 13
  Suwa 125–7, 129, 131–5
Dainichi (Nyorai) 17, 88, 118, 125–6, 128–9
  as *kami* 128
Dainichikyō 146–7
dance 97, 99–102, 156, 158–9, 161, 226, 241
Dao de jing 88–9
Dao/ist 88–9, 145, 286
Davidson, Augusta M. Campbell 6, 31
Dazaifu Tenmangū 176–7
Deal, William 84, 102
death 223–4
death and life 30, 149, 168–9
  moment of 148
  see also birth-and-death
deconstruction 51, 68
decree 250, 253–4, 257–8
dedication 20, 132, 134, 147, 202, 223, 265, 270
deer 132, 134
definition/s
  of pilgrimage 175, 223
  of religion/religious 70, 85, 232–3, 274, 298–9, 306
  of Shinto 3, 4, 9–10, 19, 21, 28–9, 35, 38, 46, 48, 60, 63–5, 71, 73–4, 117, 224, 237, 256, 299, 306

Deguchi Eiji 296, 300
Deguchi Nao 283, 288, 292, 294, 297
Deguchi Onisaburō 276, 285, 288–91, 293–9, 296
Deguchi Yasuaki 287, 288, 301
deification 47, 223
deity/deities/divinities 11–12
  Buddhist 82–3, 99, 126, 129–30, 200, 202, 208, 212, 214
  clan/tutelary 23, 87, 90, 106–7, 233
  office of 10, 257, see also Jingi-in, Jingikan
  Shinto general 10, 17, 20, 104, 106–11, 113, 115–18, 123, 127, 132, 134, 136–8, 166, 178, 183, 241–2, 257, 269, 263–6, 305–6, see also Amaterasu
  various and intermediate 13, 66, 79–80, 82, 85, 89, 94, 99, 111, 117, 136, 173, 186, 191, 199–201, 207, 221–4, 227, 245, 280, 289, 298
Demachi 13
demon/s 109, 115–16, 137, 152, 224, 280, 288, 299
  she-demon 156, 159
Dengyō 207
denomination/s 13, 25, 30, 68, 201, 214, 255
Department of Shinto Affairs 10
descent (divine kinship) 114, 123–4, 235
  of Amida 144–5
  of divinity 274
Dharma (Buddhadharma) 90, 138, 140–2, 144, 146, 151, 188, 203, 207, 255
  body of 86, 92
  decline/final (*mappō*) 140, 146–9, 189, 195, 222
  nature 117
  realm 99–100
dialogue 92, 94, 151, 170, 201, 207, 214
Diamond Realm 138, 146–7
directional influences (*hōi*) 245
directives
  Meiji 242, 256
  see also Shinto Directive
disestablishment of Shinto 7, 19, 233, 306
diversity in Shinto 7, 14, 184, 241–2, 305–7
divination 62, 189–90, 199, 266

divine 6, 89, 91
  agreement, blessing, oracle, will, etc. 113–14, 132, 134, 250–1, 263–4, 273, 277, 280, 292–3, 295, 297–9
  beings and objects 115, 144, 166, 168, 179, 241, 244, 254, 298
  land 114, 118
divinity, see deity
Dobbins, James C. 74, 203, 217
dogma 65, 280
Dolce, Lucia 119
Dōmoto, Masaki 155, 171
donation 73, 140, 145, 148, 174, 179
dōri 110–11, 113, 116–18
dōtoku 45, 53, 251
dōwa 274
dragon-serpent 94
drama 11, 169, see also Noh
dream 202, 206
dual system 122, 124–5, 130, 135
dualism 286
Dumoulin, Heinrich 49

Ebisu 245, 306
Edicts, Separation 136
Edo Period 67, 178–9, 186, 193–4, 197, 238, 252–5, 273, 276, 286
  Edo Bakufu 252–5
Ekan 200, 206–7, 209, 217
ekō 188
Elders of Zion 292
ema 25
emaki 156
embodiment 91, 94, 152, 170, 224
emic concepts 14, 234
emperor/s 23–4, 38, 46–7, 50, 62, 65, 107–8, 112–13, 124, 131, 174, 252–4, 281, 283–7, 293–9
Emperor (Tennō)
  Go-Daigo 46–7
  Go-Toba 104
  Gozu 107
  Jinmu 19, 105
  Kinmei 124, 261
  Meiji 24, 29, 37, 264–5
  Shijō 202
  Shōwa (Hirohito) 174
  Sutoku 116
emptiness 154–5, 161

enchanted 152–3, 155, 163, 166, 169
Engishiki 10
Enkū 194
enlighten/ment 90–102, 156–9
  of or by *kami* 89, 100–1, 116–17, 154
  of space 152–5
  original 81, 85, 93–4, 97–100, 152, 154, 161, 168–9
enmusubi 245
ennichi 13, 215
Ennin 202, 207–8
Ennōkyō 241
Enryakuji 83, 105–6, 109, 202, 212
enshrinement 23, 25–7, 113, 121, 125–8, 130, 144–5, 183, 188, 196, 200
enthronement
  of emperor 5, 131
  of *ōhōri* 130–1
esoteric/ism 172
  Buddhist 10–11, 81, 85, 87, 90, 92–101, 103, 121, 125–32, 138, 169, 194, 221
  Shinto 64, 90, 101, 103, 124–5, 129, 135
essence 4, 6, 36, 41, 47–8, 50, 55, 58, 60–1, 69, 72, 92, 94, 96–7, 99–101, 117, 134, 285, 294
essentialism/ist 4, 6, 8–9, 13, 20–1, 31, 34–41, 50, 52
ethnic/ethnos
  Hindu 67, 70
  Japanese 3, 16, 59, 62, 71–2, 231–2, 236, 240–1, 248, 285, 306–7
evil 145, 160, 191, 222, 245, 293
  demons/spirits 115–18, 266
  kami 118
  karma 83, 187–8
  Mara 137
exorcism 222
exoteric teachings 87, 94
expedient means 85, 168, 277, 296

faith 4, 43, 61, 71, 79, 141, 188–9, 191, 195, 247, 279, 291
  national 3–6
  shinkō 43, 115, 251, 256–8, 260–1, 273, 278–9
faith-healing 237, 270–1, 273, 281, 285, 289

Faure, Bernard 12, 31, 87, 102, 153, 171
feast 131–2, 134
federation (Shinto) 234
Fedianina, Vladlena 12, 120, 218, 222
female roles 147, 161, 164, 166, 243
festival/s 23, 29, 106, 133–4, 24, 263–4, 266
  Great Pillar Festival 121
filial piety 58
fire 94, 166, 168
  fire-walking 266
Fisher, Elaine 68–9, 74
folk/lore 5–6, 19, 60, 62, 79–80, 102, 123, 155–6, 159
Forbes, Roy 269–71, 277, 301
founder/s 85, 186, 198–9, 204, 206, 212, 202, 235, 237, 241–2, 247, 250–1, 259, 261, 266, 279–80, 289, 297
Foundress (Tenrikyō) 240, 278
Four Noble Truths 93
fraternity/ies 242, 252
fuda 196
Fudō Myōō 212
Fugen 126–7, 129, 131, 212
Fuji (Mount, Way of) 238, 250–3, 258–9
Fuji Sengen Shrine 252–3
Fujidō 238, 250, 252–3, 259
Fujihara Masatoshi 197
Fujii Manabu 195–6, 198
Fujikō 252–3
Fujimaki Kazuho 287, 301
Fujimori Kaoru 114, 119
Fujiwara family 104, 106–16, 222, 250
  Akimitsu 116
  Kamatari 115
  Kanezane 104
  Motokata 116
  Tadamichi 116
Fukata Chiyoko 241
fukumairi 173
funeral/s 141, 186, 207, 253–4, 258
  Shinto-style 257
funi 84–6, 88, 160, 224
Furoaki 106
Fushimi Inari Taisha 23, 29
Fusōkyō 236, 238–9, 247, 250–1, 253, 255, 257–60

gables (of Ise) 63–4

314 *Exploring Shinto*

Gakkai, 20
Gandhi, M. K. 41–2, 44
Geertz, Clifford 299
Gekū/*gekū* 27, 180–4
generation/s 18, 112, 195, 124, 250, 253
generic 24, 26–7
Genji 161–7, 169, 171
Gentarō 195–6
Gigen 86
Ginzburg, Carlo 40, 52
Gion 107
gōbara 130
god/s (*kami*) 18, 28, 35, 43, 52, 61, 104, 106, 108, 114, 138, 166, 173, 176–7, 187–91, 203, 223, 226, 232, 243, 271, 245, 284–5, 289, 293–5
  gods and buddhas 11, 14, 136, 164
  gods of heaven and earth 10, 59, 65–6, 187, 189–91, 199
  living gods 269, 272, 279–81
  tenjin 188
goddess
  Amaterasu 23, 27, 30, 110, 112–14, 138, 164, 237, 254, see also Amaterasu
  Benzaiten 12
Godenshō 200, 213
Goff, J. E. 162, 171
gohei 265, 267
Goi Masahisa 241
gojinji 165
gōkakukigan 245
Gokuraku 143
goma ceremonies 273
gong (hanging) 25
gongen 207
  Kumano Gongen 107
  Sannō Gongen 212–13
gongeshin 116
goryō 116
goshintai 132
gotaueshiki 180
Gōzei 186, 193–7
Gozu Tennō 107
Grapard, Allan G. 87, 102, 152–3, 166, 171
graveyards 160
Great Sun Buddha 137–40
Grotenhuis, E. 153–4, 171

gū 20, 26
guidance 21–2, 43, 48, 89, 98, 100, 194, 222, 231, 253, 306
gūji 4, 143, 147, 242, 267
Gukanshō 104–6, 108–12, 114–16, 119

Habu, Junko 122
Hachiman 105–6, 108–10, 113, 117, 306
  shrine 20, 105, 108–9, 261
Hagiwara Tatsuo 141, 150
haiden 25, 27, 127–8
Hakone Shrine 200–1
Hakue 206, 217
Hakusan
  mountain 14
  shrine 37, 44, 50
Halbfass, Wilhem 67, 74
Hannyashingyō 146
Harada Kaori 155, 160–1, 171
harae 116–17
Hardacre, Helen 10, 32, 51, 64–6, 74, 237, 248, 261, 293, 301
harvest 30, 132, 134, 180
Hasegawa Kakugyō 238, see also Kakugyō
Hasshameguri 173–4
hatsu-miya-mairi 245
Hayatama 107
head priest 143, 147, see also *gūji*
healing 145, 237, 245, see also faith-healing
health 245, 265, 285
Heart-Fuji 258–9
heaven/s 137–8, 254, 258–9, 279
heavenly boys and maidens 202, 208, see also maiden/s
heavenly deities 115, 123, 188–9, 224, see also gods of heaven and earth
Heavenly General 274–5
heavenly pattern (*tenri*) 275
heavenly rock cave 138, 141
Heian Period 83, 111, 126, 144–5, 204, 223, 246
Herbert, Jean 6, 32
heresy 194, 253, 271, 276, 283, 295, 301
heretic/al 46, 56, 194, 280, 286, 290
hermeneutics/ical 84–6, 95, 135
heroes 19, 29, 47
heuristic 9, 28

hidden 28, 89, 138–9, 163, 166, 195, 283, 291
Hie Shrine 64, 106, 109
Hiei (Mt) 83, 86–7, 90, 93, 102
hierarchy of divinities 81, 84, 110, 118, 183, 221–2, 224, 285
Higashi Honganji 194, 208
High Treason Incident 282
hijiri 83
hikime 266
hime/-gami 53, 106, 180
Himukai Shrine 26–7
Hindu-dharma 69–71
Hinduism 31, 42, 57, 66–72, 74–5, 232, 235
Hindutva 70–71
Hiraizumi Kiyoshi 34, 37–55
Hirano Daimyōjin 106
Hirata Atsutane 252
  school (-ha) 253, 290
Hirata Kanetane 252
Hirota, Dennis 198–9, 204, 217
Hitachi province 194–5
hiwatari 266
Hiyoshi (Hie) Shrine 7, 105–6, 109
  taisei hōkan 263–4
Hokkaido 179
hokora 17
Hokuriku 264
Holtom, Daniel Clarence 5–6, 32, 237–8, 248
Hon-miya (Suwa) 127–8
Honchō (Jinja) 7, 16, 20, 23, 28, 234, 306
honden 25, 27, 127
Hōnen 204
hongaku 93, 97, 119, 154
Honganji 194, 200, 203, 206–8
  Higashi 208
  Nishi 193–5, 255
hōni 95
honjaku funi 85
honji suijaku 81–4, 88, 102–3, 109–10, 117–19, 126, 131, 135, 151, 192, 197, 212–13, 216–17, 220–2
honzon 195
Hōonkō 206
hōraku 104–5
Hoshino Genpō 187, 198

household 195, 272
  Imperial 16, 19, 23–4, 242
Huayan school 95
Hyakuma Yamamba 155–61
hyakunijūgosha 182
hyakuōshisō 112–13
hyakushu 105, 108–9, 112, 114–15, 117
Hylkema-Vos, Naomi 4, 32
Hyōdo, Akiko 297, 301
hypostatization 94, 97

Iburi Izō 277
Ichien 137–8, 150
Ichizen 207–9, 217
identification/s (between divinities) 11, 63, 84–9, 101, 117, 138, 158, 160, 169–70, 222, 224, 227, 289
identity
  ambiguous of actors 152, 155, 158, 164–5, 167
  multiple religious 186, 201, 218–20, 234
  social/ideological 12, 20, 23, 29, 45, 58, 67–8, 70–2, 91, 146, 184, 186, 201, 203, 216, 219–20, 224–5, 226–7, 235, 269
ideology 12, 15, 19, 28, 34, 43, 51–2, 57–9, 66, 71, 111, 149, 151–2, 155, 232, 234, 247, 285, 306
Ikeda, Amira 292–8, 301
Ikeda, Eishun 302
Imaki 106
Imamiya Shrine 17
Imbe (priestly line) 114
imi 137
imperial
  accession rites 16, 131
  ancestors 18
  court/household 16, 19, 24, 106, 110, 112, 114
  ideology 58–60, 65–6, 71, 73, 113
  line 29, 47, 109–10, 112, 136, 208, 222, 226, 242, 254, 282, 288
  loyalism 38, 41, 44–8, 50–1, 263
  mausolea 257
  regalia 23, 107
Imperial Way Ōmoto 292
imperialism 34, 38, 47, 50–1
impermanence 48, 160, 163–5, 169, 194

impurity 30, 89
Inagaki Hisao 193, 198
Inari 7, 13, 17, 23, 29, 107, 261, 306
incarnations (of Kannon) 109, 115
indigenous viii, 3, 8, 28, 50, 52, 65–6, 70, 79, 112, 122–3, 136
initiation 129–32
inner (shrine etc) 27, 128, 138–42, 146, 148, 168, 180, 200, 202, 204, 212, 258, 264
innovation 59, 246
Inoue Enryō 281
Inoue Hiroshi 72, 74
Inoue Nobutaka 60, 62, 74, 82, 102, 119
Inoue Takami 126
Inoue Tetsujirō 58
internationalism 284, 287
invention 9, 28, 67–8, 71, 135–6, 149, 272, 297
Irago 147–8
Ise 7, 27, 63–4, 73, 75, 113, 136–50, 162–3, 168, 175–84, 226, 242, 251, 264–5, 276–7
Ise Jingū/Shrine 7, 12, 14, 16, 18, 19, 23–4, 27, 29–30, 105, 107, 109–10, 117, 137, 146, 164, 182, 200, 223–4, 226, 263, 306
Ise-mairi 175, 179, 184
Ishida Ichiro 111–15, 119
Isobe lineage 140–1, 146–7, 149
Isomae Jun'ichi 38, 54, 58, 74, 281, 301
Isonokami Shrine 271
ISSA 19–20, 218, 250, 260–1
issai shujō 90
Issaikyō 102
itinerants 83, 162
Itō Satoshi 83, 102, 139
Itsukushima (no Myōjin) 107
Iwainushi 106
Iwakura Mission 256
iwakura shinkō 128
Iwakura Tomomi 256
Iwami province 194
Iwasawa Tomoko 12, 121, 135, 218, 220, 224
Iwashimizu Hachiman 105, 109
Iwato 138
Izanagi 166
Izanami 166

Izawa no miya 180
Izumo lineage 123–4, 242, 289
　Ooyashirokyō 239, 241–5, 289
　province 106, 245
　Shrine 7, 24, 29, 175–6, 241–5, 251, 290, 306

Jainism 70, 235
Jang, Seokman 281, 301
Japanese paper 286
jashin 115, 292, 298
Jelesijevic, Dunja 11, 151, 172, 218, 222–3, 225
Jesus 279–80
Jews 45, 71, 292–3, see also Judaism
Jiba 176, 277
jibutsu 202
jichinsai 245
Jien 104–19, 218, 222
Jikkōkyō 236, 238–9, 251
Jikkōsha 238
jin 10, 26, 80, 82, 124
jinchō 124–5, 127–32, 134–5
jingi (gods) 10, 59, 65–6, 108, 124, 186
jingi fuhai 186
Jingi-in 254–5
Jingikan 10, 66, 257, 261
jingū 10, 19, 23, 26–7, 29, 47, 106–7, 263, 267
Jingū Hōsaikai 290
Jingū (Ise) 7, 12, 16, 18–19, 23, 27, 29–30, 136, 179–84, 242, 251, 276
Jingū Takahisa 287
Jingū-kanchō 287–90
Jingūkyō 251
Jingūji 126, 129–30, 136, 142
jinja/Jinja 19, 126, 251, 293
　in shrine names 7, 17, 24, 106, 176, 181, 261, 263, 269–72
　jinja shintō (Shrine Shinto) 19, 231, 257, 260–1
Jinja Honchō 7, 16, 20, 23, 28, 233, 306
Jinmu Tennō 19, 105, 182
Jinnō shōtōki 43–4, 49–50, 52–3, 55
Jinsei Tengan Gakkai 240
jinzūriki 90, 100
jizai 91
Jizō 17, 212
jōbutsu 154

Jōdo Shinshū 199, 220
Jōdo wasan 190
Jōdoshū 203, 211
Jōi 143
Jōkakuji 143
Jōkan 123–5, 128, 131
Jōmon culture 121–2, 128
Jōsenji 145
Josephson, Jason A. 270, 299, 301
jōsho 243
Jōshōji 143
Jōzen 143
Judaism 232
Jūichimenkanzeon 212
junpai 177–8, 182, 207, 217
junrei 177
Jussha Mairi 174

Kachi 148
Kadoya Atsushi 139
Kajimoto Narajirō 273, 301
Kakugyō (Hasegawa/Fujiwara) 238, 259
Kakunyo 191–2, 200, 203, 206, 208, 213
kalpa 111–13, 115, 118
Kamakura Period 126, 246
  shogunate 46, 104–5, 222
kami (Shinto divinity), *passim*; for concept, see also *jin, shin*
Kami-Buddha 84
kamidana 195–7, 225
kamigakari 267, 285
Kamigamo Shrine 106
kamisha/shimosha 122
Kamo Mabuchi 49, 105–6, 109–10
Kanaya Makoto 287, 301
Kanazashi clan 122–5, 130, 135
Kaneko, Akira 274, 292, 301
kanjō 129, 131–2
Kannon 109, 115, 126–7, 144, 173, 175, 178
kannushi 146, 290
Kano Masanao 294, 301
kanpeisha 23, 174, 183, 252
karma 63, 83, 143, 158, 187–8, 267
Karube Tadashi 40, 54
Kasahara Kazuo 192, 198
Kasama Inari 23, 29
Kashima 107, 194

Kashiwahara Yūsen 195–6
Kasuga Shrine 105, 108–10, 112–14, 117, 171, 306
Katō Genchi 3–5, 21, 32–3
Katsurajima Nobuhiro 275–6, 298, 301
Kawai Eijirō 41
Kawamura Kunimitsu 288, 298, 301
Kawazura Bonji 283–9, 291, 293, 296, 299–302
kechien 143
kegare 30
Keiran shūyō shū 82, 86–94, 96–103, 221, 223
keishinkō 242
Kenmu restoration 46–7
keshin 90, 115, 213
Ketsumiko (*kami*) 107
kettle (divination) 266
kiai 265
Kibe/ha 196, 201, 203, 206, 215
Kibe Shrine 212–13
Kido Takayoshi 255
Kigensetsu 182
Kikufuji Akimichi 193, 198
Kim, Tae-hoon 282–3, 301
King, Richard 69, 72, 74
Kinmei Tennō 124, 261
Kinpusenji 47
Kinshokuji 196, 201–4, 206–17, 225
Kinsui Gyoshi 290
Kirishitan 253, 257
Kitabatake Chikafusa 43, 50, 53, 58–9
Kitano Tenmangū 23, 105–6, 109, 115, 176–7, 179
Klein, Susan Blakeley 169, 172
kleśā (three poisons) 93
kō 176, 242
Kōda Chūsaburō 275, 302
Kodama Michiaki 142, 150
Kodama Shiki 196–8
Kōdō Ōmoto 294–5, 297
Kōfukuji, 116–17, 196
kofun 61, 123
Kōgakkan 7, 54–5, 180, 183
Kojiki 7–8, 18–19, 24, 28, 35, 58, 65, 123, 166, 260, 264, 270–1
Kokugaku/*kokugaku*, 28, 34–5, 49, 59, 61, 64, 263, 270, 273, 278–9, 287, 296

Kokugakuin University 7, 16, 57, 60, 126–8, 290
kokutai 6, 36, 46, 58
Komachi (Ise) 142, 146, 148
Kōmoto Mitsugi 282, 302
Kongōchōkyō 146–7
kongōkai 138
Kongōshōji 142
Konjin 289
Konkōkyō 18, 235, 237, 239, 247, 251, 295
Konpira Shrine 261, 306
Kōshū 86–7, 89
Kōtaijingū gishikichō 137
Kotohiragū 23
Kōtoku Shusui 37
kōtsū anzen 245
Kraus, Johannes 49
Kristensen, W. Brede 21, 32
kuden 86–7
Kudo 106
Kumano 107
Kuninotokotachi (*kami*) 289
kunitsukami 10
Kurama/dera 263
Kuramochi Nagako 167, 172
Kurata Chikyū 240
Kurata Usan 240
Kuroda Toshio 34, 54, 62, 74
Kurozumi Munetada 235, 237, 261
Kurozumikyō 18, 59, 236–9, 246–8, 251, 261, 290, 295
Kusunoki Masashige 47
kyō (teaching) 234–6, 264
Kyōbushō 252, 256
kyōgamine 142, 145
Kyōgyōshinshō 187–90, 192
kyōha 231, 234–5, 246, 248, 251, 253
Kyōha Shintō 18–19, 234, 239–40, 247, 257, 260, 268
   Rengōkai 234, 240, 252
kyōkai 243, 277–8, 284, 289
Kyōrei-sai 266
kyōshu 267
kyōso 235, 242, 266, 302–3
kyū-bukkyō 246

Lake Biwa 12
Lake Suwa 121–6

law 277, 284, 299, 300
   religion in 28, 234, 264, 289, 295–6, 297
   see also *dōri*, Ritsuryō
lay people 93, 98, 137, 141, 188–9, 199
legal/ism 59, 67, 240, 247, 257, 266, 268–9, 277–8, 284, 289, 291, 295–300
lèse-majesté 280, 296
Lévy, Christine 37, 54
light 88–9, 92, 101, 144, 156–7, 164, 241
liminality 156, 158, 163, 225
lineage/s 124, 235, 250, 266
   Buddhist 87, 92, 208
   kami/imperial 29, 46–7, 65, 136, 242, 282
   kami/priests 139–49, 263
   thought 34, 36, 59, 95, 240
linkages (of shrines) 16, 20, 179–80, 226, 245
Lipner, Julius J. 68–70, 74
location/s (shrines and religious foci) 14, 17, 22, 108–9, 122, 125–8, 153–4, 156, 178, 180, 209, 212, 216, 243, 251, 261, 277
Lorenzen, David N. 67, 74
lotus 126, 144, 146, 148, 202
Lotus Sūtra 83, 85–6, 117, 128, 143–7, 168–9, 195
Lowell, Percival 265, 267
loyalty/loyalism 30, 37–8, 41, 44, 46–48, 51, 58–59, 178, 233, 236, 242, 247, 263

madness 272, 280
Maeda Tamaki 47, 54
Mae-miya (Suwa) 127–8, 130–2, 134
Mahāvairocāna 118
Mahayana (*mahāyāna*) 95, 144, 154, 169
maiden/s (shrine/heavenly) 162, 164–5, 202, 208, 225
mairi 174–5, 179, see also *o-Ise-mairi*
Maitreya 138–9, 141, 148, 238
Makinouchi Yū 300, 302
mamori 177, 196
mandala 63, 126, 128, 130, 138, 140, 146–7, 154, 171
mandara 138
mandorla/s 146–8
manga 7, 18–19

manifestation/s (of divinity etc.) 83, 85, 88–94, 96–7, 99–101, 109–11, 117, 126, 128, 131, 151, 192–3, 195, 197, 202, 207–8, 212, 221–2
Mañjuśrī 112
Mankakuji 147–8
mannin anpuku 259
Manpukuji 200
mantras 129, 131–2
Manyōshū (Man'yōshū) 61
mappō 111–13, 140, 222
Mara 137
Martin, Jean-Marie 36, 54
marukoto 237
Maruyama Toshiaki 284, 302
Marx/ism, 38, 40, 42, 45
mason society 292
massha 17, 183
materialism 38, 40, 43, 45
Matsukata Fuyuko 37
Matsunaga, Alicia 212–13, 217
Matsuo Jirō 38, 54
Matsuura Takeshirō 178–9
mausolea/um 174, 207, 210, 212, 257
Maxey, Trent E. 71, 74
McKenzie, Timothy S. 282–3, 302
medium/s 79, 132, 134, 206, 241, 264
meguri 158, 173–5, 179–82, 184
Meiji (Restoration/Period) 24, 43, 46, 59, 61, 65–7, 73, 130, 134, 200–1, 224, 226–7, 238, 263, 276, 282, 284–6, 291, 306
  Emperor 29, 264
  government 38, 80, 135, 149, 250–61, 278, 291
  Shrine 19, 29
Meinecke, Friedrich 39–40, 48–9
Meirinsha, 273–4
Mencius 46
Meotoiwa 181, 183
merit 140, 145, 158, 174
metaphor/ical 69, 88, 93, 99, 154, 156–7, 164, 234
michiyuki 156
Michizane, see Sugawara Michizane
Miidera 116
miizu, Miizukai 284, 286–7
Minamoto clan 108, 110

Minamoto Yoritomo 104
minzoku/gaku 5, 39, 45
Miroku (Bosatsu) 149, 238
mirror/s 23, 63, 142, 144–5, 179, 264
Mishaguji (*kami*) 129–32, 134–5, 221
misogi 284, 287
Misogikyō 59, 239, 251
mission/aries
  Christian 49, 52, 261, 281
  of *kami* 89, 197
  Iwakura Mission 256
  Ōmoto 296
  Shinto 261, 264–5, 267, 287
  Tenrikyō 239, 251, 269, 283, 302
Missions Étrangères 36
Mitakekyō 239
Miwa Shrine 64, 124
miya 124, 127–8, 130–2, 134, 180
Miyai Kanejirō 289
Miyakawa (river) 179
Miyake Yoshinobu viii
miyamairi 245
Miyasaka Yūshō 126
Miyasuhime (*kami*) 107
Miyazaki Sadayuki 284–5, 302
Mizukami Fumiyoshi 118–19
modern 4–5, 15, 51, 57, 59–61, 64–73, 149, 209, 212, 233–5, 237, 242, 269, 286
  early modern 7, 156, 219
  modernism 276
  modernity 10, 56, 67, 70, 227, 285
  modernization, 23, 70, 288
Moerman, D. Max 12, 136, 150, 218, 222, 224
Monju (Bosatsu) 112
monkey/s 90–91
Mononobe clan 147
monotheistic 59, 70
morals/morality 35, 40, 45, 58, 62, 71, 251, 256–7, 273–4, 283, 290
Moreya/Moriya clan 122
Moriya Mitsusane 125, 127–30, 221
Morrow, Avery 268, 303
Motoori Norinaga 35, 59
mound/s 141–2
Mount (Asama) 142–7, (Fuji) 238, 250–1, 258, (Ontake) 264, 266, (Osore) 264

mountain/s 14, 18, 29–30, 106–7, 109, 121, 128, 141, 144–5, 152–9, 222–3, 225–6, 236, 238, 247, 251, 258, 263–4
    asceticism 83, 288, 305, see also Mount Fuji/Ontake/Osore
Mountain Crone 155, 158, 222, 226
mudra 129, 131–2, 144
Muhammad 279–81
Mujū Ichien 137–9, 141, 150
Mukyōkai 300
Murakami Shigeyoshi 288, 302
Muromachi Period 126, 131, 162
Muryōgikyō 143
musa (unconditioned) 95
Myanmar 66
myō (invisible world) 111
Myōenji 255
myōgō 88, 91
Myōgonji 13
Myōhōrengekyō 143, 145, 195
Myōi 143
Myōjin 106–7, 110
myōkōnin 186, 193–5, 197–8
Myōon Benzaiten 13
myōshū (invisible ones) 190
mystical/icism 43–4, 48, 50, 233, 258, 286
myth/s 7, 18, 64, 114, 138, 242, 270
    mythic/al 8, 15, 18, 24, 26, 28–9, 79, 94, 131, 162–3, 166, 222
        mythology/ical 65, 123, 151, 166, 232–3, 237, 241

Nachi (Kumano) 107
Nagaoka Takashi 268–9, 271–2, 276, 302
Nagaoka Tenjin Shrine 176
Nagaokakyō 176
Nagoya Tokimasa 47, 54
naikū 27, 180–4
Nakamura Kokyō 296
Nakatomi harae kunge 116–17
Nakatsutsu (*kami*) 107
Nakayama Asanosuke 182, 184
Nakayama Kaoru 287, 302
Nakayama Miki 269–279
Nakayama Shinjirō 288
Nakayama Shinnosuke 276–7
Nakayama Shōzen 272
Nakayama Shūji 269, 271–2, 274
Nakayama Yoshiko 264
Nakayama Zenbei 275
Namu Amida Butsu 188, 195
Nanbokuchō 47
Naniwa 105, 115, 204
narukama-shinji 266
nat 66
nationalism/ist 4, 6, 34, 43–5, 70, 286
native 35, 60, 65, 68, 79, 81, 121–2, 130, 136, 187–8, 191–2, 197
nativism/ist 34, 43, 136
Naumann, Nelly 65, 75
Nazi/ism 34, 36–7, 40, 48–9, 51
negi 143, 147, 263
nenbutsu 161, 188, 190–1, 193–7
nenjūgyōji 5, 33
Neo-Confucianism 254
Nichiren 194–5, 246
Nihongi 28, 35, 270–1
Nihonjinron 51
Nihonshoki 28, 58, 65, 114, 251, 260–1, 264
    Twenty-five shrines 176–8
    Twenty-two shrines 109
Nijūō (Shin Buddhism) 207, 217
Ninigi no mikoto 19, 114
nippai 237
nirmaṇakāya (as *kami*) 90, 94
nirvāṇa 154, 188
Nishi Honganji 193–5, 255
Nishigaki Seiji 175, 184
Nō drama, see Noh
Noh 11, 151–7, 159–63, 165, 167, 169–72, 218, 220, 222–3, 225–6
nondual/ism 81, 84, 86, 88, 91, 99–101, 153–4, 158–61, 169–70, 238, 250
nonduality 81, 84–6, 88, 91, 93–4, 96–7, 99, 101, 221–2, 224
Nonomiya (Noh drama) 152, 155–6, 161–3, 165–7, 169, 222, 225
norm 194, 296
normative 8–10, 20–1, 62, 69, 186
numinous 82
nun/s 143, 147
Nyorai
    Amida Nyorai 204
    Dainichi Nyorai 17, 88, 118, 137
    Tahō Nyorai 86
    Yakushi Nyorai 145, 212

ōbō 277
Occupation 6, 33, 276, 300
offering/s 29, 30–31, 104, 148, 160, 196, 243–4
Ofudesaki 271, 275, 283, 292, 303
Ofumi 192, 195
Ōharano 107
ōhōri 124–5, 130–2, 134–5
Oikawa Chihaya 19, 32
o-Ise-mairi 73, 137, 175, 179, 184
ōjin 応身 90, 213
ōjin 王神 (of Amaterasu) 118
Ōjōyōshū 198
Okada Shōji 60–2, 75, 119
Okamoto Hideo 148, 150
Ōkasedera 137
okō 132, 134
Ōkuninushi 19, 29, 106–7, 123, 242
Ōmikami 29, 110
Ōmiwa Kyōkai 277
Ōmoto 239–40, 268–9, 283, 285, 287–300
Ōnakatomi 140–1, 143, 146–7, 149, 263
Ōnamuchi 106–7
Onbashira festival 121, 126
Ono Sokyō 19, 32, 92
onryō 116
Ontake (Mt) 264, 266
Ontakekyō 236, 239, 251, 287–8, 291, 295
onyama seiten 258–9
Ookuninushi 243, 245
Oomotokyō 10, 240, 302, see also Ōmoto
Ooms, Herman 65, 75
Ooyashirokyō 18, 24, 231, 241–3, 245
oral tradition 17, 86, 92, 125, 162, 222
Origin (Initial) 274–5
original enlightenment/ground, etc. 81, 83, 86, 90, 92–100, 116, 117, 154, 161, 221
original religion 4, 80
original Shinto 4, 35, 44, 49–51, 60, 72
origin/s of shrines/temples/movements 18, 121, 177, 179, 182, 201–2, 208–9, 220, 237, 250, 297
origin-trace, 81–85, 97–9, 109–11, 118, 126, 139, 151–2, 192, 220–1
orthodox/y 14, 68, 92, 194, 201, 215, 225–6, 278, 287

Osashizu 275, 278
oshie 235–6, 251
Ōtani-ha 255
outer shrine 27, 138–43, 145, 147, 168, 211
outsider/s 11, 68, 280
Oyagami (Tenrikyō) 277–8
Oyagami community 269–70, 273–4, 276–8
Ōyamakui 106–7, 109
Ōyamato Shrine 269–72
Ōyashirokyō 239, 289, see also Ooyashirokyō

palace 23, 26–7, 47, 63, 65, 114, 124, 176
pantheon 12, 80, 82, 85, 199
paradise 50, 140, 145
parishioners 195–7, 225, 271
Park, Yeonjoo 12, 79, 87–8, 91, 102–3, 218, 221, 223
particularistic 306–7
patriotic/ism 58, 174, 178, 200, 238, 252, 282–3
Pennington, Brian K. 69–70, 75
Péri, Noël 36, 54
persecution 10, 270–1, 278
personification 13, 112, 170
pilgrim/age/s 12, 14, 19, 20, 73, 154–6, 158, 173–84, 223–4, 226, 250, 258, see also o-Ise-mairi
pillars (at Suwa) 121, 128, 132
placation of (kami) 159
pluralism/istic 186, 201, 204, 220, 246–7, 307
Plutschow, Herbert E. 105
poem/s 61, 104–6, 108–10, 112, 114
polytheism 70, 261, 276, 285
possession (spirit) 79, 167, 267, 269–70, 285, 298
prayer 16, 25, 29, 48, 106, 132, 146, 177, 186, 194–5, 237, 244–5, 263, 265, 271, 273, 276, 293, 306
precinct/s 108, 128, 154, 183, 199–201, 208–9, 212–15, 225
premodern 68–9, 73, 153, 209, 214, 219, 224, 227
priest/s 4, 7, 16–17, 20, 30, 37, 51, 58, 60, 62–5, 67, 73, 124, 131, 139, 141, 143–5, 147–9, 187, 200, 203, 206,

322 Exploring Shinto

222, 224, 233, 237, 242, 245, 247–8, 252, 261, 263–4, 269–71, 277, 287, 289–90
  Buddhist 62, 104–5, 193, 195, 197, 203, 206, 225, 255
priestess 162
priestly (lineage etc) 28, 140–2, 146, 149, 235, see also lineage
primal religion 30
primitive 36, 50, 79
prince 105, 161–2, 176, 256, 264
princess 136, 168, 180
principle/s 80, 91, 95, 97, 100–1, 160, 254, 256, 283, 289
  dōri 110–18
prohibition
  governmental 135, 252–4, 264
  religious 137–8, 189, 200, 224
Protocols 137, 292–3
provisional (*kami*, manifestation, teachings) 10, 14, 98, 109–10, 116–17, 126, 195
Pure Land 140, 142–5, 147–8, 156, 188, 190–1, 194, 246
purification 30, 116, 132, 153, 162, 165–6, 184, 225, 243–4, 258, 265, 284, 287
purity/impurity 30, 89, 132, 178
  ideological 15, 35–6, 41–3, 49, 60, 70, 72, 260
Pye, Michael 218, 223, 226, 251, 260

queen of *kami* 118

Raigo (monk) 116
raigō 144
Rambelli, Fabio 11, 33, 82, 102, 116–17, 119, 152, 154, 172
rank/ing 145, 168, 207–8
Rappo, Gaétan 8, 34, 37, 47, 54, 56
realm (various Buddhist and Shinto) 63, 99–100, 126, 138, 143, 146–7, 153–4, 157, 166, 168, 226, 241, 292
rebirth 134, 143–5, 147–9, 153–4, 169, 187, 193
recitation (Buddhist) 13, 144, 188, 191, 194–5
reform/s 63, 69–73, 83, 127, 238, 246–7, 289–90, 292, 294

refuge/s (religious) 187–8, 195
regalia 23, 107
registration 28, 243, 254, 257, 269, 271–2
reichi 237
Reikai monogatari 288
Reinders, Eric 11, 33
relics 144, 128
religion/s, *passim*
  as concept 4–5, 49–50, 59, 63, 68, 70–1, 80, 227, 231–2, 235, 256, 258, 261, 265, 268–9, 271, 273, 276–7, 281, 287, 290–3, 297–300
religiosity 153, 160–1, 220, 226, 300
relocation 17, 136, 263
Rengōkai (Sect Shinto) 234, 239–40, 252
Renmonkyō 289–90
Rennyo 186, 191–3, 195–7, 203
Rescript on Education 58
restoration 47, 287, 297
  Meiji 43, 46, 59, 73, 124, 200, 238, 252, 261, 263, 269–70, 306
revelation/s 240, 251, 268, 273
revolution/ary, 40–1, 45–6, 48, 72–3, 298
Revon, Michel 35–6, 54
Rhodes, Robert F. 12, 186, 198–9, 218, 220, 225
rice 30, 61, 107, 122, 180, 242
Rinzai Zen 13
Rishukyō 146
rites/ritual/s (various) 11, 45, 79–80, 116, 151–3, 174, 189, 199, 224, 227, 235–6, 279
  Buddhist 138, 140–1, 149, 190, 204, 206
  court/central 10, 16, 59, 61–5, 82, 254, 256–7
  initiation 131–2
  life 30, 245
  Noh 151–3, 159, 161, 165, 167, 169–70
  Shinto 20–1, 25, 30–1, 60, 62–5, 73, 109, 116, 128, 130–1, 134, 137, 139, 147, 153, 180, 224, 226, 232–3, 236–7, 243, 245, 260–1, 263, 265–6, 273, 284, 287
  shrine relations 17, 29, 226
Ritsuryō system 60–1, 65, 72, 261
ritualist/s/istic 81, 149, 159, 161, 165, 170, 261
Rogers, Ann T. 192–3, 198

Rogers, Minor L. 192–3, 198
Rokkakudō 211
rokkon shōjō 258–9
Rokujō (Lady) 161–2, 164–9
rope 25, 132, 182
Rots, Aike Peter 63, 75
Rousseau, J.-J. 46
Roy, Rammohan 69–70
Ruesch, Markus 12, 217, 220, 225
Ruppert, Brian 84, 102,
Ryōbu Shintō 35, 58
Ryōgen 115
Ryōjitsu 143
ryōkai mandara 138
Ryōtei 200, 207–8, 210–11, 217
Ryūen 147

sacred/sacralized 79, 111, 128, 130–2, 134, 137–41, 164, 166, 196, 279, 287
  places 108, 128, 131–2, 138–41, 152–4, 156–7, 175–7, 219–20, 223, 225–6, 237, 263
  power 29, 82
sacrifice (blood) 5, 132, 134, 224
Saichō 202, 207
saiseiitchi 254–6
saishi 59, 61–2, 64–6
sakaki 30–1, 161, 164–5, 167–8
Sakakura Tomoo 282–3, 302
sake (saké) 23, 143, 196
Sakura Shrine 267
Śākyamuni 85–6, 88, 109, 112, 128, 146, 148–9, 212, 253
salvation/salvific
  Buddhist 83, 111, 140–1, 172, 186, 191, 197, 200, 206
  Buddhist, for Shinto priests 141, 143–4, 147–8
  Shinto and various 81, 89, 96, 101, 107, 115, 126, 271
  Tenrikyō 280
Salvation Army 288
samādhi 188
samsara 153, 169
Sanari K. 156–60, 163–8, 172
sanctuary/sanctum 127–8
sandoku 93
sangakushinkō 251
sangoku 112, 119

Sangū dokuhon 182, 184
Sannō 58, 86–91, 106, 109
Sarasvatī 13
Sarutahiko Shrine 181
Sasaki Gesshō 204, 207, 209, 217
Satō Hiroo 102, 111, 119
Satow, Ernest 36
Savarkar, V. D. 70
Sawada, Janine Tasca 273, 302
Scheid, Bernhard 34, 49–50, 52, 55, 172
Schrimpf, Monika 33, 248
secret/secrecy 63, 86, 129, 131, 138, 140, 172, 222, 292
sect/s (general) 17, 68, 202, 231–40, 247–8, 253, 258, 260–1, 277, 279, 281, 288, 294
  Buddhist 199, 202–3, 211, 215
  Shintō (various) 7, 24, 231–40, 242, 266, 289–90
Sect Shintō 18–19, 59–60, 231, 234, 236, 237, 238, 240, 250, 252, 256–7, 260–2, 267–9, 276–8, 283–4, 287, 289, 291, 296, 300, 306
sectarian 3, 19, 67, 71–2, 199, 231, 214, 234, 237, 241, 305
secular/ization 227, 232–3, 269, 276–7, 280, 296, 300
Seirenji 195
Seishi Bosatsu 144
Sekaikyō 284
Seki Hideo 141, 143, 145–6, 148, 150
Senge Michihiko 241–2
Senge Takatoshi 242, 248
Sengzhao 85, 102
Senjuji 207–8
Senjukanzeon 212
sentient beings 83, 89–90, 92, 95–6, 101, 126, 148, 151, 154, 169
Separation Edicts 136
serpentine 94, 223
sessha 17, 183
setsuwa 43, 156
Shaka (Śākyamuni) 253, 255
shaking 99–102
shaku/shakumon 85, 88, see also *suijaku*
shaman/ism 62, 79–81, 101, 124, 130
Shamon Seikan 147
Sharma, Arvind 67, 70, 75
Shasekishū 137–8, 150, 222

Shibata Hanamori 238
Shichifukujin 173, 223, 245
shichigosan 245
shide 25
ShijōTennō 202
Shijū jōketsu 92
shikakushin 116
shiki (consciousness) 94
shikinensengū 180
Shimada Hiromi 270, 272, 274–5, 302
Shimaji Mokurai 255–6
Shimazono, Susumu 301
shimenawa 25, 132, 182
Shimogamo Shrine 106
shimosha 122
Shimotsuke 174
Shin Buddhism 10, 12, 186–97, 199–216, 220–1, 225, 255–6
shin (*kami*) 11, 26, 80, 82
shin-bukkyō 246
shinbu (shaking dance) 99
shinbutsu 11, 80, 151–2, 155, 157–9, 161–71, 218, 222–3
    bunri 11, 13–14, 53, 276
    -hanzenrei 254
    shūgō 11, 80, 82, 84, 119
Shingaku 273–4, 286
shinganjōju 245
shingo 243–4
Shingon (Buddhism/monks) 12, 56, 118, 128, 142, 194, 197, 273
shinji 131–4, 266
shinjitsushinjin 188
shinkō 43, 107, 109, 115–16, 128, 256
shinkoku 114
Shinkyō Shintō 19
shinkyō (mirror) 179
Shinmeigū 264
Shinmyō 143
Shinpūkai 289–91
Shinpukuji 139
Shinran 186–91, 197–204, 206–10, 212–15, 217, 220
Shinrikyō 239, 251
shinshin kenzen 245
Shinshū (Jōdo) 199, 214, 220, see also Kibeha
    Takadaha 206

Shinshūkyō 18, 59, 237, 239, 247, 251, 260–7
shinshūkyō (new religions) 260
Shinto Directive 257, 266, 300
Shintō Jimukyoku 250
Shintō Honkyoku 239, 274–8, 290
Shintoist/s 8, 15, 81, 261, 263, 284, 287, 290
shintōkei 240–1
Shintōshūseiha 239, 251
Shintōtaikyō 239
Shintōtaiseikyō 251
Shintōzan 237
Shirane, H. 156, 172
Shishino Fumio 238, 247, 256, 258–60
Shishino Nakaba 250, 252–3
shite (Noh) 152, 162, 164–70
Shitennōji 105, 115
shōbaihanjō 245
shogunate (Kamakura) 46, 104–5, 222
Shōkannon 212
Shōkokuji 13
Shokunihongi 136–7, 150
Shōtoku Taishi 115
Shōzōmatsu wasan 189
shrine (Shinto), *passim*; see also *jinja*
Shrine Shinto 6, 31, 231, 257, 260
shū (term) 231, 235
Shugendō 247, 261
shugenja 83
shūgō 11, 80, 82, 84, 119, 151
Shūgyokushū 105, 108–11, 113–14, 118–19
Shuha Shinto [sic] 257
shūha (shintō) 231, 235
shuin/chō 173–4, 180
shūkyō (as term) 231, 235, 256, 268–9, 271, 276, 284, 297–8
Shūkyō nenkan 240, 243, 248
Shunjo/Ekan 200, 206–7, 209, 217
Shūsaikai (Dai Nihon-) 297
Shūseiha 239
Sikhs 70
skilful/means 14, 135, 255
Smart, Ninian 8
Smith, Wilfred Cantwell 21, 33
snake 92, 94–100, 221, 223
Sokotsutsu (*kami*) 107

sokuikanjō 131
sōmoku-jōbutsu 154
Son-en 105
Sonoda Minoru 4, 25, 33
Soshitchikyō 146–7
sōshōshūkyō 265
Sōtō Zen 13
soul/s 6, 34, 42
source (spiritual) 49, 58, 135, 140, 151, 191, 197, 240, 271–2, 285–6
Souyri, Pierre-François 38, 55
spirit/mind (of nation etc.) 6, 30, 34, 36, 42–5, 49–51, 58, 61, 63, 252, 257, 284–5, 287, 291, 293
spirit/s 28, 79–81, 101, 106–7, 109, 115, 132, 134, 160, 178, 187–91, 224, 226, 237, 241, 244, 264, 266, 288, 297
  of a particular person 143–4, 147, 162
  restless 116, 160, 162, 167, 177
spiritual/ly/ity 25, 45, 126, 140, 151, 157, 164, 191, 232–3, 241, 263–4, 267, 271, 281–2, 286
Stalker, Nancy 285, 291, 294, 299, 302
Stone, Jacqueline I. 85, 90, 95, 97–8, 102, 121, 154, 172
stupa 128, 142, 145
suchness 63, 94–5
Sueki Fumihiko 90, 102
Sugawara Michizane 13, 106, 109, 115–16, 175–8, 184, 223, 306
suijaku 81–4, 88–9, 109–10, 117–18, 126, 131, 135, 151, 192, 197, 212–13, 216, 220–2
Sūkeikai 181
Sumiyoshi Shrine 107, 261, 306
Sun Goddess 23, 27, 113–14, 138, 164, 237
śūnyatā 154
supernatural 90, 152–3, 157, 159, 187–8
superstition 5, 72, 278, 280, 285, 287, 289, 296
Śūraṅgama Sūtra 188
Susanoo 107
sutra/s 13, 83, 85, 117, 128, 137, 140–9, 168–9, 174, 188, 190, 195, 224
  burials 140–1, 143–5, 149, 224
  copying 145, 174

Suwa Shrine etc. 2, 17, 121–35, 218, 220–1, 224, 261, 306
Suwa Enchū 126
Suwa Yorinaga 131
Suwa Yoritake 130
Suwaryū Shintō 125
Suzuki Sayaka 164, 172
Suzuri-ishi 128
swastika 13
sword 23, 107, 157
symbol/ism 13, 17, 75, 79–80, 91, 94, 96–100, 121, 123–4, 128, 131, 134, 152, 155–6, 158–9, 165–7, 169–70, 178, 202, 206, 212, 223, 258, 282
syncretic/ism 14, 49, 72, 80, 105, 109, 121–35, 218–19, 276
synthesis 11, 14, 43, 46, 273

taboo 137–8, 166, 224
Tahō Nyorai 86
Taigan 195
Taigyaku jiken 37, 41, 282
taima 179
Taimitsu 86–8, 92, 94
taisei hōkan 263–4
Taiseikyō 239, 251, 273, 289
Taisha/*taisha* 7, 12, 17, 23–4, 26, 29, 107, 183, 241–3, 245, 252–3, 261
Taishakyō 18, 24, 239, 242, 290
Taishō/Period 180, 297, 281–2, 284–5, 290, 293–4, 296
Taiwan 29, 293–4
taizōkai 138
Takada-ha 206–7
Take Kakuchō 212, 217
Takeda Michio 289, 302
Takeinadane (*kami*) 107
Takemikazuchi (*kami*) 106–8, 123
Takeminakata (*kami*) 123–4, 131
Takemitsu Makoto 18, 33
Taketsunumi (*kami*) 106
Takidaijingūji 136
Takihara no miya 180
talisman 196
tama 134–5
Tamayori-hime 106
Tamonten 207
Tamura Yoshirō 95, 103

326 Exploring Shinto

Tanaka Takako 86–7, 90, 103
Tanaka Yoshitō 38, 57–61, 63, 71, 75
Tani Seigo 37, 39–41, 48, 50–1, 55
tathāgatagarbha 95
tathatā 95
Teeuwen, Mark 8, 31, 57, 60, 63, 66, 73–5, 82, 93, 102–3, 131, 137, 139, 150, 152, 172, 175, 185
temizuya 25
temple (Buddhist), *passim*
Ten Branches of Shin Buddhism 214
Ten Shrines 174
tenchiheian, manninanpuku 259
Tendai/Tendaishū 10, 12, 79, 81–103, 104–19, 154, 156, 161, 202–3, 208, 211, 213–14, 218, 221–2
Tenjin(-sama) 13, 106, 109, 176, 178, 232, 306
tenjin (*ten*, heavenly gods) 115, 188–9, 203
tenjin chigi 10, 187, 208
Tenmangū 17, 20, 23, 176–9
Tennō 28, 207–8, 215, see also Emperors (various named)
Tenri (place) 176
Tenrikyō, 237, 239–41, 251, 265, 268–83, 285, 287–9, 291, 293–7, 299–303
Tenrin 273–5
Tenri-Ō-no-Mikoto 271, 275–6, 280
Tenshō Kōtai Jingū Kyō 10
theatre 152, 171–2, 220, 222, see also Noh
theology (Shinto) 8, 59, 65, 287
this-worldly benefits 178, 277
Thomas, Jolyon B. 281, 302
Three Treasures 115, 137–8, 140
thunder 106
Tiantai school 85, 95, see also Tendai
Tōdaiji 148
tomb/s 61, 123, 160
torii 13, 17, 25, 27, 162–3, 167–9, 178
Toyokawa Inari 13
Toyouke Daijingū 183
transaction/al 30, 178, 226
transformation/s (of *kami* etc.) 92, 121, 153–4, 168, 170, 188, 190, 213
treason 37, 282
Triplett, Katja 4–5, 12, 33, 218, 245, 248

Trubnikova, Nadezhda 116–17, 119
truth/s (spiritual) 14, 85, 89–91, 93, 95, 97, 101, 160, 285
Tsubaki Ōkami Yashiro 16–17
Tsuchiya Senkyō 59, 75, 87
Tsukiyomi no miya 180
Tusita Heaven 138–9, 141
tutelary deity 87, 106–9, 136, 194, 222
Tyler, Royall 155, 172
typology 4, 6, 17, 19, 22–3, 117

Uchimura Kanzō 280, 295, 300, 303
Udagawa Bunkai 280, 303
Uemura Fukutarō 278, 303
Uemura Kazuhide 39–42, 50, 55
ujigami 23, 124, 194–5, 233–4
ujiko 23, 233–34
Umehara Takeshi 95, 103
universal/ism 118, 128, 221, 240–1, 289, 300, 306
universe 118, 166, 191, 264
Uragami 253
Ury, M. 166, 171
Ushitora no Konjin 289
Uwatsutsu (*kami*) 107

Vairocana 85
Vedas/Vedānta 68–70, 72, 74
vengeful spirits 116
vibration 99–101
Vimalakīrti Nirdeśa 85, 102
virtues (Shinto/Confucianism) 58, 293
vision (religious) 258, 297
visualization 99, 129
Vivekananda, 69–70
votive 13, 25, 146
vows of Amida/Hōzō 123, 186, 188, 191

Wachutka, Michael 36, 55
waka 104–5, 112, 114, 119
waki (Noh) 162–3, 166–7, 170
Wakai Toshiaki 37, 55
Wakeikazuchi (*kami*) 106
Wakita Haruo 161, 172
wakō dōjin 88–91, 97, 99–101
Wakōji 275
wasan 189–90

Watanabe Osamu 299, 303
Watarai 28, 140–1, 143–7, 149–50
　Masahiko 143–4
　Tsuneyuki 147
Watson, Burton 169, 172
Watsuji Tetsurō 51, 303
Weinstein, Stanley 246, 249
White Light Association 241
wisdom (Buddhist) 85, 112
woman/women 99, 156, 158–9, 161, 188
Womb Mandala/Realm 126, 138, 146
Woodard, W. P. 6, 33
Worldism/World Teaching 284–5

Yakushi Nyorai 145, 212
yakuyoke 245
yamabushi 269–70, 305
Yamamba (Noh drama) 152, 155–62, 169–70, 222–3, 226
yamameguri 158
Yamamoto Hajime 105–14, 118–19
Yamamoto Hiroko 99, 103, 125, 134
Yamato 110, 123–4, 180, 275
Yamato Takeru 19, 107
Yamatohime 264
Yamazaki Ansai 58
Yanagita Kunio 5, 33
Yasukuni Shrine 24, 31–2
Yasumaro Yoshio 268, 280, 286, 291, 295, 303
Yayoi Period 15, 65, 122
yōhai 17, 27
Yomi no kuni 166

Yoneda Minoru 41–2, 55
Yoshida Jinja/Shintō 7, 28, 64, 237, 269–71, 276, 306
Yoshida Kanetomo 49, 58, 221
Yoshida Kazuhiko 83, 85, 103
Yoshida Kunihiro 18, 33
Yoshida Shōin 255
Yoshimura Masamochi 237, 247, 261–6
Yoshimura Masanori 237, 247, 260–3, 266
Yoshimura Tadaaki 266
Yoshimura Taiji 263
Yoshino 47
Yuiitsu Shintō 28, 221
Yuimakyō 85
Yuki Shrine 263
yurai 26, 182

zasu (Jien) 104
zazen 194
Zeami 155, 171
Zen 13, 49, 161, 194, 197, 246
zenaku funi 160
Zenchiku 161, 169, 171–2
Zenkōji 155–6, 175, 204, 206, 211, 217
zenshin (benevolent *kami*), 83, 115
zenshinkyō (teaching of all *kami*) 284
Zhiyi 85
Zhong, Yijiang 241, 249
Zhuangzi 286
Zonkaku 186, 192, 197, 203–4, 207–8, 221
Zōō 193

www.ingramcontent.com/pod-product-compliance
Lightning Source LLC
Chambersburg PA
CBHW050837230426
43667CB00012B/2032